ECONOMIC IMPERATIVES AND ETHICAL VALUES IN GLOBAL BUSINESS

The South African Experience and International Codes Today

ECONOMIC IMPERATIVES AND ETHICAL VALUES IN GLOBAL BUSINESS

The South African Experience and International Codes Today

by

S. Prakash Sethi
Baruch College

and

Oliver F. Williams
University of Notre Dame

KLUWER ACADEMIC PUBLISHERS
Boston / Dordrecht / London

Distributors for North, Central and South America:
Kluwer Academic Publishers
101 Philip Drive
Assinippi Park
Norwell, Massachusetts 02061 USA
Telephone (781) 871-6600
Fax (781) 871-6528
E-Mail <kluwer@wkap.com>

Distributors for all other countries:
Kluwer Academic Publishers Group
Distribution Centre
Post Office Box 322
3300 AH Dordrecht, THE NETHERLANDS
Telephone 31 78 6392 392
Fax 31 78 6546 474
E-Mail <services@wkap.nl>

 Electronic Services <http://www.wkap.nl>

Library of Congress Cataloging-in-Publication Data

Sethi, S. Prakash.
  Economic imperatives and ethical values in global business : the South African
experience and international codes today / S. Prakash Sethi and Oliver F. Williams.
    p. cm.
  Includes bibliographical references and index.
  ISBN 0-7923-7893-8 (alk. paper)
    1. Business ethics--South Africa. 2. Economics--Moral and ethical aspects--
South Africa. 3. Corporations, Foreign--South Africa. 4. Anti-apartheid
movements--South Africa. 5. South Africa-Social conditions. I. Williams, Oliver F.
II. Title.

HF5387.5.S6 S485 2000
174'.4--dc21   00-055993

Printed on acid-free paper. Printed in the United States of America

To Reverend Leon H. Sullivan

A Person of Uncommon Wisdom and Generosity

Contents

List of Acronyms

ACOA	American Committee on Africa
AHI	*Afrikaanse Handelsinstituut* (Africaans Chamber of Commerce)
AMCHAM	American Chamber of Commerce in South Africa
ANC	African National Congress
ARMSCOR	Armaments Development Corporation of South Africa
ASSOCOM	Associated Chamber of Commerce in South Africa
AZAPO	Azania People's Organization
BCA	Black, Colored, and Asian
CAAA	Comprehensive Anti-Apartheid Act of 1986.
CCSA	Christian Council of South Africa (the precursor to the SACC)
CODESA	Congress for Democratic South Africa
CORE	Congress of Racial Equality
COSATU	Congress of South African Trade Unions
DRC	Dutch Reformed Church (usually used in reference to the NGK)
EPG	Eminent Persons Group, of the Commonwealth Countries
ICCR	Interfaith Center on Corporate Responsibility
IMF	International Monetary Fund
IRRC	Investor Responsibility Research Center
ISU	Industry Support Unit (of the Sullivan Principles)
MK	Shorthand for *Umkhonto We Sizwe* (Spear of the Nation)
NAACP	National Association for the Advancement of Colored People
NAFCOC	National African Federated Chamber of Commerce

NGK	*Nederduits Gereformeerde Kerk* (Dutch Reformed Church)
NUM	National Union of Mineworkers
OAU	Organization of African Unity
PAC	Pan Africanist Congress
SACBC	Southern African Catholic Bishops' Conference, Pretoria
SACC	South African Council of Churches, Johannesburg
SACTU	South African Congress of Trade Unions
SASA	South African Signatory Association (of the Sullivan Principles)
UDF	United Democratic Front
WARC	World Alliance of Reformed Churches
WCC	World Council of Churches

Foreword by Rev. Leon Sullivan

The authors of this book pay me a great compliment in that they credit my work with the Sullivan Principles in South Africa as the stimulus for a major change in the way business today views its role in society. I will let the reader be the judge of that, but I can say that this volume brings together an excellent, comprehensive account of what I was trying to do with the Principles and of the many battles that had to be won for their success. Perhaps no other two scholars in the world have had more "hands on" experience with the anti-apartheid movement and the related economic and political issues in South Africa. During the 15+ long years of struggle, they were not only on the ground observing and analyzing the situation, but also becoming involved in improving the implementation of the Principles. By cajoling the corporations and nongovernmental organizations—both secular and religious—they were able to enhance the cause of the Sullivan Principles. It was because of the trust and esteem in which they were held by all concerned that their advice and counsel was sought and listened to by all sides. Working with thousands of documents and letters in the archives, and with personal, on-the-record interviews with a large number of significant players, they have created a unique combination of a scholarly and first-hand account of events. This research is backed by exhaustive data analysis, with the result ' that we have a highly objective, empirically based, and yet personal perspective of this grand experiment. Through lucid and incisive writing, they have recreated the tensions and the tenor of the times from the mid-seventies until the dismantling of statutory apartheid in April 1994 with the first democratic election.

My basic position in 1975, when I first raised the apartheid issue with United States business leaders, was that we couldn't check our moral and religious values at the office door. Apartheid was an evil, and business had great power in South Africa. Where there is power, there is also responsibility. I prayed about this long and hard. I pushed the companies as much as I thought I could. There were advances and there were setbacks, but finally we prevailed and the Blacks of South Africa secured their freedom. My effort in behalf of the Sullivan Principles was only one of a number of significant efforts of the anti-apartheid movement. All of those other efforts must be recognized, as well.

The Sullivan Principles and the manner in which they were implemented in South Africa were in the nature of a grand experiment in the sociopolitical change and economic uplifting of the Black people of South Africa. What is even more important is that the Principles were driven by an ethical and moral imperative, and were voluntarily implemented by a group of enlightened United States multinational corporations. No grand design or vision is ever perfect. We fall prey to human follies, limited understanding of the future, and necessary compromises to seek not what is perfect but what is possible. Thus, any such effort is subject to criticism from those who seek ideological purity and those who seek to minimize the impact of change from the status quo.

One point the authors do capture well is that my guiding vision was then—and remains today—that overcoming political apartheid is not enough. The dual focus of overcoming political and economic apartheid has been my life's work. My experience in the United States civil rights movement taught me that mobilizing the resources to teach disadvantaged Blacks important job skills was just as important as working for political rights. I preached to business that they had the power to right some of these wrongs, and some businesses responded with generous and careful programs. It is those businesses that have my highest admiration and blessings. Others who continue to focus single-mindedly on making money will, no doubt, find that new champions for the poor and dispossessed will rise to the occasion. As the authors suggest, there is a new paradigm for the role of business and society.

I would leave it to the capabilities of these two scholars to interpret the workings of the Principles, and to the readers to assess the validity of their assertions and interpretations. One thing, however, is certain. The working of the Sullivan Principles in South Africa offers invaluable lessons that are increasingly relevant in today's highly contentious global business environment, especially with respect to human rights, individual freedom, sweatshop working conditions, a living wage, social equity, moral fairness, and protection of the environment. They offer practical lessons from the one and only full-scale experiment in crafting a code of conduct, ensuring its implementation, and creating mechanisms for independent monitoring, verification of results, and public dissemination of findings. As such, this book should be required reading for all those who must contend with such problems in the global context. A failure to attend to the book's lessons would condemn us to repeat our mistakes. This would be a tragedy of monumental proportions: it would inflict unnecessary economic costs on all the parties involved, be the cause of avoidable human pain and suffering, and exacerbate political instability and social unrest in the countries involved.

Leon H. Sullivan
Phoenix, Arizona

Preface

Nowhere in the annals of the history of international business, and especially the history of multinational corporations (MNCs), has there been an experiment so unique, and yet so profound, as the operations of the United States companies in South Africa under the White-dominated regime that practiced legalized apartheid. The experiment started modestly when a small group of major United States-based MNCs, inspired by a Black clergyman, agreed to abide by a set of six principles that called for, among other things, the elimination of all types of discrimination between White and Black workers; the recognition of Black unions; and providing help for the Black communities in the areas of education, health care, and other social-support activities.

The six principles that came to be known as the Sullivan Principles—named after their originator, Rev. Leon H. Sullivan—would become synonymous with the ascendance of moral principles over purely economic interests, with the power and influence of religious groups and social activists to change corporate behavior, and with the capacity of multinational corporations, however reluctantly, to bring about social and political changes in the host countries of their overseas operations. From its modest beginnings, the Sullivan Principles program mushroomed into one of major national and international importance, and became a lightning rod in accelerating the process of sociopolitical change in South Africa.

The Sullivan Principles constituted the first of the voluntary codes of ethical conduct that were applied under realistic operating conditions and that involved a large number of corporations, recipient constituencies, and an institutional framework for project implementation, monitoring, and performance evaluation. The Principles program had a large measure of moral authority to validate corporate actions and, where necessary, to exhort companies to undertake activities that they might otherwise consider ill advised. It also presented an excellent laboratory to examine the efficacy of various modes of corporate action undertaken in a hostile sociopolitical environment. It was a setting, moreover, in which the corporations' economic and social goals conflicted, and in which corporations' own South African managers did not fully support either the rationale for the Principles or the manner in which they were being applied to the subsidiaries in that country.

The operation of the Sullivan Principles during its eighteen years was not smooth, nor should it have been expected to be. The Principles program was unprecedented, undertaken in a tense and emotionally charged sociopolitical environment, and characterized by a large measure of mutual distrust between the corporations and their critics. Nevertheless, the Principles program served an extremely useful purpose both as a symbolic gesture indicating the moral repugnance of all civilized people against the evil of apartheid, and as a practical measure for providing sorely needed help to South Africa's poor and disenfranchised people.

Despite all the real or alleged weaknesses of the Principles program, no one with any knowledge either of multinational corporate codes of conduct or the developments in the field of corporate social responsibility could fail to recognize its crucial role in helping to legitimate such codes. Most corporations of any size now proudly display codes of conduct that outline, in varying degrees, their commitment to preserving the environment, offering fair wages and safe working conditions, and dealing equitably with customers and other stakeholders. Although a great deal of old rhetoric persists, and some of these codes have more to do with good public relations than substantive corporate actions, the fact remains that the legitimacy of these demands is now accepted by all sides. Debate has accordingly shifted to the content and implementation of these codes.

There is every indication to suggest that the business community, in general, and multinational corporations, in particular, will face increasing pressure to abide by codes of conduct in situations of perceived social wrongs—whether or not the corporations are the culprits or even directly involved, and whether or not they are in a position to bring about effective change. In an effort to inform such efforts, it would be a worthwhile objective to create an accurate and comprehensive record not only of the events surrounding the anti-apartheid movement in the United States and other parts of the world, but of the many ways in which that movement altered the economic and political landscape of South Africa. Such a record would demonstrate the immense complexity that characterizes all significant issues of public import. More importantly, the record would capture the very hazardous, unpredictable, and intense nature of the process through which important public issues are handled and resolved. It is a process that involves social institutions, and human beings—with all that is noble in them, and also with the ignoble cruelty that afflicts all of us. A study of that process would provide ample lessons for the corporate community, social activists, religious institutions, international organizations, and national governments about the effective strategies and tactics for dealing with similar issues.

This book, however, has a broader purpose. We intend to offer an analytical framework that will help us to understand business and society conflicts within a normative, economic, and contextual framework, and to evaluate the likelihood of success or failure of various strategic options and implementation formats that might be available for use in a given situation.

At the *macrolevel*, this book will look at:

- The sociopolitical environment that gives a particular issue of public policy its ideological-moral legitimacy, emotional intensity, and political potency; the role that different groups play in creating ownership of such an issue; and the process through which a supportive public-opinion environment is created.

- The linkages between domestic events and international events—linkages that are likely to enhance or weaken the saliency of a public policy issue—and the process through which these linkages are strengthened by advocacy groups.

- The linkages between moral/ethical values and economic considerations—linkages that define the operational characteristics of the social conflict, especially as to who does what to whom and with what effect, both on the conflict itself and on parties not otherwise involved in it.

- The manner and degree to which industry structure, competitive intensity, and companies' level of profitability influence these companies either to cooperate with various advocacy groups or to resist their demands.

- The different approaches that might be considered in developing codes of conduct. Should they be voluntary or mandatory in character? How should compliance be monitored and evaluated? Are there specific approaches that might be suitable for specific types of issues and external sociopolitical conditions?

At the *microlevel* this book will look at:

- What happens to parent-subsidiary economic relationships when the MNC's head office imposes certain moral/ethical operational rules on the local subsidiary. Available research on MNC parent-subsidiary relations suggests that there is strong tendency for the subsidiary's management to conceal information from the head-office staff when such information would adversely affect the operational autonomy of the local subsidiary even though the information might be beneficial for the MNC's home-country or global operations.

- How adhering to parent MNC's social-policy goals might expose local managers to hostile peer-group reactions and create an adversarial relationship with local governmental agencies whose support is vital to the successful operations of the local subsidiary. The risk is that the aggressive pursuit of parent MNC's social goals might result in a weakening of the local subsidiary's competitive position.

- How the parent MNC might resolve the issues of performance measurement and evaluation, and of management compensation when the pursuit of social-policy goals potentially has an adverse impact on the subsidiary's economic performance. An alternative approach is determining how a company might develop monitoring and evaluation measures when performance on social-policy goals is considered an integral part of a subsidiary's overall performance.

- What measures companies can take to ensure that they are not held hostage, either by advocacy groups in their home country or recipient groups in the host country, to ever escalating standards of performance that disregard the company's vital strategic interests in its global operations.

- How MNCs resolve issues of internal conflict between managers and employees, and also between various groups of managers who may hold different views as to the desirability of adhering to parent MNC's social-policy goals; how such conflicts and the selected mode of conflict resolution affect the operations of the company; and how the potential for harm might be minimized.

The seeds of this book were planted in the authors' minds fifteen years ago, the product of our intensive involvement in the anti-apartheid debate in the United States and also of our participation in various activities and groups—both in United States and South Africa—engaged in the abolition of apartheid. In the process, we actively worked with, and listened to, a great many individuals and groups whose views and actions influenced and shaped our thoughts as to the salience and effectiveness of different approaches to voluntary social action, the importance of recognizing moral values as a necessary condition to economic action, and the possibilities and limitations of engaging large corporations to become agents of positive social change.

This book became an active project almost five years ago when, following the democratic, nonracial elections, the people of South Africa took the destiny of that nation into their own hands, and the Sullivan Principles program was formally dissolved. In the course of writing the book, we benefited from the cooperation and support of a large number of people who willingly shared their views, challenged our opinions, and, in the process, helped us understand events, interpret data, and project our conclusions into future as to their relevance. It would be well-nigh impossible to mention each and every friend, colleague, and casual acquaintance who helped us at each step of our journey—from active participants in one of the most notable struggles for human freedom and dignity of the last quarter of the century, to scholarly interpreters of those events and what they might mean for the future of business-society relations. We are more than happy to share credit for this book with all those we expressly recognize and those whom we may have unwittingly omitted. Nevertheless, we reserve for ourselves the sole responsibility for any flaws in our reasoning and shortcomings in our conclusions.

Among the people who helped shape the course of events, both large and small, in South Africa and whom we were privileged to come to know and learn from are: Heribert Adam, Millard Arnold, Allan Boesak, Paul Buley, Mangosuthu G. Buthelezi, Aldredge B. Cooper, Herman Cohen, Chester Crocker, Msgr. Donald DeBeer, Zach DeBeer, Les de Villiers, Chris Dhlamini, Willie Esterhuyse, George Franklin, John Garbers, Wim R. Gevers, April Glaspie, Bobby Godsell, Richard Goldstone, Rudolf Gouws, David Hauck, Anthony H. Heard, Archbishop Lawrence Henry, Father Theodore M. Hesburgh, C.S.C., Archbishop Denis Hurley, James A. Joseph, Senator Nancy Kassebaum, Hellen Kitchen, Philip Krawitz, Jim Leatt, Helga Liebenberg, George Lindeque, Senator Richard G. Lugar, Penuell Maduna, Trevor Manuel, Thabo Mbeki, Donald McHenry, Tito Mboweni, Rev. Smangaliso Mkhatshwa, E.K. Moorcroft, M.A. Moosa, Nthato Motlana, Sam Motsuenyane, Sipho Mzimela, Beyers Naude, Martin Nasser, J. Daniel O'Flaherty, Gerrit C. Olivier, Millie Olivier, Imam Rashied Omar, Peter-John Pearson, Alan Paton (deceased), Sister Edith Raidt, Cyril Ramaphosa, Gedeon J. Rossouw, A.M. Rosholt, Kate Savage, Michael Savage, Nick Segal, Walter Sisulu, Frederick van Zyl Slabbert, Eon Smit, Franklin Sonn, Louise Tager, Sampie Terreblanche, Archbishop Buti J. Tlhagale, Bob Tucker, Archbishop Desmond Tutu, Virginia Van der Vliet, Meg Voorhes, David Welsh, Harold Wolpe, and Denis Worrall.

In developing the factual background for the book, we interviewed, on the record, a large number of people for their roles during the course of events in South Africa. These people included: James Armstrong, Simon Barber, Roger D. Crawford, William D. Donovan, Jr., William Dunning, Christianne Duval, J. Wayne Fredericks, Thomas L. Grooms, George Houser, Sal G. Marzullo (deceased), John O. Mongoven, Herman Nickel, John S. North, Rafael D. Pagan, Jr. (deceased), George Schroll, Leon Sullivan, Helen Suzman, Arthur Swartz, and D. Reid Weedon, Jr.

Our research could not have been conducted without access to the most complete trove of documents pertaining to the Principles program and the activities of the United States signatory companies in complying with the Principles. The documents are housed in the Urban Archives of the Samuel Paley Library of Temple University (International Council for Equality of Opportunity Principles, Acct. 654). We wish to thank the staff of the Urban Archives for their gracious assistance. Another major source of data—especially pertaining to the withdrawal of United States companies from South Africa, and to state and local laws against companies doing business in South Africa—was provided by the Investor Responsibility Research Center, Washington, D.C. We are grateful to Ms. Meg Voorhes and other professionals at the IRRC for their cooperation in this effort. Robin Hoen, Executive Director of USSALEP (United States–South Africa Leadership Development Program) was most helpful in providing an overview of the work of nongovernmental organizations in South Africa, including the crucial financial support they received from United States businesses.

As is common in academic research, we were fortunate to draw on the assistance of a number of graduate students of our respective universities at different times from 1995 to 1999. At the Zicklin School of Business, Baruch College, the City University of New York, a major burden of library research and other support activities was carried out by, among others, Umit Akgoz, B. Elango, Mingwei Guan, Rafael Olano, Rob Panco, and Linda Sama. At the Center for Ethics and Religious Values in Business of the College of Business Administration of the University of Notre Dame, Meghan Dunne served as a research assistant. Deborah Coch and Gillian Pancotti, administrative assistants as Notre Dame and CUNY, respectively, provided much-needed technical and administrative support. We also want to thank our copyeditor, Stephen Scher, and our editor at Kluwer, Ranak Jasani. To all these wonderful people, we are most grateful.

We began this book in earnest in 1995 with the conviction that the whole era of the Sullivan Principles was a remarkable chapter in corporate America's history, and that the story needed to be told in full. After years of involvement in overcoming apartheid in South Africa, we were convinced that the events in that country were a source of important lessons not only for business, but for religious groups and nongovernmental organizations. It is in that spirit that the policies and tactics of key actors are scrutinized and criticized here. Criticisms are offered in the hope that it will help both individuals and corporations to avoid similar mistakes in the future. We must acknowledge, too, that we are far from certain that we ourselves would have done any better had we been making the decisions. And even the best insight and moral judgment may suffer from the "law of unintended consequences." We therefore set forth our thoughts with genuine humility.

Finally, it is our pleasure to dedicate this book to Rev. Leon H. Sullivan, a person of uncommon wisdom and generosity.

Oliver F. Williams, C.S.C.
Notre Dame, Indiana
S. Prakash Sethi
New York, New York

PART I

THE SETTING

Chapter 1

A Multinational Code of Conduct for South Africa
An Idea That Was Long Overdue

1. IN THE BEGINNING: THE ANNOUNCEMENT OF THE SULLIVAN PRINCIPLES

On the first day of March 1977, the Reverend Leon H. Sullivan, pastor of the Zion Baptist Church in Philadelphia, made a momentous announcement: twelve major United States multinational corporations with operations in South Africa had voluntarily agreed to abide by a code of conduct governing their operations in that country, with special attention to situation of Black workers (see exhibit 1).* These workers were subjected to various forms of discrimination under the apartheid laws and customs then prevailing in South Africa. The announcement was the culmination of a drawn-out effort, led by Rev. Sullivan, to cajole and persuade leaders of some of the major United States corporations to make a hitherto unprecedented public commitment.

The original twelve signatories of the Sullivan Principles, as the code of conduct came to be known, were American Cyanamid, Burroughs Corporation, Caltex Petroleum Corporation, Citicorp, Ford Motor Company, General Motors Corporation, IBM Corporation, International Harvester Company, Minnesota Mining & Manufacturing Company, Mobil Corporation, Otis Elevator, and Union Carbide Corporation. Three companies—Firestone, Goodyear, and Motorola—that participated in the initial discussions, which started with a summit meeting in January 1976, did not join as original sig-

---

* Unless otherwise noted, all direct quotations and paraphrased statements attributed to various individuals in this chapter and in other parts of the book are based on written communications or in-person, on-the-record interviews with the authors.

Exhibit 1. Statement of Principles of U.S. Firms with Affiliates in the Republic of South Africa

Each of the firms endorsing the Statement of Principles have affiliates in the Republic of South Africa and support the following operating principles:

1. Non-segregation of the races in all eating, comfort and work facilities.
2. Equal and fair employment practices for all employees.
3. Equal pay for all employees doing equal or comparable work for the same period of time.
4. Initiation of and development of training programs that will prepare, in substantial numbers, Blacks and other non-whites for supervisory, administrative, clerical and technical jobs.
5. Increasing the number of Blacks and other non-whites in management and supervisory positions.
6. Improving the quality of employees' lives outside the work environment in such areas as housing, transportation, schooling, recreation and health facilities. We *agree* to further implement these principles. Where implementation requires a modification of existing South African *working conditions*, we will seek such modification through appropriate channels.

We believe that the implementation of the foregoing principles is *consistent with respect for human dignity and will contribute greatly to the general economic welfare of all the people of the Republic of South Africa.* (emphasis added)

natories. The reasons for these companies' reluctance to join the Principles were best summarized by L. W. Wise, one of General Motors' staff members, in his "memorandum to file" after speaking with Keith McKennon of Dow Chemical Company. McKennon noted that Dow had some reservations about joining the Principles. In particular, McKennon "envision[ed] a chain reaction of proposals on a variety of subjects" by activist groups. Such proposed "standards of behavior," initiated by "outside parties,"[1] would interfere with or curtail management's discretionary power. In a similar vein, P. Malozemoff, chairman and chief executive officer of Newmont Mining Corporation, wrote to Sullivan on 18 August 1977, saying that whereas "we sympathize entirely with the objectives of your effort," the company would not join the collective effort. Referring to his company's 1974 annual report, Malozemoff concluded: "While we disagree in no way with the Statement of Principles which you have sent us, we prefer for the present to maintain the above as Newmont's formal statement of its position on this all important subject."[2] For Malozemoff, Sullivan's goals for the workplace were well worthy of compliance; it was the further move to diminish management's discretionary power that was unacceptable.

2. THE SULLIVAN PRINCIPLES AND THE STRUGGLE FOR THE CORPORATE SOUL

Rev. Sullivan wanted to project the Principles in moral and human terms. Along with the majority of public-interest groups involved in the anti-apartheid movement, he viewed the White minority government of South Africa as inherently evil and illegitimate, and to be opposed by any possible means, including the denial of the fruits of foreign investments. However, he soon recognized two immutable facts: companies were highly averse to injecting ethical criteria into their business decision making, and they were equally averse to interfering with the laws of a foreign government, no matter how vile. Such interference was perceived as improper and unwise business behavior that must be avoided. Sullivan discovered, too, that seeking the United States companies' total withdrawal from South Africa was doomed to failure for a variety of ideological, political, and practical considerations.

We believe that large corporations—despite their agreement to the Sullivan Principles—failed to recognize the import of the new landscape, one in which moral and ethical imperatives were explicitly stated as integral both to the corporation's internal decision making and to its external, public persona. This failure was characteristic even of that handful of enlightened corporations that were willing to take the lead in this unprecedented and, from their perspective, highly risky venture into the great unknown. Wayne Fredericks, a Ford executive and longtime South Africa expert, best expressed the cautionary attitude of United States executives in South Africa:

> My view in the very beginning and throughout all these years, and even through the Sullivan Programs, was that there was great caution on the part of American executives, and great caution on the part of South African executives, that you don't want to confront the South African government. I would frequently suggest things, and the executives would say we can't do that because we would be arrested, or our managers would be arrested. I would then ask, "Well, could you provide for me a list of all the people who have been arrested so far?" And of course, there was no such list. I mention this because in my view, during this whole period, much more could have been done than was, in fact, done.

In this failure, these corporate executives were not alone. The history of social conflict between corporations and public-interest groups during the last thirty or more years is replete with instances in which corporations failed to appreciate the moral and ethical context within which emerging social conflicts were being framed. Instead, corporations emphasized the economic nature of such issues and therefore insisted on addressing them primarily as economic conflicts that could be isolated and then, once resolved, allow the corporations to revert to their "business as usual" mode of operation.

The most recent, and perhaps the most expensive and explosive, example of this phenomenon was the infant formula controversy, in which Nestle and other multinational corporations were accused of overpromoting their commercial infant formula products to poor people of the Third World, who did not need and could not afford such products. Thus, companies were blamed for pursuing their own commercial gain even though they thereby contributed to infant malnutrition and mortality. The controversy led to a worldwide boycott of Nestle products and made the company a pariah among large segments of the population throughout the world. As a response, the World Health Organization (WHO) enacted in 1981 the *International Code of Marketing of Breast-Milk Substitutes,* which called for changes in corporate marketing practices of infant formula products. Moreover, the controversy propelled Nestle to create an independent audit commission to assure the public that it was, indeed, complying with the provisions of the WHO code. The controversy thus set a precedent—something that corporations signing the Sullivan Principles had feared—for the outside monitoring of corporate claims of compliance with similar codes. Unfortunately, it is not clear that the controversy left any permanent imprint on the corporate culture and institutional memory of either Nestle or the other producers of infant formula.[3] One would fervently hope that a similar fate would not befall the Sullivan Principles, and that we are not all destined to fight these battles over and over again, and at an enormous cost to our social harmony and economic and political fabric.[4]

3. THE REV. LEON SULLIVAN: THE MAN AND THE CAUSE

A brief look at the roots of Rev. Sullivan's upbringing and formative years is quite revealing. It hints at the factors that helped him coalesce a broad-based and yet highly diffused "protest movement" into an "action movement" with a sharply defined purpose that was closely linked with the necessary means that would translate this purpose into meaningful and measurable outcomes.

Born in 1923, Leon Sullivan was raised in a poor family in Charleston, West Virginia. Gifted intellectually, the six foot five inch young man also demonstrated athletic ability and won an athletic scholarship to West Virginia State College, from which he graduated in 1943. Enrolling in New York's Union Theological Seminary, Sullivan served in Harlem and was mentored by Adam Clayton Powell, the legendary preacher and congressman. From the start, Sullivan was known as a powerful and dynamic orator. After seminary education, he served at several churches and in 1950 finally settled as the pastor of Zion Baptist Church in Philadelphia. Under his leadership, the congregation grew to be one of the largest in Philadelphia, reaching some six thousand members.

Active in civil rights issues, Sullivan championed the cause of eliminating discrimination against Blacks in the workplace. He argued that winning civil and political rights for Blacks was only half the battle and that the struggle must continue in the arena of economic rights. He reasoned that since Blacks were major consumers in the Philadelphia area, they ought to have a proportionate share of the jobs. Observing that there were clear patterns of employment discrimination in the city, from 1959 to 1963 he led a campaign of "selective patronage" under which businesses would hire blacks or otherwise face a potential boycott. As opportunities for Blacks began to increase, it became clear that they often lacked the necessary education and skills business required for better jobs. Again, Sullivan took the initiative and founded a series of training facilities to enable Blacks to acquire the necessary skills to succeed in business; they were called the Opportunities Industrialization Centers (OIC). These facilities are now operating in many United States cities and in a number of African countries.[5]

Sullivan entered the world of "big business" in December 1970, when the chairman of the board of General Motors, James M. Roche, visited the Zion Baptist Church and asked him to consider joining the GM board of directors. The timing of this event may have been influenced by the preceding GM annual stockholders' meeting in May 1970; Ralph Nader's Campaign to Make General Motors Responsible had lambasted the company for having no Black board members and very few Black dealers. In any event, Sullivan accepted Roche's invitation and was elected to the GM board. He attended his first board meeting in Detroit on 21 May 1971, and immediately made a splash that was not soon to be forgotten. The meeting happened to be the occasion when the Domestic and Foreign Missionary Society of the Episcopal Church sponsored the very first resolution on South Africa in GM history. Though the resolution calling for GM's withdrawal from South Africa was overwhelmingly defeated (garnering only 1.29 percent of the vote), Sullivan seized the moment to make an impassioned plea to his fellow board members that they consider the moral issue involved in operating in a country that systematically denied rights to people on the basis of skin color. He argued that all multinational corporations ought to withdraw from South Africa until apartheid was dismantled. Needless to say, he did not carry the day. However, he did cause GM to consider offering a more concrete response to the moral challenge he had presented.

GM's rejection of Sullivan's proposal was not surprising, nor is the shareholders' rejection of the Episcopal Church society's resolution; shareholders rarely approve resolutions opposed by management—especially resolutions of "conscience" or those pertaining to broader societal issues. Nevertheless, such efforts serve an important purpose by generating both corporate and public awareness of such concerns and of the corporate actions that relate to them.

Sullivan's concern for the plight of Black South Africans continued to grow in the wake of his confrontation with the GM board. In the summer of 1975, during a visit to Johannesburg, South Africa, he met with Black political activists, groups representing labor unions, and small businesses. He recalls:

> During these discussions, again and again, particularly from the blacks and labor representatives with whom I talked more than any others, I was urged to try to see what I could do to make American companies, and other companies from around the world, positive instruments for change in the elimination of segregation and apartheid.[6]

A letter dated 21 August 1975, from the general secretary of the Garment Workers' Union of South Africa, is representative of the comments Sullivan was receiving.

> Basically, the point to be made is that rather than encourage the withdrawal of American capital from South Africa (we regard this as a negative act (a) it would not have 100% success and is therefore a meaningless gesture and (b) it is negative in itself), you could take a positive stance and call for American companies in South Africa to recognize the same working conditions they employ in America.[7]

Focusing on the use of corporate power to advance the welfare of Blacks (a teleological stance) marked Sullivan's involvement with South Africa for over ten years. That is, the utilitarian (focus on moral consequences) in Sullivan won over the deontological (focus on ethical duties) in Sullivan. Making the American multinational corporation into a change agent for South African society was, however, easier said than done.

4.   FORMING A CONSENSUS: BRINGING THE CORPORATIONS ABOARD

Having realized the futility of seeking corporate withdrawal from South Africa, Sullivan sought to make United States companies change their mode of operations in South Africa in ways that would provide Black workers, in large part, what they would gain in a free and open society. At the same time, he hoped to create momentum against South Africa's discriminatory laws aimed at people of color, and thereby to erode the authority of the existing government. Any change was better than no change, and any positive change for South Africa's Blacks that also struck a blow against the authority of the White government was even better.

It was only after much thought and prayer that Sullivan decided on his strategy of persuading business to work as a change agent in the fight against apartheid, "Not sure myself that it could or would work, but knowing that if it did not work, at least I would have given it a try: and I knew that God would be with me." Frank Cary—the chairman of IBM, who was on the Advisory Council for Sullivan's OIC endeavor—was one of the first business leaders to hear of Sullivan's South African project. After some small, preliminary meetings, Cary, along with Tom Murphy, chief executive officer of General Motors, hosted a meeting for nineteen top executives from fifteen of the largest corporations with South African operations. It was held on 29 January 1976 at the IBM training facility in Sands Point, Long Island. The meeting started Sullivan on a journey that would cause a major paradigm shift in the way business views its role in society. In Sullivan's words:

> I told these business leaders of the dimensions of the crisis as I saw it. I also told them of the moral implications to take a stand for what was morally right. I told these business leaders it was time that they took a stand against injustice in the Republic of South Africa. I urged them to join together and take the "first step" and set an example for businessmen in other parts of the world to begin doing something about the situation.

As a result of this historic gathering, the business leaders agreed to consider supporting a set of principles regulating the companies' behavior in South Africa. A draft of the Principles was to be formulated by Sullivan and circulated to the top executives, who would then offer changes or deletions. The process would go on until enough companies had agreed to a common code. Sullivan's own idea was that the Principles would be designed to erode apartheid not only in the workplace, but also in the wider society. He envisioned the companies as change agents that would use their power to pressure the South African government into dismantling apartheid laws, which would gradually lead to full civil and political rights for all.

There is widespread consensus that the Principles were the product of Sullivan's inspiration and dedication, which operated in tandem with changes in the sociopolitical environment and with forces of social activism that sought to dismantle the apartheid regime in South Africa. What is not generally recognized, however, is the importance of top management's involvement, both in the original deliberations and in the subsequent implementation; it was this involvement that gave the Principles their vitality and made them into a potent force of change in the South African operations of United States companies, in particular, and in the business practices of other major corporations, in general. The scope of management's involvement is apparent from the list of corporate executives (see table 1) that attended Sullivan's crucial meeting of 9 February 1977, which immediately preceded the public announcement of the Principles.

Sullivan wanted to make compliance with the Principles into a prerequisite for any further investments by United States companies in South Africa. The companies strongly resisted this requirement, however, which was thus excluded from the final version. In a memorandum to Ford executives, Wayne Fredericks commented on the 9 February 1977 meeting between Sullivan and representatives of the United States companies:

> Three different versions of Statement were circulated and discussed including one which contains a sentence regarding further investment decisions. . . . Rev. Sullivan urged inclusion, stating that his association with a watered-down Statement would, in the eyes of his constituencies, make him appear to be a tool of the corporations. Nonetheless, a majority of the companies present opposed inclusion of the sentence, and it will not appear in the final draft. Several expressed the view that the Statement even without the sentence, implicitly connects future investment decisions to progress on the principles, and that this should be sufficient.[8]

This perspective further reinforces our view of the tunnel vision of the United States executives. Rather than looking at the Principles as a major instrument of social change and positioning American corporations as the catalyst for such change, corporate executives saw the Principles primarily as a means of containing anti-apartheid activists and of preempting further United States governmental intervention into corporate affairs pertaining to South Africa. According to one executive who attended the meeting, "There was general feeling that the *Statement of Principles would be helpful in avoiding U.S. legislation on this issue*" (emphasis added). In a similar vein, Fredericks echoed the sentiments of the executives by saying that a "principal value of the Sullivan initiative could be its utility in warding off undesirable legislation and in cooling proposals for a White House Conference on South Africa. It also might persuade church groups to withdraw shareholder proposals relating to investment in South Africa." Fredericks realized, however, that "the elimination of any explicit reference to future investment decisions may lessen the likelihood of [the Statement of Principles'] serving the above functions" and diminish "Secretary Vance's enthusiasm for the document, given the comment he made to Sullivan about the importance of that reference." In addition, dropping the explicit reference to future investments would surely lessen the impact on the South African government; the deputy economic advisor to Prime Minister Vorster, in discussions with Fredericks in December 1976, cited external investments as a major concern

Table 1. Attendance list for Sullivan's meeting on South Africa, 9 February 1977

Company	Name	Title
Opportunities Industrialization Center	Rev. Leon H. Sullivan	Founder and Chairman of the Board
	Rev. Gus Roman	Special Assistant
American Cyanamid Company	C. E. Austin	President, Cyanamid Europe/Mid-East/Africa
Burroughs Corporation	R. W. Macdonald	Chairman of the Board
Caltex Petroleum Corporation	J. M. Voss	Chairman of the Board
Citicorp	R. E. Terkhorn	Vice President
Firestone Tire and Rubber Company	J. M. Cornely	Vice President and President, Firestone International
Ford Motor Company	D. Kitterman	Managing Director—Ford Motor Company, South Africa
	J. W. Fredericks	Executive Director, International Governmental Affairs
General Motors Corporation	T. A. Murphy	Chairman of the Board
	T. S. McDaniel	Director, Treasurer's Office Administrative Section
Goodyear Tire and Rubber	J. E. Purcell	Regional Director, Goodyear International
International Business Machines Corporation	F. T. Cary	Chairman of the Board
	W. E. Burdick	Vice President, Personnel
	R. H. Bierly	Director, Equal Opportunity
International Harvester	B. McCormick	President
International Telephone and Telegraph Company	K. M. Perkins	Vice President and Deputy Director, Corporate Relations
Minnesota Mining and Manufacturing Company	R. H. Herzog	Chairman of the Board
	J. A. Thwaits	President, International Operations
Mobil Corporation	W. P. Tavoulareas	President
Motorola	R. W. Galvin	Chairman of the Board
Otis Elevator Corporation	R. A. Weller	Chairman of the Board
	S. French	Vice President, Public Affairs

to the South African government, a problem intensified by depressed gold prices.

When Sullivan started his campaign for the Principles, he found very few companies that were willing to take the first step. It was not so long before that a number of United States companies were severely chastised for interfering in the internal affairs of foreign countries; for example, ITT in Chile. There was widespread concern that influencing politics of host countries tended to be more costly than beneficial. Hence, firms operating in South Africa felt that they must abide by the host country's laws, including apartheid-related laws. Since "staying out of politics" was a very strongly held attitude on the part of the companies, how to deal with the South African government became a major concern for the prospective signatory companies.

This attitude was best articulated, from the corporate perspective, at a meeting of the Conference Board on South Africa that was held in New York City on 15 March 1978. The meeting was attended by top officers of twenty-six United States companies, most of which were signers of the Principles. Although no formal minutes "were allowed to be taken," the informal notes of Sal G. Marzullo of the Mobil Corporation are illuminating:

> It was agreed that business cannot do more than improve the conditions of its workers. We cannot transform the nature of South African society and we will have serious problems with South Africa if we try. But we must do all that we can as quickly as we can to improve the social and economic well-being of all of our black and other non-white employees.[9]

In developing his approach to implementing the Principles, Sullivan followed the experience he had gained in local economic boycotts in the United States; rather than revealing his ultimate goal and asking for total compliance from the companies, he would make moderate but realistic demands on them—and then ask progressively for more. He also realized that, though he may eventually have to ask for total withdrawal, it was important for companies to make significant changes in their operations before they exited South Africa. The status quo was not an acceptable option under any set of circumstances. Sullivan comments:

> The only institutions in South Africa that had the ability or power to change practices in the country were private corporations. I realized that companies were willing to acquiesce in complying with segregation laws because it helped them with cheap labor. Therefore, in order to change these practices in South Africa, I had to start somewhere. I knew that this would be a formidable effort but that it could not be done with protests or marches, couldn't be done with ANC [the African National Congress] as ANC was doing wonderful things on the political front. It had to be done internally, inside the companies, and with a force strong enough that change in operating practices would be impossible to resist. I believed that these changes would not leave the South African government unscathed. Apartheid was like a tightly knit fabric and that once you begin to unravel it at any point, it would keep unraveling until the entire structure fell apart.

I designed the Principles in a way that I could modify them. I called it 'amplification' and I amplified them step-by-step every six months. The executives of the companies did not like it because they said that I kept raising the bar, changing the goal-post. They said they didn't have the authority to do that. I said, it says here in the Principles, I am the authority with the help of God, and who could oppose it! I was able to amass large financial resources behind the movement, behind the Principles. Groups like TIAA-CREF, CALPERS, and a host of other pension funds, state and local employee funds, and Church groups threw their financial and political weight behind the Principles. From the initial slow start, the movement became a juggernaut and there was no stopping it.

Conversations with executives who were involved at the operational level in implementing the Principles reinforce the impression that during the initial stages, corporations were primarily motivated by a desire to get the issue "off the table" of public debate. They wanted to reach a *modus vivendi* that would diffuse the issue at the least cost in political ill will and economic damage to their businesses, both in the United States and in South Africa. Issues of moral concern were either not present or were carefully suppressed from public view; executives did not want to be seen as giving in to non-economic pressures, or as acting outside their professional responsibilities of protecting the well-being of their corporations and shareholders. Both the pragmatic emphasis of the corporations and their effort to project themselves as already in compliance with the Principles are apparent in the "Q & A" that Ford Motor Company prepared when it became a signatory (exhibit 2).

We do not mean to imply that corporations were amoral or were indifferent to the ethical and moral dimensions of the debate. Instead, they were adhering to the prevailing dogma of proper corporate conduct. To wit, ethical beliefs must be practiced at the individual level and in a personal—not a business—context. S. G. Marzullo, who was a Mobil vice president and a key player during all phases of the discussion and implementation of the Sullivan Principles, best summarized this ambivalence in attitude:

> In the beginning, the corporate chairmen who attended the preliminary meetings with Leon were looking for a way to help Leon to get the pressure off the companies by religious and social groups. The broader issues, i.e., those of the character of the South African government and the morality of operating in a country that was oppressive against the majority of its own people, were deliberately kept away from the deliberations. After all, South Africa was not the only country with totalitarian or corrupt government. Mobil operates in over 120 countries in the world and only a handful of those are true democracies, or even pretend to be democracies. We simply cannot be the world's policeman. Moreover, even in countries with corrupt and reprehensible

Exhibit 2. Ford Motor Company *Q & A* on South African Statement of Principles

1. Q. Why did you sign the Statement of Principles?

    A. Ford Motor Company already has made progress in seeking for all employees of its South African affiliate equal opportunity regardless of race. The Statement of Principles reiterates our position and is another step toward upgrading the quality of life for blacks and coloreds in the Republic of South Africa.

2. Q. Why wasn't the Statement stronger? For example, why didn't it state that future U.S. investment should be withheld until racial equality is possible under South African law?

    A. The Statement of Principles was a cooperative effort between the Rev. Leon Sullivan and representatives of the companies signing the Statement. It is hoped that the document will lead toward equality for all races in South Africa without disruptive actions that could severely damage the country's economy.

3. Q. How will you look upon future investment in South Africa?

    A. As we have said, the Statement of Principles reiterate Ford Motor Company's long-standing position on equality for all races in South Africa. If and when we feel it necessary to invest in South Africa we will do so on the basis of our market needs, the economic climate and the direction of our long-term goals.

4. Q. What do you think should be the next step to achieve racial equality in South Africa?

    A. Negotiation is the surest way to achieve long-term goals.

5. Q. Don't you think that if your company and other U.S. corporations withdraw from South Africa, racial equality would be achieved faster?

    A. No.

governments, we are a positive force of change and public well being. We provide jobs, and we help people improve their lives.

Marzullo also conceded that both he and most other executives involved with the Principles were caught unaware of Sullivan's larger design: the so-called amplifications of the Principles, which progressively committed the corporations to spending ever larger sums of money and also thrust them into the political arena.

In the end, despite all the good that these corporations did by staying in South Africa and implementing the Principles, they were ultimately perceived by the public just as they were before. That is, the corporations were perceived as seeking markets and profits, and as devoid of the moral convictions and commitments that distinguish us as human beings and that make for humane societies.

5.   FEAR OF COMMUNISM

The major incentive Sullivan used to persuade CEOs to accept the Principles in his 1976 Sands Point meeting was that unless Blacks in South Africa perceived capitalism as their friend and ally, Communism would ultimately prevail.[10] This argument resonated with many United States companies, which viewed their presence in South Africa as a means of spreading the free enterprise system. Communism could never view even the best multinational companies as agents of development, but only as instruments of dependency.

That Communism was on the minds of Americans on both sides of the aisle is evident from a 1979 letter to the executive officers of Caltex Petroleum Corporation from Republican Congressman Paul N. McCloskey, Jr., of California:

> I join Andy Young in agreement that thus far U.S. business activity in South Africa is constructive rather than harmful to overall U.S. interests. But if apartheid continues to be strengthened and communist intrusion into Africa is enhanced as a result, Congress could very likely react unfavorably to continued U.S. business investment.[11]

The influx of troops and support from the Soviet Union and Cuba in the 1977–78 Ogaden War in Ethiopia added to the Cold War mentality and increased United States-South African cooperation. It was only the demise of the Soviet Union that allowed the situation to be normalized.

6.   SEEKING SUPPORT FROM THE GOVERNMENTS OF SOUTH AFRICA AND THE UNITED STATES

From the very start, the United States multinational corporations were adamant that the Principles must have the tacit approval of the South African government. Sullivan had to accept this condition. These companies also insisted on keeping the United States government at arm's length—and out of the deliberative process—lest it appear that the companies were responding to United States government's pressures and were not acting of their own accord and in the spirit of enlightened corporate citizenship. Thus, we had the ironic situation of American companies trying to fend off their own democratic government, one that opposed apartheid and was an implicit ally of their efforts to act in a nondiscriminatory manner and protect human rights. Just as ironically, the companies were seeking, hat in hand, the blessing of the very government that was the root cause of the evils of apartheid that the Sullivan Principles sought to demolish.

Tom Murphy of General Motors commented that South Africans must undertake the solution in South Africa. Murphy was concerned about the safety of his own people in South Africa, and he did not want a confrontation with the government. The United States companies also wanted to avoid publicity out of fear that their actions might be viewed by the South African government as interference from the outside. Cyrus Vance and Donald McHenry, the United States secretary of state and ambassador to South Africa, respectively, did not share this concern, however. Wayne Fredericks of Ford was able to recall the comments they made at a meeting of various CEOs from the Sullivan group on 23 February 1977. Secretary Vance noted that, though there was no predictability about the South African government, he expected that there would be no problem in implementing the Principles. He felt that the South African government would be "hesitant to take any action against American companies because of their relationship and the importance of the U.S. in that relationship, and if they did so, U.S. government would express its opinion vocally."

This schizophrenic posture on the part of the United States companies may be interpreted in different ways—some cynical and some pragmatic. Whereas the United States companies were being reluctantly led by Sullivan and impelled by public pressure, they were unwilling to jeopardize their vital economic interests in South Africa by challenging the hegemony of that country's authoritarian regime. Moreover, the companies were adamant that they *could not and should not do anything that would oppose the laws and policies of the South African government.* For example, in a 1 November 1976 letter to Sullivan, the chairman of the board and chief executive officer of 3M, R. H. Herzog, responded to an early draft of the Principles:

> The "Statement of Principles" attached to your letter reflects employment goals and practices we are supportive of worldwide and not only in the Republic of South Africa. *To the degree that South African law and South African Government policy allows*, our subsidiary there has taken aggressive action to conform to these principles. If through the offices of Dr. Kissinger, the Principles could receive official South Africa Government approval, it would certainly heighten our subsidiary's ability to enhance their current programs.[12] (emphasis added)

A similar reluctance to challenge South African laws, even those enforcing apartheid, is apparent in a letter from J. M. Voss, chairman of the board of Caltex. Voss, writing on 20 January 1977, was responding to Sullivan's letter of 23 December 1976, which included a draft of the "Statement of Principles." Voss had no problems with the Principles insofar as they concerned the workplace, but he registered serious reservations about challenging any South African apartheid laws. Voss wrote to Sullivan:

> I returned to my desk yesterday and, having studied your letter and the "Statement of Principles," would like to make the following comments:
>
> First and foremost, I reaffirm Caltex's acceptance from a moral and humane point of view of the concepts and, in our case, the utilization of fair and equal employment practices for all employees, as well as the policy of equal pay for equal work.
>
> Secondly, Caltex has training programs in place and supports programs, which have as their objective, the improvement of the quality of their employees' lives outside the work environment.
>
> Finally, Caltex is, as you know, strongly opposed to Apartheid and will continue to seek to attain the establishment of the other Principles set out in the "Statement" so far *as that is possible within the laws of the Republic of South Africa. To the extent feasible to achieve these objectives*, we will also in all appropriate ways assiduously seek the requisite changes in legalization and regulations of an Apartheid character.[13] (emphasis added)

Following meetings with the South African ambassador to Washington, Roelof K. Botha, a significant change was made in the language of the document: a reference to the *laws and customs* of South Africa was deleted and substituted with the words *working conditions* (see the Statement of Principles [exhibit 1]). Critics of Sullivan's endeavor were quick to note this change. The 7 March 1977 issue of *Africa News*, for example, noted that the *Johannesburg Star* "reports that Botha won concessions in wording from the group, although both Sullivan and Botha deny it."[14] Sullivan later clarified his position, saying that he was primarily focusing on the language of the six principles at that time and thus was willing to make the proposed change.[15]

Referring to the original twelve signatories, Sullivan reminds us that "a number of the twelve were held on the list by a shoe string."[16] To get a consensus and announce the Principles program, Sullivan was willing to compromise and then incrementally expand the scope of the Principles in due time. However, this particular compromise did not sit well with at least one United States company. W. B. Nicholson, vice chairman of Union Carbide Corporation, wrote to Sullivan on 8 March 1977, congratulating him on the March 1 announcement but quite concerned about the change.

> We conclude that the version shown to Secretary Vance is much to be preferred over the final draft submitted to Ambassador Botha.

The one variance, namely the substitution of the term "working conditions" for "laws and customs" serves to weaken the statement considerably in our view. We do not have knowledge of the circumstances which
gave rise to the last minute change, but we do have the described reaction
and would like to let you know about it.[17]

On 16 March 1977, Sullivan answered Nicholson's objection by stating
that he was trying "to broaden the base and to follow through on the six
principles in the Statement."[18]

From the vantage point of the 1990s, many may question why Sullivan
sought the approval of the South African ambassador. However, in the
context of the 1970s and the prevailing conception of business's role in society, it was unthinkable to corporate managers that the Principles not receive
some tacit approval from South African officials before being announced.
The issue debated in 1976–77 was whether this approval ought to be negotiated by the United States Department of State or by the companies themselves. Although the 3M CEO argued for the United States secretary of state
to negotiate approval of the Principles, most companies argued for a direct
meeting between some of their CEOs and South African officials. For
example, in the 22 February 1977 letter to Sullivan, the vice president of
Citibank, Robert E. Terkhom, made just that point:

> While we agree that it is a good idea to consult the Secretary of State be-
> fore delivery of the Statement to the South African Government, we do
> not believe that State Department should be asked to deliver this mes-
> sage. We prefer this effort to remain a private initiative, which the sign-
> ing corporations would communicate directly to the South African Am-
> bassador or other appropriate representative of the South African Gov-
> ernment.[19]

Similarly, the president of Mobil Oil Corporation wrote to Sullivan on 18
February 1977:

> As to our program from this point forward, I would hope we all could
> conclude that it might prove counter-productive if the Statement of Prin-
> ciples [was] handled in such a manner as to invite government-to-
> government confrontation. While I think it is certainly a constructive
> move to make what we are doing known to the Secretary of State, it is
> my belief that we might well impair our ability to produce the kind of
> conditions in South Africa which will be necessary if we are to be able to
> implement all of the points outlined in the statement. Since this will be an
> undertaking by private corporations, it seems to me we should be the
> parties which make it known, together with yourself, to representatives of
> the South African Government. An appropriate method for doing this
> might be a meeting of our group with South Africa's ambassador without

involvement of the U.S. Government representatives. We, as a company, would certainly be happy to be identified with the statement in an implementation program of that nature.[20]

Following this advice, IBM's Frank Cary, GM's Tom Murphy, and Sullivan met with Roelof Botha and secured his agreement subject to the significant caveat discussed above. They also met with Secretary of State Cyrus Vance (Jimmy Carter was inaugurated as United States president in January 1977, at which point Vance replaced Henry Kissinger).

7. FORMING A CONSENSUS: ATTITUDES OF RELIGIOUS AND OTHER ANTI-APARTHEID GROUPS

Sullivan's 1 March 1977 announcement of the Principles met with a mixed response. The American Committee on Africa—whose spokesman, ordained minister George Houser, had testified before Congress for economic sanctions against South Africa as early as 1966—called the Principles "an exercise in triviality." Mainline religious groups were, for the most part, doubtful of the usefulness of the Principles, but there was also some initial cooperation. For example, within three weeks of issuing the Principles, Sullivan met with the executive director (Tim Smith) and other key members of the Interfaith Center on Corporate Responsibility (ICCR), a coalition of major Protestant groups and numerous Catholic dioceses and religious orders. ICCR had already presented many numerous shareholder resolutions asking companies to withdraw from South Africa. The very month the Principles were issued, ICCR filed such resolutions against five of the signatory companies. Nonetheless, even as ICCR was asking companies to withdraw, the group was also attempting to persuade them to join the Principles program. Tim Smith, in a 29 March 1977 letter to Sullivan, captured the complexity of the position of most church groups at that time.

Dear Mr. Sullivan:

I was recently at a meeting in Moline with John Deere executives discussing Southern Africa. They indicated that they had not been approached to sign your set of principles but said they would be very willing to do so. Mr. William Hewitt is the Chairman and personally indicated his interest.

We will also continue to raise with G.E. and ITT why they have not signed and would be pleased to raise this with any other companies you may wish, arguing that it is a minimum standard of decency in the workplace that should be applied. However, it is also the consensus of most of the Churches that have been working on this problem that *such changes in the workplace have not and will not lead to the basic social changes* that are vitally necessary in South Africa. This is one of the major points that Sally Motlana raised in her comments at the meeting. It seems to be an analysis bolstered by solid facts. However, we can all agree that companies have an obligation to act responsibly and humanely in the workplace and of course Church groups will continue to endorse this concept.

You had said at lunch that you were willing to raise some larger issues with some of the signatories, e.g., the role of Citibank's loans, G.E. attempting to sell a nuclear reactor to S.A., Union Carbide investing on the border of a Bantustan.

We look forward to hearing reports from you on the fruits of these conversations. Let's keep in touch.[21] (emphasis added)

It would appear that in the early stages of discussions, ICCR was willing to give the Sullivan Principles some measure of public support. Furthermore, Sullivan wanted the 1977 Principles to encompass political and civil rights in the wider society and not simply call for changes in the workplace. Sullivan's 11 April 1977 response to the above letter is telling in that he acknowledged his desire to push for political and civil rights but judged that he must do so incrementally.

My Dear Mr. Smith:

We will be having meetings during the next month with a number of companies trying to get them to sign the Statement of Principles and then to follow through on the implementation. We will be in touch with John Deere executives, as you suggest, to see if they will sign the Principles.

As you indicated in your letter, I will let you know if there are other companies with which you might be helpful to be signers, as you are doing now with G.E. and ITT. It is clear in my mind, as you have stated, that companies do have an obligation to act responsibly and humanely in the workplace. *Of course, it is my desire that much more will come out of the Statement of Principles in the longer run as we push to see how far we can go.*

Also, as you have requested, I will be willing to raise larger issues with Citibank regarding loans; with Union Carbide regarding investing on the Border of Bantustans; and with G.E. regarding attempting to sell a nuclear reactor to South Africa. I do not know what successes I can have, but I will, very willingly, raise the questions. I cannot give you a time frame, but I will do this as soon as possible and will let you know the response.

I will keep in touch as you have requested.[22] (emphasis added)

Another response to the Principles—a quite favorable one—had the effect of uniting many church groups against the program; namely, that of the top officials in the South African government. Since the Principles focused on the workplace, South African officials could easily embrace them. Dr. Connie Mulder, minister of information and the interior, spoke in Parliament in Cape Town, praising the Principles. The Embassy of South Africa used Mulder's comments to attempt to counter any move by United States groups to force disinvestment in the country. For example, in a 20 April 1977 letter, an official in the Embassy of South Africa wrote to the chairman of the Endowment Committee on the Board of Regents of the University of Maryland:

> Apparently, some sources expected the South African Government to respond negatively to these recommendations [the Sullivan Principles]. In fact, the South African Government has expressed its strong support for the objectives outlined in the six points mentioned above.

> Speaking in Parliament in reaction to the six general guidelines, Dr. Connie Mulder, Minister of Information and the Interior, publicly commended the American business initiative launched to contribute to the well-being of black workers in South Africa. Dr. Mulder said South Africa welcomed the American companies initiative to implement and expand development programs already in operation in South Africa. He went on to say that as a result of these existing programs, the black man found himself outstripping his counterparts on the African continent and many other areas of the world in all fields of human endeavor. According to most press accounts it is clear from the tone of the South African Government's reply that the government is leaving the door open for constructive participation in the employment and welfare goals of American firms. Dr. Mulder also noted that these programs should be implemented on a non-discriminatory basis world-wide if American firms and the American Government were truly concerned with the welfare of blacks and other groups.

> Thus, the South African Government has endorsed the efforts by several leading American corporations to advance job opportunities and welfare of all their employees in South Africa regardless of race.[23]

The Principles also had the strong support of the Carter administration. For example, William E. Schaufele, Jr., assistant secretary of state for African affairs, said in a 16 April 1977 statement:

Although there is clearly room for improvement in the performance of their labor practices, South African-based American companies have shown considerable sensitivity in dealing with their black employees. By their example, they have already set in motion some of the kinds of changes that are so desperately needed.

A recent step in the right direction was the March 1, 1977, announcement by 12 major U.S. corporations with business interests in South Africa expressing support for a set of principles designed to promote equal employment rights for blacks and nonwhite minority groups.[24]

Even stronger praise for the Principles and of the United States corporations came from the Secretary of State Cyrus Vance in his 5 October 1977 address to the signatory company officials at a dinner meeting at the Hotel Pierre. He saw United States business as involved in a very important endeavor, one that advanced United States foreign policy.

Your presence here is also a tribute to Leon Sullivan whose drive, whose perseverance and whose vision have been devoted to the task of seeking to better the working conditions and the living conditions of black and colored and Asian workers and their families in South Africa. We applaud and encourage his efforts to persuade more companies both in the United States and abroad to support the Statement of Principles. I think it's important to note that Leon's efforts have, as I said, lit a fire and have contributed greatly to the increased interest of other countries in the question of employment practices in South Africa.

As some of you probably know, some two weeks ago the foreign ministers of the European common market announced a code of conduct for employment standards for companies who are headquartered in the common market countries and they will be encouraged to adopt this standard of conduct. This found its source and arose from the efforts which Leon has started here in this country. In our view the common market code has many commendable features. Moreover, in South Africa, the Urban Foundation, which is a private non-profit organization which is pledged to improve the quality of life of South African urban communities, which is a local foundation, is presently developing its own code of employment practices. And, again, this relates back to the spark which Leon lighted.

Let me tell you from the standpoint of the State Department, we pledge our full cooperation and our support as you work to provide a better life and wider opportunities for your employees. We believe that your efforts will set an example which will hasten the day when all the people of South Africa will realize their full human and spiritual potential. So,

Leon, the message that I want to bring to you tonight is that you can count on us in the government to support you in every way for this private effort, and I emphasize that it is a private effort as you said. But I want you to know it has the full support of the United States government. And at any time that we can do anything to help you in this most important effort we're there and just call us.[25]

Within the next several years, the number of United States companies signing the Principles rapidly increased, the accountability structures for monitoring the program were set in place, the Principles themselves were further amplified (far beyond what the original CEO's envisioned), and events in South Africa took an ominous turn. Finally, of course, apartheid was dismantled.

In the remainder of this chapter, we will trace the events in South Africa immediately following the initial, 1 March 1977 announcement of the Principles. Subsequent chapters offer a careful history and analysis of the major events of the following twenty years.

8. REACTION TO THE PRINCIPLES IN SOUTH AFRICA

South African activist groups, including the South African Council of Churches, did not react favorably to the Principles. Nor was there any tangible support from the South African business community, which saw the Principles as driven primarily by the United States companies' own problems in America. The South African business community also took umbrage at the implication that it was the United States companies who were at the vanguard of business effort to improve the lot of Black workers in South Africa. The business community felt that South Africans were more experienced and better attuned to the cultural sensitivities and economic realities of South Africa and that South African companies were making significant efforts to achieve similar ends through peaceful means and within the prevailing legal and political framework in South Africa.

Even the influential *Financial Mail,* the politically liberal business magazine, was lukewarm in its praise for the Principles and saw some major gaps in its scope. Witness the following points made in an article from the 4 March 1977 issue:

- The most obvious omission in the Statement of Principles is the question of trade union rights for Africans. Continued refusal to recognize African unions constitutes a perpetuation of racial discrimination. Many of the problems with which the Principles deal come about precisely because Africans are denied collective bargaining rights.

- The Statement of Principles needs to be given teeth. American parent companies should take a much closer interest in the everyday operations of their South African affiliates; some firms prefer the "ostrich approach" and really do not want to know what is going on.

- Those companies that are in the forefront of equal rights for African employees (for example, Africans supervising Whites) should come out of their closets and publicize their actions. If they are subjected to behind-the-scenes pressure from the government, the companies should expose these pressures publicly.

- An American chamber of commerce should be established in South Africa to provide guidance to the business community and to give United States firms a unified voice for social change.[26]

9.   CONCLUDING REMARKS

Admittedly, the final version of the code, announced on 1 March 1997, was not nearly as strong as Sullivan had wanted. It was what the companies were willing to enforce—which was no trivial consideration. That multinational corporations would join together voluntarily and agree to work for the advancement of human rights, in a country that by law and custom had denied those rights, was unprecedented. It was a unique set of events, personalities, and situational dynamics; most of the parties realized that they were breaking new ground and treading into uncharted territory. Sullivan was quite astute in realizing that he was "pushing the envelope" through sheer force of personality, faith in his cause, and willingness to acknowledge and address the real constraints that corporate leaders confronted from their other constituents. He was willing to trust the sincerity of the corporate leaders and to accept their commitment to what was, under the circumstances, a remarkable effort to transform the workplace in South Africa. Sullivan was also an astute tactician. As subsequent events would show, through a process of patient tenacity and negotiation, he was able to escalate the standards of performance and expand the area of activities covered by the Principles. He thereby achieved a substantial part of his original agenda—the same one that anti-apartheid activists had wanted and accused Sullivan of betraying in his dealings with multinational corporations.

ENDNOTES

1 L.W. Wise, "Memorandum to File," 6 September 1979.

2 P. Malozemoff (chairman and chief executive officer, Newmont Mining Corporation), letter to Leon H. Sullivan, 18 August 1977.

3 S. Prakash Sethi, *Multinational Corporations and the Impact of Public Advocacy on Corporate Strategy: Nestle and the Infant Formula Controversy* (Boston: Kluwer Academic Publishers, 1994); Oliver F. Williams, "Who Cast the First Stone," *Harvard Business Review* 62, 5 (1984): 151–60

4 Oliver F. Willams, ed., *Global Codes of Conduct: An Idea Whose Time Has Come* (Notre Dame, IN: University of Notre Dame Press, 2000); S. Prakash Sethi and Paul Steidlmeier, *Up Against the Corporation Wall: Cases on Business and Society*, 6th ed. (Upper Saddle River, NJ: Prentice Hall, 1997); Steven Greenhouse, "Nike Plant in Vietnam Is Called Unsafe for Workers," *New York Times*, 18 November 1997; Steven Greenhouse, "A Deep Split on Policing of Sweatshops: Apparel Talks Seek a Code of Conduct," *New York Times*, 21 November 1997; "Mattel Creates System to Monitor Conditions in Overseas Factories," *Wall Street Journal*, 21 November 1997; Steven Greenhouse, "Measure to Ban Import Items Made by Children in Bondage," *New York Times*, 1 October 1997; David Gonzalez, "Youthful Foes Go Toe to Toe with Nike," *New York Times*, 27 September 1997; "McDonald's Sues London Activists for Libel," *Times* (London), 12 January 1995; "Marathon McDonald's Libel Trial Near Climax," Reuters, 15 June 1997.

5 For a good account of Sullivan's work, see Leon H. Sullivan, *Build Brother Build* (Philadelphia: Macrae Smith, 1969).

6 Leon H. Sullivan, "Speech Given to the Summit Conference of Black Religious Leaders on Apartheid," New York City, 13 April 1979, 7. Unless otherwise specifically indicated, all speeches and correspondence quoted are from the Temple University Archives, Acc. 654–6C, International Council for Equality of Opportunity Principles, Papers from 1974–1987.

7 Quoted by Leon H. Sullivan in statement to the House Committee on International Relations, joint hearing of Subcommittees on International Economic Policy and Trade, and on Africa, 95th Congress, 2d sess., 6 July 1978, 5.

8 W. Fredericks, memorandum to T. Mecke and R. Markley, 11 February 1977.

9 Sal G. Marzullo, minutes of a Conference Board Meeting on South Africa, 15 March 1978.

10 Interview with the Reverend Leon H. Sullivan, 21 July 1995.

11 Paul N. McCloskey, Jr. (U.S. congressman, 12th District, CA), letter to the executive officers of the Caltex Petroleum Corporation, 16 November 1979.

12 R. H. Herzog (chairman of the board and chief executive officer, 3M), letter to Leon H. Sullivan, 1 November 1976.

13 J. M. Voss (chairman of the board, Caltex), letter to Leon H. Sullivan, 20 January 1977.

14 "U.S. Firms Pledge Discrimination Ban in South Africa," *Africa News*, 7 March 1977, 4–5.

15 See "Annals of International Trade: A Very Emotive Subject," *New Yorker*, 14 May 1979, 10.

16 Sullivan, "Speech Given to the Summit Conference of Black Religious Leaders on Apartheid," 9.

17 W. B. Nicholson (chairman, Union Carbide Corporation), letter to Leon H. Sullivan. 8 March 1977.

18 Leon H. Sullivan, letter to W. B. Nicholson, 16 March 1977.

19 Robert E. Terklom (vice president, Citibank), letter to Leon H. Sullivan, 22 February 1977.

20 William P. Tavoulareas (president, Mobil Oil Company), letter to Leon H. Sullivan, 18 February 1977.

21 Timothy Smith (director, ICCR), letter to Leon H. Sullivan, 29 March 1977.

22 Leon H. Sullivan, letter to Timothy Smith, 11 April 1977.

23 Carl F. Noffke (information counsellor, Embassy of South Africa, Washington, DC), letter to Hugh McMullen (chairman, Committee on Endorsements and Gifts, Board of Regents, University of Maryland), 20 April 1977.

24 William E. Schaufele, Jr., "Steps by U.S. Business Community," *Department of State Bulletin*, 9 May 1977, 469–70.

25 "Remarks of Cyrus Vance, Pierre Hotel, October 5, 1977," Temple University Archives.

26 "A Damp Squib Unless . . .," *Financial Mail*, 4 March 1977.

Chapter 2

The Emergence of the Anti-Apartheid Movement

The anti-apartheid movement and the development of the Sullivan Principles must be interpreted in the historical context both of South Africa and of the confluence of events in and between the United States and South Africa from the early 1960s through the 1980s. In this chapter, we first discuss the pivotal role of the Dutch Reformed Church and its rationale for supporting apartheid. We then turn to an analysis of the evolving anti-apartheid position of the mainline Protestant churches and the Roman Catholic Church. In this context, we will be highlighting the connection between the churches in South Africa and those in the United States. The remaining sections of the chapter examine the relevant political dynamics of South Africa, the United States, and the United Nations. Although some of these themes are discussed in greater detail in later chapters, the overview presented here provides a context for the unfolding story.[1]

1. THE RELIGIOUS RATIONALE FOR APARTHEID: THE DUTCH REFORM CHURCH

The first Dutch Reformed Church (DRC) minister arrived in South Africa in 1665. Missionary work among the slaves and Khoikhoi was discouraged, however. The "heathen" could not be baptized, although some exceptions were made in cases where a White person guaranteed the Christian training of a Black candidate. It was not until 1786 that this missionary work became a full-scale ministry.

Missionary activity increased with the arrival of Wesleyan Methodists and members of the London Missionary Society. The Methodists made the

journey with some five thousand British immigrants in 1820. This large influx of new arrivals from England added many former city dwellers to the
Cape Colony. The increased missionary activity among the Africans produced some tension. A scholar at the University of Cape Town, John W. de
Gruchy, expressed the problem well:

> The basic reason that Dutch and English settlers alike resented the pres-
> ence of some missionaries was . . . because the missionaries not only
> evangelized the indigenous peoples, but took their side in the struggle for
> justice, rights and land. The missionaries, being white, regarded
> themselves as the conscience of the settlers and the protectors of the
> "natives." . . . The church's struggle against racism and injustice in South
> Africa only really begins in earnest with their witness in the nineteenth
> century.[2]

Scholars have noted that in the nineteenth century—the seminal period in
the development of what would become the Republic of South Africa—there
were at least two distinct theories concerning the best approach to missionary work with the Africans.[3] One group advocated the acculturation of
Blacks into the White communities as the most appropriate way to convert
Blacks to the Christian way of life. Another, more dominant approach was
that tribal life and culture should be infused with Christianity but not merged
with White, Western culture. Separateness was thought to be essential to
promote and protect the way of life of the African. This theory was congru-
ent with the political vision of those who saw separateness as the only way
to ensure the safety of the White communities. The practice of having separate churches for the races grew to be standard practice not only for the
Dutch Reformed Church, but also for other Protestant denominations such as
the Baptists and Lutherans.

Roman Catholics and Anglicans could not accept the principle of separate churches, although in practice the typical congregation was, for the most
part, of one skin color only. In any event, the early Boer republics were all
governed by the principle that the Blacks were inferior beings who should
live under the unconditional authority of Whites. As early as 1839, the White
members of a Dutch Reformed congregation in the eastern Cape petitioned
to have separate communion based on race. At that point, and for scriptural
reasons, the General Synod rejected the request. In 1857, however, acknowledging the weakness of Whites who could not accept Blacks and Coloreds,
the synod approved separate communion and services. The so-called daugh-
ter churches for Coloreds, Indians, and Africans emerged in the wake of this
separatist policy.

Slowly but surely, the racist customs became statutory. For example, in
1924, when the National Party won control of the government, James

Hertzog became prime minister and soon enacted laws that ensured Afrikaner dominance. Of particular significance was the "civilized labor" policy. The government would hire "civilized"—that is, White—workers in preference to "uncivilized"—that is, Black—workers. The effect of this policy was dramatic. The impact on railway workers was typical. In the first ten years of the Hertzog administration, the percentage of Blacks dropped from 75 to 49 percent, whereas the percentage of Whites rose from 9.5 to 39 percent. In 1936 Hertzog passed the Representation of Natives Act, which took the eleven thousand Black Africans in the Cape off the common voters' roll. He also strengthened the pass laws and authorized the government to exercise "forced removals" of Blacks when necessary for the convenience of White areas.

In order to understand the root convictions of the National Party, consider the party's rationale as detailed in a 1948 statement:

> On the one hand, there is a policy of equality which advocates equal rights within the same political structure of all civilized and educated persons, irrespective of race or color, and the gradual granting of the franchise to non-Europeans as they become qualified to make use of democratic rights. On the other hand there is the policy of separation, which has grown up from the experience of the established European population of the country, and which is based on the Christian principles of justice and reasonableness. . . . We can only act in one of two directions. Either we must follow the course of equality, which must eventually mean national suicide for the white race, or we must take the course of separation ("apartheid"), through which the character and the future of every race will be protected and safeguarded, with full opportunities for development and self-maintenance in their own ideas, without the interests of one clashing with the interests of the other.[4]

To understand the struggle over apartheid in the last thirty years, it is important to realize the religious dimension of the problem. Among the 1.5 million White members of the Dutch Reformed Church of the 1970s and 1980s were the power brokers of government policy in the Republic. Almost all the top government officials, National Party Parliament members, provincial and town council members, police, and military officials belonged to DRC congregations. Although most mainstream Protestant churches and the Roman Catholic Church openly criticized the policy of separate development, the DRC did not.

An important distinction in analyzing the teachings of a church lies in the difference between official teaching and what is actually taught and believed by the people in the pews. During the 1970s and 1980s the DRC functioned as a civil religion par excellence, providing the people with a religious sanction for a bold Afrikaner nationalism. The Afrikaners understood themselves as struggling for dignity and identity in the face of oppression from both the British and the Africans, and they found a vision, a rationale, and a source of strength in the Dutch Reformed Church.

In 1974 the General Synod of the Dutch Reformed Church promulgated a document detailing the church's position on racial matters. Titled *Human Relations and the South African Scene in the Light of Scripture*, the document builds its case from Scripture, focusing on the creation narratives and the protohistory of Genesis 1–11.[5] The twin themes of the unity and equality of all peoples and the ethnic diversity among peoples are taken (1) to emerge from Scripture and therefore (2) to be in accord with the intentions of the Creator. Consider, for example, a text from the Acts of the Apostles:

> From one single stock he not only created the whole human race so that they could occupy the entire earth, but he decreed how long each nation should flourish and what the boundaries of its territory should be. And he did this so that all nations might seek the deity and, by feeling their way towards him, succeed in finding him. (Acts 17:27)

Although the document accepts the unity of all peoples as the ultimate destiny of ethnic groups, human sin has made diversity a fact of life that finally can be overcome only in the next world, in God's Kingdom. The story of the tower of Babel tells of the results of sin.

> Now Yahweh came down to see the town and the tower that the sons of man had built. "So they are all a single people with a single language!" said Yahweh. "This is but the start of their undertakings! There will be nothing too hard for them to do. Come, let us go down and confuse their language on the spot so that they can no longer understand one another." Yahweh scattered them then over the whole face of the earth, and they stopped building the town. It was named Babel therefore because there Yahweh confused the language of the whole earth. It was from there that Yahweh scattered them over the whole face of the earth. (Gen. 11:5–9)

To be sure, the Synod's 1974 document acknowledges that the message of the Gospel has social significance. For the DRC, the Scriptures—rather than blurring "all distinctions among peoples"—are interpreted as saying that Christians must ensure that diversity does not degenerate into estrangement. The document, however, in what seems to be a fatal flaw, equates *diversity* with *separation*. Thus, for example, the document states, "In specific circumstances and under specific conditions the New Testament makes provisions for the regulation on the basis of separate development of the co-existence of various peoples in one country."[6] Although the Christian task of avoiding estrangement in the midst of *diversity* is a manageable one, it is quite another story to overcome estrangement in the face of a rigid government policy of *separation*. As a matter of fact, the policy of separation had brutally increased injustice and systematically destroyed the family in Black African communities.

The DRC document, though clearly rejecting racism and discrimination on the basis of skin color, advocates the policy of separate development. Since apartheid is often associated with racial discrimination, the term *apartheid* is avoided. It was of no consequence that the policy of separate development had required an abundance of legislation demeaning to the human dignity of Blacks; the one clear advantage of the legislation was, indeed, that it maintained the power and privileges of the Whites. Nonetheless, some of the most incisive criticism of the DRC in South Africa came from its own theologians; there was a growing conviction that Dutch Reformed practice was "more determined by the interests of the Afrikaner than the Word of God."[7]

To understand how such a fundamentally religious people as the Afrikaners could bend the Word of God to their own interests, it is well to remember that civil religion is an ever present temptation, a temptation to which we in the United States have often succumbed.[8] The Afrikaners, in the face of great adversity, triumphed over enemies in the major events of their history—the Great Trek, the many wars, the 1948 National Party Victory, and the 1961 founding of the Republic. Through these events, many came to believe that God was acting in their history as he had done in Israel. They were a chosen people destined by God to bring an abundant life to all southern Africa. With this sense of divine calling and mission, central policies such as separate development were not simply strategies devised on the basis of prudential judgments. However, this overarching worldview was slowly losing its compelling power for the DRC as it became more and more apparent that separate development was impossible to reconcile with a biblical vision of justice and love.

One of the most hopeful signs that the process of dismantling apartheid was indeed underway was a statement released by the August 1985 annual meeting of the Presbytery of Stellenbosch of the DRC.

> We recognize that, in the South African society, racial discrimination plays a fundamental role in both structural and personal matters; we confess that this is contrary to the biblical principles of love of one's neighbor and justice.

> We also acknowledge that the ideal of apartheid did not succeed in creating social justice but has, on the contrary, led to human misery, frustration and injustice.

We confess that the Nederduits Gereformeerde Kerk has often insensitively and uncritically tolerated the negative realities and consequences of apartheid.

We therefore hereby declare ourselves prepared

a) to assess the apartheid system in all its consequences truly honestly and critically;

b) with all other people in our country, to seek prayerfully for a meaningful alternative for our land, and to do whatever we can to alleviate the suffering caused by the system.[9]

2. OVERVIEW OF CHURCH STRATEGIES (1970–85)

The Dutch Reformed Church had the largest White population of all the churches in South Africa. Within the DRC there are three denominations, each having racially separate bodies. The three White denominations of the DRC are the NGK *(Nederduits Gereformeerde Kerk)* with 1.8 million members; the NHK *(Nederduitsche Hervormde Kerk),* a more conservative church with 250 thousand members; and the *Gereformeerde Kerk,* an ultra-conservative denomination with 125 thousand members. The DRC (in this case, both the NGK and the NHK) made a distinction between racism and the policy of separate development, the former being sinful and the latter being acceptable. Since the NGK and the NHK would not condemn apartheid as a sin and a heresy—as the non-White branches of the NGK, with some 1.8 million members, had done—the World Alliance of Reformed Churches suspended them from membership. A growing minority of NGK members wanted to move toward a multiracial church and society. However, there was little support in the White DRC bodies for disinvestment or any other pressure strategies.

In the 1970s and 1980s, the major Protestant denominations showed a prophetic shift in the social action agenda. However, very few of the Whites in these denominations had much power and influence in the government. Their membership was also relatively small (table 2).

The mainline Protestant denominations in South Africa are joined together in the South African Council of Churches (SACC), which has a long history of opposition to racism and apartheid. In conjunction with the Christian Institute, an ecumenical center, SACC sponsored a series of studies on apartheid. In a 1976 report, SACC proposed a code of conduct for industries

Table 2. Church Membership by Race and Denomination

	Whites	Blacks	Coloreds	Asians
Anglicans	450,000	800,000	350,000	9,000
Methodists	400,000	1,500,000	140,000	4,000
Presbyterians	130,000	360,000	8,000	2,000
Lutherans	40,000*	700,000	100,000	1,000
Roman Catholics	400,000	1,700,000	260,000	21,000

*In 1984 the Lutheran World Federation (LWF) suspended the Evangelical Lutheran Church of Southern Africa for its failure to reject apartheid.

operating in South Africa. With six of its seventeen provisions being similar to the Sullivan Principles, the emphasis was on affirmative action strategies to better the lot of Blacks.

In 1978 Bishop Desmond Tutu was elected general secretary of SACC. He repeatedly employed a strategy of political and economic pressure, including the *threat* of disinvestment, as a means of persuading the White government to negotiate with the Blacks. In the face of much opposition, he courageously condemned violence and sought alternative strategies (besides economic and political pressure) to bring about changes in the government's racist policies. Rev. Beyers Naude replaced Tutu in the general secretary post at SACC in 1985. A former minister of the Dutch Reformed Church (NGK section), Naude was "banned"—a governmental order restricting a person's rights—for seven years (1977–84) for his work with the Christian Institute. In Naude's case, the banning order forbade him to speak in public, meet with more than two persons at once, and be quoted in the media. Naude, like Tutu, saw the threat of disinvestment as a way to avoid violence: "I believe that under certain circumstances a Christian is morally justified to ask for disinvestment in the same way as he is morally justified to call, for instance, for strike, boycott or a radical peaceful measure in order to avert a greater danger."[10] In April 1986, in hopes of increasing the pressure on the South African government to dismantle apartheid, Bishop Tutu made a dramatic plea for global economic sanctions against the Republic.

The Roman Catholic Church, too, had a long history of opposing apartheid, but it did not have much influence on the consciences of the White policymakers in South Africa. Its membership is predominantly non-White: 1.7 million Blacks, 260 thousand Coloreds, 21 thousand Indians, and 400 thousand Whites. The president of the Southern Africa Catholic Bishops' Conference (SACBC) during the 1970s and 1980s was the unusually talented churchman Denis E. Hurley, O.M.I., archbishop of Durban. Although, out of concern for the poor, the bishops' conference had adopted a very cautious approach to economic sanctions, it took prophetic stands on forced removals, the police conduct in townships, and the situation in Namibia.

The government had a long-standing adversarial relationship with mainstream Protestant churches and the Catholic Church. In 1984, in a case widely covered in both the international and the South African media, Archbishop Hurley was charged with making untrue and defamatory statements about Koevoet, the police counterinsurgency unit in Namibia. Officially charged under Section 27B of the Police Act of 1979, Archbishop Hurley pleaded not guilty and was fully prepared to document the injustice. After six months of harassment, the government finally withdrew the charges, saying it "had based its case on an erroneous news report." An excerpt from the archbishop's statement after the withdrawal of charges summarizes the stance of the mainstream churches: "These people fail to accept that political behavior is subject to the moral law. It is the church's duty to promote good ethical behavior in politics as much as in personal life."[11] It is perhaps an understatement to say that church-state relations, at least for the mainstream churches outside the DRC, were tense in South Africa.

3.   A BRIEF HISTORY OF CHURCH ACTIVISM

Church groups in South Africa, by the force of circumstances, became involved in political issues in a manner that was almost unthinkable prior to 1950. From the 1950s to the 1980s, there was a gradual shift in church policy from merely making statements against apartheid to formulating strategies and taking action to undermine the apartheid government.[12] This remarkable transition, outlined in the "Chronology of Church Involvement" (table 3), occurred under the influence of some new ideas in theology— Vatican II and Black, Liberation, and political theologies—that advocated direct action to change unjust social structures. What was especially compelling in South Africa was the spiral of violence caused by state repression and militant opposition.

Until the mid-1970s, both the SACBC's and the South African Council of Churches' statements reflected a concern to use every lawful means to overcome apartheid. Thus, although the SACBC condemned apartheid as evil in its 1957 statement, it gave no support or encouragement to the African National Congress defiance campaign against apartheid. In fact, the SACBC at that time held much the same view about overcoming apartheid that continued to dominate the United States business community into the 1970s and early 1980s. The SACBC's 1957 "Statement on Apartheid" taught that

Table 3. Chronology of Church Involvement

1957	The South African Catholic Bishops Conference (SACBC) issues the landmark "Statement on Apartheid." Apartheid condemned as evil, yet a very incrementalist approach encouraged as the means of overcoming it.
1960	Cottesloe Consultation convened by the World Council of Church (WCC) held in Johannesburg. Dutch Reform Church (DRC) withdraws from WCC and the South African Council of Churches (SACC) after they criticize apartheid.
1960	(March 21) Sharpesville incident.
1960	(April 18) Defiance campaign suppressed after banning of ANC and PAC.
1962	SACBC issues statement, urging the use of "every lawful means . . . in order to overcome injustices."
1962	Second Vatican Council of the Catholic Church provides a new religious paradigm, suggesting action for social justice.
1963	(June 11) Nelson Mandela captured, and he and most ANC leaders sent to Robbin Island. ANC now relies on sanctions supported by a worldwide network of anti-apartheid organizations.
1966	SACBC issues pastoral letter, urging that all legal means should be used to change unjust laws, such as racial discrimination, migratory labor laws, and laws denying political rights.
1966	George Houser (ACOA) testifies before U.S. Congress, advocating sanctions similar to ones legislated 20 years later.
1968	SACC issues "A Message to the People of South Africa," which outlines the basis for later civil disobedience position.
1972	SACC establishes the Division of Justice and Reconciliation following the WCC Special Fund of the Program to Combat Racism.
1974	SACC adopts a resolution supporting conscientious objection based on presence of structural violence in South Africa.
1976	Soweto mass violence.
1977	(March) Sullivan Principles promulgated.
1977	(September) Steve Biko murdered.
1977	SACBC issues "Declaration of Commitment," which outlines a new understanding of its mission: evangelization includes transforming the concrete structures that oppress people.
1978	Bishop Tutu appointed general secretary of SACC (first Black G.S.).
1979	Catholic seminaries finally integrated after setting the policy in 1972.
1979	SACC vice president Allan Boesak at the General Conference proposes massive civil disobedience. Bishop Tutu advocates "economic pressure" to hasten political change.
1980	SACC conference proclaims that churches must adopt political action.
1982	SACBC issues report on Namibia highly critical of South African security forces for violating human rights.
1985	(November) SACC issues a resolution calling for "disinvestment and similar economic pressure."
1985	(December) WCC consultation in Harare with SACC calls for "immediate and comprehensive economic sanctions and a refusal to refinance SA's foreign debt."
1986/87	State of emergency widens.
1986	(April) Bishop Tutu calls for global economic sanctions against Republic of SA. (May) SACBC issues "Pastoral Letter on Economic Pressure for Justice."

the condemnation of the principle of apartheid as something intrinsically evil does imply that perfect equality can be established in South Africa by a stroke of the pen. There is nothing more obvious than the existence of profound differences between sections of our population which make immediate total integration impossible. . . . Nor is it unjust for a state to make provision in its laws and administration for the differences that do exist. It would be unreasonable, therefore, to condemn indiscriminately all South Africa's differential legislation.

This policy would undergo a fundamental change over the next thirty years. The intellectual root of this change was the theology taught not only in the 1968 SACC statement, but also in the 1962 Roman Catholic Vatican II documents. When confronted with increasing violence, this new theology justified both the Protestant and Catholic churches in actively opposing the government and even in advising the global community to use economic sanctions against South Africa. Thus, in 1985 SACC called for disinvestment by the world community, and in 1986 SACBC issued its "Pastoral Letter on Economic Pressure for Justice." Whereas SACC called for outright disinvestment, SACBC—following a characteristically cautious tack—advocated that economic pressure "be implemented in such a way as to not destroy the economy." The document expressed concern that sanctions not harm the least advantaged.

4.   THE UNITED STATES RESPONSE TO CHURCH ACTIVISM IN SOUTH AFRICA

The concern of United States groups over South African racist policies dates back to 1912, when the National Association for the Advancement of Colored People (NAACP) provided assistance to what later became the Africa National Congress of South Africa. It was not until 1953, however, that the momentum for change began to build; that year marked the founding of the American Committee on Africa (ACOA) by George Houser, a White, Methodist minister. Under Houser, ACOA campaigned for total United States disinvestment from South Africa. In 1957 ACOA sponsored a Declaration of Conscience campaign with the "World-Wide Day of Protest," which featured Eleanor Roosevelt and Martin Luther King, Jr. For the most part, however, the ACOA campaign of the 1950s did not attract much interest in the United States.

In Houser's judgment, it was the media attention given to official violence against Blacks in South Africa that eventually caught the attention of the American public.[13] For example, on 21 March 1960, in connection with a demonstration against the pass laws in Sharpeville, the police killed 67 and wounded 180 people. In 1976 security forces fired upon 15,000 school children demonstrating in Soweto. Finally, between 1984 and 1987, the unrest and violence throughout the country substantially strengthened the growing American interest in support of disinvestment.

To be sure, the television and other media coverage of these tragic events brought the apartheid problem into the living rooms of middle America, but does it explain entirely the ever expanding pressure for total disinvestment? Houser and others think otherwise. Instead, they focus on the perception that business was, at least until 1984, too cozy with the White government in South Africa and relatively unconcerned about the plight of the non-White majority who suffered under apartheid. Based on this perception, whether accurate or not, the anti-apartheid movement in the late 1960s devised strategies that focused on the role that United States business played in South Africa in sustaining the government's apartheid policies. A major offensive was launched by the church groups in 1975. It was largely led by the Interfaith Center on Corporate Responsibility (ICCR), a coalition of Protestant denominations and an ad hoc group of Catholic dioceses and religious orders, housed in the New York City headquarters of the National Council of Churches. ICCR called for the prohibition of bank loans to the Republic of South Africa. Forty-seven banks, including some of the major banking institutions in the United States, were threatened with a mass withdrawal of deposits and continued shareholder pressure unless loans to the Republic of South Africa ceased. Although the campaign did not have any immediate, significant effect on banks' loan policies, it did give much visibility to the apartheid problem.

Initially, as the ICCR and its religious investors challenged managers to take responsibility for supporting the evils of apartheid with their bank loans, bank managers argued that their sole responsibility was to find reliable businesses that would yield reasonable income on their loans commensurate with the safety of the principal. As the campaign progressed, however, Tim Smith, executive director of ICCR, observed a gradual opening on the part of managers to hear and act upon the social and moral concerns of the church groups.

Businesses came to realize that what was at stake was the very legitimacy of business in the minds of some important constituencies. What was happening here was a gradual paradigm shift from the *market capitalism model* to what has been called the *business ecology model*.[14] The religious coalition was finally successful in terminating all loans, but the process took over ten years. It was, moreover, never clear to the interest groups whether the banks were acting on principle or protecting their self-interest. Although at least two banks (Chemical and Chase Manhattan) expressly cited their opposition to apartheid as the reason for ending the loans, most bank officials publicly cited economic grounds alone.

5.   THE POLITICAL CONTEXT OF THE ANTI-APARTHEID MOVEMENT – SOUTH AFRICA

In 1983, with the addition to the Republic of South Africa Constitution that expanded Parliament from one to three chambers, Coloreds and Indians obtained a parliamentary franchise. A distinction was made between "own affairs" and "general affairs," with "general affairs" (foreign affairs, defense, security) being controlled by a cabinet comprising selected members of all three chambers, and "own affairs" being governed by the particular racial chamber. Although the White National Party maintained control under the new constitution, the party did, at least, acknowledge the citizenship of Indians and Coloreds. The remaining 73 percent of the population, the Black Africans, had yet to receive any sort of parliamentary franchise. For this reason, many Indians and Coloreds were antagonistic to the new constitutional structure and unwilling to accept the franchise until all could participate. Without the broad support and participation of the Indians and Coloreds, the new chambers of Parliament were reduced to "puppet legislatures" whose members were viewed with contempt by the body politic.

The years from 1965 to 1985 were both exhilarating and frightening for South Africans. Prime Minister Verwoerd (1954–66) led the nation in an era of unparalleled prosperity and power. In 1960 the electorate (all White) approved by a slim majority the motion that South Africa become a republic. A short time later the nation withdrew from the British Commonwealth. For the Afrikaners, a dream had been realized: they were finally free of the British. For the English-speaking segment of the population, however, there was a sense both of alienation from South Africa and of isolation from the rest of the world.

Opposition to the racist policies of the government continued to grow. Nelson Mandela, a law school student of the prestigious University of Witwatersrand, accepted a leadership role in the African National Congress. After being frustrated in all attempts to effect change through nonviolent pressure, Mandela took leadership of a group (*Umkonto We Sizwe*, "Spear of the Nation") that planned to use sabotage in places that would not involve danger to lives. For this and other activities, he was sentenced to life imprisonment in 1964, where he remained for twenty-seven years. To counteract the growing unrest in the society, the government passed a number of laws that curtailed civil liberties.

At the same time, Afrikaner entrepreneurs were emerging as a force in business life in South Africa. Until the 1960s, a tacit understanding existed that the English-speaking South Africans would run the business world and the Afrikaners would manage the government. This situation began to change in the mid-1960s. By 1980 the Afrikaans Institute of Commerce, the *Afrikaanse Handelsinstituut*, had become a powerful voice in the commercial world. Achieving success and power in business led to a healing of the rift between the White English- and Afrikaans-speakers. Many areas of cooperation developed between the two White "tribes." With this healing, however, arose a renewed fear of the Black "threat" to the nation and increasing defensiveness toward criticism of apartheid from the international community.

The nation was stunned in 1966 when Prime Minister Verwoerd was stabbed to death by a messenger in the House of Parliament. The Minister of Justice, B. J. Vorster, was elected prime minister by the National Party Caucus and continued the National Party policies. Political unrest continued. The Black communities were especially angry over Pretoria's policy of sending urban Black dependents to the homelands. This "endorsing out" strategy broke up families and inflamed anger. In June 1976 Soweto students rebelled, ostensibly over the mandatory use of Afrikaans in schools, but also as a general condemnation of the whole system. More than 175 people were killed. Not since the 1960 Sharpeville demonstrations, where the police killed sixty-seven Black Africans, had the violence been so great. Reports of police brutality were widespread, and at least one Black leader who died in prison—Steve Biko—was judged to have been the victim of the government. (In 1997, the Truth and Reconciliation Commission found that Biko had indeed been murdered by the police.)

In 1978, when Vorster retired for reasons of health, P. W. Botha assumed the role of prime minister. Compared to previous leaders, Botha was a reform (*verligte*, or "enlightened") Nationalist. He told his White constituency that they must "adapt or die." He dramatically increased the education budget for Black Africans, dismantled more color-bar legislation in the workplace, granted Blacks the right to form and join unions, abolished the Mixed Marriages and the Immorality Acts, and provided a token franchise for Indians and Coloreds. However, his critics in the Progressive Federal Party (the White opposition) continued to point out that all his reform measures assumed the legitimacy of "Grand Apartheid"; that is, of a society based on ethnic groupings enforced by law.

5.1   Pieter W. Botha: "Cooperative Coexistence"

Analysts, both domestic and international, had long argued that P. W. Botha was increasingly alienating his potentially large, moderate constituency by the absence of any clear overall vision of the society he was trying to fashion through his reforms. Botha was often trapped between the reactionary right and the strident and demanding left. On the one hand, some Whites, growing insecure at the thought of being overrun by Blacks in the country, were moving to the right on the political spectrum and were resisting all change. On the other hand, many moderate Blacks, increasingly frustrated with the pace of political reform, were moving to the left and resorting to violence in hopes of hastening their freedom. The people knew well that the riots in Sharpeville (1960) and Soweto (1976) achieved more for the cause of reform than did any of their elected officials' activities. The Black leaders in the townships, a product of the South Africa government, were generally considered unimportant and held in contempt by the populace.

Botha had been advised by many, especially the South African business community, to be less of a party politician and more of a statesman, and to lead his people with a clear vision of a dynamic society that enshrines a justice that knows no color bar. At one point, Botha seemed to understand and accept the advice. Officials of his administration conveyed to the United States government, as well as to South Africa's business leaders, that he would advance his agenda for substantive reform at a National Party Congress in Durban on 15 August 1985. The Durban speech, however, proved to be a diatribe against other nations' interference in the internal affairs of South Africa. Not only did the address fail to restore the confidence of the moderates in his own country, it so frightened the international banking community that a financial crisis followed in short order. Led by the United States' Chase Manhattan Bank, major banks from Britain, Japan, Switzerland, and West Germany refused to renew short-term loans to South Africa. Called "rolling over," this renewal process had, heretofore, been automatic because South Africa was considered a good borrower. Foreign banks already had an estimated $24 billion invested in the nation, but this lifeline was about to be effectively withdrawn.

In September 1985, in a speech at a party congress at Port Elizabeth, Botha delivered an address that was the closest he had come to offering his administration's vision of South Africa's future.[15] Botha candidly admitted that "constitutional rights for Blacks in the central government have . . . been a point of dispute in South Africa right from the start." Departing from National Party doctrine, Botha rejected apartheid as a solution and instead offered a new vision that he called "cooperative coexistence."

I have already repeatedly stated that if "Apartheid" means:

- Political domination of one group over another
- The exclusion of any community from the political decision-making process
- Injustice and inequality in the opportunities available to any community
- Racial discrimination and encroachment upon human dignity,

Then the South African Government shares in the rejection of the concept.[16]

Rejecting a universal franchise in a unitary state—for "Africa taught us that it means the dictatorship of the strongest black group"—Botha offered a vision of a federation of "units . . . recognized on a geographic and group basis." While acknowledging that much was yet to be negotiated, Botha offered the following broad contours of constitutional reform:

- The Republic of South Africa forms one State. It is an explicit implication of the Government's view that independence will not be forced on the self-governing areas and that they form part of the Republic until they should decide to become independent. In this regard, however, the Government also respects the decision of the four states that previously formed part of the Republic, to take independence. As a result of the large degree of interdependence between the independent states and the Republic, the Government nevertheless acknowledged the possibility of co-operation with these states in an overall framework.
- It follows this point of view that there should be one collective South African Citizenship for all who form part of the Republic. For this reason I announced on 11 September this year among other things that the South African Citizenship of those black persons who permanently reside in the Republic, but who lost their Citizenship as a result of independence, will be restored.
- Thirdly, my Government stated clearly that all groups and communities within the geographical area of this state must obtain representation to the highest level without domination of the one over the other. Therefore I do not understand why the Government is time and again still expected to say that it is prepared to share its power of decision-making with other communities. It is accepted National Party policy and surely it is evident in views repeatedly expressed by the Government.[17]

In the Port Elizabeth speech, later amplified at Cape Town, Botha called on the President's Council, an appointed group from the three-chamber central government, to broaden its role so that Blacks could be represented on a national level. The President's Council comprised sixty members: thirty-five appointed by political parties and twenty-five appointed by the president. Channels for important negotiations with Black leaders were at least being discussed. In a 31 January 1986 speech to Parliament at Cape Town, Botha again spoke of this "National Statutory Council" but failed to provide specifics of the plan; the speech was not well received by Black leaders. In April 1986 Botha surprised many by announcing that the hated pass laws would no longer be enforced and would be abolished. Even so, Botha's vision for South Africa—which included the continued segregation of schools, housing, and "culture"—was far less ambitious than that of the country's most progressive leaders.

5.2   The Progressive Federal Party

One of the most surprising features of South African political life during these years was the vitality and strength of the opposition party, the Progressive Federal Party. Led by a talented and articulate Afrikaner, Frederik van Zyl Slabbert, the party championed the cause of the Blacks and argued for immediate negotiations for reform. In Slabbert's words:

> Nothing is a greater threat to the rights and protection of minorities than to entrench racial and ethnic groups in a new constitutional dispensation. This is one of the fundamental shortcomings of the Government's constitutional reforms, both in the tricameral parliament and in the latest constitutional initiatives between Black and White. If racial and ethnic groups, as defined in law by the Government should form the building blocks of a new constitutional dispensation for South Africa, then a future picture of siege and conflict will become a reality.[18]

After hearing State President P. W. Botha's agenda for overcoming apartheid at the official opening of Parliament on 31 January 1986, Slabbert decided to resign from Parliament, saying that the reform proposals were "not good enough. It is a false start."

5.3   The African National Congress

The African National Congress (ANC) was anathema to P. W. Botha. In his words, "And if communist-controlled organizations such as the ANC should have their way with support from abroad, it will be a dark day for South Africa."[19] The government's position on the ANC was outlined in a speech by the deputy minister of information, D. J. Louis Nel.[20] In essence, he said that the ANC is a "terrorist and Communist-backed organization" whose stated aim is "the total disruption of the Black communities."

In the government's view, the ANC was seeking total change through violence and revolution, and had formed "an alliance with the South African Communist Party, who endeavor to establish a Marxist-Socialist state in South Africa." The ANC did not want a reform that would result "in the sharing of power by all South Africans irrespective of race, color or creed." Instead, according to Nel, it sought a revolution and the "seizing of power by a militant few." Addressing a Youth Year rally in Bloemfontein, P. W. Botha reiterated a common theme: much of the campaign against South Africa comes from supporters around the world of the "godless Marxist ideology."[21]

For their part, ANC leaders Nelson Mandela and Oliver Tambo had always claimed that they were not Communists. They had accepted money and arms from the Soviet Union and cooperation from the small South African Communist Party. Norway and Sweden contributed substantial funds for nonmilitary ANC programs, and it is reported that the ANC raised almost $30 million a year around the globe. According to its leaders, ANC violence began in the 1960s only in response to the government's own violence. For the most part, the ANC used sabotage designed to provoke the government and to raise the anxiety of the White citizenry. In 1980 an attack on the Sasol oil installations was given wide publicity, and in 1984, forty-four bombing incidents were attributed to the ANC.

The bible of the ANC was the Freedom Charter, a document that renounced apartheid and called for a multiracial democracy. Drawn up by a "Congress of the People" in June 1955, the charter would, if implemented, pose a considerable threat to the existing economic framework of South Africa: "The national wealth shall be restored to the people. The mineral wealth, the banks and monopoly industry, shall be transferred to the ownership of the people as a whole."[22]

Most Blacks identified with Nelson Mandela and the ANC. They saw this approach as the most tangible way to oppose apartheid. Surveys of the Black community continued to indicate Mandela as the people's choice for leadership. Having been jailed for over twenty years, he was typically perceived as a hero or martyr. For most Blacks, the ANC had come to symbolize the struggle for freedom against oppression. Whether most Blacks also subscribed to the full program of the ANC, or even understood what that program entailed, was quite another matter.

A growing number of Whites in South Africa had come to see the fallacy of the Botha government's position on the ANC. A prominent Dutch Reformed cleric—Nico Smith, former theology professor at the University of Stellenbosch and member of the Broederbond—asked permission to lead a delegation of clerics to meet the leaders of the outlawed ANC in the exiled headquarters at Lusaka, Zambia. The government refused this request, but Smith had made his point: the government should be meeting with the ANC! Eight students at Stellenbosch University, long the training ground for Afrikaner leaders, announced plans to travel to Lusaka to meet representatives of the ANC. The government responded by withdrawing the students' passports.

A month later, in November 1985, the editor of the *Cape Times*, Tony Heard, published an interview with exiled ANC president Oliver Tambo. Since Tambo was a "banned person," however, he could not be quoted, according to South Africa's very restrictive security laws, without the permission of the minister of law and order. For publishing the interview, Heard was charged under the Internal Security Act and could have received as much as a three-year jail sentence. The interview itself was quite instructive, belying many governmental stereotypes of the ANC and showing that a genuine chance existed for political negotiations. In Tambo's words, "There is always the possibility of a truce. It would be very, very easy, if, for example, we started negotiations."[23]

5.4   The United Democratic Front

In 1983 the President's Council proposed the outlines of a tricameral parliament (subsequently adopted and implemented in 1984). At the same time, the so-called Koornhof Bills—legislation designed to strengthen the government's control over Black labor—were being discussed. Mobilized in opposition to these government moves, numerous groups came together to pool their resources and offer a united front for a free, democratic, and multiracial country. The resulting United Democratic Front (UDF) was a coalition of some six hundred groups—political clubs, professional societies, student organizations, community groups, and labor unions. Founded by the president of World Alliance of Reformed Churches, Allan Boesak, the UDF saw its role as one of coordinating the actions of the coalition's organizations. With perhaps as many as two million members, the group actively sought to abolish apartheid and institute majority rule. When the state of emergency was declared in July 1985, many UDF leaders were detained in jails across the nation. The government repeatedly claimed that the UDF was a front for the banned ANC since the UDF had adopted the ANC Freedom Charter.

The underlying concern of the UDF was that the National Party government was involved in an effort to modernize apartheid, not to abolish it. In the UDF's view, the Koornhof Bills attempted to divide Blacks, giving urban Blacks more rights and security, and pushing "homeland" Blacks out of the mainstream economic and political community of South Africa. In this way, the argument went, Whites could appease the international community but still retain control. By the same token, the new constitution was perceived as an instrument of neo-apartheid.

5.5 The Azanian People's Organization

The Azanian People's Organization (AZAPO), a Black consciousness group, was opposed to any sort of multiracial government. For members of this movement, the proper name of the country known as South Africa was Azania, a Greek form of the Persian word *zanj-bar* (Zansibar), meaning "land of the blacks." Founded in 1978 after other Black organizations were banned, AZAPO comprised a relatively small group of Blacks. In 1983, however, AZAPO brought two hundred organizations together to form the National Forum (NF), which declared its intention to abolish apartheid and the "system of racial capitalism." Considerably to the left of the UDF, the NF was locked in a struggle against "the system of racial capitalism which holds the people of Azania in bondage for the benefit of the small minority of White capitalists and their allies, the White workers and the reactionary sections of the Black middle class."[24] In many Black townships, internecine violence flared up between members of the UDF and AZAPO, each fighting for community dominance.

5.6 Mangosuthu Gatsha Buthelezi and Inkatha

Mangosuthu Gatsha Buthelezi, popularly known as Gatsha Buthelezi, was the hereditary leader of South Africa's six million Zulus. In this period, Chief Buthelezi was the chief minister of the Kwazulu homeland administration and extremely popular with the Zulus, most of whom lived in or near the "homeland," which was laced throughout Natal. The original plan of the National Party was gradually to make all of the so-called homelands constitutionally separate from South Africa.

Buthelezi's power base in South Africa was a highly organized Black political organization known as Inkatha (the full title is *Inkatha Yenkululeko Yesizwe*, which means the "National Cultural Liberation Movement"). Inkatha was a million-member organization, predominantly Zulu but open to all Blacks. Most members of Inkatha lived in the areas of Kwazulu, although branches operated throughout the Transvaal townships, the Orange Free State, and Cape Town. As president of Inkatha, Buthelezi was in a position to hold substantive negotiations with the Nationalist government.

Buthelezi was opposed to independent Black homelands. Instead, he argued for sharing power with the White government in an undivided South Africa. As a longstanding advocate of the free enterprise system, Buthelezi saw free enterprise for Blacks *within* South Africa—rather than the constitutional independence of the homelands—as the best way to improve the quality of life for Blacks. In this light, his repeated condemnation of the disinvestment lobby is understandable. Buthelezi championed new investments and traveled around the globe encouraging new foreign investments in South Africa. He recognized that his view "is rejected vehemently by the ANC's Mission in Exile, by the UDF and by AZAPO." Though not denying the validity of some of these groups' critiques, Buthelezi advocated a more pragmatic approach: "I am committed to tactics and strategies which will work today and which will not prejudice tomorrow, and I say simply that leaders in South Africa have no option but to let the day after tomorrow look after itself."[25]

5.7 Labor Unions in South Africa

After the 1976 riots in Soweto, the South African government responded to increasing pressure from the business community by forming several commissions to study public policies relating to Black workers. One of the commissions was specifically charged to make recommendations regarding the reform of labor legislation concerning Africans. Led by a scholar in industrial relations from Pretoria, Nicholas Wiehahn, the commission suggested major reforms, one of which was that Africans be allowed to join registered trade unions. In 1979, this Wiehahn Commission recommendation was accepted by the government; within months, more than 10 percent of Black workers belonged to African trade unions.

Unlike labor unions in the United States, African trade unions—whose members lacked the franchise—had no effective access to the political arena. Collective bargaining was Africans' only means of achieving their goals. For example, demanding housing near the work site was a way for workers without the franchise to try to change—through the collective bargaining process—the Group Areas Act. Similarly, when public policy did not outlaw discriminatory hiring and promotion practices, such matters became part of the collective bargaining agenda. Job security was another issue that took on crucial importance in South Africa; when Black Africans were dismissed, they had to leave their current, urban residence and return to a homeland within seventy-two hours.

The collective bargaining process was thus being used to air and resolve grievances well beyond the scope and competence of many industrial managers. South African business was confronted with issues that properly belonged in the political domain. With such burdensome problems in mind, most businesses in South Africa were aggressively lobbying the government to improve the broad spectrum of social and political rights for workers.

In December 1985, thirty-six labor unions with a combined membership of more than five hundred thousand workers formed a new labor federation, the Congress of South African Trade Unions (COSATU). COSATU's president, Elijah Barayi, made it clear that the federation's agenda was primarily political, including the abolition of the pass laws, disinvestment by foreign companies, and nationalization of the mines. COSATU member unions were some of the largest in South Africa: the Federation of South Africa Trade Unions (FOSATU), the National Union of Mineworkers, and the General and Allied Workers Union. The formation of this federation heralded a new militancy in the struggle for political rights.

The Council of Unions of South Africa (CUSA) had actively supported certain kinds of disinvestment. Many union federations, however, offered more qualified support, wanting to exploit the threat of disinvestment for all the leverage possible without risking an increase in unemployment. Other Black labor unions took a different approach to the issue. Lucy Mvubelo, general secretary of the largest Black trade union in South Africa, the National Union of Clothing Workers, opposed all economic sanctions:

> To proponents of isolation, disinvestment, and embargoes, I must say: Don't break off contact, and don't advocate disengagement and withdrawal of foreign investments. Only indigenous movements—the trade unions, the political groupings, the schools, the business associations— within South Africa can bring about significant, positive change. Outsiders can influence it, but only through participation, not by isolation.[26]

This position was clearly a minority one among the trade unions.

5.8   The South African Business Community

When the Afrikaner National Party came to power in 1948, the business leaders were largely English-speaking Whites who were deeply resented by the new rulers. This resentment, stemming from years of British imperialism and the brutal Anglo-Boer war, became entrenched in habits that maintained sharp divisions between business and government—even though a number of Afrikaners emerged as major business leaders in recent decades. But a new era was heralded in with the 1979 Carlton Conference, when President Botha outlined a partnership in which government would support the free enterprise system by creating a climate of confidence and stability, and by removing statutory racial discrimination that prevented full participation of Blacks in the economy. For its part, the private sector was charged to ensure economic growth that would create much needed jobs for the expanding population.

Six years after the Carlton Conference, in the face of massive unrest in the society, it was clear that the honeymoon was over for business and government. Frederick du Plessis, chairman of Sanlam, a major conglomerate in South Africa, summed up the business response to the Botha administration when he likened the country to a car without a driver. Gavin Relly, chairman of the Anglo-American Corporation, succinctly stated the challenge: "It is necessary for the government to enter into negotiations with representatives of all groups in South Africa for a system of genuine power sharing." The Association of Chambers of Commerce (ASSOCOM), the South African Federated Chamber of Industries (FCI), the National African Federated Chamber of Commerce (NAFCOC), and the *Afrikaanse Handelsinstituut* (AHI) all called upon the government to "negotiate with acknowledged Black leaders about power sharing."

That leading citizens should champion such desperately needed reforms is not particularly unusual in a society, but that business as an institution of society should be on the leading edge of social change was remarkable and perhaps unparalleled. In September 1985 ninety major South African companies published an advertisement in the nation's leading newspapers presenting their agenda for reform. Robin Lee, managing director and chief executive of the Urban Foundation in South Africa (a foundation funded by business to improve the welfare of Blacks) summed up the new mood of business: "What is needed now is almost a quantum leap from conventional views of corporate social responsibility . . . to a definite, organized and visible role in bringing about rapid social and economic change."[27] What Leon Sullivan had advocated in 1976 was slowly becoming a reality.

In the same month that the newspaper advertisement was published—and as an indication of how rapid and dramatic a change the business community envisioned—eighteen of South Africa's most prominent business and media leaders traveled to Lusaka, Zambia, to meet with the ANC. Tony Bloom, chairman of the Premier Group, was straightforward in expressing the point the delegation was trying to make: "I believe the ANC are people with whom serious negotiations can be undertaken."[28] The business leaders present were Gavin Relly, Hugh Murray, Tony Bloom, Peter Sorour, Zach de Beer, Tertius Myburgh, and Harold Pakendorf. Representing the African National Congress were Oliver Tambo, Chris Hani, Pallo Jordan, James Stuart, Thabo Mbeki, and Mac Maharaj. Although Gavin Relly was quick to point out that "immediate universal suffrage, with no protection for minorities or safeguards for institutions" (a demand of the ANC), would never be acceptable, he did acknowledge that the meeting was valuable and laid the groundwork for "constructive understanding." Most people in South Africa hoped for national conciliation, and many believed that the business community had blazed the trail that the government must follow.

6. THE POLITICAL CONTEXT OF THE ANTI-APARTHEID MOVEMENT – UNITED STATES

There was a growing expectation in the United States that business should be involved in social issues. Advocacy groups, encouraged by the success of Ralph Nader's initiatives, began to grow in importance. What gave rise to this rather sudden increase in nonmarket forces or interest-group activism? Was the church involvement in the United States simply a response to the call of the churches in South Africa? One of the formative experiences that may have set the tone for activism in the United States was the civil rights movement of the 1960s. Those who participated in that momentous social and political change, whether actively or passively, came to feel a new power to transform society. Evil did not have to be tolerated; unjust social structures could be changed with strategy and persistence. In the United States the antiwar movement, the rise of local community organizations, and the experience of the civil rights movement (along with its use of the media and its creation of heroes) provided, in our judgment, the model and the power that brought subsequent activist movements to birth.

At the same time, several other important developments provided fertile soil for the growth of activist movements. During the previous decades the media achieved significant power to shape public opinion on social issues, and informed public opinion generated financial and other support for a wide variety of organizations championing such issues. In addition, whereas the two major political parties used to be the vehicles that carried the concerns of the people into and through the public-policy process, the two parties had come to be perceived as ineffective in this regard. Interest groups came, instead, to perform many of the roles that the political parties had, in effect, abdicated. The need for United States businesses to avoid racist policies in South Africa had an especially compelling claim on Americans because of their own, often unsuccessful, experience in trying to overcome a racist past.

For a variety of reasons, concern over apartheid moved to center stage in the United States during the 1980s, but the issue was by no means a new one for Americans. Americans for South African Resistance came together in 1952; later called the American Committee on South Africa, the organization coordinated the liberation movements of South Africa that had supporters in the United States. The 1960s saw many Black dreams come to fruition in legislation enacted by the Johnson administration. During that same period, social activists—college students, civil rights leaders, and church groups—began exerting pressure against endowments that held investments in firms operating in South Africa and against banks that made loans to the South African government. The goal of the activists was ultimately to dismantle apartheid through pressuring the Republic of South Africa government. The role of the anti-apartheid movement and its impact on United States companies to withdraw from South Africa are discussed in detail in chapter 12.

7.   INTERNATIONAL SANCTIONS

International sanctions against South Africa were never totally effective; for example, the oil embargo never stopped the supply of oil.[29] Whether sanctions were nonetheless successful—did they hasten the end of statutory apartheid?—is much more debatable. In an economic sense, sanctions add to the cost of doing business. Thus, all sanctions can be overcome if one is willing to pay the price. From the perspective of those imposing sanctions, each successive, more stringent level of enforcement results in added costs, which become prohibitive beyond a certain point. That is why no regime of sanctions is either totally successful or a complete failure, even under conditions of armed conflict; for example, in World War II, blockades were constantly mounted and repeatedly breached. The question is therefore one of rational choice. Beyond the political and moral symbolism, the extent of sanctions must be carefully ascertained, taking into account both the direct costs involved in imposing the sanctions and the sanctions' potential impact on those being constrained or censured.[30] More research is needed on strategic or "smart" sanctions that are designed to reach the power brokers and to avoid harming the poor and the powerless.

It is beyond the scope of this book to discuss the arguments, pro and con, in the debate on use or effectiveness of economic sanctions, either in general or with respect to South Africa. Although the opposing groups continue to adhere unswervingly to their positions, it is highly doubtful that the world community would ever have mobilized massive and coordinated economic resources or military forces to inflict serious harm on South Africa's White-dominated government. Most published studies of economic and military sanctions imposed on other countries have concluded that sanctions have been, at best, a crude tactic, one that has, in the long run, invariably been found to be ineffective.[31] In the final analysis, there has rarely been enough determination and commitment of resources by nations who sought changes in the conduct of offending, repressive regimes. Such regimes adroitly play on the reluctance of democratic nations to initiate military action as the ultimate recourse—even under conditions that are far more inhumane and violative of human rights than the conditions prevailing in South Africa.

A further complicating factor in the case of South Africa was that a number of major industrial powers had important economic stakes in the country and were unwilling to jeopardize those interests for the sake of pursuing a dubious strategy of sanctions. They also claimed that a path of peaceful persuasion—that is, a carrot-and-stick approach—would lead to better results. In any case, it is doubtful whether any logical or historical arguments would have made any difference in the opinions and beliefs of those who advocated sanctions, who would simply consider such arguments as self-serving.

The South African government was able to meet its essential needs for imported materials through the collusion of (1) nations who were less sympathetic to the sanctions rationale, and (2) rogue businesses, including many large multinationals that stood to make enormous profits by violating those sanctions.[32]

As early as 1960 the African states had asked the Arab nations to prevent their oil from being sold to South Africa. However, it was not until 1973 that the Africans received a positive response. In that year, hoping to enlist the OAU (Organization of African Unity) nations in an alliance against Israel, the Arab nations (with the exception of Iran) cut off oil suppliers to South Africa. With the fall of the shah of Iran in 1979, the new Iranian government also joined the boycott. The net effect of the boycott was to force South Africa to pay more for oil on the world market and thus to slow economic growth. In April 1986 P. W. Botha stated that between 1973 and 1984 South Africa paid SA Rand (ZAR) 22 billion more for oil than it would have paid without the sanctions. When de Klerk took office as state president in 1989, he often argued to his White constituency that reformist measures dismantling apartheid were required in order to influence the relaxing of sanctions. Finally, in December 1993, after the new constitution was agreed upon and the election date set, the president of the UN General Assembly announced that the oil embargo was lifted.

The United Nations had taken an unequivocal stand against South Africa since 1952. In 1960, following the Sharpeville shooting by police, the UN Security Council went on record as "deploring" the moves of the South African government. In 1963, the Security Council encouraged all states to embargo the sale of arms, ammunition, and all types of military vehicles to South Africa. In 1977 the embargo on the sale of arms and nuclear weapons technology was made mandatory. No further mandatory sanctions were proposed because the United States and United Kingdom were prepared to exercise their veto out of Cold War concerns. Cut off from arms purchases, South Africa diverted vast sums to expand the quasi-governmental arms manufacturer ARMSCOR. Within ten years the company had grown to be the third largest in the country, and South Africa became a net arms exporter.

In 1985, Commonwealth members passed the Nassau declaration, which asked member nations to ban or restrict trading in oil, computers, arms, and Krugerrands. Loans were also restricted. In 1986, following a failed summit to influence South Africa to move toward dismantling apartheid, Commonwealth nations banned bank loans and the purchase of iron, steel, coal, and uranium from South Africa. The United Kingdom withheld approval on the 1986 measure, agreeing only to a voluntary ban on new investment (and, even then, only pursuant to the principle of following the EC on the other issues). Also in 1986, the United Nations tightened the 1977 embargo to include "all military, paramilitary and police vehicles and equipment, as well as weapons and ammunition, spare parts, and supplies for the aforementioned." Again in 1986, the United States passed the Comprehensive Anti-Apartheid Act (CAAA), which is discussed in a later chapter.

8.   THE UNITED STATES POSITION: A CHANGING CONTEXT

In large measure, the reason that United States companies in South Africa were targeted by groups wanting apartheid dismantled was because the United States government was itself so unresponsive. The government believed that the Cold War demanded that Communism be fought on all fronts and without compromise; this anti-Communism effort therefore required that racial concerns be overlooked or given short shrift. Ambassador Philip Crowe summed up the government's position in a 1961 letter to *U.S. News and World Report:* "The net of it is that South Africa has faced the issue of Communism squarely and is willing to go a long way toward combating it. Russia's threats and saber-rattlings do not scare here as they seem to frighten most of the emerging nations of the continent."[33] (The roles of both the United States government [under various administrations] and the United States Congress are analyzed in chapter 11.)

Until 1989, when the Cold War environment changed dramatically, both Republican and Democratic administrations were primarily governed by global strategic interests when it came to South Africa. From 1950 through the 1980s, the United States in its policy toward South Africa attempted to walk a fine line. It avoided taking any action that would seriously and adversely affect economic ties between the two countries. At the same time, it urged South Africa to abandon its apartheid policies.

President Carter, though not severing any significant economic ties, pushed the anti-apartheid pole to the limit with his public hostility to the regime. Ambassador Andrew Young even offered advice to the Blacks based on his own experience in Georgia. Although the Blacks in Africa may not have made the gains in political and economic rights during the Carter administration that they had hoped for, they at least had confidence that the United States was on their side. Perhaps more importantly, United States Blacks knew that their government stood squarely opposed to racism in South Africa.

On 21 November 1984, shortly after Ronald Reagan's landslide victory over Walter Mondale, three prominent Black leaders, concerned over the arrest of sixteen trade union leaders in South Africa, staged a protest at the South African Embassy. These three (Civil Rights Commission member Mary Frances Berry, Washington, DC; Congressman Walter Fauntroy; and Trans African executive director Randall Robinson) were arrested for demonstrating within five hundred feet of the embassy. They were released, but their protest, covered by television and newspapers, caught the public eye; prominent Blacks and Whites repeatedly turned up at the embassy to be arrested in a ritualistic fashion.

Randall Robinson and his colleagues named the movement the Free South Africa Movement. From examining the roster of key Jewish, Catholic, Black, labor union, and Democratic Party leaders who took their turns getting arrested at the embassy door, it was clear to many that the anti-apartheid issue might be just what was needed to bring the old Democratic coalition together. The South African government continued to provide grist for the mill by making widely publicized arrests and by its shootings in the Black townships.

ENDNOTES

1 Sections of this chapter closely follow an earlier work by one of the authors. See Chapters 2 and 3 of Oliver F. Williams, *The Apartheid Crisis* (San Francisco: Harper & Row, 1986).

2 John W. de Gruchy, *The Church Struggle in South Africa* (Grand Rapids, MI: Eerdmans, 1979), 13.

3 Cf. Peter Hinchliff, *The Church in South Africa* (London: SPCK, 1968), 46–47.

4 Quoted by Gideon S. Ware, *A History of South Africa* (New York: Homes & Meier, 1974), 167–68.

5 *Human Relations and the South African Scene in the Light of Scripture* (Cape Town: Dutch Reformed Church Publishers, 1975).

6 Ibid., 32 ff.

7 De Gruchy, *Church Struggle in South Africa*, 81. For an analysis of the development of the prophetic dimension of the church in South Africa, see Peter Walshe, *Church Versus State in South Africa* (New York: Orbis Books, 1983). See also Marjorie Hope and James Young, *The South African Churches in a Revolutionary Situation* (New York: Orbis Books, 1981).

8 For example, see Robert N. Bellah, *The Broken Covenant: American Civil Religion in Time of Trial* (New York: Seabury Press, 1975).

9 Quoted and discussed in David J. Bosch, "Reconciliation: An Afrikaner Speaks," *Leadership* 4, 4 (1985): 64–65.

10 "Beyers Naude in Conversation with Alan Paton," *Leadership* 3, 4 (1984): 85–89.

11 Ted Botha, "State, Church Polarization," *Pretoria News*, 28 February 1985.

12 Cf. Tristan Anne Borer, *Challenging the State: Churches as Political Actors in South Africa* (Notre Dame, IN: University of Notre Dame Press, 1998).

13 Interview with George Houser, 15 October 1994.

14 George A. Steiner and John F. Steiner, *Business, Government, and Society*, 5th ed. (New York: Random House, 1988), 9.

15 See P. W. Botha, abridged text of speech presented 30 September 1985 (available from the South African Consulate General, New York, NY 10017).

16 Ibid., 2.

17 Ibid., 4.

18 Brian Stuart, "Remove Doubt about Reform Objectives, says Slabbert," *Citizen* (Johannesburg, South Africa), 16 July 1985.

19 P. W. Botha, abridged text, 2.

20 See D. J. Louis Nel (deputy minister of information, South Africa), speech presented 16 October 1985 (available from the South African Consulate General, New York, NY 10017).

21 "P. W. Warns of 'Deep Potholes' Ahead," *Citizen* (Johannesburg, South Africa), 13 July 1985.

22 Quoted in "Quarterly Trends Monitor, June 1986," a publication of the United States-South Africa Leader Exchange Program, Inc. (USSALEP).

23 "Pretoria Takes Action against Editor," *New York Times*, 9 November 1985.

24 Howard Barrell, "The United Democratic Front and National Forum: Their Emergence, Composition and Trends," *South African Review* 2 (1984): 11–15.

25 Mangosuthu G[atsha] Buthelezi, "Black Demands" (paper presented at the Business International Conference on South Africa: The Evolving Challenge to International Companies, London, England, 5 June 1985), 6.

26 Lucy Mvubelo, foreword to *The Politics of Sentiment,* by Richard E. Sincere, Jr. (Washington, DC: Ethics and Public Policy Center, 1984), ix.

27 "Reform the 'only hope' for South Africa," *Cape Times,* 31 July 1985.

28 Hugh Murray, "A Moment in History," *Leadership* 4, 3 (1985): 30–35.

29 Richard Hengeveld and Jaap Rodenburg, eds., *Embargo: Apartheid's Secrets Revealed* (Amsterdam: Amsterdam University Press, 1995).

30 Gary Clyde Hufbauer, Jeffrey J. Schott, and Kimberly Ann Elliott, *Economic Sanctions Reconsidered: History and Current Policy,* 2d ed. (Washington, DC: Institute for International Economics, 1990); Gary Clyde Hufbauer, Jeffrey J. Schott, and Kimberly Ann Elliott, *Economic Sanctions Reconsidered: Supplemental Case Histories,* 2d ed. (Washington, DC: Institute for International Economics, 1990).

31 Hufbauer, Schott, and Elliott, *Economic Sanctions Reconsidered: Supplemental Case Histories*; Les de Villiers, *In Sight of Surrender: The U.S. Sanctions Campaign Against South Africa 1946–1993* (Westport, CT: Praeger, 1995); Merle Lipton, "Sanctions and South Africa: The Dynamics of Economic Isolation," Special Report No. 1119, *The Economist* Intelligence Unit (London: *The Economist,* 1988).

32 S. Prakash Sethi, ed., *The South African Quagmire: In Search of a Peaceful Path to Democratic Pluralism* (Cambridge, MA: Ballinger, 1987); Lipton, "Sanctions and South Africa."

33 Quoted in de Villiers, *In Sight of Surrender,* 10. For an overview of this policy, see Peter J. Schraeder, *United States Foreign Policy toward Africa* (New York: Cambridge University Press, 1994).

Chapter 3

The First Step toward Implementation
Bringing Life to the Principles

The initial announcement of the Principles generated widespread press coverage, both for their substance and for the unusual nature of the action to be undertaken. It was unprecedented that CEOs from some of the largest United States corporations would voluntarily and collectively commit themselves to an externally created set of guidelines for their operations. It was also significant that

- the Principles were adopted despite their explicit ethical foundation in human rights. More than corporations in any other part of the world, large United States-based corporations have consistently and vociferously opposed mixing ethical or even political criteria in their economic decision making. Corporations are viewed as essentially private institutions that are designed for economic activities undertaken for the benefit of their owners; namely, the shareholders. Mixing ethical and political rationales with economic decision making is therefore viewed not only as contrary to the shareholders' economic interests, but also as detrimental to larger issues of public policy in a democratic society. That these very corporations use all types of political and other arguments when doing so advances their economic interests is beside the point and only serves to support those who would argue not to use private economic organizations for broader social and political purposes, no matter how justified those purposes might appear at a particular time.

- the Principles were to be implemented in a foreign country where they would be in conflict with local laws, thus raising the issue of intervention in another country's internal affairs.

- the implementation of the Principles, when limited to United States companies alone, might have put them at a competitive disadvantage with respect to their competitors, not only from South Africa, but also from Japan and Europe.

- senior executives committed themselves to the Principles despite what was, in many cases, a gross disproportion between the small size of the companies' South African (versus worldwide) operations and the extensive burdens senior management took on in connection with the Principles. Indeed, our analysis shows that it was the personal involvement of senior corporate executives that made possible not just the formulation and adoption of the Principles, but also their rapid implementation.

This last point was thoughtfully commented upon by Wayne Fredericks, a Ford representative who was also a confidant of Sullivan and among the most active members of the "founding collective" of midlevel corporate executives whose involvement was critical to the formulation and implementation of the Principles.

> CEOs and Executive VPs of most of the corporations doing business in South Africa had, on the whole, no experience in South Africa. Some of them may have taken short visits to South Africa. And in those days, when you visited South Africa you were really kept in tow by one particular group which was the White power structure both at the economic level and at the political level. So, during those days, people making decisions at the top had no contact with the Blacks, Coloreds and Asians at the bottom who were struggling for recognition and acceptance.

> We must also not lose sight of the economic context of South Africa regardless of its moral context. I recall my discussion with a senior executive who lamented, "Wayne, this program you describe is a very important one and I'll support it, if I can financially, through the company, but I can't give any time to it." He said, "I already give 25% of my time to less than 1% of my company's interests. How can I do any more." And this was one of the leaders. One can see a sense of a kind of personal anguish in this. He wanted to do more, but it isn't what he was hired to do.[*]

There were other obstacles, too, that confronted Sullivan in his effort to formulate and secure support for the Principles:

- Contrary to what one might expect on the basis of the swift enactment of the Principles, neither the African-American community nor the general public was much aware during the 1960s and 1970s of the struggle for equal rights in South Africa. Nor was this struggle a high priority of the mainstream leadership of African-American organizations.

---

[*] Unless otherwise specifically stated, all direct quotes or paraphrased statements attributed to various individuals in this chapter, and in other parts of the book, are based on written communications or in-person, on-the-record interviews with the authors.

- The political constituency for the Principles in South Africa—that is, the affected Black majority—was nonexistent; neither the Black population, nor its leadership, the exiled African National Congress and the suppressed union leaders, had any effective means of expressing their opinions.

- There was some dialogue and consultation between the Black church leaders in South Africa through the South African Council of Churches (SACC) and the National Council of Churches (NCC) in the United States. However, all available evidence indicates that SACC's stance toward the multinational corporations was aggressive rather than conciliatory, and that it leaned toward the withdrawal of all foreign investments from South Africa as a means of putting pressure on the White government.

In view of the foregoing obstacles—corporate, social, political—the Principles were a testimony to the growing power of public-interest groups, especially those with religious affiliations, to confront large corporations and impel them to examine the moral import of their economic actions. This period was, in particular, one in which religious and other public-interest groups involved in South Africa were grappling with the activities of large corporations in developing countries; for example, the marketing of infant formula, the overpromotion and selling of expensive prescription drugs, and the exploitation of local workers, especially women and children, through sub-poverty-level wages and inhumane working conditions. Within a larger context, such confrontations marked the emergence of a new trend in social activism, a trend that has become both more pronounced and, indeed, institutionalized.

What is also crucial to understanding the enactment of the Principles is the particular character of Sullivan's engagement with the corporate world. Although Sullivan was an African-American, it is highly doubtful that his success with the Principles was due to his influence in the African-American community. Instead, his success was based on other factors: his magnetic personality, passion for the cause, powerful oratory, and acute sense of timing. An even more important factor was his awareness of the role of economics as a means of empowering the Black community. A final but important consideration was his superb understanding of the strategies and tactics that could be employed in dealing with corporate America. He was thus able to overcome his weakness in not having the support of large constituencies of consumers and voters. By negotiating from high moral ground, he directed the bargaining framework away from economics, his alleged weakness with respect to the corporations, and toward his strength: the ethical context of business. He further disarmed his opponents by demonstrating a grasp of the "limits of their acquiescence" and by deliberately refraining from pushing them beyond those limits.

Another reason for the successful enactment of the Principles can be seen in the sharp contrast between the process Sullivan followed and the failed efforts of the United Nations to create a Code of Conduct for Transnational Corporations[1] (UN Code) and of the WHO in its sponsorship of the International Code of Marketing of Breast-Milk Substitutes (Infant Formula Code).[2] The UN Code was doomed to failure from its very inception. It was designed by a bureaucratic agency of the UN, largely at the behest of the developing countries (which constituted the majority of the member states). Initiated in the heyday of the nonaligned movement, the UN Code sought to impose standards of conduct on multinational corporations (MNCs) that had little to do with ethical concerns and everything to do with extracting a larger share of revenues from the MNCs than developing countries could receive under competitive market conditions. The UN Code did not impose any obligations or standards of accountability on the developing countries for their own acts of omission and commission. The UN Code ignored the legitimate concerns of the industrially advanced countries, which were the major source of foreign aid for the nonaligned nations. Finally, the UN Code failed to involve the MNCs actively in the negotiation process. Thus, the process had all the prospective beneficiaries present at the negotiating table and none of the players who would have to foot the bill; lacking any real leverage, and fighting among themselves, the representatives of the industrially advanced countries were reduced to finding a graceful exit. The debacle was complete; after fifteen years and millions of dollars in expenses, the "final" version of the UN Code has yet to be brought before the General Assembly.

The failure of the UN Code points to three reasons that were crucial to the successful enactment of the Sullivan Principles. The parties that had to implement the Principles were intimately involved in the development of their structure and content. There was a genuine effort to understand and to take into account the legitimate interests of all the important stakeholders, whether or not they were involved in the negotiating process. From the outset, the objective of the exercise was to make progress and move forward, rather than be consumed by public posturing, grandstanding, or public humiliation of those whose views and prior actions were deemed despicable. Thus, the "purity" of ideals or principles was secondary in importance to the need to make progress toward the desired outcomes.

The Infant Formula Code likewise suffered from a variety of fatal flaws, with the result that despite all the hoopla following its passage, the code's implementation was, at best, highly sporadic and, at worst, largely superficial. Moreover, it is highly doubtful whether the code ultimately had any significant effect either in reducing infant mortality or in increasing breast-feeding.[3] Just like the UN Code, the Infant Formula Code was the creation of developing countries. Acting in concert, they enacted a code that paid little regard to the practicalities of the situation, included no measures for holding countries responsible for their own conduct, and made no provision for the

WHO to exert pressure on countries that lagged behind in implementing the code. Ironically, it was the countries that were most vociferous in seeking enactment of the code—and in criticizing the industrially advanced countries and infant formula manufacturers—that were the slowest in implementing the code and in monitoring the performance of their domestic companies.[4]

The role of activist groups in the infant formula controversy was also problematic. They were conspicuously silent when it came to holding developing countries responsible for their conduct—even though it was those countries that had the greatest stake in solving the problem. Instead, activists sought to impose code standards universally—even in countries where women and families were quite capable of making informed choices and could well afford to use commercially made infant formula products.

A final problem in attempting to resolve the infant formula controversy was the lack of unanimity among infant formula manufacturers. Their intense competition in the marketplace carried over into the negotiations; their efforts to cooperate and their changing coalitions—no more than marriages of convenience—repeatedly broke down into backstabbing and mutual recriminations.[5]

By contrast, the Sullivan Principles had a fortunate set of circumstances surrounding them. The companies involved had built an overall consensus about what needed to be done and what resources were required to do the job. The Principles also received the commitment of the companies' top management. Moreover, unlike the above cases, there was a prime mover, Sullivan, who was solely responsible for dealing with the companies. He was thereby able to prevent the internal dissension, competing perspectives, and ideological divides that are the bane of social movements.[6] Any of these problems would have killed the Principles before they had any chance of being implemented. Finally, although Sullivan had extensive and continuous discussions with various anti-apartheid groups, he alone made the final decisions on contentious issues. This process allowed the companies to commit themselves to the Principles with some degree of assurance that all parties would operate within a shared framework and with due respect for their mutual and reciprocal obligations.

1. GETTING ORGANIZED: THE FIRST IMPLEMENTATION

After the euphoria associated with the 1 March 1977 announcement of the Principles had passed, the twelve signatories were given their marching orders by Sullivan. The companies were told that immediate steps should be taken to put Principle 1 into practice. In Sullivan's words: "The first priority is the removal of all racial restriction signs and the beginning of the process of the desegregation of all plant facilities. This we hope you will begin at once. Please write me and let me know how you are making out in this regard."[7]

The amazing thing is that the top officers took Sullivan's request so seriously. Several examples illustrate the power Sullivan held over the companies at that time. On 11 April 1977, J. A. Thwaits, president of international operations of 3M, responded to the request Sullivan had sent to Ray Herzog, chairman of the board and chief executive officer of 3M.

> As I believe you are aware, our company in South Africa has been supportive of these Principles for some long time and had been putting them into effect prior to our officially supporting the Statement of Principles. With respect to your specific question on signs relating to eating, comfort and work facilities, I would advise that from my observations on a recent visit these do not exist within our company's facilities there.[8]

On 15 April, the president of Cyanamid Europe/Mideast/Africa, C. E. Austin, responded to Sullivan as follows:

> We have noted your request that the twelve companies which originally endorsed the Principles make a special effort to implement item number one relating to non-segregation. I am glad to inform you that we have already taken down the signs in our Lederle pharmaceutical plant at Isando and our chemical plant at Witbank. In our administrative offices in Edenvale, we have never had any signs.[9]

On 18 April, the vice chairman of Union Carbide Corporation, W. B. Nicholson, responded as follows:

> I talked with Rev. Roman on Friday last and gave him an oral report concerning our experience with signs.

> In brief, in four locations (three of which became operational over the past two years) we have had no signs. At a fifth location, the signs were taken down about a year ago without repercussion. At a sixth, removal was accomplished just last week. This accounts for all of our mining and manufacturing operations.

> At our head office in Johannesburg, which is our only office location, signs were removed from male toilet facilities some time ago. One sign remains on a female toilet facility. We are feeling our way with respect to this last sign because we occupy rented space and are not the only tenant in the building, and also because resistance has been evident.

You can see from the above report that our signs are essentially all down. We want to keep them down, and believe the best way to accomplish the aim is to be quiet about it.[10]

From the 1 March 1997 announcement until the 5 October dinner meeting later that year with Secretary of State Cyrus Vance (see chapter 1), the signatory companies had been meeting regularly to discuss and report on their progress in implementing the rudimentary elements of the Principles. At the October dinner meeting, Sullivan asked the top executives from signatory companies—some fifty companies had now signed on to the Principles—if they would begin thinking about how best to organize their common endeavor, and then submit their reflections to him.

Meanwhile, events in South Africa began to capture the minds and hearts of Americans. The Black consciousness leader, Steve Biko, died a brutal death while in detention, which caused widespread unrest in the Black townships. On 19 October 1977, Prime Minister John Vorster, responding to the unrest, arrested fifty black leaders and banned (outlawed) eighteen anti-apartheid organizations. President Jimmy Carter, under pressure to do something, argued for a UN embargo on arms shipments to South Africa; on 4 November 1977, the embargo was passed by the UN Security Council.

Sullivan's response to the sad events in South Africa was to see the glass half full rather than half empty. He urged the companies to widen the circle of those involved with the Principles program. In his 23 November 1977 letter to Thomas A. Murphy, chairman of the board of the General Motors Corporation, Sullivan noted:

You can expect interest around South Africa to be intensified within the next six months, as a result of the Biko exposures and the recent jailings and bannings. It is, therefore, most important that we get as much broad support behind the Statement of Principles throughout America and around the world, as possible, for the effort to maintain and gain effectiveness.[11]

Although United States companies were responding to Sullivan's plea by signing up for the Principles and also expanding the scope of their activities to erode apartheid, they were simultaneously coming under increased pressure from the church groups to consider withdrawing from South Africa. The church groups' efforts were largely coordinated through the Interfaith Center on Corporate Responsibility (ICCR). As we shall discuss in the latter part of this chapter, this dual and inconsistent posture of ICCR—urging the companies to become signatories to the Principles and also pressuring them to withdraw from South Africa—was a contributing factor in diluting both the magnitude and direction of the Principles' impact. The ICCR's posture weakened the hand of United States companies in pressuring the South African government to accelerate the changes required to dismantle apartheid. That posture also made it more difficult to induce multinational corporations from other countries to make commensurate efforts in improving the conditions for Black workers in their South African operations.

2.   THE INDUSTRY RESPONSE

With the ICCR withdrawal pressure threatening to undermine his program, Sullivan began to move ahead with an organizational strategy for implementing the Principles. A number of companies responded to Sullivan's call for the creation of systems and procedures that would accelerate the implementation process.

It was in this context that W. B. (Bill) Nicholson, vice chairman of the Union Carbide Corporation, wrote to Sullivan on 20 October 1977. Nicholson was an advocate of the Principles and favored an "evolutionary" approach to dismantling the "highly structured system of racial separation and discrimination." However, he came to realize that the process of that evolution was, to date, moving too slowly.

May I suggest, of the fifty-odd companies now in place, a continuing and more structured program specific to on-site observance of the six principles. A first step would be to identify major issues which stand in the way of, or otherwise bear on full implementation. Then a position could be developed on each issue. Collaborative assessment of the issues could be undertaken between regular group meetings by teams formed for the purpose, drawing from the designated representatives of the signatory companies. By way of example, three such issues are:

Education. Nothing is more basic nor a greater determinant. The six principles cannot be fully reduced to practice without vast change in the availability and quality of education for blacks. What can be done from the outside to inspire wholesale progress?

Laws, regulations and social practices. The Government has said it does not condone discrimination. But there is little or no evidence, in terms of changes in relevant laws, regulations and practices that the Government means what it says. Specifically, what kind of Government action is called for and what can be done to excite it?

Internal forces for change. Positive forces are at work within South Africa, e.g., the Urban Foundation. Can linkage be accomplished with these forces from the outside and benefit gained thereby? Let us identify these internal developments and endeavor to build constructive relationships.

Such address to mainstream issues could end up simply with the provision of evidence for the individual U.S. company, or it could lead to some kind of programmed group effort. Fifty-odd companies acting in concert on major, specific issues is an attention-getting prospect. The leverage potential is impressive.[12]

The upshot of Nicholson's letter to Sullivan was that Nicholson and two other officers of Union Carbide (Fred O'Mara, executive vice president, and Dwight Wait, chairman of Union Carbide Africa and Middle East) were invited to meet with Sullivan at the Zion Baptist Church in Philadelphia on 17 November 1977. Also at the meeting were the Rev. Gus Roman, an assistant to Sullivan, and Larry W. Wise of the General Motors Corporation. This meeting was a crucial one for the future shape of the Principles program. The minutes, taken by O'Mara, illustrate how carefully the group was thinking about the process of implementation.

It was agreed that uniform reporting of progress would be beneficial to the total effort and that Union Carbide would develop a format for reporting progress under the six principles. The proposed format will be sent to Reverend Roman who will have it critiqued and then will be proffered to all signatory companies. Reporting in this format would be at six month intervals with interim reporting of special events as required.

In Dr. Sullivan's recent meeting with Secretary Vance, the Secretary asked that Dr. Sullivan continue to give his leadership to the group and Dr. Sullivan has agreed.

Discussion then centered around the need for education and four levels of need became evident.

    a. Literacy

    b. Secondary Schooling

    c. Vocational or Technical Training

    d. Professional Training

It was recognized that education needs are massive and that "giant steps" and time are required.

The matter of a more structured approach to the implementation of the six principles was examined and discussed in detail. It was recognized by all present that a structured approach will somewhat limit Dr. Sullivan's flexibility and that he must and will take this into consideration. On the other hand, it was agreed that such an approach would maximize the impact of the total group of companies, an impact which is sorely needed. Finally, Mr. Nicholson was asked to prepare in some detail a proposed organization structure and modus operandi for this effort and send it to Rev. Roman who will solicit comments from a selected number of the 54 signatories. This document along with the draft of a reporting form will then be presented to the group of 54 at the January meeting, probably January 17.

In implementing an organizational structure, it is recognized that there are differences in management philosophies and interests which will have to be resolved in the structured approach. It is felt that people of goodwill can make such resolutions and go forward with the effort.

It is further recognized that a financial assessment on each of the group will be required to fund all out-of-pocket expenses of an organization.

The participation of non-U.S.A. companies was discussed. There is currently participation by some Swedish and Danish companies. Participation of French, German, Netherlands, U.K. and Japanese companies is desired. Dr. Sullivan plans to make contact with companies in these countries early in 1978. He asked Union Carbide's help with these contacts. We believe we can be of help in all of these countries except the Netherlands. Union Carbide has started gathering lists of those companies who have operations of some kind in South Africa as our first step toward implementation. It was suggested that IBM and possibly GM could also be of help.

Dr. Sullivan asked what we would do if at some point the South African government drew the line and said "this is as far as you can go in these efforts." Union Carbide replied that we hoped that our group efforts would be well enough thought through and adeptly presented in the interest of the government so that the group could make steady progress without such confrontation. If a serious confrontation was generated, we would have to seriously rethink our entire posture.

It was recognized by all that progress so far can be best described as desegregation rather than integration but that it was truly progress and will lead to evolutionary change.

Rather than having three separate groups it was agreed that all signatories should now be in one group. The first meeting of entire body will be on January 17.

The possibility of the loan of an executive from one of the signatory companies on a full time basis will be explored by Reverend Roman. All agreed that this would be very desirable, particularly in the context of the growing consensus that an organization was required.[13]

At this meeting the seeds were planted for the organization that would finally guide the Principles program. Key ideas that would soon come to fruition were:

- The need to use a standard reporting form that would be filed at regular intervals. (Initially, the intervals were six months; annual reporting was instituted later.)

- The need to develop a structured approach to implementing the Principles. The idea of using a task group for each of the Principles eventually grew out of this suggestion.

- The need to have a full-time executive to coordinate the overall program of implementation.

2.1   Nicholson's Draft

In a letter of 28 November 1977, Bill Nicholson of Union Carbide forwarded his draft for the "organization of the ongoing work of the signatory companies in the implementation of the adopted principles." There were four essential features of his proposed organization. First, a Council would be chaired by Sullivan, administered by a full-time executive secretary, and include one senior officer/director from each signatory company. Second, the Council itself would be guided by a charter; "essentially the published Statement of Principles equates to a charter." While "political actions per se would be avoided," the Council would lobby "for modification of South African laws, regulations and customs *to the extent needed to facilitate observance of the adopted operating Principles*" (emphasis added). Third, a Steering Committee consisting of "twelve carefully chosen members of the Council, the Executive Secretary and one member of Sullivan's organization would meet bi-monthly and would oversee specific programs of implementation of the Principles." Fourth, the Steering Committee would have the following duties:

- To monitor progress of signatory companies in the implementation of programs based on the six operating principles

- To develop standards and guidelines for consistent use in these operating programs

- To identify and assess major issues standing in the path of full observance of the adopted principles

- To develop recommendations to the Council on ways in which these principles can be more completely and expeditiously supported

- To undertake tasks, approved by the Council, which are aimed at resolution of identified issues and removal of obstacles to progress[14]

Nicholson's draft envisioned project teams or task forces, each chaired by a member of the Steering Committee, to carry forward the objectives of the program. A team would have six to eight members, each recruited from a signatory company.

2.2   Formation of Task Groups

Nicholson's letter of 28 November 1977 and his proposed organizational plan met with the approval of Sullivan, who sent a 22 December letter to that effect to all CEOs of signatory companies. The signatory companies, now numbering fifty-four, were asked to send a representative to a 9 February 1978 meeting at the General Motors Building in New York City. The agenda for the meeting was to establish plans for that calendar year. Sullivan asked all the CEOs not only to consider organizing task groups to further the work of the Principles, but also to serve on one or more of the task groups themselves. He suggested task groups on educational programs, health care and housing, other equal employment codes and related efforts, and periodic reporting. "We are hopeful that group endeavors can be established which can assist us in better understanding our undertaking and thereby accomplishing our objectives more effectively."[15]

The idea of task groups was favorably received by the corporate community. For example, in a letter of 6 January 1978, Rawleigh Warner, Jr., chairman of the board of Mobil Corporation, responded as follows to Sullivan's 22 December letter: "It may well be, as you suggest, that the time has come to focus on specific areas of implementation through the organization of task groups. We will be happy to join in that effort if that is your conclusion."[16] Warner also indicated that he would send a top officer of Mobil, Ed Waggoner, to the 9 February meeting.

Sullivan used the 9 February meeting to establish a consensus on the task group idea, and, to the same end, he called another meeting for 2 March. Key members of the Principles program continued to nudge Sullivan toward finalizing plans for the organization. For example, Fred O'Mara of Union Carbide, writing on 22 February concerning the upcoming 2 March meeting, concluded by saying: "We hope that at your meeting next week the signators will come to agreement on both the reporting and monitoring mechanisms and the need for a structured cooperative implementation effort."[17]

Finally, in April 1978, Sullivan announced the formation of seven task groups that closely followed the structure of the original Principles: (1) Equal and Fair Employment Practices; (2) Equal Pay; (3) Education;

(4) Training; (5) Management and Development; (6) Health Care and Housing; and (7) Periodic Reporting and Economic and Community Development.

The task groups were each composed of members of the signatory companies and were given the assignment of providing "a series of guidelines and objectives for the companies to more clearly and forthrightly pursue the aims of the Principles."[18] One of the concerns of the United States companies was that Blacks be given the same rights as Whites to form and join trade unions that were officially registered with the government. As of 1978, Blacks did not have these rights, but the government had, in fact, set up a commission in 1977 to study the matter. Chaired by Professor Nicholas Wiehahn, the commission (which came to be known as the "Wiehahn Commission") was reportedly making good progress in formulating recommendations for major changes the union rights of Blacks. It is significant that some top United States corporate leaders wrote approvingly to Sullivan about the impending change. For example, on 22 February 1978, Fred O'Mara of Union Carbide wrote to Sullivan after a three-week visit to South Africa. Reflecting on his trip, O'Mara wrote:

> One of the subjects discussed was Black unionism and its lack of standing in a legal sense in South Africa. The Wiehahn Commission, chaired by Professor Wiehahn, is studying the whole subject of black unionism and also the subject of job reservation. In our conversations with Professor Wiehahn, he indicated that the Commission would make its recommendations to the Government late this spring. Until legal standing for black unionism is attained there is really no frame of reference against which either management or unions can negotiate and there is no recourse in case difficulties arise. Therefore the recommendations of the Wiehahn Commission are an important factor.[19]

Sullivan had tried unsuccessfully to include union rights in the original Principles, but several of the founding twelve companies opposed such an inclusion. The move to include union rights was now gaining momentum, however. On 9 May 1978, James W. Rawlings, vice chairman, Union Carbide Africa and Middle East, wrote to Sullivan about some of the goals envisioned for the companies of the Principles program: "The Government of South Africa can, I believe be persuaded . . . to provide a non-discriminatory legislative context for labor unions having black members and to make other changes in the law where it conflicts with the objectives to which you have applied so much energy."[20]

Although it was not until 1 May 1979 that the Wiehahn Commission published its recommendations for granting Blacks the same trade union rights as Whites, the task group with responsibility for the second principle

("Equal and fair employment practices for all employees") took the bull by the horns and in mid-1978 added a section advocating Black union rights. Following the Wiehahn proposal, legislation was passed in South Africa in 1979, in the wake of which the Kellogg company signed a formal union agreement. By the end of 1981, five additional United States companies had signed union agreements.

2.3   First Amplification of the Statement of Principles

When all the task groups finished their first assignment, Sullivan announced (6 July 1978) what has come to be known as the "First Amplification of the Statement of Principles." The full text of that amplification, as released in 1978, is as follows:

PRINCIPLE I – Non-segregation of the races in all eating, comfort and work facilities.
  Each signator of the Statement of Principles will proceed immediately to:
  • Eliminate all vestiges of racial discrimination.
  • Remove all race designation signs.
  • Desegregate all eating, comfort and work facilities.

PRINCIPLE II – Equal and fair employment practices for all employees.
  Each signator of the Statement of Principles will proceed immediately to:
  • Implement equal and fair terms and conditions of employment.
  • Provide non-discriminatory eligibility for benefit plans.
  • Establish an appropriate comprehensive procedure for handling and resolving individual employee complaints.
  • Support the elimination of all industrial racial discriminatory laws which impede the implementation of equal and fair terms and conditions of employment, such as abolition of job reservations, job fragmentation, and apprenticeship restrictions for Blacks and other non-white.
  • Support the elimination of discrimination against the rights of Blacks to form or belong to government registered unions, and acknowledge generally the right of Black workers to form their own union or be represented by trade unions where unions already exist.

PRINCIPLE III - Equal pay for all employees doing equal or comparable work for the same period of time.
  Each signator of the Statement of Principles will proceed immediately to:

- Design and implement a wage and salary administration plan which is applied equally to all employees regardless of race who are performing equal or comparable work.
- Ensure an equitable system of job classifications, including a review of the distinction between hourly and salaried classifications.
- Determine whether upgrading of personnel and/or jobs in the lower echelons is needed, and if so, implement programs to accomplish this objective expeditiously.
- Assign equitable wage and salary ranges, the minimum of these to be well above the appropriate local minimum economic living level.

PRINCIPLE IV – Initiation of and development of training programs that will prepare, in substantial numbers, Blacks and other non-whites for supervisory, administrative, clerical and technical jobs.

Each signator of the Statement of Principles will proceed immediately to:

- Determine employee training needs and capabilities, and identify employees with potential for further advancement.
- Take advantage of existing outside training resources and activities, such as exchange programs, technical colleges, vocational schools, continuation classes, supervisory courses and similar institutions or programs.
- Support the development of outside training facilities individually or collectively, including technical centers, professional training exposure, correspondence and extension courses, as appropriate, for extensive training outreach.
- Initiate and expand inside training programs and facilities.

PRINCIPLE V – Increasing the number of Blacks and other non-whites in management and supervisory positions.

Each signator of the Statement of Principles will proceed immediately to:

- Identify, actively recruit, train and develop a sufficient and significant number of Blacks and other non-whites to assure that as quickly as possible there will be appropriate representation of Blacks and other non-whites in the management group of each company.
- Establish management development programs for Blacks and other non-whites, as appropriate, and improve existing programs and facilities for developing management skills of Blacks and other non-whites.
- Identify and channel high management potential Blacks and other non-white employees into management development programs.

PRINCIPLE VI – Improving the quality of employees' lives outside the work environment in such areas as housing, transportation, schooling, recreation and health facilities.

Each signator of the Statement of Principles will proceed immediately to:

- Evaluate existing and/or develop programs, as appropriate, to address the specific needs of Black and other non-white employees in the areas of housing, health care, transportation and recreation.
- Evaluate methods for utilizing existing, expanded or newly established in-house medical facilities or other medical programs to improve medical care for all non-whites and their dependents.
- Participation in the development of programs that address the educational needs of employees, their dependents and the local community. Both individual and collective programs should be considered, including such activities as literacy education, business training, direct assistance to local schools, contributions and scholarships.
- With all the foregoing in mind, it is the objective of the companies to involve and assist in the education and training of large and telling numbers of Blacks and other non-whites as quickly as possible. The ultimate impact of this effort is intended to be of massive proportion, reaching millions.

PERIOD REPORTING

The signator companies of the Statement of Principles will proceed immediately to:

- Utilize a standard format to report their progress to Dr. Sullivan through the independent administrative unit he is establishing on a 6-month basis which will include a clear definition of each item to be reported.
- Ensure periodic reports on the progress that has been accomplished on the implementation of these principles.

* * * * *

Consistent with the desire of the signatory companies to contribute toward the economic welfare of all people of the Republic of South Africa, they are urged to seek and assist in the development of Black and other non-white business enterprises, including distributors, suppliers of goods and services and manufacturers.

There will be a continuing review and assessment of the guidelines in light of changing circumstances.[21]

The first amplification of the Principles proved the worth of the task group concept, and the original seven task groups, most with counterpart

groups in South Africa, continued to function effectively under their amplified charter. Each task group met at least three times annually to assess what
remained to be accomplished and how best to achieve those goals. Sullivan
often used those meetings to raise expectations for companies' performance
on various social issues, and he also prod the groups to consider even more
amplifications (by 1986 there were five amplifications).

2.4   Reaction to the Principles from ICCR

From the very beginning, the Interfaith Center on Corporate Responsibility and many of its strong supporters were hostile to the Principles and what
they represented. Tim Smith was careful not to openly criticize Sullivan or
his motives. But he was unequivocal in his dismissal of the Principles as a
vehicle for improving the lot of Black workers in South Africa or even as a
transitional step toward reaching the avowed goal of the movement; that is,
dismantling apartheid and establishing a nonracial, democratic society in
South Africa. Instead, he saw the Principles as an impediment to the success
of the anti-apartheid movement and was quite dismissive of the economic
hardship that would be inflicted upon the Blacks of South Africa if all foreign investors departed (which, of course, few did).

Smith avoided open conflict with Sullivan and maintained a cordial dialogue with him, even going so far as to urge companies to become signatories to the Principles. At the same time, however, Smith was using a variety
of tactics—including shareholder resolutions, campaigns at level of both
state and local government, and mass meetings on college campuses—in his
aggressive campaign for total withdrawal.

From the perspective of ICCR, the Sullivan Principles diverted attention
from the fundamental issues, central among which was the struggle for
Blacks' political rights. Smith's first response to the announcement of the
Principles was a quick and sharp retort:

> Is the "Statement of Principles" a case of offering a stone when a child
> asks for a fish? The issue in South Africa at this time is black political
> power; it is not slightly higher wages or better benefits or training pro-
> grams, unless these lead to basic social change. As one South African
> leader put it, "These principles attempt to polish my chains and make
> them more comfortable. I want to cut my chains and cast them away."[22]

George Houser, executive director of the American Committee on Africa
(ACOA), called the Principles an "exercise in triviality." Coordinated by
ICCR, a group of twenty-six representatives of various Catholic organiza-
tions and major mainline Protestant denominations in the United States

issued a letter to United States corporations doing business in South Africa. The letter reiterated the need for disinvestment:

> We call on all U.S. corporations investing in South Africa to adopt a policy to cease any expansion and begin to terminate present operations in the Republic of South Africa unless and until the South African government has committed itself to ending apartheid and has taken meaningful steps toward the achievement of full political, legal and social rights for the black majority."[23]

Sullivan hoped to heal the breach with ICCR by noting that his aim, too, was the total dismantlement of apartheid and the political empowerment of Blacks in South Africa:

> The Statement of Principles that you received represents only a "first step" in an attempt to see if American-based companies operating in the Republic of South Africa can be a significant influence for change in getting rid of apartheid as a system and totally unacceptable way of life. The ultimate objective of my effort is to assist in the ending of apartheid and the ending of the oppression and destruction of human life that has already reached unendurable, inhumane, and savage operations.[24]

Along the same lines, in a letter addressed to Father Robert C. W. Powell, director of the National Council of Churches of Christ in the United States (ICCR's parent organization), Sullivan explicitly stated his ultimate goal of having companies aggressively oppose the government. In particular, he aimed to have all companies participate in intensive lobbying efforts that would communicate to the South African government that participating American businesses wanted to see the end not only of discriminatory laws relating to employment, but of oppression, terrorism, and, ultimately, the apartheid system itself.[25]

This measured and pragmatic response, however, was not satisfactory to ICCR, where a "prophetic" perspective—a strategy of high-profile confrontation—appeared to have been deliberately chosen on the basis of religious convictions. During the same month that Sullivan announced his Principles, ICCR filed shareholder resolutions against five signatory companies. Thus, the period of early growth of the Principles also coincided with increased pressure on the United States companies from ICCR, which was urging them to withdraw from South Africa. For example, during the very time that Bill Nicholson of Union Carbide was proposing a structure and organization for the Principles program, his CEO, W. S. Sneath, received a 7 November 1977 letter from the chairperson of ICCR (Sister Regina Murphy) and five other members asking the company to withdraw from South Africa. Referring to the banning and arrests in October 1977, the letter stated "we have concluded that U.S. companies are unable to act as a force for significant change but instead tend to support the status quo." Such tactics were, indeed, having an impact; universities with large endowments were beginning to question the presence of United States corporations in South Africa.

From the perspective of those in the business community, what was lacking in the prophetic rhetoric of ICCR was logic and reasoned argument. How did "polishing the chains and making them more comfortable" undermine—or, indeed, even relate to—the efforts of the many groups rising up in opposition against South Africa's White minority government? Was anyone arguing that the Blacks of South Africa would cease to struggle because there was a small alleviation in their poverty and utter misery? Did not such a complex problem as apartheid warrant a plurality of strategies? If all foreign investors departed, what would the impact be on the economic system of post-apartheid South Africa and on the well-being of its Black citizens? These were the questions that many conscientious and ethically sensitive business leaders were asking.

Like many religious people speaking prophetically, ICCR and its advocates glossed over both the inconsistencies in their position and the manner in which they implemented their strategy. For example, ICCR representatives were unable to explain how the withdrawal of United States companies alone—which represented, at most, roughly 10 percent of total direct foreign investment in South Africa—would, in itself, alter the political landscape. To have any major impact, ICCR's strategy required the participation of such other countries (and their companies) as the United Kingdom, Germany, and Japan, whose combined investments accounted for more than half of all direct foreign investments in South Africa and an even greater share of total international trade with that country.

One of the authors of this book (Sethi) raised these issues with Tim Smith in extended discussions during the 1970s and 1980s, but to no avail. For example, why were ICCR and its supporters not pressuring companies from the three countries just mentioned above, and why were they not publicly calling for their church brethren in those countries to take the same, aggressive stance toward their own countries' involvement in South Africa? Smith argued that the activists and church groups in those countries were equally committed to supporting the withdrawal of foreign investments from South Africa, but that they were less successful because governmental support was lacking and the countries' companies were belligently opposed to disinvestment. This explanation, however, begs the question rather than answers it. To wit, if the foreign corporations representing a majority of investments and dominant trading positions in South Africa were unable or unwilling to leave South Africa, how is the departure of United States companies alone going to bring about any substantial change?

Even if ICCR and its supporters were unable to mount pressure against foreign companies in *their* own countries, it does not explain why anti-apartheid groups did not mount any boycott campaigns against the United States businesses of those companies—as against the Swiss company Nestle during the infant formula controversy. For example, Japanese automobile companies were major players in South Africa. Why not take action against them in the *United States?* Despite persistent questioning by one of the authors (Sethi), however, Smith refused to offer a plausible explanation why ICCR would not take a public stance against the Japanese companies in the United States or ask the American public to boycott Japanese cars and Japanese consumer electronics products. The apparent answer, and the one Smith would not acknowledge, was that he knew he could not get the American public to give up their Japanese cars or their Japanese consumer electronics. Thus, whereas the pressure on the American corporations to withdraw from South Africa was being presented by ICCR as a matter of "ethics and princi-ple," ICCR's strategy reflected a pragmatic political judgment. The organi-zation exerted pressure where it would yield the best results in terms of maintaining and reinforcing its "ideological and political" stance; whether such posturing would enable ICCR to achieve its express goal—the exit of American corporations from South Africa—was essentially irrelevant.

ICCR saw itself as following—and as consistently following—an ethics of principle; the paramount importance of condemning an evil overrode the consideration of consequences or results. The organization followed a simi-lar strategy and undertook similar actions in other high-profile social and public policy controversies involving large corporations. For example, in the case of the infant formula controversy, ICCR and its supporters strongly op-posed the efforts of moderate church groups, most notably the Methodist Church, to initiate a dialogue with Nestle. The goal of these moderate groups was to negotiate a closure to the Nestle boycott that would require the com-pany to commit itself to complying with the Infant Formula Code, and to subject itself to strict, independent (that is, external) monitoring of its com-pliance efforts. (More recently, ICCR's approach to the dialogue on sweat-shops and the apparel industry may mark the beginning of a less confronta-tional strategy.[26])

Unfortunately, even Sullivan's more measured approach, which would begin in the workplace and only later move toward political involvement, was strongly resisted by the corporate CEOs who had agreed to be the sig-natories of the Principles. Sullivan had presented the CEOs with an opportu-nity—if, indeed, "opportunity" is an appropriate and applicable concept in this instance—for the corporations to move beyond the conventional and ordinary, to recognize the changes that were taking place not just in the United States, but in the world, and to help shape the future. These managers may have been competent, well intentioned, and caring, but visionary they were not.

For example, in his 22 November 1977 response to an inquiry of Hugh Calkins, chairman of the Corporation Committee on Shareholder Responsibility of Harvard University, Tom Murphy, chairman of General Motors, wrote:

> Let me say that we in General Motors share your concern for the human rights of all people in that country. The recent actions of the South African government are distressing and indeed regrettable especially in light of the progress GM and others have worked so hard to achieve. I can assure you that General Motors has in the past, and will continue in the future, to avail itself of every opportunity to aggressively pursue improved conditions for General Motors South African employees, *especially in the areas of wages, benefits, training, education, housing and recreation.*
>
> In this respect, we continue to strongly support the Statement of Principles developed earlier this year by Dr. Leon H. Sullivan. As you are probably aware, General Motors was one of the original twelve companies which endorsed the Principles in March of this year.[27] (emphasis added)

Thus, despite the political upheavals that were accelerating in South Africa and were given vent in the United States and other nations, United States corporations were justifying their presence in South Africa by citing their participation in the Sullivan Principles program as an end in itself; they refused to see the Principles as just the first step toward Black emancipation in South Africa. Not only did the corporations walk away from explicitly accepting the notions of human rights and moral duty, they backed away from acknowledging that in a world that is increasingly linked economically, corporations can and should be an engine of positive political and social change. Although these corporations well understood—as a basic premise— that capitalism and economic freedom cannot exist without commensurate political freedom, they were unwilling to discard short-term economic advantages for the long-term goal of economic prosperity for South Africa. It was just such prosperity, however, that would serve as the essential foundation for stable, democratic freedom in that country. By the same token, it was the future prospect of such prosperity that would have provided corporations all the moral justification they needed to promote social and political change.

ENDNOTES

1 Senate Committee on Foreign Affairs, *U.N. Code of Conduct on Transnational Corporation: Hearing before the Subcommittee on International Economic Policy, Trade, Oceans, and the Environment.* 101st Congress, 2nd sess., 11 October 1990.

2 World Health Organization, *The International Code of Marketing of Breast-Milk Substitutes* (Geneva: World Health Organization, 1981); S. Prakash Sethi, *Multinational Corporations and the Impact of Public Advocacy on Corporate Strategy* (Boston: Kluwer Academic Publishers, 1994).

3 S. Prakash Sethi, "A New Perspective on International Social Regulation of Business: An Evaluation of the Compliance Status of the International Code of Marketing of Breast-Milk Substitutes" *Journal of Socio-Economics*, 22, 2: 141–58.

4 Ibid. See also Sethi, *Multinational Corporations.*

5 See references *supra* note 2. See also Oliver Williams, "Who Cast the First Stone," *Harvard Business Review* 62, 5 (1984): 151–66.

6 Williams, "Who Cast the First Stone."

7 Leon H. Sullivan, letter to David R. Foster (chairman and chief executive officer, Colgate-Palmolive Company), 25 May 1977.

8 J. A. Thwaits (president, international operations, 3M), letter to Leon H. Sullivan, 11 April 1977.

9 C. E. Austin (president, Cyanamid Europe/Mideast/Africa), letter to Leon H. Sullivan, 15 April 1977.

10 W. B. Nicholson (vice chairman, Union Carbide Corporation), letter to Leon H. Sullivan, 18 April 1977.

11 Leon H. Sullivan, letter to Thomas A. Murphy (chairman of the board, General Motors Corporation), 23 November 1977.

12 W. B. Nicholson (vice chairman, Union Carbide Corporation), letter to Leon H. Sullivan, 20 October 1977.

13 Minutes of 17 November 1977 meeting with Leon Sullivan and others at the Zion Baptist Church, enclosed with letter sent by F. B. O'Mara (executive vice president, Union Carbide Corporation) to Leon H. Sullivan, 22 November 1977.

14 "A Proposal for Organization of the Efforts of the Signatory Companies toward More Complete and Expeditious Implementation of Operating Programs Based on the Statement of Principles," enclosed with letter sent by W. B. Nicholson (vice chairman, Union Carbide Corporation), 28 November 1977.

15 Leon H. Sullivan, letter to W. S. Sneath (chairman and chief executive officer, Union Carbide Corporation), 22 December 1977.

16 Rawleigh Warner, Jr. (chairman of the board, Mobil Oil Corporation), letter to Leon H. Sullivan, 6 January 1978.

17 F. B. O'Mara (executive vice president, Union Carbide Corporation), letter to Leon Sullivan, 22 February 1978.

18 Leon H. Sullivan, statement to the House Committee on International Relations, joint hearing of Subcommittees on International Economic Policy and Trade, and on Africa, 95th Congress, 2d sess., 6 July 1978, 10.

19 O'Mara, letter to Sullivan, 22 February 1978.

20 James W. Rawlings (vice chairman, Union Carbide Africa and Middle East), letter to Leon H. Sullivan, 9 May 1978.

21 Quoted by Leon H. Sullivan in statement to the House Committee on International Relations, 13–16.

22 Timothy Smith, "Whitewash for Apartheid from Twelve U.S. Firms," *Business and Society Review* 74 (1977): 59–60.

23 Sister Regina Murphy and twenty-six other members of ICCR, letter to General Motors, 31 October 1977.

24 Leon H. Sullivan, letter to George Houser, 25 April 1977.

25 Leon H. Sullivan, letter to Father Robert C. S. Powell, 5 January 1977.

26 For a discussion of the sweatshop issue in the apparel industry, see Oliver F. Williams. ed., *Global Codes of Conduct: An Idea Whose Time Has Come* (Notre Dame, IN: University of Notre Dame Press, 2000). For the infant formula discussion, see references at chapter 1, note 3.

27 Thomas A. Murphy (chairman of the board, General Motors), letter to Hugh Calkins (chairman of the Corporation Committee on Shareholder Responsibility, Harvard University), 22 November 1977.

Chapter 4

Shaping the Organization
Institutionalizing the Implementation Process

Any program or activity—no matter how passionate the cause, no matter how important the outcome—is likely to lose both its vital energy and sense of urgency as attention shifts from lofty principles and goals to the concrete, routine, often monotonous tasks of implementation. Indeed, the highly intense crusaders and visionaries who launch major enterprises of any sort are not generally known for their patience or for their capacity to devote the same level of energy to the myriad and mundane details that translate visions of the future into activities, tasks, and discrete outcomes. Nor is it reasonable to expect the rank and file of organizers, managers, and workers to maintain a spirit of passionate belief and dedication; for them, "working for the cause" still comes down to the daily grind of "making a living."

This situation is not unique to public-interest groups or public-purpose organizations. It is equally endemic to business ventures, both large and small. Large organizations invariably suffer from agency costs as they seek to motivate mid- and lower-level managers and workers to align their personal goals with those of the organization. In the case of small, entrepreneurially driven organizations, the problem typically lies in the inability of the visionary founders to loosen their grips on the organization, thereby providing professional managers the authority and discretion they need to transform small organizations into the complex ones essential for growth and expansion.

**1.   DESIGNING AN IMPLEMENTATION
          STRUCTURE FOR THE SULLIVAN PRINCIPLES**

The implementation phase of the Principles owed its success to a very
large measure on two factors:

- The establishment of an effective organizational structure, which included
  the use of professional managers from the very first and continued through
  the early years of implementation

- The creation of an effective, independent monitoring system with enough
  resources to evaluate corporate performance, and with the authority to make
  public its findings, thereby rewarding well-performing corporations and
  bringing pressure to bear on those that lagged behind

1.1   Defining the Criteria for Successful Implementation

From its very inception, the implementation process of the Sullivan Principles was endowed with substantial resources, both monetary and physical
(buildings, motor vehicles, and so on), and with a cadre of dedicated (and
highly competent) corporate executives who would play a vital role in its
success. And the Principles were, indeed, a success—at least if success is
measured primarily in terms of the requirements for compliance as set forth
in the Principles, and as evaluated and reported by the independent
monitoring system. However, there are other ways of measuring success, and
the Principles were surely seen as unsuccessful by many activists, by various
religious groups, and even by important segments of the Black population
and leadership in South Africa. These groups believed that the only
measures that could be deemed successful were ones that would deny the
country access to foreign capital, technology, and export markets and would
thereby force the abolition of the apartheid regime in South Africa. To them,
the Principles were a placebo designed to lull people into false hope and
complacency, thereby delaying the inevitable confrontation with the South
African government. Therefore, the success of the Principles in alleviating
the suffering of a minute number of South Africa's Blacks—in particular of
those employed by United States multinational corporations—was irrelevant,
at best, and counterproductive, at worst.

In view of these divergent, mutually exclusive conceptions of what was
the appropriate course of action for corporations dealing with South Africa,
United States corporations were in a no-win situation. They were spending
enormous resources on implementing the Sullivan Principles but nonetheless
failed to mollify large segments of their external constituencies, including
their critics. These groups became more vocal, even strident, with the passage of time and the continued failure of South Africa's government to initi-

ate the necessary political and economic reforms that would lead to equal rights for the majority of the Black people of South Africa. This erosion of external support, coupled with the increased hostility toward the signatory corporations, ultimately weakened the corporations' own, internal support for the Principles.

1.2   The Dual Governance Structure for Implementing the Principles

In consultation with members of the religious community and executives from some of the leading signatory companies, Sullivan devised a dual organizational structure. One part of the structure would perform the oversight function—somewhat akin to a committee comprising the outside members of a board of directors. A new not-for-profit organization, the International Council for Equality of Opportunity Principles (ICEOP), was specifically created for this oversight function. The other part of the structure would act as the supervisory board and oversee normal operational details—somewhat akin to the internal, or management, representatives of a board of directors. This function was vested in a second newly created organization, the Statement of Principles Industry Support Unit (ISU). Figure 1 describes the organizational structure for implementing the Principles, a structure that emerged in 1980 and remained basically unchanged until Sullivan separated himself from the Principles program in June 1987. Exhibit 4 provides a listing of the persons who filled various units, committees, and boards as of March 1986.

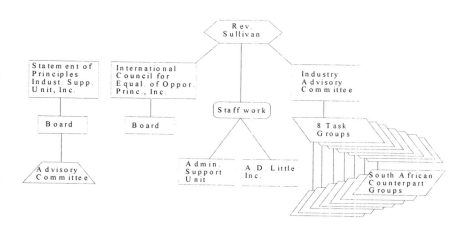

Figure 1. Organization Chart of Sullivan Principles Program

Exhibit 4. Organizational Structure and Operating Units of the Sullivan Principles Program

International Council for Equality of Opportunity Principles, Inc.

Board of Directors

Leon H. Sullivan, Chairman

Gus Roman
Ralph Abernathy
Roy A. Allen
Jerome Cooper
Thomas J. Ritter
Harrison Trapp
Wade Wilson
Paul Vivisaker

Daniel W. Purnell
Executive Director

Administrative Support Unit

Leon H. Sullivan
Chairman

Daniel W. Purnell
Executive Director

Arthur D. Little, Inc.

D. Reid Weedon
Senior Vice President

J. Wayne Fredericks
Ford Motor Company

William Hamilton
General Electric Corporation

D. B. Bolen
E. I. Dupont De Nemours & Co.

Charles Bolling
SmithKline Beckman Corporation

William D. Broderick
Ford Motor Company

Elizabeth L. Clark
Upjohn Company

George Franklin
Kellogg Company

J. Wayne Fredericks
Ford Motor Company

Tom L. Grooms
Deere & Company

William Hamilton
General Electric Company

Statement of Principles Industry Support Unit, Inc.

Sal G. Marzullo, Chairman
Mobil Corporation

Gus Roman, Pastor
Berean Missionary Baptist
Church, Brooklyn, New York

Industry Advisory Committee

Trevor Hoskins
Goodyear Tire & Rubber Co.

Charles Infante
Dow Chemical Company

Lauren P. Katzowitz
Exxon Corporation

Sal G. Marzullo, Chairman
Mobil Corporation

Welcome Msomi
Sterling Drug, Inc.

Ralph L. Phillips
Mobil Corporation

Daniel W. Purnell
ICEOP

James W. Rawlings
Union Carbide Southern Africa, Inc.

W. Mark Schmitz, Secretary
General Motors Corporation

Harrison J. Trapp, Pastor
Thankful Baptist Church
Philadelphia, PA

P. F. Rosen
Coca-Cola Company

Charles E. Russell
IBM Corporation

W. Mark Schmitz
General Motors Corporation

George J. Schroll
Colgate-Palmolive Company

D. Reid Weedon, Jr.
Arthur D. Little, Inc.

The oversight aspect of the governance structure was largely dictated by the concerns of various constituencies seeking a role in monitoring corporate actions under the Principles. If the chart seems unwieldy, it was deliberately so. Sullivan was concerned that the hostility of various groups advocating sanctions and total withdrawal from South Africa would further undermine the credibility of the Principles if these groups lost confidence in the monitoring process and perceived corporate actions in South Africa to be less than those advocated by the Principles. Such a large oversight structure, however, ran the risk of becoming unfocused; subgroups within the signatory companies could seek to further their own visions of how, in practice, the Principles should be interpreted or applied. In some cases, these subgroups had mutually exclusive goals or represented constituencies with varying degrees of commitment to the Principles. Sullivan contained this risk, however, by maintaining centralized control and also through the force of his own personality.

As time progressed and the task of monitoring became more elaborate and time consuming, Reid Weedon of Arthur D. Little, Inc. (ADL), who was the person responsible for creating and implementing the monitoring system, became the de facto policymaker. Weedon has stated that in practice he and Sullivan decided most policy matters after consulting with the companies, either as represented in the task groups or the ISU. As Weedon gained Sullivan's trust, he assumed ever greater responsibility for policy-related decisions, eventually coming to make all the decisions himself and simply keeping Sullivan informed of what decisions were made and why.[1] Weedon's ascendance to such a powerful position was possible, perhaps, only because activists were unconcerned about the effectiveness and transparency of the signatory companies' performance. Just how those companies operated in South Africa was more or less irrelevant to the activists, who simply wanted multinational corporations to leave the country altogether. Activists' only interest in the Principles was to discredit them per se, thus undercutting any role for them in the anti-apartheid debate.

1.3 International Council for Equality of Opportunity Principles (ICEOP)

Sullivan's strategy in broadening the oversight function and expanding the support base for the Principles in the religious community is best described in the minutes of a 13 November 1979 ICEOP meeting in New York City. At the meeting, Sullivan announced that "the International Council for Equality of Opportunity, composed of churchmen and educators, would assess the progress made by the companies. They will assist in the monitoring and will make on-site visitations and inspections."[2]

Sullivan realized that he must find a way to enhance the perceived legitimacy of the Principles, especially with church groups and educators. The pressure was mounting on college campuses and among church groups to make the Principles operational and their impact more visible. The ICEOP was chaired by Sullivan and at that time included eight other prominent clergy and notable citizens as members: Rev. Gus Roman, secretary/treasurer; Bishop Alfred G. Dunston, African Methodist Episcopal Church, Philadelphia, PA; Dean Paul N. Ylvisaker, Graduate School of Education, Harvard University; Dr. Andrew F. Brimmer, Board of Governors, Federal Reserve Bank (ret.), and president, Brimmer and Company; Dr. Ralph D. Abernathy, West Hunter State Baptist Church, Atlanta, GA, and past president, Southern Christian Leadership Conference; Rev. Jerome Cooper, Philadelphia; and Rev. Roy Allen, Detroit.

Unfortunately, as it turned out, ICEOP, despite its charter and express purpose, played little, if any, role in the monitoring process. This limited role may have seemed appropriate at the time, but it ended up having unintended—and adverse—consequences for the Principles program. In particular, ICEOP's limited role disrupted the link between the Principles—the initially designated "moral goals"—and outcomes (corporate conduct). As a consequence, the monitoring process was robbed of its moral underpinnings. Indeed, as ADL's Weedon took over sole responsibility for the monitoring process, operational goals and means became interchangeable. He not only created the audit instrument, he took it upon himself to modify the instrument on an ad hoc basis—essentially without oversight or accountability, but with strong endorsement from Sullivan. As Weedon himself admitted, though the ICEOP never had much influence in shaping or monitoring the Principles program, that body did provide some legitimacy for the program in the eyes of the Black community.[3]

In another meeting of ICEOP, held in Philadelphia, Pennsylvania, on 10 December 1979, Sullivan outlined his strategy—and solicited those of others—for enlisting and expanding the clergy's support for the Principles. Dr. Deotis Roberts, a professor of religion at Howard University, offered to "develop a theological interpretation and construct" for the Principles. He spoke critically of the Theology of Liberation and its prophetic stance against capitalism. "He carefully explained that many who advocate the Theology of Liberation are not carefully examining its implications and its lack of Christian foundation."[4] It was clear from the minutes that Sullivan was skillfully building a coalition of clergy to act as spokespersons for the Principles. He was nonetheless attentive to those lay persons and clerics at the meeting who saw a need to improve upon the Principles. The minutes report that Sullivan and Roman agreed:

- Companies do only as much as they are forced to do.

- The much-alleged progress by the present South African government must be carefully evaluated; though some say there are signs of progress, others call it window dressing.

- Immediate action is needed to avert violence; expectations have been raised.

- The Principles themselves raise expectations. Blacks and other non-Whites want complete freedom, not polished chains.

- The Principles are being evaluated constantly by friends and critics to determine their effectiveness. Measurable progress is necessary.[5]

When the board of directors of the ICEOP had its first meeting on 17 November 1979, Sullivan outlined the history of the Principles program, and Weedon provided a summary of the Principles' progress. Present at the meeting was Rev. John J. Ridyard, director of the Catholic Foreign Missionary Society of America, who reported on his recent trip through England, the Netherlands, and Switzerland. In discussing the Principles with industry, the clergy, and union officials, he found that despite their general agreement with the Principles, they repeatedly expressed two concerns; namely, that the effect of the Principles be effectively monitored and that they be made international in their application rather than being implemented only by American multinational companies.

The minutes indicate that Sullivan, in response to a question about support for the Principles within the minority community, reported that "the response in the United States was overwhelmingly in support of the Principles and the Organization of African Unity continues to support the Principles as a viable alternative to withdrawal." Through the ICEOP, Sullivan was obviously trying to consolidate minority support for the Principles—support that, much to his chagrin, was not fully achieved. Other business recorded in the minutes included the election of officers: chairman of the board, Sullivan; vice chairman, Bishop Alfred G. Dunstan; secretary and treasurer, Rev. Gus Roman; and executive director, Rev. C. T. Vivian. It is also recorded that the ICEOP received funds from the Joyce Foundation (five thousand dollars) and the Warner-Lambert Company (three thousand dollars).

A key vote at the meeting was that ADL be awarded a contract to "develop and analyze questionnaires and publish reports of the effect of the Principles as implemented by the several companies in South Africa, for the sum of $50,000." In approving the contract, the directors of the ICEOP were, of course, doing no more than formally ratifying what Sullivan had already worked out in detail with all of the companies involved.

1.4   The Statement of Principles Industry Support Unit

As mentioned earlier, the nominal role of ISU was to act as a supervisory board for the Principles program and to oversee normal operational details. In practice, ISU provided funding to ICEOP and ADL for activities relating to the promotion and implementation of the Principles. ISU was formally organized as a nonstock, nonmembership organization. The legal consequences of this form of organization were that the ISU was controlled and managed by its board of directors, was self-perpetuating, and was not directly accountable to its members. Financed by contributions from the signatory companies of the Sullivan Principles, ISU was established at the companies' initiative and designed specifically to keep the control of the funding in the hands of the companies. Its board of directors constituted its governing body. The directors were elected by consent of a majority of the corporations participating as members of the Statement of Principles Advisory Committee. ISU's president also acted as liaison to the executive director, to the ICEOP, and to Sullivan himself.

The creation of the ISU, its organizational structure, and operational domains came about through the reports of the various task groups organized by Sullivan during the initial stages of the Principles program. As explained in chapter 2, but worth repeating here, these task groups, organized in April 1978, closely followed the structure of the original principles: (1) Equal and Fair Employment Practices; (2) Equal Pay; (3) Education; (4) Training; (5) Management and Development; (6) Health Care and Housing; (7) Periodic Reporting and Economic and Community Development. The task groups were each composed of members of the signatory companies and were given the assignment of providing guidelines and objectives for companies, which would enable the companies to implement the Principles in an authoritative and unambiguous manner. Most of the task groups had counterpart groups in South Africa, and each met at least three times annually to assess what remained to be accomplished and how best to achieve it. Sullivan often used the meetings of these task groups to raise expectations—which he called "goalposts"—for companies' performance and for the task groups themselves.

As originally established, the formal ISU charter was as follows:

> ***PURPOSE OF THE ORGANIZATION:*** To broadly facilitate the promotion and implementation of the six principles. It is not intended that the ISU engage in any way or be funded for activities extending beyond the Principles into areas involving Dr. Sullivan's broader personal objective. Members of the ISU will not be authorized to speak for or represent the views of the Signatory companies, individually or collectively, on any issue.

FUNDING: The signatory companies provide the funds.

Make funds available to provide suitable office facilities for the ISU and to reimburse all necessary travel and administrative expenses incurred by ISU personnel in the promotion and implementation of the six principles.

Reimburse all expenses of Dr. Sullivan and ISU personnel incurred in attending meetings.

Consider funding on a case by case basis, appropriate consulting services for Dr. Sullivan (Arthur D. Little & Co.) or the ISU.

PERSONNEL: All ISU personnel, including the Executive Secretary and the Administrator, are nominated by Dr. Sullivan and approved by the Directors of the Charitable Corporation. The Executive Secretary and the Administrator work under the general guidance of Dr. Sullivan.

The Administrator's function:

1. *Communications:* To establish and administer a communication system which will (a) keep all signatory companies informed with respect to the current status of all Task Group activities. (b) Keep all signatory companies currently informed of any expansion of the Principles under consideration by Dr. Sullivan. (c) Provide Dr. Sullivan with individual company views and consensus views on any matters concerning the six principles or their implementation.

2. *Administration:* To keep appropriate financial records of the ISU in accordance with the directions of the Treasurer of the Charitable Corporation, and to keep appropriate records of all other matters concerning activities of the ISU. To arrange and coordinate all meetings between Dr. Sullivan (and/or the Executive Secretary) with signatory companies, Task Group Leaders, Chief Executive Officers of signatory companies, the six principles Industry Advisory Groups, and other individuals and groups which are consistent with promoting and implementing the six principles. To provide Dr. Sullivan and the Executive Secretary with other administrative assistance which they may request in order to promote and implement the six principles, including but not limited to the preparation of press releases, letters and memos, and the making of travel arrangements.

The Executive Secretary's functions:

1. To promote the six principles by seeking additional signatory companies, or by seeking greater cooperation with existing signatory companies.

2. To explain the Principles and the status of their implementation to various publics including but not limited to churches, students, university administrators and government representatives.

3. To report generally on progress in implementing the Principles

4. To conduct liaison activities with the various monitoring groups in order to provide feedback to Dr. Sullivan and the signatory companies on the findings of these monitoring groups with respect to the implementation of the six principles.

5. To conduct such other activities as Dr. Sullivan directs with respect to the promotion and implementation of the six Principles.

1.4.1   Unique Characteristics of ISU and Their Impact on the Implementation of the Sullivan Principles in South Africa

The effective implementation of the Sullivan Principles was largely the handiwork of ISU and its affiliate in South Africa. The operating executives of ISU were drawn from the group of senior middle-level corporate executives, selected from various corporations, who were at the forefront of involving their CEOs in the Principles, of guiding them through various phases of developing and implementing the Principles, and of maintaining the link between the corporations and Sullivan. These executives had the personal commitment, professional expertise, and corporate support that created a formidable set of resources and guaranteed that the signatory companies would take the necessary actions both in the United States and in South Africa to implement the Principles in the most enlightened and proactive manner.

1.4.2   Strengths of the ISU Structure and Operational Procedures

Although the ISU was an industry-based organization, its function and structure was distinctive in ways that allowed it to escape many problems characteristic of voluntary, industry-based groups:

- The Principles were designed to address a common problem that afflicted all companies, not just companies in a particular industry. Accordingly, the company groupings within the Principles program were not by industry but were more a function of companies' operations in South Africa.

- Being part of the Principles program generally provided companies with a competitive advantage because of the positive reputational effects emanating from their participation. By the same token, however, there was a tremendous loss of public credibility if signatory companies were seen as giving less than 100 percent to the implementation effort. The companies' performance was monitored and rated by an outside agency. Various groups, including city and state purchasing authorities and public pension funds, used these ratings to determine the eligibility of those companies wishing to do business with them. Thus, public disclosure of poor performers had a direct, adverse effect on a company's business. Public disclosure was consequently instrumental in reducing the free-rider problem and in forcing companies to follow the lead of the best-performing companies lest their reputations be tarnished. Finally, disclosure strengthened Sullivan's hand in further expanding the scope of the Principles to require signatory corporations to undertake more responsibilities—not only in the economic arena, but also in the political one—toward dismantling apartheid in South Africa.

- The signatory group included some of the largest and highly regarded companies in the United States—companies that could ill afford the stigma of not delivering on their commitment to implement the Principles. This source of pressure was especially significant because the companies were already under extreme pressure (from other sources) to discontinue their operations in South Africa. Thus, any erosion of public confidence in their commitment to the Principles would nullify any positive goodwill that they hoped to generate through participation in the Principles program.

- The Principles, from their inception, had the benefit of the direct, personal involvement of many high-profile CEOs from major corporations. This involvement ensured that ISU would have not only the full support of the member corporations, both in the United States and South Africa, but also the necessary resources to operate effectively.

- ISU executives were senior middle-level managers in their respective, signatory corporations and participated in ISU with the encouragement and support of their corporations. These executives were experienced at playing the corporate game of finding resources and molding corporate policies at the operational level for maximum effect. Since they continued to perform their regular corporate duties while serving on the ISU, they intertwined the role of decision makers and implementers, thereby reducing the friction that inevitably occurs when an outside agency seeks to imposed external standards on the inner workings of field operations.

The organization also gained from a continuity of leadership. Over a period of eighteen years, there were only four chairmen. James W. Rawlings of Union Carbide, the first, served three years (1976–79). He was followed by Mobil Oil's Sal Marzullo (1980–90), who was the principal spokesperson and ISU's "face" to outsiders during the most tumultuous period of the organization's history. Though Marzullo resigned in 1990 when Mobil decided to leave South Africa, he retired from Mobil soon thereafter and served as the ISU's paid administrator from 1991 to 1994. William Dunning of Caltex chaired the organization from 1991 to 1993. Gillette's William Donovan, who took over the leadership in 1993, oversaw ISU's dissolution in 1994 following the landmark, fully democratic elections in South Africa and the formation of that country's new, nonracial government.

1.4.3   Problems and Shortcomings of Emanating for ISU's Organizational Structure

Despite the various advantages noted above, ISU's organizational structure and operating procedures were not without problems. Except for the last few years of its existence, ISU did not have a separate office or independent staff. Instead, it was housed in the United States corporate headquarters of the current ISU chairman. Thus, during the tumultuous decade of the 1980s, the identity of ISU, in terms of its public persona, was closely tied to Sal Marzullo, who actively represented ISU in various public and private forums, including congressional committees, State Department meetings, and various organizations of the United Nations.

The continuity provided by Marzullo's leadership gave ISU the flexibility to respond quickly and effectively to what public concerns there were about ISU operations. Unfortunately, this same continuity of leadership also created a sense of passivity, even apathy, among a large number of the signatory companies, who were quite content "to pay their dues" and leave all the public talking to Sal Marzullo and a short list of ISU board members. ISU also had problems collecting dues from its members; leading companies within the ISU were often forced to make up the difference to meet the organization's financial obligations.

As we shall discuss in subsequent chapters, ISU's small group of executives were stretched thin by trying to fulfill their dual role: in addition to being executives responsible for specific activities within their corporations, they had to cope with the ever expanding demands of ISU. In practice, this dual burden resulted in the executives' "doing what must be done to meet the deadlines of annual reporting and making the numbers to satisfy Reid Weedon." In the process, efforts to encourage broader participation in the Principles program (both by signatory and by nonsignatory companies) were shortchanged, as were opportunities for the cross-fertilization of ideas and for the development of innovative approaches to implementation. What emerged was a highly routinized relationship between the companies as represented by ISU and the monitoring system as represented by Reid Weedon.

Sullivan's role in the monitoring system was largely ceremonial. Although Sullivan was the prime mover in the realm of ideas for expanding the scope of the Principles, he left the task of translating the Principles into concrete corporate objectives almost entirely in the hands of Reid Weedon. Weedon, in turn, heavily influenced Sullivan concerning "what needs to be done and how it must be done." As we shall also see in a subsequent chapter,

Weedon had in place no "real" structure for external accountability. The external oversight under the aegis of ICEOP existed on paper only. Weedon himself well knew that he had devised and implemented the oversight process all by himself, while keeping Sullivan informed of his actions. In the final analysis, it was Weedon's vision that became, for all intents and purposes, the operating standard of the Principles.

1.4.4 ISU's Organizational Structure and Operational Procedures in South Africa

As recorded in the media, the responses to the initial announcement of the Sullivan Principles mirrored the range of responses of South African business executives who were asked to join the Principles program and implement the code. From our research, at least three distinct attitudes to the Sullivan code emerged on the part of South African managers of United States companies:

1. The code merely put into words what many companies were already doing, albeit with a low profile. For example, in the *Sunday Times* of 3 July 1977, a spokesperson for IBM in South Africa noted, "The fair practices manifesto has changed little. Like many non-American companies, United States firms are continuing to implement practices begun years ago. But we often preferred to keep a low profile, believing we could achieve more without too much publicity."[6] This remark is somewhat misleading, however. For example, with the advent of the Sullivan code, almost all signatories had to construct multiracial eating and bathroom facilities. Training Blacks for supervisory positions and upgrading pay scales were also new undertakings for the majority of the firms.
2. The Principles could easily expand and become a troublesome interference in South African society. In particular, African trade unions were feared. For example, *Business Week* reported in its 24 October 1977 issue that "a member of the S.A. Foundation, a businessmen's lobby, said that, 'if anything unreasonable, like the recognition of black trade unions comes, . . . it would be most unwelcome.'" The article further stated, "Fearing that African unions would quickly become lightning conductors for nationwide strikes and political unrest, the South African government has been leaning heavily on employers to ignore them and has been harassing many of their organizers."[7] Finally, the article noted that of the more than three hundred United States companies operating in South Africa in 1977, Ford Motor Company was the only one to accord Black unions even a limited form of recognition.
3. The third type of attitude was expressed well in a hard-hitting piece in South Africa's equivalent of *Business Week,* a journal called the *Finan-*

cial Mail. In its 4 March 1977 issue, an article entitled "A Damp Squib Unless . . . " stated that "The American business manifesto needs to go a lot further, and be followed up with determination."[8] The key point of the article was that any Principles or code must include trade union rights for Africans because "many of the problems which the manifesto [the Principles] seeks to tackle arise in large part from the fact that Africans are denied collective bargaining rights." The article also argued that the United States parent companies should pay much closer attention to the everyday operations of their South African subsidiaries than they had been up until then. The *Financial Mail* obviously wanted to see apartheid dismantled. However, the editors were concerned that United States companies were not sufficiently serious about such an endeavor. Goeffrey Windsor of Dresser SA was quoted in the magazine as saying, "It really seems to be just a lot of talk." Peter Scholtz, another manager of the subsidiary of a United States firm, Koehring, SA, stated, "I expect Koehring will probably keep their noses out of what is happening." The *Financial Mail* itself raised a tough issue when it noted, "There is a genuine question in Washington as to whether the recent anti-apartheid gesture by the U.S. firms was aimed more at the White House and liberal American stockholder groups than at the Vorster government and its policies."[9]

From the practical perspective of implementing the Principles, executives of United States companies' South African subsidiaries fell into two discrete categories. Those holding the attitudes described under 1 and 2 above were unlikely to do more than what was absolutely necessary to implement the Principles and to maintain their own individual positions in their corporations. Those holding the attitudes described under 3 above were likely to be more aggressive in implementing the Principles and expanding their scope. With all three of the above attitudes present in South Africa, however—even within the same corporation—the decisive factor in determining the pace of change turned out to be the intensity of interest demonstrated by senior managers in the United States.

2.   A BRIEF OVERVIEW OF SA ORGANIZATIONAL DEVELOPMENT

Roger D. Crawford—in 1999, a senior manager with a Johnson & Johnson subsidiary in South Africa—was involved with the Principles program almost from its inception and continuing until its abolition in 1994. He makes the case that the organization of the Principles program in South Africa went through five stages in its eighteen-year history:

1. 1977–81 No coordination of effort and no synergy
2. 1981–82 Development of a critical mass, and economy of scale
3. 1982–85 Organization developed
4. 1985–86 Social justice added to objectives, plus challenge to the government
5. 1986–94 Organization formalized

During stage 1, most companies moved immediately to remove "Whites only" signs on toilets and to construct multiracial bathrooms and eating facilities. This effort was in response to instructions received in a personal letter Sullivan sent to CEOs in the United States. The companies also began funding projects in the townships—such as assisting in school funding, day-care centers, clinics, and so on. There was, however, little coordination of these efforts and little cooperation in creating joint projects.

During stage 2, there was considerably more cooperative effort and co-ordination of activities on the part of the signatory companies. Thus, one saw evidence of the first signs of creating critical mass and of benefiting from economies of scale. Stage 3 began in 1982 with the appointment of Roger Crawford as national coordinator of the Principles program in South Africa. Crawford was given a two-year paid leave of absence from Johnson & John-son to provide leadership to the organization. A national advisory council was also established in South Africa. Chaired by Bill Magruder, a managing director of Union Carbide in South Africa, the council consisted of the six heads of the South African counterpart task groups (Housing, Education, Health Care, Small Business Development, Rural Development, and Advo-cacy/Communications).

An example of the coalitions that developed in this period was the East Rand Task Force of Sullivan signatories (ERTF). Chaired by J. L. Clarke, the managing director of Gillette South Africa, the ERTF's seven aims and objectives were:

1. To further the objectives behind the Sullivan Principles within the region common to the Task Force and to do so with the cooperation of, and in consultation with, the community
2. To identify projects that would be of interest to the members of the Task Force and would benefit by group activity rather than by single company activity
3. To disseminate information on the activities of the functional and re-gional task forces and to undertake projects that were complementary to these activities
4. To be a resource on Sullivan-related activities to members, new mem-bers, and non-members on the East Rand and to encourage non-American companies to participate in group activities

5. To communicate activities and experiences to other Sullivan signatories
6. To work toward becoming totally representative of Signatory companies on the East Rand by encouraging membership of all the active Signatory companies
7. To further these activities by formal meetings at least 10 times per year[10]

This group effort achieved success that would have been beyond the scope of any individual company. For example, it transformed a government-controlled, so-called Colored-only training facility—the Highveld Technical College, on the campus of St. Anthony's in Johannesburg—into a multiracial organization. It was as a coalition of important United States companies that ERTF was able to accomplish this opening to other racial groups (notably, Africans). This same coalition also initiated the Springs Legal Aid Clinic, an organization that enabled those charged with breaking apartheid laws to mount a legal defense. Such opposition to the policies of the South African government was highly unusual; the individual companies were, indeed, reluctant to challenge the government or its laws for fear of losing government contracts. This fear was especially great because many of the largest companies in South Africa were quasi-governmental; that is, they were owned and controlled by the South African government. Although they supposedly operated as market-driven private companies, they were, in fact, organs of the state and acted in concert with, and under the direction of, the South African government. These companies—utilities, steel and arms producers, airlines, trains, shipping, and health care—constituted a major part of South Africa's economic activity. A capacity to act collectively under the aegis of ERTF thus provided individual companies some measure of protection against retaliatory action by the South African government.

Stage 4 of the Principles' organization began in 1985 and lasted for about a year. That period was marked by a dramatic shift in activity: the companies openly opposed apartheid laws and publicly challenged the South African government to create a more just and democratic society. The impetus for this initiative came from the fourth amplification of the Sullivan Principles in 1985, known as the "Social Justice Amplification" (chapter 8).

Stage 5—the final stage of the implementation of the Principles in South Africa—was marked by the establishment in 1986 of a formal organization called the Signatory Association of South Africa (SASA). Roger Crawford, Director of Human Resources for Johnson & Johnson, was elected chair of the association; the practice of borrowing a manager for two-year terms to work full time for the association was terminated in favor of electing officers from signatory companies to manage the association as a collateral duty. Denise Buckle, originally a secretary for the group, was promoted to senior administrator, and the association rented a suite of offices with the American Chamber of Commerce of South Africa (AMCHAM), an association of

United States companies and of South African companies doing business within the United States.

The major challenge during this stage was to implement the phase 3 plan that was developed in 1985, partially in response to the fourth enhancement of the Principles (discussed in Chapter 8). A highly unusual aspect of this phase 3 plan was the decision of the Signatory Association of South Africa to undertake an advertising campaign and create a highly visible public profile of the changed stance of the United States companies in South Africa— which were actually challenging the South African government and its apartheid laws. The public persona of the United States companies' position toward apartheid had thus come a full circle. What started out to be a drive to: (a) attempt to forestall the divestiture movement in the United States, and (b) to dismantle the apartheid infrastructure in the United States companies' South African plants, became a public campaign for the dismantling of apartheid's political structure and institutions. This stance was precisely the one that had been adamantly opposed by the United States companies and their CEOs during the early phases of the anti-apartheid campaign and the initiation of the Sullivan Principles.

ENDNOTES

1 Telephone interview with Reid Weedon, 4 April 1997.
2 Notes on the General Signatories Meeting, held at Pfizer Corporation headquarters, New York, 13 November 1979, 2.
3 Telephone interview with Weedon.
4 Minutes of the board meeting of the International Council for Equality of Opportunity Principles, Inc., 10 December 1979, held at the Progress Plaza, Philadelphia, 2.
5 Ibid., 3.
6 "U.S. Firms in SA Stick to Equal Pay Rules," *Sunday Times* (London), 3 July 1977.
7 "South Africa: Multinationals Are Caught in the Middle," *Business Week*, 24 October 1977.
8 "A Damp Squib Unless . . .," *Financial Mail*, 4 March 1977.
9 Ibid.
10 J. L. Clarke (managing director, Gillette South Africa Limited), letter to Reid Weedon (Arthur D. Little, Inc.), 8 July 1978.

Chapter 5

Measuring Progress
An Independent Monitoring System

Through our long experience in analyzing and evaluating multinational codes and the reasons for their relative success and failure, we are led to conclude that corporate efforts and proclamations concerning their codes of conduct are generally met with public skepticism and disbelief. Codes are often viewed as "hollow words" designed to assuage the public's sense of moral outrage, and as little more than an exercise in public relations. These sentiments are not entirely without foundation, especially when one views the context in which such codes are often proposed and the scanty public disclosure companies provide concerning their actual compliance with the codes.

These multinational codes are typically written in broad terms and presented as expressions of general principles. They lack specificity and are subject to divergent interpretations. Very rarely, if ever, do corporations allow their compliance with codes to be monitored by external, independent bodies whose findings are then made public.

In order to have any meaning in terms of gaining public credibility, codes of conduct must meet two sets of considerations:

- The need for specific, quantifiable, and objective measures that convert general principles into operating standards. That is, how effective is the audit instrument that would be used to evaluate the substance of the company's espoused commitments expressed in the code?

- The need for a credible, independent monitoring commission. How independent is it? How comprehesive is its reporting system? How willing (and able) is the commission to receive and investigate complaints from both inside and outside the company? Is the commission able to make its findings public?

These two conditions are inextricably linked in a symbiotic relationship. A highly precise and quantifiable audit instrument is necessary in order to ensure that different auditors examining the same phenomena would draw similar conclusions; that is, the facts or field conditions should not be subject to varying interpretations. Lacking such an objective and quantifiable system, the effectiveness of the independent monitoring system is seriously eroded, if not effectively nullified. Similarly, a corporation's assertions of meeting its code-related commitments are unlikely to be believed unless they are verified by an independent group of monitors whose integrity is unquestioned by most informed and objective observers.

The monitoring and reporting system of the Sullivan Principles incorporated some features of objectivity, precision, and transparency outlined above. However, as we shall discuss in this and other parts of the book, the system fell considerably short of the level of independent investigation, objective measurement, and detailed external reporting.

1.   THE ANTECEDENTS TO THE DEVELOPMENT OF THE MONITORING SYSTEM

From the very inception of the Principles program, both Sullivan and the companies were in agreement on the need to ensure compliance with the Principles, and to report the companies' performance to the public. However, there were major differences between Sullivan and the companies concerning the need for monitoring as such, the manner in which it should be conducted, and the form and detail in which such findings should be reported to the public.

From ICEOP's perspective, monitoring was necessary because "companies will only do as much as they are forced to do." Furthermore, ICEOP was extremely sensitive to the external criticisms concerning the problematic and uncertain benefits of the Principles to the Black people of South Africa. In order to meet the concerns of "friends and critics to determine their [the Principles'] effectiveness," ICEOP was insistent on the need to make "measurable progress" that was constantly evaluated.[1]

The companies' concerns were somewhat different. They were primarily interested in ensuring that their combined performance was seen as a collective effort on their part, and in demonstrating their commitment to the Principles. They were also concerned that the monitoring process not be used to highlight comparative performance of individual companies except in a very general manner. They felt that such an approach would place companies in competition with each other and thereby undermine the cooperation that was considered necessary for the overall success of the Principles. The companies were afraid that detailed publication of individual companies' performance and compliance efforts would be exploited by the groups that were unsympathetic to the Principles or to the companies' stance of staying in

South Africa. Moreover, because companies would be fearful of exposure to the harsh light of public scrutiny, they would be afraid to experiment with bold approaches to implementing the Principles; rather than being praised as innovative risk takers, the companies may end up being criticized for embarking on experiments that failed. There was also some concern that the South African government would react negatively to some of the initiatives taken by the United States companies if they were to become public and were interpreted as an affront and an open challenge to South African laws and policies.

2. EARLY EFFORTS BY THE UNITED STATES COMPANIES AT DEVELOPING A MONITORING SYSTEM

From the very beginning, and despite their resistance to monitoring and public reporting, many company executives felt strongly that a uniform system of reporting would be necessary for the Principles to have any meaningful impact. W. B. Nicholson, vice chairman of Union Carbide and a strong advocate of the Principles, took the lead on this problem. During a meeting between ISU members and Sullivan on 17 November 1977, Union Carbide officials agreed to develop a draft of a reporting form. A month later (22 December), Fred O'Mara, executive vice president of the Union Carbide Corporation, wrote to Sullivan and forwarded a draft of a reporting form. Summarizing their 17 November meeting, O'Mara stated: "This form is to be critiqued and modified by you and Reverend Roman per suggestion of a selected few of the signators. The final form would then be presented to the CEO meeting in mid to late January. The purpose of the form is to make for more definitive reporting on a regular basis."[2]

After much comment and discussion, especially on the part of the task group on periodic reporting and economic and community development, a format for the questionnaire was approved. The questionnaire addressed issues concerning the number of employees from different racial groups (Black, White, Colored, and Asians), pay scales, benefit plans, training programs, and programs to improve the quality of life outside the work environment (housing, transportation, schooling, recreation, health facilities, and legal advice).

Each signatory company was asked to report for the six-month period ending 30 June 1978. Further, in order to provide some context for the data, each company was asked to report for the six-month periods ending in 31 December 1972, 31 December 1976, and 31 December 1977. As might be expected, the data for the period ending 31 December 1972 was difficult to obtain. The 31 August 1978 letter from Richard R. Farrow, vice president–personnel of Warner-Lambert International, presented a typical response. After stating that he was enclosing the "Sullivan Summary Report Forms" for the four indicated six-month periods, Farrow indicated that his company was unable to reconstruct the complete data for the earliest period (ending 31 December 1972), but was providing, instead, certain data that was "reasonably accurate."[3]

Although the reporting instrument was not especially refined in 1978, it was a fairly comprehensive and effective instrument in view of the voluntary nature of data submission. And yet, despite public pressure from groups such as the ICCR, the United States companies were unwilling to release individual company performance data to the public. Instead, it was decided that a composite report, one that summarized the total endeavor of all the signatories, would be prepared and publicly released—even though it was apparent that such a report would not satisfy outside critics. Since Sullivan had neither the time nor expertise to prepare the report, the Steering Committee, at Sullivan's request, contracted with Reid Weedon's consulting firm, ADL, to prepare the summary report for public dissemination. In November 1978, Weedon issued the "First Report on the Signatory Companies to the Sullivan Principles," which was then made available to the public.[4] In all, fifty-seven United States companies submitted reports for eighty-one subsidiaries or locations in South Africa. A summary of the highlights of the report (exhibit 5) indicates how much remained to be accomplished.

In the second report, issued in April 1979, which measured the progress from June to December 1978, Weedon and his ADL associates assigned ratings to each company. One hundred sixteen companies were now enrolled in the program. The ratings were as follows:

I.	Rated as "making acceptable progress"	66 companies
II.	Rated as "cooperating"	23 companies
III.	Did not respond to survey	10 companies
IV.	Enforcers without operations in South Africa	6 companies
V.	Recent signers not yet reporting	11 companies

The report indicated that signatory companies had over fifty thousand employees, less than half of whom were Whites. Sullivan was concerned and disappointed that the performance of over 40 percent of the companies was rated less than acceptable—a rating that required companies to

- submit questionnaires for the periods ending in June and December 1978

- fully implement Principle I of the Sullivan code

- demonstrate a substantial commitment to implement the other five Principles

Exhibit 5. First Report on the Signatory Companies to the Sullivan Principles: Summary of Major Findings

1. Nonsegregation of the races in all eating, comfort, and work facilities.
    *   56 locations reported that all facilities were common.
    *   8 locations reported that some facilities were still separate.
    *   17 locations reported that all facilities were separate.
    *   5 of the 17 reported that facilities were still separate because of the laws of South Africa.
2. Equal and fair employment practices for all employees.
    *   68% of reporting units have common benefit plans for all.
    *   76% of reporting units have procedures for dealing with complaints without regard to race.
    *   16 reporting units out of 81 have trade unions; only one of these is for black workers exclusively.
3. Equal pay for all employees doing equal or comparable work for the same period of time.
    *   90% of blacks employed in a wage basis earn less than $360 per month. 9% of white employed in a wage basis earn less than $360 per month; 56% earn more than $535 per month
4. Initiation of and development of training programs that will prepare, in substantial numbers, blacks and other nonwhites for supervisory, administrative, clerical, and technical jobs. Here, the numbers were not encouraging. For example, the chart below gives the information the Ford Motor Company provided for some job categories of its operation in South Africa.

Black Trainees

Job training	1976	1977	1978
Foreman training	3	5	12
Mfg. engineering	0	0	3
Tool setter training	11	7	10
Computer operator	0	0	0
Total	14	12	25

5. Increasing the number of blacks and other non-whites in management and supervisory positions.
    *   Only 7% of the companies responding had blacks at the management and supervisory level.
    *   In 81% of the companies whites hold the majority of these positions.
    *   At General Motors only 4 of 1100 salaried workers were blacks.
6. Improving the quality of employees' lives outside of the work environment in such areas as housing, transportation, schooling, recreation and health facilities. While the amount of money spent and the number of employees served was not provided, the report indicated the following percentage of the companies assisting in the indicated area:

Type of Aid	% of Companies
• Financial assistance — housing	51%
• Subsidized schooling	39%
• Tuition refund	36%
• Bursaries or scholarships	19%
• Free bus service	19%
• Adult education	18%
• Company-subsidized housing	13%
• Upgrading of local schools	12%
• Literacy training	10%
• Automobiles for non business use	6%
• Rental allowance	4%
• Automobile loans	3%
• No outside assistance provided	35%

3.   MONITORING AND EVALUATION OF CORPORATE PERFORMANCE: THE NEXT PHASE

The first set of reports revealed a number of deficiencies in the reporting system, especially with regard to ranking and evaluating individual companies' performance. After much discussion within the task group on periodic reporting, it was agreed that, beginning in the report for the period ending 30 June 1979, each company would receive one of three possible ratings on the basis of the Sullivan Summary Report Forms submitted: I, making good progress; II, making acceptable progress; and III, needs to become more active. It was also decided that, beginning with the twelve months ending 30 June 1980, the reporting would be done on an annual basis rather than semi-annually.

During 1979 two other initiatives were undertaken to address the question of monitoring the performance of the United States companies in South Africa under the Sullivan Principles. This question was framed in terms of what should be expected of these companies and how they should respond to the concerns of important stakeholders and the public-at-large both in South Africa and the United States. The first initiative related to the meeting at the Carnegie Corporation in New York, and the second to a trip to South Africa by a team of ICEOP members that was led by Gus Roman, aide to Sullivan.

3.1   The Carnegie Meeting

On 15 June 1979, Alan Pifer, president of Carnegie Corporation of New York, called a meeting[5] "to provide an opportunity for discussing ways to monitor the labor practices of American firms in South Africa in an effort to ascertain their compliance with the six Sullivan Principles." The meeting was attended by a group of forty-two educators and other distinguished persons. The educators, who represented universities and colleges owning stock in corporations doing business in South Africa, included the presidents of Colby, Columbia, Cornell, Georgetown, Rutgers, and Smith. Other schools represented were Bryn Mawr, Carleton, Dartmouth, Harvard, Haverford, Oberlin, and Wesleyan. The presidents of the Rockefeller Brothers Fund and the Clark, Ford, and Rockefeller Foundations were also in attendance, as were a variety of government, business, and labor leaders.

The primary focus of the meeting was to ascertain whether the monitoring mechanisms for the Sullivan Principles provided an accurate picture of how well the United States companies were advancing the cause of human rights for Blacks in South Africa. For the institutions represented at the meeting, answering this question was no academic exercise. The institutions were facing increasing pressure from students, faculty, and concerned citizens to withdraw their investments from companies with operations in South African. Issues of moral standards and human rights with regard to South African investments were engendering increased controversy, and it was becoming harder to defend those investments. The burden was on the leaders of these academic and philanthropic institutions to show that United States companies were advancing the human rights of Blacks. Companies' performance under the Sullivan Principles was therefore an overriding concern.

The report of the Carnegie meeting indicated that many of the Black leaders in South Africa were skeptical that the Principles could accomplish much in such a hostile environment. These leaders were, however, willing to support the Principles if certain changes were made:

- In order to achieve both more credibility and greater legitimacy, the Principles program needed to strengthen its connection with, and gather better information about, the signatory companies' Black workers—in particular, through discussions with those workers and with union organizers to ensure that the Principles program's areas of emphasis were valid in the South African circumstances.

- The monitoring function needed to be kept separate from both the Sullivan organization and the corporations themselves, and needed to be based, in whole or in part, in the United States, with substantial input from South African labor. (Skepticism was expressed regarding programs for change that only involve management's speaking with management.)

- A strong enforcement plan needed to be developed, preferably from the outside and with recognition that the South African government did not welcome the changes being promoted.

Roman, as an aide to Sullivan, reported on the current state of the monitoring question. He indicated that Sullivan had contracted with ADL to develop a questionnaire for signatories that would indicate the extent to which each company was meeting the requirements of the Principles. A summary report was also to be prepared on the basis of the completed questionnaires. The gathering was told that ADL was working on the third such summary report, and that a rating scale was to be introduced. Roman made it clear that the ADL report "should not be considered monitoring in the true sense of the word" since "no fixed goals and timetables have yet been promulgated by Reverend Sullivan." Roman also outlined the task-group structure of the Principles and explained the role of the ICEOP: chaired by Sullivan and including such distinguished Black leaders as the Reverend Ralph Abernathy, the group's purpose was "to set policy for the Sullivan Principles and to guide the task forces in deciding how the principles are to be monitored."[6] Roman indicated that, as of that time, ICEOP had no funding but anticipated receiving some in the near future. Roman further indicated that a small delegation would soon visit South Africa for three weeks to study ways to improve both the implementation of the Principles and the reporting process.

The sense of the Carnegie meeting was "that the Sullivan Principles are a responsible but necessarily limited piece of the work that needs to be done; but in order to bolster that effort and to satisfy the more rigorous demands of the students and faculty who have called for divestiture, an independent monitoring mechanism should be considered."[7] Moreover, any monitoring program needed to credible, reliable and, independent; since the companies themselves would probably end up financing the ADL reports (which, in fact, was precisely what happened), the Carnegie participants felt that that monitoring endeavor would not be perceived as objective.

Another point raised at the meeting was similar to a criticism that was raised in March 1977 when Sullivan first announced his Principles. To wit, given Sullivan's insistence on building a consensus among the companies before making public any new challenge for them to meet, he was perceived by some critics as being too willing to compromise. "His painstakingness looks to many outsiders like a reluctance to push the corporations 'too far.'"[8] The group also raised a question that continued to haunt even the most ardent supporters of the Principles; namely, "the degree to which any improvement in the U.S. corporate behavior will have an impact on the South African government or its apartheid policy."[9]

3.2   The Trip to South Africa

The trip Gus Roman led to South Africa took place from 5 to 29 August 1979. It was funded by a grant of thirty thousand dollars from the Edna McConnell Clark Foundation of New York. Accompanying him were Weedon and Ellen Rupert of ADL, and Daniel Purnell of Sullivan's staff. It is noteworthy that the group did not include any members of ICEOP (with the exception of the two staff members). Nor did it include any members of the academic and philanthropic institutions that were represented at the Carnegie meeting. Thus, despite the earnestness of the Roman group to seek out new information and divergent viewpoints, the group was essentially insular in its orientation. Especially in view of Sullivan's preference for "inclusiveness," we believe an important opportunity was lost by not involving other important stakeholders in this early, fact-finding phase of developing a more effective monitoring process.

This constrained approach resulted in the exclusion even of moderate but highly credible groups (such as the Investor Responsibility Research Center [IRRC], based in Washington, DC) whose extensive experience in, and knowledge of, South Africa could have been quite useful to the Roman team. Thus, although the Roman-led delegation sought the views of divergent groups in South Africa, these views were channeled through an analytical process designed to filter out all those opinions and perspectives that were at odds with the limited goals that had been set forth by the corporate community (ISU) and tacitly approved by Leon Sullivan and Reid Weedon .

Since ISU members still felt a strong need to control the information made public about individual companies' implementation of the Princicples, the unwillingness of ISU members to include outside, nonmember representatives in the fact-finding group was to be anticipated. And Weedon and ADL could be counted to go along with this approach because of their desire to keep the Principles program going and prevent it from being subjected to potentially severe external criticism, which might irreparably rupture its cohesiveness.

We believe that by yielding to such an overcautious approach, the Roman team failed to enhance or even protect Sullivan's vision for implementing the Principles. With hindsight, the consequences of this insularity became all too evident in terms of its eroding the credibility of the monitoring process and its seriously undermining the value and validity of the Principles in the eyes of both its supporters and its detractors. It should, therefore, not be surprising that despite the many findings of the Roman team's report, little change of any significance occurred in the design of the monitoring process. The team failed to recommend any measures that would enhance either the objectivity and verifiability of corporate performance under the Principles, or the credibility of its public reports, whose collective statistics and very general rating system continued to mask the performance of individual companies. Ironically, these failures set in motion a process that would ultimately lead to the denigration not only of the goals that the Principles were designed to accomplish, but of the Principles themselves.

During their visit to South Africa, the Roman team visited twenty-four United States company operations in South Africa and met with government and other officials. In addition, each of the seven task groups initially organized in the United States with officials from the parent companies now had counterparts in South Africa, and each of these groups was solicited for suggestions for improving the monitoring and reporting process.

The team's eighteen-page report made some important observations.[10] One especially noteworthy point pertained to critics' objection "that self-reporting by the companies did not assure an accurate and valid system of reporting progress."[11] Given the highly contentious external environment, there was the question of whether the United States companies in South Africa would report information accurately, especially information that might reflect adversely on a company's compliance ratings. The report noted, however, that the on-site monitoring that was conducted by the team during its August 1979 visit had the effect of putting the companies on notice that they would always be subject to such scrutiny. This assertion, however, could not be taken at face value in the absence of any provision or recommendation for systematic and regular outside field audits to be undertaken by independent and otherwise credible monitors.

The report noted that the Roman team's on-site monitoring had generated findings "very similar" to IRRC's monitoring activity, which was quite expensive and funded by a group of institutional investors. "We have a comparable number of comprehensive reports on these companies at minimal costs, when compared to the IRRC budget."[12] Again, this observation seems to be self-serving. One gets the sense that Roman's team wanted to continue using the ADL monitoring process without considering any other alternatives, whether internal or external (for example, monitoring by or though IRRC). The net effect of this August 1979 visit was that ADL's Weedon continued to be the sole arbiter of what information would be collected, how would it be collected and evaluated, and in what form that information would be made public.

In June 1979, at the same time that Roman was presenting his report, there were four other "monitoring-like activities" that had the potential to develop into a full-fledged monitoring system. Roman spoke of initiatives by the Trade Union Council of South Africa (TUCSA); the *Post*, a newspaper under the leadership of Percy Qoboza; the Investor Responsibility Research Center (IRRC); and the United States government labor attaché's office in Johannesburg. Largely for reasons of funding and trained personnel, three of these endeavors never amounted to much. Moreover, although IRRC did develop a very helpful reporting format for some companies, it was unable to develop a comprehensive monitoring program for the entire group of companies operating in South Africa. In order to achieve this broader goal, IRRC needed the support and cooperation of both Sullivan and the member companies of ISU, neither of which was forthcoming.

A year later, with the issue of monitoring still in the air, Thomas A. Murphy, chairman of the General Motors Corporation, wrote a most revealing letter to Frank T. Carey, chairman of IBM. The 2 June 1980 letter presented Murphy's strategy for maintaining some control over the monitoring process:

> Following up on our conversation the other evening in Washington, attached are draft copies of the letters which David Rockefeller and I have agreed to sign seeking support from the Sullivan signatory companies for the Industry Support Unit. I would hope that you would consider signing the letters with us in order to maintain some degree of control over the direction of this initiative.
>
> As you know, the only alternative we have to Dr. Sullivan's efforts at monitoring is the continued and even expanded involvement of Arthur D.

Little, Inc. which is to be paid for through signatory company support of the Industry Support Unit (ISU). I should emphasize that the ISU was established at our initiative and designed specifically to keep the control of the funding of this aspect of the Sullivan initiative in the hands of the companies. None of the funds provided the ISU could be expended without the expressed consent of the companies on the ISU Board.

. . . Since the funding of the ISU is so important to maintaining the Principles initiative from which we have all gained, and to keep some control over the direction of the initiative, we would like to have you join David and me in signing the attached letters.[13]

It was apparent from the letter that Murphy and Rockefeller (of the Chase Manhattan Bank) were concerned that the monitoring function could come under the control of those who were hostile to business; funding the ISU was seen as a way to prevent such a loss of control. What follows is the full text of their crucially important letter advocating direct funding of ISU:

FOR NON-CONTRIBUTING SIGNATORY COMPANIES

As you are aware, the Statement of Principles Industry Support Unit (ISU), which was designed to provide support for the implementation and advancement of the Six Principles, has been an integral part of the Sullivan Principles initiative. In this regard, the activities funded by the ISU serve to advance significantly the credibility of the Principles initiative and to interpret the importance of this effort to key sectors of the public —although it should be noted that these activities do not include "monitoring."

We believe that the Principles initiative is a more constructive approach to change in South Africa than the often-suggested alternatives of withdrawal and economic sanctions. The initiative, through the ISU, is dependent on financial assistance to facilitate communication and cooperation between Dr. Sullivan, the Task Groups and Signatory Companies as well as to provide staff, administrative and consulting services.

As described in the enclosed report, the ISU faces serious financial difficulties. Further, we are particularly concerned because the ISU budget crisis has forced Arthur D. Little, Inc. (ADL) to suspend its services. In this regard, we believe that the professional expertise and independent viewpoint of ADL has contributed significantly to the initiative and its credibility.

To date, only $338,500 of the $566,000 budget for the fiscal year ending June 30, 1980 has been raised, principally because 64 of the 135 Signatory Companies have not supported the ISU. Inasmuch as your company or foundation has not yet contributed to the ISU, we hope that you will demonstrate your support by making a contribution of $2,000 (endorsers) to $14,000 (reporting Signatory Companies with worldwide revenue exceeding $1 billion), to cover both the first and second fiscal years of the ISU's operation. As a matter of information, the ISU is an exempt organization under Section 501(c)3 of the Internal Revenue Code and, accordingly, contributions to the ISU are eligible for consideration by most company-sponsored foundations.

The Principles initiative is a unique, reasoned response to an extraordinarily difficult issue. We believe that the ISU merits your full support and hope that you will join us in ensuring its continuance.[14]

4.   MONITORING: THE CRUCIAL ISSUE

Despite the continuing efforts by ADL and the signatory companies, the issue of monitoring remained largely unresolved and became increasingly contentious. The gap between the ADL reports and the expectations of the anti-apartheid groups was quite large and could not be bridged without radical restructuring of the reports' contents, the verification process, and the public reporting there of. Thus, with the passage of time, the mutual distrust and antagonism between the two sides began to feed on itself. Eventually, this distrust would play a major role both in the increasingly strident and confrontational stance of critics and in broadening their support, both in the United States and South Africa.

Educators and religious activists favored an independent monitoring group, and Sullivan was inclined to support this position. Nevertheless, United States companies were, for the most part, content to have ADL review the reports filed by the companies and, on that basis, assign a rating. Since ADL's audit was fundamentally a desk audit, however, and did not provide for a systematic, regular, field investigation of corporate activities, the continued use of the ADL audits confirmed the fears and concerns of corporate critics and their dissatisfaction with Roman's report and recommendations.

5.   THE WHARTON INITIATIVE

In his search for a monitoring system that would be acceptable to all parties and that would also have significant public credibility, Sullivan was led to contact Professor Herbert L. Northrup, head of the Industrial Research

Unit at the Wharton School of the University of Pennsylvania, to see if he would undertake such an assignment. In a letter of 6 July 1980 (exhibit 6), Northrup recommended a framework for organizing and implementing an independent monitoring system. This extremely important letter sets forth some important conditions that must be met for such a system to be objective, credible, and acceptable.

Exhibit 6. Letter from Prof. Herbert R. Northrop to Rev. Leon Sullivan
***

The senior staff of the Wharton Industrial Research Unit and I appreciate very much your offer for us to take over the monitoring of The Sullivan Principles for companies operating in South Africa, and the time that your staff and especially yourself spent in explaining your views and plans relating to this task. We have explored the various issues involved and, with this letter, set forth our views on the principles which we believe should govern how monitoring should be organized and what monitoring should entail.

I. MONITORING ORGANIZATION

We believe that successful monitoring would require the following organizational principles and practices:

1. *Independence* – The monitoring organization must be completely independent. It cannot therefore report to the International Council of Equality of Opportunity Principles but must report solely to you. Thus, the monitoring organization should not be encumbered with overseeing organizations, observers, confidential consultants, or anyone else. No other group or persons should represent the monitors or be encouraged to replicate the monitoring work in South Africa or should be in any relationship which would give them access to monitoring or company information or which would compromise the monitoring impact or dilute the authority and responsibility of the monitoring organization.

2. *Confidentiality* – All information obtained by the monitoring organization must be held in confidence by the monitoring organization and must remain the property of that organization. Information as appropriate will be reported to you, and information concerning a company will be reported to and discussed with that company, but raw data and undigested or unanalyzed information should not be released by the monitoring organization.

3. *Acceptability* – The monitoring organization must be completely acceptable both to you and to the companies involved. Only by such acceptability can the necessary information be obtained to make monitoring a success.

4. *Objectivity* – The monitoring organization must be a prestigious one which has public recognition and standing and which has the staff and the leadership whose competence, sophistication, interest, and objectivity will attest to the accuracy of the monitoring.

5. *Control* – All persons associated with the monitoring organization must be employees of the monitoring organization and under the control of the director of the monitoring organization. No other monitoring activity (other than the A.D. Little activity) should be authorized or permitted by you or by any organization associated with you. Otherwise the effectiveness and acceptability of the monitoring would be seriously compromised.

continued on next page

Exhibit 6—continued

6. *Audit Cooperation* – Data collected by the A.D. Little organization for the desk audit must be available on a confidential basis to the monitoring organization. A careful and constructive relationship <u>must</u> be developed between the monitoring organization and A.D. Little in order to maximize the results and effects of the work of both toward the common goal.

7. *Funding* – The monitoring function should not be initiated until funding is pledged. This includes initial funding to develop the methodology, planning, and content and to cover the costs of submission to a funding organization; and then funding to cover one year's effort as set forth in paragraph No. I-9 below. The funding organization should also understand that, assuming the monitoring effort is successful, funding will be requested to continue the monitoring each year.

8. *Funding Independence* – The funding organization should be independent of you, the U.S. government, and the companies monitored. In order further to insure independence, the funding should be paid directly from the funding organization to the monitoring organization.

9. *Pilot Program* – The first year of monitoring should be conceived of as a pilot operation from which all—you, the companies, and the monitors—can learn and correct mistakes and misapplications. This would permit all parties to make suggestions for improvement while avoiding hardening of attitudes or reduced cooperation in case mistakes are made or differences of opinion or procedures exist.

10. *Interracial Staff* – Every effort should be made by the monitoring organization to have an integrated, interracial staff, all members of which, as set forth in paragraph No. I-5, must be employees of the monitoring organization and subject to the control of its director.

11. *Application of Organization Principles* – The application of these organizational principles is, I am sure, obvious. Such organizational requirements envision, for example, a different role for the International Council of Equality of Opportunity Principles which would be entirely divorced from the monitoring function; there could be no monitoring – observer role for the National Council of Churches, the American Friends Service Committee, or for any other outside organization; and there could be no participation by the former monitor in any monitoring function or relationship either directly or indirectly in his role as consultant to you.

II. MONITORING PRINCIPLES

We have found considerable differences of opinion on what monitoring should entail and therefore we set forth below our concept of the principles which should govern monitoring. The philosophy underlying our approach is that monitoring would be useful both to you and to the companies involved. Monitoring should demonstrate that companies are being examined to make certain that they are expanding the opportunities for Blacks and that therefore the continued presence of American multinational companies in South Africa is consistent with the principles which you so eloquently espouse.

1. *Purpose* – The prime purpose of monitoring should be to determine whether, and to what extent, companies signatory to the Sullivan Principles are fulfilling their obligation to move toward equal opportunity for Blacks and other disadvantaged persons. Emphasis should be on employment, training, development, and upgrading, but examination should

continued on next page

Exhibit 6—continued

also be made of company activity in related social measures, such as assistance in housing and education, preemployment training and indoctrination, etc. Examination should also be made of civil rights on the job—rights to appeal discipline (grievance machinery), rights to join or to refrain from joining unions, etc.

2. *Understanding Industry Structure* – Fundamental to successful monitoring is the understanding of industry structures, which permit some industries to expand employment much more rapidly than others. Structural requirements such as different skill, training, and product warranty and safety requirements, varying sophistication of processes, etc. are often controlling. Thus, understanding of industry requirements and varying industry structure must be quite sophisticated for successful qualitative monitoring.

3. *Differences with Desk Audit* – It follows from the above that companies can be rated differently by a desk audit (A.D. Little) and by sophisticated monitoring. Such differences must be clearly explained and understood.

4. *Coverage* – It is not practical to monitor each company each year. Therefore, attempts should be made to monitor a sample of companies which rate a high grade in the desk audit, a sample of those rating a medium grade, and a sample with a low grade. This selection would be designed to explain why such companies are so rated by the desk audit, what practices are worth emulating, and what can be done to remove barriers to progress.

5. *Climate for Progress* – Improvement can be enhanced by a receptive climate. Therefore, a prime purpose of monitoring should be to enhance the receptivity to progress. This involves avoidance of sensationalism, and emphasis on constructive suggestion and criticism.

6. *Relation to Purposes Set Forth by Dr. Sullivan* – We have examined a copy of Dr. Sullivan's memorandum of June 6, 1980, and of the twelve points set forth in the "Purpose of On-Site Monitoring." We believe that the principles of paragraphs II, 1–5, set forth above, are consistent with these documents as long as the monitoring is accomplished with the organizational principles set forth in paragraphs I, 1–11. The need to eliminate apartheid is not questioned. The monitoring organization, however, cannot be the spearhead of an attack on that deplorable system if it is to work in South Africa. This again emphasizes the need for the monitoring organization to be completely independent and to concentrate on appraising the extent to which the companies have met their obligations under the Sullivan Principles and on recommendations for further improvements.

III. CONCLUSION

We have attempted in this letter to provide a framework within which we believe an independent, reputable, and knowledgeable organization could develop and operate the monitoring function and thus contribute both to the improvement of the welfare of disadvantaged citizens in South Africa and also could enhance the value and workings of the Sullivan Principles. We would certainly understand if some of our requirements seem inconsistent with your needs. It may also well be that our role, if any, would be more suited to working with and assisting companies in the improvement of their practices in South Africa than to monitoring those companies' practices. We shall therefore await your decision before determining what task, if any, we can perform.

The letter addressed two issues: the structure and character of the monitoring organization, and the principles that underlie the monitoring process. Northrup indicated that the monitoring organization should meet the following criteria: independence, confidentiality, acceptability, objectivity, control, audit cooperation, sufficient funding; independence of the monitoring organization from the funding sources; and interracial staff. The letter also recommended that the first year of the audit should be considered a pilot program that would be used as a basis for learning and for collecting input from all the parties involved. Finally, Northrup suggested that the monitoring organization be independent of all interested parties (including not just the companies, but the church groups and other groups advocating withdrawal of companies from South Africa). "There could be no monitoring-observer role for the National Council of Churches, the American Friends Service Committee, or for any other outside organization; and there could be no participation by the former monitor in any monitoring function or relationship either directly or indirectly in his role as consultant to you."[15] More controversial was Northrup's recommendation that Sullivan's present oversight vehicle, the ICEOP, should have "a different role," unidentified by Northrop, "which would be entirely divorced from the monitoring function."[16]

Sullivan's response to Northrup's recommendations was both enthusiastic and supportive. Indeed, in his letter 4 August 1980 (reproduced in its entirety as appendix 5.1), Sullivan appeared to have accepted most of Northrup's recommendations. A careful reading of Sullivan's letter, however, suggests that he may not have been entirely certain as to what he was agreeing to; his comments on certain points were somewhat at variance with the substance and intent of Northrup's recommendations. Sullivan indicated that he was in agreement with the recommendation that "the monitoring function should be left to the Wharton Industrial Research Unit under [Northrup's] direction." The ADL organization would collect data and perform a desk audit, both of which would be made available, "on a confidential basis, to the on-site monitoring organization, and vice versa from your organization, if requested by them. It is vitally important, indeed, that a careful and constructive relationship be developed by the Arthur D. Little organization and your organization, for maximized results."[17]

Sullivan envisaged a "monitoring council of up to seven persons of the highest credentials and public acceptance."[18] He also emphasized the need for cooperating with the companies and for creating a process of regular and frequent communications between the companies' representatives and the monitoring organization. The purpose of this process would be "to assist the monitoring unit and monitoring council with company insights; but it should be clear that the companies would have no organic relation with the on-site monitoring process and would have no authority in decisions made by your organization, or on the views of the monitoring council."[19]

Sullivan's also reemphasized his commitment to make these reports available to the public, but he also indicated that companies should be allowed "an opportunity for their comments and reactions. [However], the raw data and undigested and unanalyzed information would not be released by your monitoring group [to the companies or other parties]."[20]

Northrup's design for a monitoring council and its underlying rationale was a significant step toward making the monitoring process independent, objective, and credible to various stakeholders. From our perspective, however, the design also contained some serious flaws that would severely constrain its implementation and acceptance by the body politic.

A major flaw of the proposal was that the monitoring function wavered between a policing function designed to detect shortfalls in compliance, and a proactive function designed to induce companies to take positive steps in enhancing the achievement of the Principles' goals. This distinction is particularly important in the South African context because the primary reason for the companies to comply with the Principles was to protect them from the criticism of the pro-withdrawal public-interest groups and to forestall further attacks on the companies' right to do business in South Africa. Thus, the pertinent question was not whether these companies simply complied with the Principles. Instead, the driving imperative was to impel the companies to do ever more in meeting their obligations under the Principles and thereby diffuse the criticism of their adversaries. Unfortunately, this point, which was paramount to Sullivan's vision, seemed to have been lost by the Northrup proposal.

It is not clear to us as to why Northrup wanted to exclude ICEOP from any role or responsibility in the oversight function. This organization contained the very important component of religious leadership that could provide the moral and ethical voice in the implementation and interpretation of corporate activities under the Principles. Apparently, Northrup equated, albeit erroneously, ICEOP with other religious groups such as the National Council of Churches and the Interfaith Center on Corporate Responsibility (ICCR). Thus, his recommendation deprived the process of an essential moral credibility that could not be entirely fulfilled by "seven persons of the highest credentials and public acceptance."

There is no explanation why the desk audit was to be performed by ADL, whereas field monitoring was to be undertaken by the staff of Northrup's Industrial Research Unit. The letter also did not outline any process by which local nongovernmental organizations, which were independent of the adversarial position of many pro-withdrawal groups, could be used for field monitoring.

Northrup advocated different types of field audits for different companies—based on the unique characteristic of their particular industries. However, he did not specify as to what those "unique" characteristics might be that would require separate treatment. We find this approach as having the potential for arbitrariness, which would therefore make the reports' findings contentious and undercut their validity. In any case, such an approach was sure to cause internal dissension among the companies, with some feeling that they were being subjected to more onerous audits than other companies. By the same token, public-interest groups would criticize the monitoring and subsequent reports as having been too easy on some of the companies.

As it turned out, despite his enthusiastic early support for the Northrup proposal, Sullivan failed to follow through on his commitment to Northrup. The contract was never consummated. Indeed, as indicated by 20 November 1980 letter from the lawyer who prepared the "Agreement between ICEOP and the Industrial Research Unit of the Wharton School," the lawyer conducting the contract negotiations was himself taken by surprise. When the lawyer, Ira J. K. Wells, Jr., submitted his bill, he included the comment: "I was not aware until Monday of this week that the above proposed contractual agreement was not consummated. To that point I was awaiting comments on the Agreement, two copies of which I delivered to Reverend Roman some time ago."[21] Apparently, Sullivan, in his wisdom, judged that ADL was the sort of monitor that could best achieve his goals. Sullivan thereafter chose Reid Weedon of ADL to handle the task of devising activity classification, performance standards, and reporting systems for the signatory companies.

6.   ADL DEVISES A MONITORING SYSTEM

Weedon developed a monitoring system that included questionnaires, a rating system, and annual public reports. On 30 June 1979, with the third progress report issued under the Principles program, ADL introduced rating criteria. Companies were rated under nine separate categories (Principles I, Ia, Ib, IIIa, IIIb, IIIc, IV, V, and VI), with each being given one to three points (one being the best). The highest total rating that a reporting company, or "unit," could receive was a nine. Reporting units were to be grouped into the following categories: making outstanding progress, nine points; making considerable progress, eighteen points or less; need to become more active, more than eighteen points.

Separate from the overall rating points just mentioned, ADL also assigned points within each category for evaluating a unit's performance in that category. In this context, ADL found it more workable to select a number of factors within each of the categories and to assign a few points to each of the factors (instead of the originally proposed system of establishing a baseline of five points and then adding or subtracting points based on other pertinent factors). Considering the differences between companies (size, location, and type of business), Weedon decided to have more than ten points available in some categories so that a company would have a variety of ways to accumulate points. In order to avoid confusion, the second category—"making acceptable progress"—was changed to "making progress." Although ADL performed the above calculations in reaching an overall rating for each company, the ADL report did not release the actual number of points for any signatory (either overall or in any particular category). The report stated only the general, overall rating for each company (or unit).

Weedon was thus in the enviable position of both evaluating the performance of the companies and assigning them grades. The criteria he used, however, were highly flexible and subjective, and the review process was not subject to independent examination to assess its internal consistency. To outside observers, Weedon became both the judge and jury of the monitoring process, one that ultimately protected the corporations from "insidious" competition among themselves and "unwanted" criticism from outsiders. Unfortunately, Weedon's control of the monitoring process also left the corporations largely at the mercy of his notions of what needed to be done and how to do it. Many company executives were thereby denied opportunities to experiment with different approaches, ones that may have differed dramatically from those preferred by Weedon.

6.1   Payment to Arthur D. Little, Inc.

ADL was paid for its services through signatory companies' support of ISU, and the ISU budget crisis once forced ADL to suspend its services. The major issue between ISU and ADL was whether ADL would eliminate the charge of interest on the existing indebtedness and minimize its outside expenses. According to the minutes of the ISU's board of directors on 25 February 1983, ISU agreed that, subject to Sullivan's review, an annual budget of approximately $160,000 should be presented to ADL. This budget, which would initially provide $125,000 for the annual report, grading, and related processing, plus $35,000 for travel and other costs, would represent the maximum amount ISU would remit to ADL without specific approval of the ISU board.

In light of the increasing costs associated with ADL's annual reviews of the signatory companies' progress in meeting the Sullivan Principles, ADL requested an increase in its fees to $275,000, an increase of $95,000 from the $160,000. In order to recover these increased costs, the ISU board decided to increase the assessment upon all signatory companies by 20 percent in 1984.

6.2   Role of Arthur D. Little, Inc.

ADL was the sole monitoring agency for the Sullivan Principles. Moreover, in practice, Sullivan and Reid Weedon of ADL decided most policy matters after consulting with the companies, either as represented in the task groups or the ISU board. At a 21 June 1984 meeting, the ISU discussed the expanding role of ADL (and Weedon). Wayne Fredericks suggested that the role of ADL be reevaluated, with special attention both to the need for an annual survey and to Weedon's role as a spokesperson for the signatories. Discussion centered on two areas: Weedon's credibility (should he be the spokesperson for the signatories in order to enhance his credibility with external stakeholders?), and ADL's credibility and objectivity (how would an increase in Mr. Weedon's more visible role affect the perceived objectivity of ADL?).

6.3   Flaws in the ADL Monitoring System

It is important for us to summarize the major flaws in the ADL-designed system; these flaws have much bearing on our analysis of the performance data in the ADL annual reports as presented in a latter part of this book. This summary also suggests ways in which a future monitoring program could be constructed to be more objective, consistent in measurement, and informative in terms of what is made available to the public.

The rankings of the signatory firms were determined on the basis of the Sullivan Summary Report Forms submitted by the companies. This approach suffered from a number of serious flaws.

There was no way to compare the performance of individual companies within each group and to measure the degree of dispersion between the top- and bottom-ranked companies within each group.

Since all the companies were grouped only as falling into one of three categories, these categories included large number of companies, and the resulting evaluation of performance was too general to be informative.

Weedon did not provide any detailed criteria for classifying individual companies into the three categories. This failure made it impossible for anyone else to evaluate the objectivity and consistency of company groupings into the three categories.

The system of monitoring and reporting depended, for the most part, on the auditors of each individual company to verify that company's expenditures under various categories prescribed by the Principles. This flaw was one of the most serious, in our opinion, because it compromised the quality of the reported numbers.

There was no way to evaluate whether the different auditing firms used by the companies were evaluating the same numbers in the same manner. This uncertainty made cross-company comparisons difficult, if not impossible.

The auditors of each company reported only expenditures—not the quality of expenditures or their effectiveness in achieving their intended objectives.

A number of categories (and also of subcategories within each category) overlapped with one another, thereby allowing companies and their auditors to "dress up" numbers in a way that would look good on the reporting forms.

Weedon did not have any independent monitors who would systematically "spot check" companies' performance under field conditions. This procedure is a standard one that is widely practiced in sophisticated audits— where "what is available on paper" is verified in the field through detailed analysis of scientifically selected samples representing the universe of phenomena under investigation. Instead, Weedon undertook to do all field examinations on his own. Admittedly, these examinations benefited from his extensive knowledge and experience of the companies' operations in South Africa. Unfortunately, the examinations also suffered from their ad hoc and haphazard character, and they could not be relied on to provide a systematic understanding of weaknesses in the companies' performance or in the reporting system itself. As we shall show later, in allocating funds to various projects, many companies played the game of anticipating and catering to Weedon's whims and foibles, thus making choices that pleased him but were not necessarily effective means of implementing the Principles.

7.   SOME CONCLUDING REMARKS

The monitoring system eventually become the Achilles heel in, and a significant contributor to the erosion in the credibility of, the entire Sullivan Principles program. In their desire to maintain control over the monitoring system, the companies may have won the battle of information management, but they lost the war to gain public confidence and trust in the companies' claim to be playing a positive role in South Africa.

In making ADL the sole arbiter of what was to be monitored, how it should be monitored, and how and what information should be reported to the public, the companies lost sight of the very purpose that was at the foundation of the Sullivan Principles and their implementation.

We believe that it was the companies that persuaded Sullivan to opt for the weaker option of continuing with ADL monitoring under Weedon's control and supervision. The companies were obsessed with the need to control both the compliance process and public dissemination of the findings. It seems likely that Sullivan did not comprehend the implications of a weaker auditing and reporting process. It is also possible that he was unwilling to challenge the companies on this account because he felt that he would be able to use the public pulpit to raise the goalposts and thereby elicit better performance from the companies.

In our opinion, Sullivan's committed a tragic mistake and set the stage for the eventual downfall of the Principles' program, both in terms of its public credibility and acceptance, and its capacity to serve as an instrument for creating more innovative and bold efforts by American companies to meet the needs of their Black workers and, more broadly, the Black people of South Africa.

By abdicating his responsibility to insist on a more credible monitoring system, Sullivan lost the public trust in the viability of his own Principles. What is surprising to us is that there were all kinds of warning bells that both Sullivan and the companies chose to ignore. Although one can understand the companies' shortsightedness in seeking to control the dissemination of information, we are hard pressed to explain Sullivan's apparent reluctance to confront the issues concerning independent monitoring, public accountability, and the transparency of the performance information disclosed to the public.

In conclusion, we believe that the monitoring system failed to live up to both its promise and potential. The companies must bear part of the blame for their unwillingness to make public their individual performance. Sullivan must share some of the blame in acquiescing to this approach and in abdicating the crucial role of oversight, both on his part and that of ICEOP. Finally, the monitoring system further suffered because of the inability and unwillingness of Reid Weedon to institute procedures that would strengthen the process of independent monitoring and evaluation by injecting measures of objectivity, consistency, and transparency.

After Sullivan left the Principles program in June 1987, Sal Marzullo of Mobil, then chairman of ISU, executed a new contract with ADL that significantly altered its role. At its meeting of 22 July 1987, the ISU board agreed that ADL should be

- limited to the evaluation of the questionnaire

- have no role in making policy

- engaged on the basis of an annual fee that sets forth a schedule of specific services the firm would render

- barred from any outside activity relating to South Africa, such as consultation to government agencies or speaking engagements, without the prior approval of the ISU Board

The ISU board's action, we feel, speaks for itself.

APPENDIX 5.1

Zion Baptist Church
N.W. Cor. Broad & Venango Street
Philadelphia, PA. 19140 19104
LEON H. SULLIVAN, Minister

Dr. Herbert R. Northrup
Director, Industrial Research Unit
Vance Hall/CS, 3733 Spruce Street
Philadelphia, Pa. 19104

My dear Dr. Northrup:

Thank you for meeting with me to discuss the possibility of the Wharton Industrial Research Unit handling the on-site monitoring functions for the Sullivan Principles for companies operating in South Africa.

In response to your letter of July 8th, and as a result of our discussions, having explored the various issues involved, these are the points that I am hopeful we can agree upon, as mutually acceptable.

The monitoring function would be left to the professional discretion of the Wharton Industrial Research Unit, under your direction. There would be a monitoring council to which you would report, possibly several times a year, on the experiences and findings of the monitoring unit. The monitoring council would be the only group to which your on-site monitoring organization would report. You would also want to consider any suggestions, or recommendations the council might make, as long, of course, as it does not infringe on your professional judgment.

The monitoring council would consist of up to seven persons of the highest credentials and public acceptances.

It would be expected that there will be an annual public report of sufficient information, of on-site monitoring findings of individual company implementation of the Principles, and a designation of where the individual companies visited fall in a compliance rating.

As discussed, the monitoring reports would be made available to the companies to allow an opportunity for their comments and reactions, but that raw data and undigested and unanalyzed information would not be released by your monitoring group. The release of full monitoring reports to companies, however, would be left to the discretion of the companies.

In order to make the monitoring effort as acceptable as possible to the companies involved, there would be a contact relationship developed with a communication unit of various company representatives. This would assist the monitoring unit and monitoring council with company insights; but it should be clear that companies would have no organic relation with the on-site monitoring process and would have no authority in decisions made by your organization, or on the views of the monitoring council.

It is agreed that your monitoring organization would have a staff of outstanding competence, sophistication, interest and objectivity and that every effort would be made to insure a racial balance. Of course, all persons associated with the monitoring unit would be employees of the monitoring organization and under the control of the Director of the monitoring organization.

It would be understood that the Arthur D. Little Company will continue their valuable work as a vital part of the overall monitoring process.

Also, I will authorize no other organization to perform this service for me, or for any organization associated with me; although we might want to accept on-site monitoring efforts made of a high reputable character, as sufficient for the monitoring needs of a company, such as that done by the South African Institute on Race Relations, that concluded, in my view, a fine on-site monitoring report on the Ford Motor Company not long ago.

I shall request of the Arthur D. Little organization that data collected for the desk audit made by them, be made available on a confidential basis, to the on-site monitoring organization, and vice versa from your organization, if requested by them. It is vitally important, indeed, that a careful and constructive relationship be developed by the Arthur D. Little organization and your organization, for maximized results and to assure that all are working, as best as possible, toward the common goal.

I am willing to initiate contacts with Foundations to secure funding to support the on-site monitoring effort. Utilizing resources already in hand, I am prepared to commit funds already collected, or promised, to the International Council for Equality of Opportunity Principles, to conduct the on-site monitoring services. Of this amount, $10,000 will be made available to you upon agreement of your willingness to assume the on-site monitoring responsibilities and the remaining funds will be made available on a payment schedule basis.

It is understood, of course, that the $40,000 will only be an initial amount to get the program going, because the requirements will be far greater than this amount. Hopefully, the $10,000 received, will be helpful in providing resources to develop the kind of proposal needed for the broader foundation funding requirements.

I have concluded that all funds for this purpose would be payable directly to the Wharton School, thereby insuring the independence of the operation from me, the companies, or anyone else involved.

It would be understood that this first year of monitoring would be conceived as a pilot operation, but with the provisions that our funding sources would be willing to make commitments of up to two years, if the program works successfully.

It is not the intent of this endeavor to work for sensationalism, but to perform a constructive and critical service necessary for the success of the Sullivan Principles objectives, and for the success of our anti-discrimination objectives.

You understand, of course, my aim is the elimination of apartheid. All I am doing is directed towards that end. I see the Principles as a valuable catalyst in helping to bring this about, as well as to end racial discrimination in the work place, as well as outside the work place, all together.

I appreciate your concern regarding the extent to which your special role and the monitoring organization can play in spearheading that which I see as my main objective. Please know, though, that I recognize your work to be limited, and part of an overall effort to deal with a very difficult problem.

As I mentioned, Reverend Gus Roman will be my liaison between your organization and me, when I am not available, and will have continuing coordination with your organization.

I hope in this lengthy letter I have been able to capture the important matters we discussed in our meetings and our mutual agreements on the developing of an effective on-site monitoring program.

I invite the Wharton Industrial Research unit to assume this professional responsibility as the on-site monitoring organization for the Sullivan Principles in South Africa. If you agree, I will send you the $10,000 that you might begin to initiate your work, and will want to finalize whatever further agreements are necessary to get the process underway.

You will, no doubt, also want to take a trip to South Africa soon, to perhaps make a dry run on-site analysis. Hopefully, several companies would be willing to cooperate in such an initial effort. I await your reply.

Sincerely,
Leon H. Sullivan

ENDNOTES

1 Minutes of board meeting of the International Council for Equality of Opportunity Principles, Inc., 10 December 1979, held at the Progress Plaza, Philadelphia.

2 F. B. O'Mara (executive vice president, Union Carbide Corporation), letter to Leon H. Sullivan, 22 December 1977. An enclosure is entitled "Report on Sullivan Principles."

3 Richard R. Farrow (vice president–personnel, Warner-Lambert International), letter to Leon H. Sullivan, 31 August 1978.

4 The summary of the first report is from a discussion by Lee Elbinger, "Are Sullivan's Principles Folly in South Africa?" *Business and Society Review*, Summer 1979: 35–40.

5 Summary of the Discussion on Labor Practices of American Corporations in South Africa, Carnegie Corporation of New York (meeting convened by Alan Pifer, president of Carnegie Corporation), 15 June 1979.

6 Ibid., 5.

7 Ibid.

8 Ibid., 7.

9 Ibid., 8.

10 "Monitoring Report of the Statement of Principles," August 1979.

11 Ibid., 16

12 Ibid., 18.

13 T.A. Murphy (chairman, General Motors Corporation), letter to Frank T. Carey (chairman, IBM), 2 June 1980.

14 Ibid.

15 Herbert R. Northrup (director, Industrial Research Unit, the Wharton School), letter to Leon H. Sullivan, 8 July 1980, 3.

16 Ibid.

17 Leon H. Sullivan, letter to Herbert R. Northrup. 4 August 1980.

18 Ibid.

19 Ibid

20 Ibid.

21 Ira J. K. Wells, Jr., letter to Daniel Purnell (International Council for Equality of Opportunity Principles, Inc.), 20 November 1980.

PART II

THE SULLIVAN PRINCIPLES IN ACTION
Application of the Principles at the Corporate Level

Chapter 6

Eli Lilly & Company, Inc.
Application of the Sullivan Principles at the Corporate Level

Eli Lilly & Company was one of the earliest signatories to the Sullivan Principles.[1] Joining the Sullivan Principles was, indeed, consistent with the company's overall posture of being a socially responsive company with a long history of community involvement. The company also had the good fortune of not being initially subjected to the extreme external pressure from religious groups that confronted hosts of other large corporations in different parts of the United States. Indianapolis, Indiana—the location of the company's headquarters—was not exactly a hot bed of social turmoil.

The nature of Lilly's operations in South Africa needs to be interpreted within the framework of the pharmaceutical industry—its global competitive structure and operating characteristics, coupled with the challenges and opportunities associated with the production and marketing of pharmaceuticals. A company's *ability* to respond to societal concerns and needs depends, in large part, on its financial strength and well-being, which, in turn, are influenced by the competitive intensity of the marketplace in which it operates. However, the particular manner in which a company actually *addresses* such societal concerns is largely influenced by its culture, its leadership, and the fundamental values that the company and its management hold paramount in dealing with their internal and external constituencies.

1.   ELI LILLY: THE COMPANY AND ITS SOUTH AFRICAN OPERATIONS

Lilly is one of the world's leading pharmaceutical companies. Based in Indianapolis, in 1998 it was ranked 37 in *Business Week*'s "Global 1000" in terms of market value, and 185 in *Fortune* magazine's "Fortune 500" in terms of sales.

Lilly was founded in 1876 by Colonel Eli Lilly, a thirty-eight-year-old Civil War veteran and pharmaceutical chemist.[2] For many decades, the company was headed by a member of the founding family, although no family member is currently involved in the company's management. As a legacy of its family ownership, Lilly has always taken its social responsibilities quite seriously; the Lilly family itself founded the Lilly Endowment, which is one of the top five charitable endowments in the United States and supports a wide array of community activities, educational initiatives, and religious programs.

Lilly (South Africa) began operating in 1938, with a manufacturing capacity being added in 1964. The subsidiary currently has 230 full-time employees and ranks eighth in terms of drug sales in South Africa. The company performs about as well in South Africa as it does in the United States, and with the same major products: insulin, oral and injectible antibiotics, and drugs for diseases of the central nervous system. In the 1990s Lilly undertook a significant expansion of its operations in South Africa.

2. LILLY AND THE SULLIVAN PRINCIPLES

Lilly first became aware that there might be a problem concerning its South African operations in 1986, when a religious order submitted a shareholder resolution asking the company to withdraw from South Africa. An internal corporate review indicated that the resolution would receive little, if any, support from other shareholders. Although some managers argued that the company should simply ignore the resolution lest it encourage other groups to follow suit, management decided, in keeping with the company's policies and culture, to initiate a dialogue with the sponsoring group.

At the same time, Eugene Beasley, a Lilly board member who was also on the board of General Motors and had met Sullivan through that board, suggested that Lilly consider becoming a signatory to the Sullivan Principles. This recommendation was immediately accepted. It would thus appear that the decision to join the Sullivan Principles resulted not from a deliberate and systematic policy review, but from the initiative of the board and CEO, an action that was consonant with the company's longstanding tradition of community involvement.

The lack of extensive internal discussion about the consequences of joining the Sullivan Principles had certain drawbacks, however. Despite the company's commitment to its social responsibilities, there was no specific corporate policy on how to address problems of social injustice as such, and therefore no foundation upon which to formulate and execute a plan of action, under the Sullivan principles, for its South African operations. Consequently, in the early years of its operations under the Principles, Lilly was most comfortable in following the lead of other companies, basing its decisions on the popular tide of public opinion and majority sentiment. At this stage, most of the decisions concerning the selection of projects and the disbursement of funds were left to the company's senior executives in South Africa. Though the home office in Indianapolis was kept fully informed, its oversight was, at best, perfunctory, a measure of the home office's confidence in the local subsidiary's management and their ability to carry out the company's directives and commitment to comply with the Sullivan Principles. Moreover, the company's designation of a project manager demonstrated its willingness to allocate the resources needed to meet both the external demands and company's internal interests associated with the Principles.

During the mid-1980s the winds of change began to blow unpredictably in South Africa, thus putting pressure on companies there to take a stand and be prepared to defend it. Among other things, the leadership of the African National Congress called for a further tightening of economic sanctions against the South African government—including the withdrawal of all foreign investments. This call was supported by most of the prominent Black leaders of South Africa, with the notable exception of the Zulu leader, Gatcha Buthelezi. The call for disinvestment was taken up in the United States by religious activists and other public-interest groups, including many institutional investors and public pension funds. State and local agencies enacted laws barring companies doing business in South Africa from bidding for contracts within their jurisdictions. In June 1987 the call for disinvestment was endorsed by Sullivan himself, who indicated that he would step down as leader of the Principles program.

In response, Lilly began a campaign of more active engagement that was to see them through the next stage of their activities in South Africa, and into the future. The company's first step was to undertake a systematic review of its various options with regard to the South African question; in an effort to make prudent decisions that would not compromise its long-held corporate values, the company evaluated both its efforts to date and its relationship with various stakeholders These deliberations led management to conclude that it would continue its operations in South Africa. This decision was based on the conviction that the company's presence there would benefit both the Principles program and the company's own interest in furthering education and social progress in that country. Three key factors contributing to the company's decision not to withdraw were:

- The company's products were unique and essential to the South African market.

- Concern for company employees and job security should not be sub-ordinated to purely political interests if other means of addressing those interests were available (as Lilly believed they were).

- Staying involved in South Africa would, in the long run, be more effective than withdrawing.

Overall, Lilly felt justified in its decision because it upheld the values of an ingrained corporate culture that considered community involvement and respect for employees to be paramount. Nonetheless, Lilly was left in the position of defending its decision to critics both in South Africa and at home. Ironically, it was, in part, just because the company had taken its social responsibilities so seriously in the past that it had so little experience—and such difficulty—in handling such criticism. Despite Lilly's heavy involvement in international development projects, activists at home persisted in their condemnation and distrust of Lilly's decision to remain in South Africa, and South African Blacks were skeptical of American companies' commitment to the goals of the Black empowerment movement.

Having made the decision to stay, Lilly's top management in the United States determined that the company should strengthen its support of Sullivan-related activities in South Africa, and that it should become more directly involved in dealing with the issue both in South Africa and the United States. Lilly's public declaration of its position forced a heightened engagement with critics and led the home office to concentrate even more effort and attention on the evolving situation in South Africa. The allocation of resources among the company's South African projects came under careful scrutiny; gradually, a company policy began to emerge.

In South Africa, the project manager found that he was spending an ever greater proportion of his time—both company paid and personal—on projects related to the Sullivan Principles. A great many of company's employees were also involved in the Principles projects funded by the company. Lilly saw its continued involvement in the South African market as a role model for the industry and marketed the idea by emphasizing the benefits of involvement. Lilly (South Africa) helped form a new association, the East Rand Industrialists Association (ERIN), comprising fifty-six companies, of which approximately 25 percent were American. Lilly's project manager was named president of the association, and each of the members were tapped to work on the specific areas of South African economic development where they had the needed expertise. Lilly's own focus was threefold: education, health care, and promoting the economic well-being and political independence of South Africa.

Lilly's management quickly became adept at presenting a defense of its position that did not appear overly conciliatory towards the South African government. Staying in South Africa was, according to one Lilly executive, the "right thing," not the "perfect thing." The company had a clear internal conviction that its continued presence in South Africa could make a substantive contribution to the circumstances of Black, Colored, and Asian (BCA) South Africans. The company thus sought to appeal to the better judgment of its critics to align them to the company's viewpoint—or, at the very least, to obtain a respectful hearing.

Lilly's South African subsidiary enjoyed virtually complete autonomy from its parent in the area of project selection and funding, but kept headquarters posted on events and outcomes. Headquarters remained keenly interested in seeing demonstrable progress, however, and hoped that, in cases where sufficient local expertise developed within South Africa, the company could gradually transfer control of the projects from the company to the local community. The primary goal was to secure an economically independent South Africa, even to the point of generating management talent there that could be used at headquarters.

3. PERFORMANCE MEASURES OF LILLY'S ACTIVITIES IN SOUTH AFRICA UNDER THE SULLIVAN PRINCIPLES

Lilly consistently received top ratings for its performance under the Sullivan Principles. A brief summary of its monetary and nonmonetary contributions for the period 1987–93 is presented in tables 4 to 8. This period coincided with Sullivan's withdrawal from his association with the Principles' program, having failed in his effort to see the complete dismantling of the apartheid system in South Africa. This period also witnessed a precipitous decline in the number of United States companies operating in South Africa—from a high of 110 in 1986 to a low of 59 in 1989. The remaining signatory companies would nevertheless continue with the program and contribute additional funds that would more than compensate for the shortfall resulting from the departure of other signatories.[3]

From 1987 to 1993, Lilly's total annual contribution to the Principles program increased from ZAR 643,000 to 1,501,700, or 230 percent. In analyzing the data, certain trends are discernible. For example, there was a significant shift in the allocation of funds to activities aimed at education and preparation of Black people to gain higher-paid jobs, and to activities designed toward community development (table 4). Total expenditures in the area of education and training increased threefold during this period, from ZAR 214,200 to 653,200. Within this category, there was a significant shift away from funds allocated to teacher training, as in the early years of the Principles program, and toward the direct assistance to students (in the form of scholarships and career guidance). It is interesting to note that one of the

Table 4. Eli Lilly SA (Proprietary) Limited, Financial Contributions for Activities under the Sullivan Principles

	ZAR (1000s)	Education for Non-Employees (%)	Community Development (%)	Social Justice (%)
1987	643.3	33.2	33.3	33.5
1988	756.5	33.3	33.7	33.0
1989	915.2	46.1	53.9	NA
1990	1,066.7	50.9	49.1	NA
1991	1,322.9	42.5	57.5	NA
1992	1,566.0	48.9	51.1	NA
1993	1,501.7	43.5	56.5	NA
Total	7,777.7			

Source: Reid Weedon, "Report on the Signatory Companies to the Sullivan Principles," Nos. 11–17.

most popular programs in the initial years of the Principles program—the "Adopt-a-School Program," which was a staple of many a corporate social responsibility programs in the United States—proved not to be very successful in South Africa and was dropped there by many United States companies, including Lilly (table 5).

Table 5. Eli Lilly SA (Proprietary), Distribution of Expenditures in Education for Non-Employees, by Percentages

	1987	1988	1989	1990	1991	1992	1993
Wages and Bursaries[a]	11.5	14.1	33.5	12.9	18.3	46.6	42.3
Career Guidance[b]	5.7	3.6	3.6	43.2	34.0	33.5	41.3
Adopt-a-School	19.1	24.5	7.6	15.2	18.0	6.0	0.0
Teacher Assistance[c]	63.7	57.8	55.3	28.7	29.7	13.9	16.4
Total in ZAR (1000s)	214.2	252.3	422.3	541.6	561.6	765.8	653.2

[a] Includes wages for Technikon students and bursaries for non-employees.
[b] Includes academic support and bridging programs.
[c] Includes support for multiracial schools, goods purchased, and other expenses.

Community-development expenses also showed marked changes that reflected both the communities' changing needs and Lilly's evaluation of those needs, its experience with various types of community-development activities, and its perception that the company should concentrate its resources on a small number of projects for which the need was greatest. The total expenditures increased more than fourfold, from ZAR 213,700 in 1987 to ZAR 849,200 in 1993. Moreover, as was discussed earlier, the company had made a strong commitment to "do the right thing," not only by supporting programs, but also by becoming actively involved to ensure that funds were spent wisely and to produce the desired outcomes. For example, in

1987 a majority of funds were devoted to housing and civic improvements. By 1993, however, health care was consuming 64.5 percent of the total funds (table 6).

Table 6. Eli Lilly SA (Proprietary) Limited, Distribution of Expenditures in Community Development, by Percentages

	1987	1988	1989	1990	1991	1992	1993
Support BCA	0.9	5.9	9.2	11.7	11.5	12.3	4.3
Housing	38.7	2.8	6.4	9.3	4.0	9.3	3.6
Land Ownership	0.0	0.0	8.6	9.2	5.8	6.1	0.9
Health Care	30.8	35.0	34.6	28.2	28.7	35.3	64.5
BCA Leadership	0.0	0.0	7.4	9.4	23.0	11.3	8.5
Nonwork Training	0.0	0.0	0.0	0.0	2.3	0.0	0.0
Political Rights	0.0	0.0	10.6	6.3	3.7	6.8	8.3
Civic	29.5	56.3	8.6	9.8	20.0	13.2	5.0
Goods and Equipment	0.0	0.0	0.0	0.0	0.7	0.0	4.9
Other	0.1	0.0	2.8	16.1	0.3	5.7	0.0

Source: Reid Weedon, "Report on the Signatory Companies to the Sullivan Principles," Nos. 11–17.

The Sullivan Principles encouraged the companies to pay a living wage to their lowest-paid workers, which was interpreted to mean a wage level that would support a family of five or six members as measured from a base level determined by the government to be subsistence level. As table 7 demonstrates, Lilly consistently increased its minimum wage level above that which was mandated by the government. The excess above that level increased from 91.5 percent in 1987 to 171.0 percent in 1993. That is, by 1993 Lilly was paying over 2.7 times the minimum mandated subsistence wage to its lowest-paid workers. Within this group were 23.7 percent of the company's BCA employees.

As part of its strategy for more intensive involvement in community-related projects in South Africa, Lilly (South Africa) made certain strategic shifts in its choice of projects and allocation of funds. The company began to devote a larger proportion of its resources to those program activities where (1) it had particular expertise or (2) a long-term commitment and a large infusion of resources would enable the company to make a significant contribution to ameliorating the underlying problems. The former approach is evident in the company's activities in health care, which are described in the following section, and the second approach, in the company's activities in

Table 7. Eli Lilly SA (Proprietary) Limited, Composition of Workforce and Support for Minimum-Wage Employees

	Total Employee Number	Percent BCA Employees	Excess Percent Mandated Minimum (MML/MHL) Wage[a]
1987	177	26.0	91.5
1988	179	25.7	114.0
1989	181	24.9	123.1
1990	182	25.8	130.2
1991	188	25.5	141.7
1992	192	26.0	160.0
1993	207	23.7	171.0

Source: Reid Weedon, "Report on the Signatory Companies to the Sullivan Principles," Nos. 11–17.

[a] Represents percent excess cash pay of an employee's monthly Minimum Living Level or Household Subsistence Level (MML/MHL) for a family of five or six members.

education and community development, which are described in the section after that.

3.1 Lilly's Programs in Health Care in South Africa

As a pharmaceutical company, Lilly was especially well equipped to focus its energies on improving the quality of health-care services in South Africa and on making those services available to the most needy among the country's populace. Through its involvement and commitment, Lilly (South Africa) became a role model for augmenting activities and implementing changes among a host of nonsignatory companies in South Africa.

The company's activities in health care covered a wide spectrum. They ranged from campaigns to institute changes in the government's own programs and policies, to specific actions that helped BCA communities to uplift themselves through cooperative efforts. This approach spread throughout the South African medical and pharmaceutical fraternity, and resulted in the initiation of numerous health-care projects that otherwise might never have been undertaken. Among the health-care areas included in Lilly's projects were programs that promoted AIDS awareness, TB testing, family planning, and drug abuse, both among company employees and in their communities. These programs continue to be a training priority of the company's staff. In addition, a nutrition-information campaign was initiated in 1993 among squatter camps on the Cape Flats in response to reports of an increase in malnutrition in these areas. Upgrading of hospitals and of nursing staffs, especially in rural areas, was another major area of involvement. Finally, providing training in, and consultation on, cancer, psychiatric, and general surgical care for the BCA communities, particularly in rural areas, was an area of strong interest and one in which the company undertook significant fund-raising efforts.

In monetary terms, Lilly contributed over ZAR 7.7 million during the period 1987–93 to its health-care projects. These projects fell into four broad categories: education and training, dissemination of information, support for community health-care activities, and support for medical research and related activities at the university level (table 8). Included within these four categories were a large and diverse number of projects; for example, in 1993 alone, ZAR 699,100 was spent on nineteen different projects.

Table 8. Eli Lilly SA (Proprietary) Limited, Distribution of Health-Care Expenditures, by Percentages

	1987	1988	1989	1990	1991	1992	1993
Education and training[a]	40.0	42.2	30.2	54.4	46.4	30.0	38.0
Information dissemination	4.8	0	2.6	14.7	14.8	0	5.9
Community health[b]	24.0	43.9	38.9	13.8	17.6	33.8	23.6
University research	31.2	13.9	28.3	13.8	17.4	36.2	32.5
Total ZAR (in 1000s)	62.5	87.7	160.4	134.4	217.6	292.9	699.1

Source: Reid Weedon, "Report on the Signatory Companies to the Sullivan Principles," Nos. 11–17.

Note: The cumulative total of these expenditures is slightly different than that under the health-care category, where education and training are considered bursaries and scholar-ships given to health-care professionals, which are categorized, in turn, under the reporting guidelines as "Education and Training to Non-employees."

[a] Primarily represents direct support of students in health-related disciplines.
[b] Includes primary care in the field locations.

Lilly's executives in South Africa also engaged in lobbying efforts to ensure that health-care facilities be available to service BCA communities in South Africa.[4] The minister of health, for example, was lobbied to appoint additional staff for that particular purpose. The company held meetings with both provincial and national health-care directors to encourage increased budgets for hospitals in the provinces, rural communities, and metropolitan BCA areas. Furthermore, in order to pave the way for an integrated health-care system, Lilly's twenty-three-person marketing-management teams invited people of all racial groups to participate in a series of medical-practice seminars the company presented in five centers throughout the country.

The company supported nongovernmental health-care organizations by setting guidelines for new health-care policies. Resulting projects included a series of meetings between six pharmaceutical companies and senior staff members of the ANC health desk, as well as numerous follow-up meetings with ANC health-care officials, the minister of health, and the Pharmaceutical Manufacturing Association.

3.2   Lilly's Projects in Education and Community Development.

The second shift in Lilly's strategy involved focusing on projects in which the company's long-term commitment, coupled with the contribution of greater financial and human resources, would be especially useful. Projects in education and community development were the prime targets here,[5] but this effort fell somewhat short of Lilly's original expectations. The system of monitoring and evaluating companies' performance (through the Sullivan Summary Report Forms) required them to demonstrate efforts in each and every category listed under the Principles. This requirement often forced companies, including Lilly, to fragment their resources and efforts, even at the expense of efficient resource allocation.

3.3   The Dissolution of the Sullivan Monitoring System

The dissolution of the Sullivan monitoring system in 1994 did not alter Lilly's commitment to responsible corporate citizenship in South Africa. On the contrary, the company not only continued to meet its ongoing commitments, but it expanded its health-care activities (on which it spent ZAR 1.6 million in 1994).

3.4   A Model Program: Lilly's Involvement with the Rural Foundation

Many of the programs that the companies were initially involved with under the Sullivan Principles tended to be aimed at the numerous problems associated with rapid urbanization and with the very high profile squatter camps, such as the "Crossroads." By the late 1970s, however, there was a growing awareness that the problems of apartheid were also having an equivalent deleterious effect in the rural areas of the country, which had been gone largely unnoticed.

In 1982, as a response to this identified need in rural areas, a new organization was established. The Rural Foundation had as its mission to develop leadership in the field of comprehensive rural development. The target groups included commercial farmers, farm workers and their families, small-scale settlement farmers and their families, and other nonagricultural rural institutions, organizations, and groups. The basic operating units of the Rural Foundation were the autonomous Community Development Associations (CDAs), whose goal was to help the community to help itself. CDAs voluntarily affiliated themselves with the Rural Foundation, which then provided expertise, relevant technology, personnel, funding, training, facilities, and lobbying. The response of the Rural Foundation was, and is, one of adaptation and realignment. The support that it provides has been essential in upgrading and improving lives in the rural communities.

Lilly has been involved with the Rural Foundation since 1989. In addition to monetary support (approximately ZAR 500,000 since 1994), Lilly has continuously had a senior executive serve on the foundation's board as a representative of the private sector. The specific focus of Lilly's program interests has been in leadership development, training the trainers in primary health care, and preschool programs. The company's ongoing commitment to programs such as the Rural Foundation serves to illustrate how a basic concern for the community, coupled with involvement in meaningful programs, can last long after a code of social conduct has ended and public pressure has faded.

4.   CONCLUSIONS: SOME LESSONS LEARNED

Lilly's eighteen years of experience working with the Sullivan Principles gave the company some hard-earned insights into the challenges and opportunities facing multinational corporations and how such corporations can respond to them in a constructive manner. Some of these lessons are narrow in scope and relate more specifically to Lilly, but other lessons relate directly to the Sullivan Principles and their strengths and limitations.

In seeking public- or community-service projects to support, companies must exercise a high level of scrutiny, including cost-benefit analyses, to ensure that funds are spent in an efficient manner and are directed toward desired outcomes. Just because such projects are oriented toward service rather than business (as such) is no excuse for sloppy management.

Companies must ensure that recipient organizations have the wherewithal to manage the projects and deliver the specified services to targeted groups. To this end, company executives must lend a hand in developing administrative capabilities in the recipient organizations and in informing themselves about the scope of the projects and the specific activities to be undertaken.

Companies must develop an extensive database about the various stakeholders whose views are likely to hold sway in influencing societal expectations of corporate performance. And it is necessary to develop and maintain a dialogue with these groups in order to understand and respond to their concerns. This approach would also help companies to anticipate the need for changes in their operational policies and public posture, thus obviating the need to react to external pressures in an ad hoc (and often counterproductive) manner.

In the final analysis, it is the strength of a company's corporate culture and the maintenance of a high level of expected ethical behavior that forms the basis for its effective reaction to external forces.

In shaping its corporate decisions and policies, Lilly carefully attended to, and learned from, the ongoing debate over apartheid, the Sullivan Principles, and divestment. In so doing, the company was able to identify and respond to some of the critical factors in the unfolding of events in South Africa.

ENDNOTES

1   In the preparation of this chapter, the authors have greatly benefited from the advice and support of John S. North, the former director, international corporate affairs, Eli Lilly & Co., Indianapolis, IN. Notwithstanding his assistance, the authors are solely responsible for the text, analysis, interpretation, and conclusions presented in this chapter.

2   The description of the early history of Eli Lilly is based primarily on E. J. Kahn, Jr., *All in a Century: The First 100 Years of Eli Lilly & Company* (Chicago, St. James Press, 1989); and "Eli Lilly & Company," in *The International Directory of Company Histories*, Vol. 1 (Chicago: St. James Press, 1988–94), 645–47.

3   S. Prakash Sethi, "Working with International Codes of Conducts: Experience of the U.S. Companies Operating in South Africa under the Sullivan Principles," *Business & the Contemporary World* 8, 1 (1996): 129–50. See also Karen Paul, "U.S. Multinational Corporations in South Africa: Should There Be a Conflict between Economic Interest and Political Imperatives," in *Up against the Corporate Wall: Corporations and Social Issues of the Nineties*, edited by S. Prakash Sethi and Paul Steidlmeier (Englewood Cliffs, NJ: Prentice-Hall, 1997).

4   Eli Lilly SA (Proprietary) Ltd., "Report on Health Care Involvement" (August 1994).

5   Ibid. See also Reid Weedon, "Report on the Signatory Companies to the Sullivan Principles," Nos. 11–17.

Chapter 7

Ford Motor Corporation of South Africa
Application of the Sullivan Principles at the Corporate Level

In early February 1988, Ford Motor Company announced that it was withdrawing from South Africa.[1] The announcement was a long time in the making. The previous two years had seen almost a stampede of American companies leaving South Africa through closures, sales of assets, and a variety of other means. Quite often, these divestitures caused significant losses to the American parents when measured against the value of the companies' assets in South Africa.

Ford completed its divestment program on 30 April 1988—the end of an era for a company that had operated in South Africa longer than almost any other major United States manufacturer. Ford was one of the original group of companies that had signed the Sullivan Principles, and it had consistently received top ratings for its compliance with the Principles. However, neither Ford's good intentions nor its excellent performance under the Principles was enough to satisfy its various stakeholders and critics, who would accept no less than a total withdrawal of United States corporations operating in South Africa.

Though depart it did, Ford's actions upon leaving South Africa stand in sharp contrast to those of other United States corporations. In particular, Ford gave away over half of its equity interest to an employee-controlled trust whose income would be used to benefit various community groups. The press release stated:

> We have reached an agreement that is clearly supported by black South African trade unions, and, we believe, by a cross section of black South Africans generally. It is precedent setting in the extent of economic empowerment it gives to black workers, both through ownership and through Board representation. It is a result of thorough consultation process with interested parties. In addition to preserving thousands of jobs, it provides significant benefits to black communities and to black educa-

tion, under arrangements in which blacks themselves will manage trust funds and make decisions on resource allocation.[2]

The activist groups who were advocating divestment did not call for such an approach. Nor was such an approach expected under the Sullivan Principles. Ford established the trust on its own initiative. Moreover, just prior to leaving South Africa, Ford injected a significant amount of new funds into its South African operations. The goals were to (1) ensure the continuing financial viability of its successor, (2) provide added incentive for the new owners to continue with the company's programs that were initiated under the Sullivan Principles, and (3) demonstrate the company's good faith that, in placing the new company's stock in trust, it was not engaging in a mere "paper" transaction but transferring substantial resources for its successor to carry out its new mandate.

Ford's divestment of its South African assets (coupled with the particular method it chose for accomplishing that end) adds one more important dimension to our understanding of the consequences of codes of conduct. What we see is how such codes can transform the economic-business environment even when, as in Ford's case, code compliance is no longer necessary or possible because of legal, social, political, or economic considerations (or, by extension, even when the short-term objectives of the code have been accomplished, as with the abolishment of apartheid and the establishment of a nonracial democracy in South Africa).

1.   FORD IN SOUTH AFRICA: A BRIEF HISTORY

Ford entered South Africa by establishing a wholly owned subsidiary of Ford Motor Company of Canada, Ltd., in Port Elizabeth in December 1923. Previously, Ford had been exporting Canadian-built cars that were sold through a local distributor. The plant in Port Elizabeth was set up to gain better control over merchandising and prices. Ford of the United States acquired a majority of the stock of Ford of Canada in 1959. During the war years of the 1940s, more than half of the production in South Africa was dedicated to that country's military purposes. A new plant was built in 1948 and expanded in 1954. In 1962 the parts and accessories division was moved to a new building. In 1963 an engine plant was built. In 1973 Ford South Africa celebrated its fiftieth anniversary by opening a car-assembly plant at Struandale. At the point that the Sullivan Principles were instituted, Ford was a leader in the South African market for automobiles. The company led that market in sales in 1977 and was second in 1978, accounting for 16.7 and 16.0 percent of the market, respectively.

Despite its leadership position in the 1970s, Ford, like other firms in the South African automobile industry, was experiencing eroding profits and chronic underutilization of its production capacity. Between 1971 and 1977, South African automobile manufacturers averaged 5.5 percent return on their equity—compared to an average of 11 percent for all manufacturers in South Africa, and 14 percent for American companies worldwide. In 1977 Ford lost approximately eight million dollars in South Africa. In the three previous years, its reported profits were "negligible."

Ford's South African operations accounted for approximately 1 percent of its worldwide sales during the period 1976–78 and were an insignificant component of its global operations. During the period 1972–79, Ford South Africa had been in an overall net loss position. The company funded its operations primarily through local, short-term borrowing and through merchandise credits from Ford's European subsidiaries. Since 1975, Ford spent an average of about seven million dollars annually to maintain a viable business in South Africa. The expenditures went toward the retooling required to produce the European-type vehicles marketed there, toward meeting local-content requirements, toward the performance of routine maintenance operations, and toward the implementation of the Sullivan Principles.

2.   FORD AND THE SULLIVAN PRINCIPLES

According to a memorandum from William Broderick, a senior Ford executive, the company's attitude toward the Principles was quite favorable after the initial 29 January 1977 meeting in New York (see chapter 1).[3]

> There was general agreement among participants that such a 'Statement' was feasible, but there was need for some reworking of the Sullivan draft. There was also a consensus among participants that the Statement is intended for two different audiences—a South African one, and a U.S. domestic one—and that the more important of the two for the companies is the South African one. With that in mind, the Statement should avoid language or positions that could make it counterproductive.

Ford South Africa had already made progress in seeking equal opportunity for all its employees, regardless of race. It was, indeed, the first automotive company in South Africa to hire non-White workers in assembly plants. In 1975 Ford South Africa's 5,081 workers included 1,088 Black, 1,929 Colored, and 2,064 White workers. The Statement of Principles further reinforced this position. According to Wayne Fredericks,

> Ford saw supporting and implementing the Sullivan Principles as the most appropriate and effective means available for U.S. companies with

South African affiliates to contribute to the process of constructive social change in South Africa. They believed that the cooperative, persistent and voluntary implementation of the Sullivan Principles, both in and outside the workplace, constitutes the most effective and pragmatic contribution to achieving social justice and racial reform that South African affiliates of U.S. firms can make, consistent with their economic and commercial purposes and their capabilities. Given both those purposes and the relatively small percentage (less than 5%) that U.S. investment constituted of total private investment in South Africa, the role of American affiliates though important was necessarily limited. They nonetheless hoped that the achievement of American affiliates would constitute an example which other companies, and group of companies would emulate.

Ford believed that the Sullivan Principles would not only be more effective, but generate better results over the long term for the citizens of South Africa, if the Principles program continued as a voluntary effort rather than as a legislated mandate imposed by the United States government. Ford's executives were aware, however, that many people did not agree with this position, and they also recognized that the voluntary approach fell short, and would continue to fall short, of perfection. But the executives believed that the alternative suggested—pulling out of South Africa—raised even greater problems. Fredericks did not believe that a confrontational approach would contribute to improving the status of Blacks in South Africa. Nor did he believe that, as a foreign-owned firm, Ford had either the competence or the authority to involve itself in the internal political matters of that country. The company nonetheless did "have both the right and the obligation to treat all its employees equally, to provide ample opportunity for advancement through training and educational programs, and to help make it possible for its employees and their families to lead productive and healthy lives in their local communities." Furthermore, a total withdrawal from South Africa would have the effect of immediately confronting over 5,600 Ford employees, 64 percent of whom were Black or Colored, with the loss of their livelihoods and uncertain prospects for the future.

3.   CAMPAIGN AGAINST FORD BY ANTI-APARTHEID ACTIVISTS

Anti-apartheid groups exerted persistent pressure on Ford (and other United States companies) for deciding to remain in South Africa, and as part of a campaign spearheaded and largely coordinated by ICCR, Ford was subject to numerous shareholder resolutions urging the company to withdraw. The following 12 December 1997 letter by Ford, in response to one from Sister Regina Murphy (chairperson) and twenty-five other members of ICCR, presented Ford's position to the divestiture issue:

> Ford Motor Company takes exception to your conclusion that 'US companies are unable to act as a force for significant change in S.A. but tend to support the status quo.' Experience has shown that change in South Africa, under the best of circumstances, will be a different process. The issue on which people differ is the appropriate role for the affiliate of an American business corporation to play in the process of change. In our view, more will be accomplished in the long run on behalf of all the people of South Africa by the presence of companies like Ford, providing that such companies actively implement principles similar to those articulated in the Sullivan Statement.[4]

Two months later, Timothy Smith, director of ICCR, wrote to Henry Ford, chairman and CEO of Ford Motor Company:

> I am writing at the request of several church groups which hold stock in Ford Motor Company. As you know, the *New York Times* reported that during your trip to South Africa you stated that Ford was planning to expand there. . . . In light of commitment in the Ford Annual report last year that there would be no expansion unless there was progress on the Six Principles, do you consider that South Africa has now allowed adequate progress on these principles to legitimize Ford's expansion?[5]

Henry Ford's response to John Sengstacke, publisher of the *Chicago Daily Defender,* presented Ford Motor Company's position on South Africa: the company should stay in that country, had an important role to play there, and had maintained its presence there despite the continuing losses from its South African operations. The letter also reiterated that Ford's stance of staying in South Africa should not be construed as an endorsement of the policies of the South African government.[6]

Among the dignitaries writing to Ford was Father Theodore Hesburgh, president of the University of Notre Dame. Below are excerpts from letters exchanged between Hesburgh and Ford executives.[7] The exchange started with a Hesburgh letter of 9 November 1978 to Lee Iacocca, Ford's president.

> As owner of 10,000 shares of Ford Motor Company common stock, Notre Dame shares responsibility for corporate practices in South Africa. University trustees have approved the enclosed Policy Statement regarding Investments in South Africa. . . . Notre Dame will be following with genuine concern the implementation of programs for racial progress.

> Because of South Africa's official policy of apartheid . . . various United States educational, religious, and civil rights groups are increasingly

opposed to U.S. involvement in South Africa. Corporations themselves are faced with a variety of imposing—if not convincing—arguments for either continuing to carry on business in South Africa and by their presence help to effect constructive change, or for withdrawing in the hope of influencing the apartheid regime to change its ways.

Either courses of action involve ambiguity, and no-clear-cut solution presents itself. Consequently, it does not seem that the University of Notre Dame, in its efforts to formulate a responsible shareholder policy, can advocate a stance for simply remaining or withdrawing. On the other hand, apartheid seems to be so clearly opposed to any reasonable concept of human rights that the University cannot use the ambiguity of the situation to avoid all responsibility.

The resolution went on to state that the university would support a shareholder resolution for a company to withdraw from South Africa in cases where the company had not adopted principles, such as the Sullivan Principles, whose objective was to provide improved opportunities and employment practices for non-White South Africans. Furthermore, to carry out such a policy, the university administration would inform the management of its portfolio companies of the university's resolve as set forth in the policy statement.

Iacocca responded by saying, "As a recent visitor to South Africa, I feel deep concern regarding apartheid policies and urge Ford Motor Company to set a visible, positive example in broadening the opportunities and enhancing the lives of Black and Colored South Africans."

Another inquiry, addressed to Henry Ford, came from Marion Freeman, cochair of Notre Dame's University Committee on Social Responsibility. Sidney Kelly of Ford responded:

I enclose for your information a copy of a letter . . . which outlines the way in which we are implementing the Statement of principles. . . . Other information you requested is as follows:

Ford South Africa as of October 1977 had a total of 4,849 employees. Of these, 1,667 were colored and 1,110 were black. There were no Indian employees.

Hourly employee job categories and wage ranges are listed on the attached chart. . . .

In 1977 Ford South Africa sold a total of 763 cars and 944 trucks to the government of South Africa. This represents 4% of total sales.

Ford South Africa has no current plans for expansion. During his recent visit to South Africa, Henry Ford II stated in a press conference, 'No, we have no plans to expand our operations here in South Africa. We are now, as I said a moment ago, operating at something less than 60% of our capacity and it will be several years before, in our opinion, we will use our total capacity that's already available and in place. So, it would be a long time before we would need to consider a capacity increase.[8]

Ford received similar inquiries from other academic and religious institutions, including Ohio State University, Brandeis University, and the American Lutheran Church, to name a few.

In a letter addressed to the Nigerian ambassador to the United States, who had written to Henry Ford on behalf of the Black African nations, Henry Ford stated:

Contrary to some press reports, Ford has no intention of expanding its South African operations in the foreseeable future. . . . We do, nonetheless, plan to maintain our present operations in South Africa. Our continuing presence should in no way be interpreted as an endorsement of the policies of the South African government. . . .

Despite the fact that Ford South Africa lost money in 1977, and earned only marginal profits in 1976, we are more than doubling our 1978 spending in equal employment activities over 1977 levels, including $1.1 million to be spent for training programs. We believe that efforts to improve conditions for our black and colored employees should be among our top priorities, and we have taken steps to see that the funds required to do a good job will not be constrained by the profit outlook.[9]

3.1 Shareholder Resolution for Ford to Terminate Its Operations in South Africa.

In its proxy statement of February 1977, Ford indicated that the American Baptist Home Mission Society, the United Presbyterian Church in the United States of America, and the United Christian Missionary Society, all of which owned the company's common stock, intended to present the following proposal at the company's annual meeting:

Whereas in South Africa the black majority is controlled and oppressed by a white minority which comprises 18% of the population.

Whereas South Africa's apartheid system legalizes racial discrimination in all aspects of life and deprives the black population of their most basic human rights e.g. Africans cannot vote, cannot collectively bargain, must live in racially segregated areas, are paid grossly discriminated wages, are assigned 13% of the land while 87% of the land is reserved for the white population.

Whereas the South African system of white minority rule called apartheid has been widely condemned by the US governments and numerous international bodies.

Whereas black opposition to apartheid and black demands for full political, social legal rights in their country has risen dramatically within the last year.

Whereas killing, arrests and repression has been the response of the White south African government to nationwide demonstration for democratic rights.

Whereas the Prime Minister has openly declared his intention to maintain apartheid and deny political rights to South African Blacks.

Whereas we believe that the US business investments in the Republic of South Africa, including our company's operation, provide significant support and moral legitimacy to South Africa's apartheid government.

Therefore be it resolved that the shareholders request that the Board of Directors establish the following as the corporate policy:

Ford Motor Corporation and any of its subsidiaries 1) shall cease further investment in the Republic of South Africa and 2) shall terminate its present operations there as expeditiously as possible unless and until the South African government has committed itself to ending the legally enforced form of racism called apartheid and has taken meaningful steps towards the achievement of full political, legal and social rights for the majority population.

The statement submitted by these stockholders in support of their proposal stated:

In spite of changes in wages, benefits and working conditions in some US subsidiaries, the South African Government toward Black enfranchisement and full human rights has taken no measurable steps. In addition our company is required to undercut its US commitment to equal opportunity employment by following South Africa's racists employment laws and practices, e.g. there must be racially segregated facilities in the plant, no black can supervise a white, all top jobs are reserved for white employees, no African trade unions.

In addition Ford strengthens the white minority's ability to control the black population in South Africa and maintain it's illegal occupation of Namibia by selling vehicles to police and military. We believe that such sales compromise the spirit of the arms embargo against South Africa established by the US government.

In our opinion the investment of US companies act as an economic vote of confidence in the apartheid status quo. Taxes are paid to the apartheid government. Investments contribute American technology, skills and equipment. We believe that the present crisis in South Africa makes it imperative to end any form of support for apartheid and white minority rule.

The board of directors recommended a vote against the proposal. The board's argument was that "in early 1977, Ford gave its support to a Statement of Principles that will guide the operations of its affiliate in South Africa. The Principles, reviewed by the United States Department of State, have the support of most major United States firms having business operations in South Africa."

In all, Ford received a total of thirteen written communications on this question by April 1979 (after the shareholder resolution was circulated in February and March). Of these, one was from a private citizen who supported the company's position. The remaining twelve were from institutions that included seven universities, two insurance companies, a Protestant church, a Catholic religious order, and a theological seminary. Two of the universities did not address the shareholder resolution specifically, but one noted that, under university policy, sales to the police and military were deemed to constitute "severe social injury" in support of apartheid. The other university called attention to, and requested Ford's comments on, its policy statement requesting that United States corporations not sell goods or services to the South African government that are used in the direct support or enforcement of its apartheid policies. In reply, Ford sent a copy of its proxy statement, which set forth the company's position on the issue. Ford also referred both of the universities to the analysis prepared by IRRC of Washington, DC, and circulated to IRRC's affiliated institutional investors.

Of the seven institutions that opposed the company's position and voted in favor of the shareholder resolution, four limited their substantive comments to one or two sentences. Three institutions (two universities and a Protestant church) went into greater detail to explain their positions. One university argued that even though its policy did not apply to the sales of products manufactured in other countries and sold in South Africa, Ford should not be satisfied to rest its policy on that technical distinction. The university supported the purpose of the legal embargo on sales to the police and military in South Africa and believed that Ford should honor that purpose even though the law did not require it to do so. The university suggested that such an approach would be consistent with the enlightened stance adopted by Ford of South Africa in is operations there.

The other university wrote that the trucks and other vehicles sold to the South African police and military allowed the South African government to continue and possibly even strengthen its policy of apartheid by assuring the government that it had the military transportation necessary to enforce the apartheid system. The university asked that these vehicles be treated as if they were of United States origin and thus subject to the United States embargo (see following section). The Protestant church representative commended Ford and expressed appreciation for its leadership efforts on behalf of Black South Africans. However, he also urged the company to go beyond the letter of the law, even without a majority vote of the stockholders, to ensure that the company would not be associated in any way with the harassment of Black people in South Africa.

An affirmative statement in support of the Sullivan Principles came from C. Peter Magrath, the president of University of Minnesota.

> I feel that the University of Minnesota has taken vigorous steps to express a legitimate moral concern over racism in South Africa. Not only have the Regents unanimously supported the Sullivan Principles, but we have also persuaded other universities with similar corporate investments to support those same humanitarian proposals. . . . Moreover, I am not convinced that such improvement would result from a withdrawal of American businesses from the nation. . . .

> Personally, I would recommend that, in the future, we consider divesting from corporations that are intransigent to our recommendations or that reject the Sullivan resolutions. We have clearly signaled our deep interest in the conditions of South African Blacks, and in doing so, I would hope that those corporations in which we hold investments might respond positively and appropriately to our concern.[10]

Although the university did not own any stock in Ford, President Magrath wrote to Ford's Wayne Fredericks, stating:

> The Regents' position (which is mine) is that we should abstain on resolutions asking corporations in which we have investments to pull out of South Africa, and that we are not in favor of divestiture. I, personally, would consider recommending at some point to our governing board that they divest from corporations that refuse, after a reasonable period of consideration, to adopt the Sullivan principles.

3.2 Ford's Position on Sales to South African Police and Military

One of the most scrutinized aspects of Ford's operations in South Africa was, as we have just seen, the sale of the company's products to units of South Africa's police and military.[11] The United States Department of Commerce prohibited the sale or transfer of United States origin commodities and technical data to the South African police and military. Ford's position was outlined in a report it published in May 1980:

FSA [Ford South Africa] sells a small number of non-U.S. origin civilian vehicles to the police and military. Such sales do not run counter to or circumvent any U.S. Government policy objective, and are not in violation of U.S. laws or regulations, nor of the laws or regulations of any country from which the vehicles or their components are supplied. . . .

In determining its position on the issue, Ford sought to ascertain whether, aside from meeting the requirements of U.S. law and policy objectives, recommending the total halting of sales of non-U.S. origin vehicles to the police and military would result in net harm or net benefit to the black population of South Africa. It is clear that if FSA were to cease its relatively limited sales to those agencies, the military and police would have no difficulty finding alternative sources of supply, given the presence of several other car manufacturer-assemblers in South Africa. Therefore, cessation of such sales would have a negligible impact on actual police and military activities.

At the same time, such an action by FSA might influence the South African Government to restrict or halt procurement of Ford vehicles for its other civilian agencies, which represents a significant volume of business. One consequence of such an action (possibly accompanied by a more general consumer boycott of our products) and the resulting sales decline, would be layoffs. That would adversely affect FSA's black and other non-white employees who constitute more than 60% of our labor force. It could also diminish FSA's ability to implement the Sullivan Principles as rapidly as it would like to, in areas such as housing, education and recreational facilities, where government cooperation (e.g., construction permits, providing teachers, etc.), is essential to satisfactory progress. . . .

A shareholder resolution calling on Ford to halt all sales of vehicles to the South African police and military was submitted at the 1979 Annual Meeting. Its sponsors were the United Presbyterian Church, three Roman

Catholic religious organizations, and Oberlin College. The resolution was defeated by a vote of 97.85% to 2.15%.

4. EMPLOYEE REPRESENTATION AT FORD SOUTH AFRICA

Ford South Africa was a leader in creating employee-representation programs in South Africa.[12] In 1973 the company and its Black employees organized a liaison committee in accordance with the Black Labor Relations Amendment Act (1973) to replace a works committee established earlier under the Native Labor Settlement of Disputes Act.[13] Of the nineteen members of the new committee, fourteen were elected by Black employees and four (including one Black) were appointed by management. Management made one additional appointment in its capacity to designate a secretary. The role of the liaison committee was to consider matters of mutual interest to the employer and to the Black employees, and to make recommendations to the employer about conditions of employment. The committee did not negotiate formal, collective labor agreements. In March 1977 the United Automobile, Rubber and Allied Workers of South Africa (UAW) demonstrated that it represented the interests of the majority of Black hourly paid employees. Ford South Africa informally recognized the union by agreeing to withhold forty-eight cents per week from each requesting employee's wages as a premium under a group insurance policy.

Ford South Africa negotiated general conditions of employment for its hourly paid employees through the Industrial Council for the Automobile Manufacturing Industry. Since the UAW represented only Black members, it was legally prohibited from participating in the Industrial Council and therefore could not formally be a party to a general collective labor agreement. However, a Black representative from each employer's liaison committee, accompanied by an official from the Black Labor Administration, did participate in meetings of the Industrial Council. Within Ford South Africa, management recognized the UAW as speaking in behalf of its members, and the company discussed work-related grievances with the union's plant-level shop stewards. In 1979, South African labor law was amended to permit the registration of unions comprising Black members (and, in some cases, also to permit multiracial unions). The UAW was registered under the new act.

5. FORD'S DIVESTMENT FROM SOUTH AFRICA

In February 1988[14] Ford announced its long-rumored decision to divest from South Africa. At the time of divestiture, Ford owned, through Ford of Canada, 42 percent of South African Motor Corporation (Samcor). Samcor was formed in 1985 from a merger between Ford and Amcar, a South African company owned by Anglo American Corporation. In November 1987, after nine months of negotiations, Ford signed an agreement with the representatives of Samcor, Anglo American Corporation, and the National Union of Metalworkers of South Africa (NUMSA) that ended Ford's direct investment in South Africa. Ford's divestment was completed on 30 April 1988 (see exhibit 7).

Exhibit 7. Memorandum of Understanding

This memorandum serves to confirm that Ford Motor Company of Canada Limited ("Ford"), Anglo American Corporation of South Africa Limited ("Anglo"), Anglo American Industrial Corporation Limited ("AMIC"), the National Union of Metalworkers of South Africa ("NUMSA") and South African Motor Corporation (Pty) Limited ("Samcor") have reached a mutual understanding on the following elements of a restructuring of Ford's participation in Samcor.

1. Ford will donate a 24 per cent equity interest in Samcor to a trust for the benefit of Samcor employees. The balance of Ford's 42 per cent equity interest in Samcor will be sold to Anglo and AMIC.
2. All employees of Samcor at the time that, or at any time after. this agreement is formalized, will be members of the trust.
3. There will be seven trustees chosen to administer the trust, five elected by and representing hourly employees and two elected by and representing salaried employees.
4. The trustees for community welfare and development activities will use all dividends received by the trust.
5. The trustees will nominate three of their number to serve as members of Samcor's Board of Directors. Of these, two will be chosen from the trustees representing hourly employees and one from the trustees representing salaried employees. All seven trustees will vote on each nomination.
6. A committee will be established, consisting of an equal number of trustees and senior management, including the Managing Director. The committee's function will be to discuss and analyze company problems and issues of mutual interest to employees and management. The committee will meet at least six times a year. Any committee member may propose agenda items. This committee is not to be regarded as a substitute for the normal collective bargaining process, which will continue to function in accordance with established rules and procedures.
7. As soon as is feasible after this memorandum has been signed by all parties, but no later than December 11, 1987, each member of the employee trust will be paid by Samcor, on a one-time only basis, the sum of SAR700.00 after deduction of income tax. Any future payments by Samcor to the trust will be in the form of dividends, with the amounts to depend on Samcor's profitability and declaration of dividends by Samcor's Board of Directors.

Continued on next page

Exhibit 7—continued

8. Samcor will provide training to the employee trustees and to the employee directors to enable them to carry out their trustee and director functions effectively. The training will be provided at or by institutions to be mutually agreed upon by Samcor and the trustees.
9. Ford will establish two community trusts, one in the Pretoria area and one in the Port Elizabeth area. Each trust will consist of eight trustees, four of whom will be Samcor employees or their representatives, and four of whom will have other members of the communities in question.
10. Ford agrees to provide training for a period of five years at its U.S. and/or European plants or at other locations agreed upon jointly, for the purpose of upgrading the skills and qualification of Samcor's black employees, so that career development and job opportunities for those employees would be enhanced upon completion of such training.
11. A shareholders' agreement will be entered into between Anglo, AMIC and the employee trust, dealing with those matters that are normally covered between shareholders in private companies.
12. All parties agree that full implementation of this agreement can be accomplished when all the legal requirements relating to the establishment of the trusts and to other aspects of the agreement are completed.

This memorandum represents a commitment among the parties to enter into specific agreements, including the trust and shareholder agreements, and execute appropriate legal documents conforming with the intent of the individual parts of the understanding stated above.

The primary reasons for Ford's divestment were not too different from those offered by many other United States companies that withdrew from South Africa: the worsening economic situation in South Africa left little room to maneuver; the continuing pressure from activists was not only taking up an inordinate amount of senior management's time, but also creating adverse publicity; and many state and local authorities in the United States had imposed restrictions on buying from companies with operations in South Africa. Nonetheless, through its particular divestment strategy (the transfer of assets), the company hoped to make a substantial contribution to the future welfare of its Black workers in South Africa. Ford was, indeed, hoping that its departure from South Africa would enable it to gain a more positive public image, both in that country and in the United States. Finally, as a matter of long-term strategy, Ford wanted to keep the door open for its possible re-entry into South Africa should circumstances subsequently warrant such an action.

5.1   Method of Divestment

Ford had first offered to donate more than half of the 42 percent it held of Samcor's equity—an amount equal to 24 percent of the Samcor's total equity—to a trust fund for the direct benefit of Samcor's employees.[15] However, during lengthy negotiations with NUMSA, it became clear that the union did not want to accept the offer. The union was worried that the new interests of its members as shareholders might conflict with their interests as workers. In addition, the union saw the company's suggestion that the trust earnings be distributed directly to employees as inconsistent with the trade union movement's recent guidelines that disinvesting foreign companies dispose of their assets in ways that benefit all of the people of South Africa.

The union made an alternative proposal to the effect that Ford turn over the same 24 percent of Samcor to a worker-controlled trust in South Africa, the revenues from which would go to community groups. Ford agreed. It was decided that the trust would be controlled by seven trustees, all employees of Samcor. Five of the trustees would be elected by hourly paid employees, and two by salaried employees, a proportion that reflected the overall composition of these two groups in Samcor's workforce. Although all Samcor employees would be the collective owners of Samcor shares through the trust, the dividends would be distributed to development projects in communities throughout South Africa. The trustees would choose the projects to receive funds. The remaining 18 percent of Ford's original 42 percent stake in Samcor was sold for a nominal sum to Anglo American Corporation, Samcor's majority shareholder. The union had asked at first that the trust be given at least 30 percent of the equity in Samcor. However, this proposal was unacceptable to Anglo American, which made clear that it would insist on a 76 percent stake in Samcor, presumably because, in South Africa, certain changes in a company's charter required the support of more than 75 percent of the shareholders. Anglo American was not prepared to give the worker-controlled trust the power to block future modifications of Samcor's charter. At the urging of Ford, the union ultimately dropped its request for larger stake in Samcor.

5.2 Union Representation on the Samcor Board

Initially, Ford had four seats on Samcor's fifteen-member board of directors. Under the new arrangement, Ford would retain two seats, and three would go to the newly established trust (resulting in an expanded board of sixteen directors). One of these three seats on the Samcor board would be filled by one of the trustees, one by a representative of the hourly paid employees, and one by a representative of the salaried employees. Furthermore, Samcor would pay for the training of these three employee-directors.

The union expressed concern that having just two directors representing its members would not give it much of a voice on the board. To overcome this concern, a separate labor-management committee was established, composed of an equal number of labor representatives and senior managers. The committee would meet regularly to discuss issues of concern to either labor or management. Both sides agreed that this joint committee would not substitute for the collective-bargaining procedures already in place.

5.3   Injection of Funds

When Ford announced its plans to disinvest, it also announced its injection of $61 million of new funds into Samcor—an effort to ensure Samcor's economic viability after Ford's departure. Some members of the United States Congress alleged that this action violated the intent of the Comprehensive Anti-Apartheid Act's ban on new investment in South Africa. However, after Ford's detailed explanation of why Samcor's continued viability depended on this injection of new capital, the Office of Foreign Assets Control of the United States Treasury Department determined that the action did not violate the act. The $61 million was used to pay off most of Samcor's debts, which made it easier for Samcor to obtain loans domestically to finance the retooling necessary for the company to remain competitive.

5.4   Non-Equity Ties

Ford also signed an agreement to provide Samcor with continued access to its trademark, to technical and management assistance, and to a supply of components. In interviews with IRRC, representatives of Ford, Samcor, and NUMSA asserted that such continuing, nonequity ties were a crucial part of the arrangement because Anglo American had made clear that it would close Samcor without them. According to a Ford statement, Anglo American "regarded itself as unqualified, as well as unwilling, to try to run the company successfully without Ford's support, including the right to use the Ford trademark." Under this arrangement, Ford Canada would receive an annual technical assistance and service fee of about $200 thousand from Samcor in payment for the use of its trademark and for the technical- and management-assistance agreements. Ford also made a commitment to pay "up to $250 thousand a year to train Samcor workers in locations outside South Africa."

5.5   Charitable Contributions

In addition to the employee trust, Ford established two community trusts, with grants of $2.3 million each, to benefit Black townships near Pretoria and Port Elizabeth, where most of Samcor's employees lived. Each community trust would be run by a board of eight trustees, four to be chosen by the union and four by Ford from the community at large. In addition, Ford committed itself to donate between $4 million and $5 million to an education trust that the company would establish. Unlike the two community trusts, this education trust would be national in scope, and its trustees would not include Samcor employees. All three trusts would be located in South Africa and operate under appropriate South African laws. Ford also donated $250 thousand to the Legal Resources Center, a public-interest law group that provided free legal services to Black South Africans, and $100 thousand to the Management Development Training Center of the National African Federated Chambers of Commerce (NAFCOC).

5.6 Sales to the Public Sector

The divestment arrangement prohibited Samcor from selling to the South African police, military, or other apartheid-enforcing agencies any products incorporating components made in the United States. Samcor agreed to adhere to this prohibition. This agreement was of little practical significance; Samcor received most of its foreign-made parts from Japan or from Ford's European subsidiaries—parts that were outside the scope of the agreement. Thus, for all intents and purposes, Samcor could (and did) sell its products to anyone it wanted, including the South African military and police.

5.7 Union and Worker Reaction

As discussed above, Ford made a strong effort to consult with the union prior to making its final divestment decision. The company also went a long way to accommodate NUMSA's concerns about board participation, formation and control of equity-holding trusts, and the distribution of dividends to community groups. NUMSA's reaction to the divestment process and its content was consequently quite favorable.

The reaction of the rank-and-file workers was not so positive, however. Workers were more concerned with the impact of the agreement on their own incomes than with the union's lofty objective of sharing the fruits of divestment with all the people of South Africa. Serious disagreements arose between the union and the workers over the terms of the trust, in the wake of which there was a wildcat strike at the Samcor plant in Pretoria, a strike that eventually included most of the plant's three thousand hourly paid workers. A Ford representative told IRRC that the striking workers claimed the union had not fully explained to them how the trust would work and that they were upset that its dividends would be paid out to community-welfare projects instead of to the workers themselves. A NUMSA spokesperson explained the conflict differently, attributing it to a long-standing rivalry between two unions that were now both part of NUMSA: the Motor Assembly and Component Workers' Union of South Africa (MACWUSA), and the National Automobile and Allied Workers Union (NAAWU), the largest union to join

NUMSA. The spokesperson stated that some former members of MACWUSA had announced their opposition to the trust, claiming that NUMSA had overstepped its mandate in signing the agreement with Ford. The MACWUSA group then circulated petitions among the workers, claiming that if workers signed the petition and opposed the trust, they would receive their share of the cash value of the 24 percent stake in Samcor, which was estimated to be ZAR 40 thousand per worker. The NUMSA spokesperson explained that when Ford and Samcor did not agree to cash in the shares, the workers went on strike.

After a mass meeting of the workers, union representatives, and senior Ford and Samcor management, the workers agreed to terminate the strike on the condition that negotiations concerning the trust would continue. According to a Ford representative, the workers committee rejected the NUMSA shop stewards because the workers felt that these stewards had not adequately represented the workers' interests in the original negotiations with Ford over the trust. According to a spokesman for NUMSA, however, the original shop stewards resigned because they stood by the original agreement with Ford. In any event, new shop stewards were elected under NUMSA's supervision. Although still recognizing NUMSA as their bargaining agent on working conditions, the workers committee asked the union to remove itself from involvement in the trust negotiations. Consequently, NUMSA agreed to set aside its mandate pending resolution of the workers committee's negotiations with Ford. However, NUMSA continued to recognize the existing agreement with Ford.

The first issue to be decided in the negotiations was whether there would even be a trust. Apparently, some of the workers did not want any kind of trust and preferred that the equivalent cash value of the 24 percent equity in Samcor be distributed among all the workers. This arrangement was not acceptable to other parties. Instead, it was agreed that any change with regard to distributing the trust fund earnings to individual workers would require the support of 75 percent of the employees. On this basis, and in the presence of Samcor's shop stewards, an agreement was signed on 24 November 1987 by the representatives of NUMSA, Ford, Samcor, and Anglo American Corporation. Ford completed its divestment program on 30 April 1988, thus ending its direct investment in South Africa.

6.   FORD RE-ENTERS THE SOUTH AFRICA MARKET

In the 1990s, political changes in South Africa, including the abolition of apartheid, led to a significant shift in public sentiment in the United States with regard to the continuation of sanctions against South Africa.[16] On 10 May 1994, the first nonracial elections took place in South Africa; Nelson Mandela was elected president of the new democratic Republic of South Africa. By this time Ford, along with a number of other companies, had started to think about re-entering the South African market, and they were strongly encouraged to do so by the newly elected South African government.

Ford estimated the automobile market in South Africa at three hundred thousand units of cars and trucks (combined) in 1994. Of these, twenty-three thousand to thirty thousand were Ford cars (sold through Samcor). Ford believed that three hundred thousand cars per year was very small for a country with a population of forty million; the South African market was therefore perceived as having great growth potential. As of 1994, seven major automobile manufacturers were active in the South African market: BMW, Delta (Opel and Isuzu), Mercedes (Mercedes and Honda); Nissan (Nissan and Fiat), Samcor (Ford, Mazda, and Mitsubishi); Toyota; and Volkswagen (Volkswagen and Audi).

At that point in 1994, Anglo American Corporation owned 76 percent of Samcor, with the remaining 24 percent controlled by the Samcor Employee Trust. In November 1994, however, Ford, Anglo American, and the Samcor Employee Trust agreed that Ford could purchase 45 percent of Samcor's equity for $14 million. The company, however, did not disclose the terms of the disbursement of the proceeds among the parties. Pursuant to the new investment, Ford and Anglo American each owned 45 percent of equity, with Samcor Employee Trust holding the remaining 10 percent of Samcor's equity. Jim Miller was appointed as Samcor's managing director and CEO. Miller had been with Ford for twenty-one years and had held the positions of director of eastern Europe and export operations at Ford of Europe. Along with Ford, Ford Motor Credit Company also entered South Africa by forming a joint venture with Anglo American, the goal of which was to provide financing support to Ford dealers and retail customers in South Africa. Twenty-five percent of the equity in Ford Motor Credit was held by Anglo African Industrial Corporation Limited, 50 percent by Amalgamated Banks of South Africa, and 25 percent by Ford Credit International. Allan Frode was nominated as the managing director of Ford Motor Credit in South Africa. He had been with Ford for twenty years and was a financial expert.

ENDNOTES

1   The authors are grateful to Wayne Fredericks, a former Ford executive and a leading advocate of the Sullivan Principles, for his assistance and cooperation in the preparation of

this case study. The authors, however, are solely responsible for all the text, analysis. and conclusions contained in this chapter.

2 Ford Motor Company, press release, 19 February 1988.

3 William Broderick (Ford Motor Company), memorandum to T. Mecke and R. Markley, 10 March 1977.

4 Sidney Kelly (Ford Motor Company), letter to Sister Regina Murphy, 7 December 1977.

5 Tim Smith (director, ICCR), letter to Henry Ford, 9 February 1978.

6 Henry Ford (Ford Motor Company), letter to John Sengstacke (publisher of the *Chicago Daily Defender*).

7 Letters exchanged between Father Hesburgh and Ford Motor Company, 1978–79; Ford Motor Company, letters from Sidney Kelly to James Kristoff, treasurer, Ohio State University, to Arnold Mickelson, 14 November and 21 December 1978, and to the American Luther Church, 15 June 1979; and Brandeis University statement of 26 April 1979.

8 Sidney Kelly (Ford Motor Company), letter to Marion Freeman (University Committee on Social Responsibility), 22 February 1978.

9 Henry Ford, letter to the Nigerian ambassador, 20 February 1978.

10 C. Peter Magrath, statement to the Board of Regents, University of Minnesota.

11 Ford Motor Company, "Ford's Position on Sales to South African Police and Military," May 1980; Report, IRRC, 17 April 1979.

12 Ford Motor Company, "Report of the International Labor Relations Staff," 30 November 1983.

13 Ford Motor Company, "Report on Union Relationships." 1973.

14 Ford Motor Company, press release, 19 February 1988.

15 The narrative in this section is based on a variety of published sources and interviews with various people both within and outside Ford and in the United States and South Africa. In particular, see Ford Motor Corporation, press release, 19 February 1988; Ford Motor Corporation, "Q & A: Possible Ford Reinvestment in Samcor," July 1993; and Jennifer Kibbe and David Hauck, "Leaving South Africa: The Impact of U.S. Corporate Disinvestment," (Washington, DC: IRRC, 1988), 2–15, 38–41.

16 The narrative in this section is based on press releases by the Ford Motor Corporation of 26 October and 28 November 1994, and 17 November 1995.

Chapter 8

Raising the Ante
Enhancement of the Principles

Leon Sullivan's rationale in creating the Principles was to have the United States companies play an important role in dismantling apartheid in South Africa. He recognized that, though perhaps unable and unwilling to exert direct political pressure on the South African government, the companies could nonetheless exert substantial albeit indirect pressure through the economic power they wielded.

In this approach, Sullivan's thinking was not too far from that of more radical anti-apartheid activists, who were well aware of that same economic power but believed that it could be used more effectively if applied negatively; that is, by having large corporations withdraw from the country altogether (hence, the strategy of pressuring United States corporations to disinvest). Though recognizing that total withdrawal may ultimately be necessary, Sullivan believed that it should not be the first step. And until withdrawal was necessary, companies should use their economic power to eliminate race-based discrimination in the workplace, improve the physical conditions in the communities where Blacks lived, and provide Blacks with the economic means (and therefore the power) to exert their influence in the political arena.

From Sullivan's perspective, the Principles were not a static, one-time-only arrangement. Instead, he considered them to be a dynamic response to changing economic and sociopolitical conditions. It was this conception of the Principles that explains his willingness to compromise on the scope of the Principles during their initial formulation. He had worked in the trenches of poverty and job creation in the Black neighborhoods of Philadelphia and New York. He understood the importance of gaining ground one step at a time and making advances only when he had secured his current position. In interviews with the authors he categorically stated, "I always had a secret agenda about moving the United States companies toward engaging the

South African government in the political arena. But I also knew that there would be no Principles if I had insisted on the inclusion of political goals at the start of this process." He went on to say that "ICCR and other anti-apartheid activists refused to confront this reality and thus criticized me and the Principles without seeing the larger picture."

Although the United States companies were willing to accept the narrowly defined agenda of the Principles, from the outset the companies were firm in their refusal to engage in activities that might be construed as interfering in the internal affairs of the South African government. It is, indeed, possible that the leaders of the United States companies might actually have believed that in cooperating with Sullivan and participating in the Principles program, they could control both the scope of the Principles and the manner of their implementation. But even within such a conception of the Principles program (which differed from Sullivan's), an analysis of the companies' public statements and their expenditure patterns in compliance with the Principles suggests that the companies believed that the Principles would make a genuine contribution to the elimination not just of discrimination in the workplace, but of apartheid itself. The companies wanted to challenge the government only through the workplace, however, because the reforms there could be justified in economic terms and, at the same time, enable the companies to avoid a direct confrontation with the government in the broader political arena.

In our view, the amplification process became unfocused in attempting to meet the twin goals of eliminating discrimination in the workplace and maintaining political pressure on the government to bring an end to apartheid; the efforts required to pursue one goal were sometimes (and increasingly) inconsistent with what were required to pursue the other. Moreover, an emphasis on achieving one goal often resulted in sacrificing progress in achieving the other. There was an unavoidable strain on scarce resources and on the time that managers had available for the Principles program, and the dual goals of the program continually sent mixed signals to the external constituencies whose support was critical in generating and maintaining public pressure on the South African government.

Another major flaw in the amplification process was the lack of leadership by Sullivan and by the group of church leaders who were supposed to oversee and evaluate not only the performance of the United States companies in the Principles program, but also that of Reid Weedon, who played a vital role in its implementation. In our extensive interviews with Sullivan, we were unable to elicit a cogent explanation of how he planned to use each amplification as a stepping stone to the next one. Nor could Sullivan explain how the successive amplifications would eventually lead to the predefined, albeit dynamically changing, goals of achieving parity among all employees in the workplace and, through the activities of United States companies under the Principles, lead to the political dismantlement of the apartheid regime in South Africa.

Thus lacking both strong leadership and a clear sense of direction, the amplification process degenerated into a series of ad hoc and discrete steps that focused on two aspects of the Principles program; namely, to improve the implementation of the Principles and to respond narrowly to the short-term sociopolitical circumstances in South Africa. Unfortunately, even within this limited scope, the amplification process failed to meet its objectives. With regard to implementation, the amplification process put considerable emphasis on the allocation of funds, which was essentially an internal political problem for the group of companies participating in the Principles program, and the process avoided issues that would have made the system of monitoring and verification more transparent, thereby improving the program's public accountability. With regard to "enhancing" the Principles—extending their scope and effect into the political arena—the amplification process was often handicapped by both internal dissension and public acrimony and distrust. The implementation of the amplified Principles therefore proved to be more symbolic than substantive—and largely counter-productive.

As we saw earlier, Sullivan's first enunciation of the Principles consisted of six statements outlining broad areas of concern that he wanted the signatory companies to address. The statements focused on nonsegregation of the races in all eating, comfort, and work facilities; equal and fair employment practices for all employees; equal pay for all employees doing equal or comparable work for the same period of time; initiation and development of training programs to prepare Blacks and other non-Whites for supervisory, administrative, clerical, and technical jobs; increasing the number of Blacks and other non-Whites in management and supervisory positions; and improving the quality of employees' lives outside the work environment in such areas as housing, transportation, schooling, recreation, and health facilities.

1.   FIRST AMPLIFICATION: JULY 1978

As originally formulated, the Principles were deficient in two important respects: there were no operational standards defining how each Principle would be implemented by the signatory companies, and there were no objective measures by which the performance of each company would be evaluated and the findings reported to public.

We have previously described in detail (chapter 3) the activities of various task groups established by the signatory companies to develop operational standards and objective measures of performance evaluation. These task groups performed an invaluable service in the creation of the standards, without which the Principles would potentially have had multiple and inconsistent interpretations—like *Alice in Wonderland,* where the interpretations of words and actions were fluid and subjective (but nonetheless all correct), with no rational basis for preferring one interpretation over another.

The opponents of the Principles program have criticized its processes as essentially insular and therefore as lacking in credibility. Although these criticisms have some merit, we believe that, in view of the fractious sociopolitical environment and the unconcealed hostility of many anti-apartheid groups toward the Principles program, this insular approach, whether by design or by accident, was beneficial to the program. It saved the program from becoming even further politicized and from losing the sense of collective solidarity that kept the program going and enabled it to attract further signatories. Moreover, this insularity enabled the signatories to generate a coherent set of activities, to define criteria for acceptable levels of performance, and to agree upon standards for public reporting.

The process involved midlevel executives who were both committed to reforms in South Africa and experienced in creating operational systems that would lead to their efficient implementation. Not only did these executives "buy into the Principles," but, through their affiliation with, and participation in, the program, they brought with them the assurance that their companies would take the implementation process seriously. In particular, these executives had the trust of their top management and also had a strong network of other midlevel executives within their organizations who could be counted upon to facilitate and expedite the implementation process. In part because the insularity discussed above, and also in part because of these executives' dedication to moving the program forward, the process of implementing the Principles avoided being bogged down in the long and debilitating "consultative process" that is the bane of nongovernmental organizations—where everyone must be heard, and consensus be built, before any decision is made. Although such a decision-making process may be desirable and even necessary for establishing goals that need to secure widespread public support, it is fatal in implementing goals that have already been established or accepted; the process degenerates into "decision by committee," where vital technical expertise is relegated to a secondary role.

The first amplification of the Principles, discussed in chapter 3, established two patterns that would continue, in one way or another, through all the successive amplifications. (1) The amplification process identified, in general terms, the tasks that must be undertaken to meet the spirit of a particular principle, but it left to the discretion of each company the determination of how those tasks would be performed and the timetable within which to achieve a specified level of implementation. (2) There were no specific quantifiable standards against which the adequacy of a corporation's performance could be measured. Even when quantifiable standards were used, they focused on defining corporate efforts or inputs (such as funds allocated) rather than on defining the outcomes that needed to be achieved through those efforts.

As we discussed earlier, this lack of an outcome-based standard was one of the most critical failures of the entire Principles program and its implementation apparatus. We also believe that this approach provided the United States corporations with a major loophole through which they could escape their responsibility for not producing significant and measurable results, while nonetheless claiming to be in compliance with the Principles. The weakness of this approach was further exacerbated by the monitoring and performance process instituted by the consulting firm of Arthur D. Little.

Consider the example of Principle 2, which called for equal and fair employment for all employees. The amplification to this Principle stated that each signatory company will "proceed immediately" to:

Implement equal and fair terms and conditions of employment

Provide non-discriminatory eligibility for benefit plans

Establish an appropriate comprehensive procedure for handling and resolving individual employee complaints

Support the elimination of all industrial racial discriminatory laws which impede the implementation of equal and fair terms and conditions of employment, such as abolition of job reservations, job fragmentation, and apprenticeship restrictions for Blacks and other non-white

Support the elimination of discrimination against the rights of Blacks to form or belong to government registered unions, and acknowledge generally the right of Black workers to form their own union or be represented by trade unions where unions already exist

It is not clear to us why the emphasis was placed on *proceeding immediately* rather than on *completing the task within a specified time period.* The amplification also called for establishing *appropriate* procedures for handling employee complaints, and asked the employer to *support* the elimination of all industrial racial discrimination laws, to *support* the elimination of discrimination against the rights of Blacks to organize unions, and so on. It could, of course, be argued that this approach offered the flexibility each company needed to devise ways to implement the measures in a manner sensitive to the particular circumstances of each company. However, this argument begs the question rather than answers it. To wit, whether or not an employer had complied with the Principle should have been judged after the fact and on the basis of criteria that were specific, quantifiable, objective, and sufficiently transparent to determine whether the company had, in fact, met the standards by achieving the desired results.

Another example of the weakness of the "effort-oriented" approach can be found in the Principle 5's amplified requirements, which dealt with increasing the number of Blacks and other non-Whites in management and supervisory positions. The amplification stated that the companies should "proceed immediately" to:

> Identify, actively recruit, train and develop a sufficient and significant number of Blacks and other non-whites to assure that as quickly as possible there will be appropriate representation of Blacks and other non-whites in the management group of each company

> Establish management development programs for Blacks and other non-whites, as appropriate, and improve existing programs and facilities for developing management skills of Blacks and other non-whites

> Identify and channel high management potential Blacks and other non-white employees into management development programs

As we discuss later (chapter 10), the United States companies did not have much to show for their efforts in this area. Promotion of Blacks and other non-Whites invariably confronted strong resistance form the White South African managers, who offered explanations hauntingly like those heard during the early days of the civil rights struggle in the United States. To wit, there are not enough trained and educated Blacks available; we cannot and must not promote unqualified people; and so on. Furthermore, it was clear that the managers saw such statements as obvious truisms. Thus, in view of our experience working in South Africa, we believe that the United States companies refrained from making the systematic effort required to identify and train Black and other non-White employees for promotion into supervisory positions. There was just too much resistance in the management ranks of their South African subsidiaries, a resistance that the United States parent companies were unwilling or unable to challenge.

The contentious nature of the above problem was frankly admitted by Wayne Fredericks, a senior Ford Motor Company executive and one of the most ardent supporters of the Sullivan Principles. In an interview with the authors, he stated that "increasing the number of blacks and other non-whites in management and supervisory positions was a very sticky issue. It took a lot of prodding to get them included in the first amplification." He went on to say that the issue involved "interpersonal relations and building of mutual trust and this is not something you could impose from the outside."

Similar arguments can be made with regard to the amplification standards outlined for the remaining Principles. There is no reason to belabor this point through further discussion, but we would invite readers to undertake their own analysis based on the complete text of the first amplification, which appears in chapter 3.

Despite its limitations, the first amplification took the important step of recognizing the necessity for companies to systematically and periodically report their progress in implementing the Principles. In particular, the amplification asked signatory companies to proceed immediately to utilize a standard format to report their implementation progress to Sullivan through the independent administrative unit he had established. (The report forms were initially submitted twice a year, but the reporting was soon changed to an annual basis.) Unfortunately, the system became—in practice—an exercise in "bean counting," and both the number of beans and their significance were left to be determined solely by Reid Weedon, who would also make public his "assessment" of what had been accomplished.

2.   SECOND AMPLIFICATION: MAY 1979

The second amplification attempted to tackle one of the more controversial aspects of the Principles—the workers' right to organize—which had been left out of the original formulation of the Principles. This amplification, which came in the form of additions to Principles 2 and 6, asked the signatories to allow their employees to unionize and to challenge influx control laws:

> Secure rights of Black workers to freedom of association and assure protection against victimization while pursuing and after attaining these rights [amplification under Principle 2]

> Support changes in influx control laws to provide for the right of Black migrant workers to normal family life

> Increase utilization of and assist in the development of Black and other non-white owned and operated business enterprises including distributors, suppliers of goods and services and manufacturers [amplifications under Principle 6]

Recall that the "right to unionize" was strongly opposed by many of the United States companies—for example, IBM—whose operations were not unionized anywhere else, including the United States. These companies felt that by insisting on workers' rights to join unions in South Africa, they would be setting a precedent that would affect their operations in other parts of the world. Sullivan nevertheless insisted, and the United States companies—confronted with both the political needs of South Africa and the political pressures at home—eventually acceded. In South Africa, because of press censorship and the lack of political freedom, Black unions (whether officially sanctioned or not) were emerging as the only potent economic and political force challenging South Africa's highly discriminatory political and economic apparatus. The unions were, indeed, the only medium through which Black voices could express their frustration and vent their anger. Black unions did not simply represent the rights of Black workers in the workplace; the unions represented and spoke for all aspects of the Black workers' lives in South Africa. In view of these considerations, the United States companies realized that South Africa was a unique situation. To be sure, the United States companies also recognized that Black unions were increasingly becoming a fact of life in South Africa, one that could not be avoided or controlled. It would therefore have been politically counterproductive for the United States companies to withhold their support, especially since anti-apartheid activists in the United States continued to chastise the companies for not recognizing the inherent right of the Black workers to organize.

The two additions to Principle 6 broke important new ground and also specifically expanded the reach of the Principles in an area that had hitherto been addressed only implicitly. The addition called for the United States companies to support changes in the influx control laws, which prevented workers' families from leaving their native homelands and living with the workers near the plant sites. These laws were designed by the South African government to ensure that only workers who provided labor would live in the White areas and that these areas would not be inundated with Black women and children. The laws also enabled the government to avoid the additional spending necessary to address the housing, educational, and other needs of Black families who would, but for the influx control laws, be settling in White-dominated areas.

This second amplification represented the first time that the Principles urged the companies to extend their reach into the political arena, specifically by challenging the South African government to make changes in a central pillar of the apartheid structure. Unfortunately, the amplification did not suggest how companies would "support" changes in the influx control laws. Nor did it set up any system—for example, task groups—to devise ways in which United States companies could undertake appropriate action. As future events would show, this amplification had, at best, a symbolic value. We could not find any evidence of specific actions taken by the signatory companies to implement this amplification. Nor did the annual public reports of these companies make reference to any specific actions undertaken or outcomes achieved in the course of implementing this amplification. However, a number of companies enabled Black workers to purchase houses in White areas, which may have indirectly had an effect in eroding the influx control laws.

The second addition to Principle 6 called for the signatory companies to support the development and growth of Black-owned enterprises in South Africa. What is perhaps most interesting (and surprising) about this amplification is that its substance was not incorporated into either the initial formulation of the Principles or their first amplification. Sullivan, of all people, was cognizant of the fact that enterprise activity among the economically deprived invariably occurred—and had to be supported and encouraged—at the lowest rung of the economic ladder. Accordingly, in the United States, Sullivan had vigorously campaigned in support of small minority-owned businesses and had urged large corporations to cooperate through their vendor and outside-supplier programs. The situation in the case of South Africa was even more critical. South Africa's pervasively discriminatory legal system included all kinds of regulations to restrict the growth of small, Black-owned enterprises. At the same time, it was apparent that the United States companies could create an enormous multiplier effect in Black economic growth by supporting such enterprises.

With regard to supporting Black-owned businesses, there was a tremendous gap between the "express intent" and "operational reality," just as there was above in the case promoting Blacks into the managerial ranks. Moreover, the underlying rationale for the failure to act was much the same: many White managers of the United States companies in South Africa were unwilling to direct business toward Blacks because they believed that any progress in that direction would unavoidably come at the expense of White-owned businesses. For the White managers, this outcome was unacceptable. Indeed, these managers—again, like those in the United States in response to the civil rights movement—also defended their unwillingness to support Black businesses by arguing that such businesses could not supply quality goods at competitive prices, that the United States companies could not afford to compromise on quality, and that setting targets (euphemism for quotas) was undesirable. Suffice it is to say that despite all protestations of vigorous and sincere effort, the record of the United States companies in promoting Black-owned enterprises in South Africa was disappointing.

3. THIRD AMPLIFICATION: NOVEMBER 1982

The third amplification was an attempt, in part, to involve employees and the representatives of Black communities in the companies' programs for implementing the Principles. Another objective was to improve the auditing process under the Principles. This amplification was accomplished by making additions to Principle 2 and by rewriting the clause on periodic reporting. The companies were to "proceed immediately" to:

Involve Black workers or their representatives in the development of programs that address their educational and other needs and those of their dependents and the local community [amplification under Principle 2]

Report progress on an annual basis to Reverend Sullivan through the independent administrative unit he has established

Have all areas specified by Reverend Sullivan audited by a certified public accounting firm

Inform all employees of the company's annual periodic report rating and invite their input on ways to improve the rating [new clause on periodic reporting]

Unfortunately, the amplification of Principle 2 made no suggestion as to how Black workers and community representatives would be involved in the decision-making process for developing programs, and we could find no evidence in the archival data whether the South African counterpart of the Industrial Support Unit established any consultative mechanisms among the company representatives for implementing this amplification. Indeed, based on our meetings with Black business groups, workers, and community representatives over a number of years in South Africa, there was widespread dissatisfaction with the so-called consultative process.

Perhaps the major source of misunderstanding—and consequently inaction—arose because of various stakeholders' differing interpretations of the meaning of *involvement* in Principle 2 and of *invite their input* in the new periodic reporting clause. From the perspective of the United States companies' management, *involvement* meant listening to the views of various stakeholders in making decisions. However, it did not mean that those views must be accepted and implemented at all times and under all circumstances. From the perspective of Black workers, involvement without having some influence on the actual decisions (or their outcomes) was nothing but a sham. In the end, the perception of Blacks was that management did what it wanted to do and was only going through the motions of listening to Black workers.

Similar cynicism was expressed in the area of incorporating the input of workers into the reporting process; our interviews with workers' representatives during the peak period of the Principles program—that is, 1982–86—indicated that they, along with community representatives, were deeply dissatisfied. Their perception was that most United States companies were unwilling to share with workers any detailed information about the performance of individual companies—even their own—under the Principles. The data were considered proprietary. Instead, workers, along with the rest of the world, were given access to the consolidated annual report for the entire group of signatory companies. This report provided, of course, only an overall, summary rating for each company; no details were provided.

The problem of involving community representatives in the decision-making process, whether on a consultative basis or as a substantive voice, was more complex. The so-called community representatives were also most likely to be the recipients of grants and funding from the signatory companies. Thus, any significant involvement from this group posed two problems for the United States companies:

1. It was not always clear who should be represented in the formal consultative process. Not only did different community groups often have different agendas, but the groups were also in competition with one another both for public support and corporate munificence. Thus, the presence of one group often led to acrimony and complaints from other groups, who felt that they would lose out in securing projects and in promoting the interests of their constituencies. In both our own field observations in South Africa and our interviews with nongovernmental organizations (NGOs) there, it was apparent that this situation gave rise to an adverse, albeit unintended, side effect. The internal dissension and mutual distrust among the NGOs was exploited and exacerbated by some of the signatory companies' South African managers, who would typically consult with, and award grants to, their favorite NGOs. To make matters worse, the list of preferred NGOs—and thus of preferred projects—would change more or less arbitrarily with changes in each company's management. A further distortion resulted from the way in which companies' performance under the Principles was measured: what mattered was not "what was accomplished," but "what was spent." In sum, the perception of NGOs was that the consultation process and the awarding of grants was arbitrary, partisan, and ultimately ineffective—a perception that bred both contempt and cynicism among the NGOs and their constituencies.

2. The groups whose cooperation was sought by the companies were sometimes maligned and accused by other groups as having been co-opted by the companies. Thus, rather than being a constructive force in the consultative process with the companies, the "in" groups often became more belligerent and demanding, thereby proving their independence both to their constituents and to their adversaries.

The third amplification's requirement that the companies should have "all areas specified by Reverend Sullivan audited by a certified public accounting firm" was allegedly designed to strengthen the audit process and thereby make it more palatable to the Principles' critics. Unfortunately, this requirement was so loosely defined and poorly implemented that it neither improved the integrity of the auditing process nor mollified critics of the that process. Indeed, the auditors responsible for certifying the veracity of the companies' claims under the Principles were the same ones who audited the companies' financial data. It appears likely that these auditors would give every benefit of the doubt to the companies—under the "generally accepted accounting principles"—in determining whether expenses could be classified as belonging to Principles-related projects. Moreover, even under the best of circumstances, the auditors verified only the expenses and not their potential effect; it was beyond the auditors' role to determine the quality—and in many cases, even the extent—of companies' efforts to promote Blacks to management and supervisory positions, or of companies' efforts to increase purchases from Black-owned businesses. When one takes into consideration that these two areas were the ones in which the companies had both the most control over the outcome and the poorest record of achievement under the Principles, it is painfully clear that the auditing process was poorly designed as an means of either motivating companies or measuring their efforts to promote the goals of the Principles program.

4.   FOURTH AMPLIFICATION: NOVEMBER 1984, AND FIFTH AMPLIFICATION, NOVEMBER 1986

More United States companies participated in the Principles program from 1984 to 1986 than during any other period. There was, moreover, an increasing demand by workers and community groups in South Africa for the signatory companies to do even more toward meeting their obligations under the Sullivan Principles and their amplifications. It is nonetheless ironic that this period immediately followed one in which there was a radical increase in the intensity of public pressure, especially by anti-apartheid activists, for the companies to withdraw from South Africa. By 1984, public sentiment had coalesced in favor of political action as such. The economic justification for staying in South Africa, regardless of its inherent merits, was no longer enough. No institution, whether economic, social, or political, could insulate itself from the political character of apartheid in South Africa. Pressures on the companies thus continued to mount, no matter what they did under the existing principles.

In 1983, the South African Council of Churches (SACC), a coalition of Protestant churches, passed a resolution asking the world community to refrain from investing in institutions that supported apartheid. Disinvestment was also endorsed by a coalition of Black trade unions—the Congress of

South African Trade Unions. The United Democratic Front (UDF) was organized that year, as well; it was a coalition of some six hundred organizations under the leadership of Alan Boesak, a minister of the so-called Colored branch of the Dutch Reformed Church, who was a fiery orator and a powerful opponent of apartheid. He was, moreover, the de facto spokesperson for the banned ANC in arguing for economic sanctions.

In June 1983, Bishop Desmond Tutu, a former head of the South African Council of Churches, proclaimed the "Tutu Principles." These principles emphasized the political nature of the apartheid struggle and downplayed the value of economic issues insofar as such issues were taken to be separate from, and interpreted apart from, the political context of the Blacks' struggle for freedom in South Africa. The pressure was now on Sullivan and the signatory companies to expand their reach and become more proactive in the political arena.

In November 1983, Sullivan announced the fourth amplification. It largely followed the Tutu Principles by asking the companies to press for the abolition of the laws and regulations that constituted apartheid. The companies were, moreover, expected to lobby the government, overtly and actively, against apartheid. In announcing his new initiative, Sullivan declared that "contrary to generally held perception to the effect that the U.S. companies would not accept a political role that called upon them to pressure the South African government, we have the evidence of 119 participating companies that have unanimously and enthusiastically accepted the new amplification."[1]

The fourth amplification, presented as an addition to Principle 6, formally addressed the "Increased Dimensions of Activities Outside the Workplace," in accordance with which companies were to:

Use influence (to) support the unrestricted rights of Black businesses to locate in the urban areas of the nation

Influence other companies in South Africa to follow the standards of equal rights principles

Support the freedom of mobility of Black workers to seek employment opportunities wherever they exist, and make possible provisions for adequate housing for families of employees within the proximity of workers' employment

Support the ending of all apartheid laws, practices and customs

Sullivan's amplification differed from Tutu's principles in one important aspect. Sullivan did not use the threat of withdrawal of all investment as leverage to move the government to dismantle apartheid.

After Tutu was awarded the Nobel Peace Prize, his campaign for economic sanctions against South Africa was given prominent global media coverage. Media attention in the United States also increased in the wake of Randall Robinson's Thanksgiving Day protest (21 November 1984) at the South African Embassy in Washington, DC, which subsequently brought different celebrities and public figures to the embassy each day to protest apartheid and support economic sanctions against South Africa. As we discussed in chapter 2, this widely publicized campaign lasted two years and was known as the Free South Africa Movement.

The additional pressure on United States companies to leave South Africa was not without an effect. In 1983 a small number of these companies made tentative efforts to lobby the South African government on noneconomic issues, which was a major new dimension in the companies' public posture in South Africa. In particular, the companies, through the American Chamber of Commerce (AMCHAM) in Johannesburg, protested a bill that would have, in effect, required employers to enforce influx control laws in the workplace. It is noteworthy that the 1984 Arthur D. Little report on the companies' progress on the Principles included the following observation on the new requirements of the program. "It is significant that there are today several areas in which companies are being requested to be active which would not have been tolerated by the companies when the program was initiated."[2]

The period from late 1984 through August 1985 marked another turning point in the anti-apartheid movement. P. W. Botha's proposal for a new, tricameral parliament outraged the Black population because they were left out of the new arrangement. The UDF grew increasingly powerful and outspoken. In the United States—in April 1985 alone—there were twenty separate sanction bills pending in the Congress. There were also widespread protests against apartheid on many college campuses, with events at Berkeley, Columbia, and Rutgers being widely reported. Over four thousand protesters demonstrated at the South African Embassy in Washington, DC, to express their anger and disapproval at the pace of changes in that country. In 1985, at a World Council of Churches consultation in Harare, the SACC issued a definitive call for comprehensive economic sanctions until apartheid was dismantled.

In July 1985, Fred Ferreira, managing director of Ford South Africa and president of the South African Signatory Association (SASA), convened a meeting of the signatory companies to develop "a more meaningful role by the broad business community in the social change process in South Africa."[3] In attendance were chairmen of the Principles task groups and board members of the AMCHAM in South Africa. Also in attendance were Dr. Robin Lee, executive director of the Urban Foundation; representatives from Black community groups, the Association of Chambers of Commerce

(ASSOCOM), and the South African Federated Chamber of Industries (FCI); and ADL's Reid Weedon. Experts such as John Kane Berman of the South African Institute of Race Relations and Professor Lawrence Schlemer of the University of Natal Institute for Applied Social Sciences offered a new strategy. After much discussion, the group charged Schlemer to draft a concept paper outlining the new direction for the Principles program, to be known as "Sullivan: Phase 3." The resulting concept paper (appendix 8.1) outlined a series of actions that the United States companies should undertake in the more proactive stance of supporting Black people's political aspirations in South Africa.

Coordinating with AMCHAM, SASA decided to use a public relations campaign developed by the firm of J. Walter Thompson (JWT). The primary focus of the campaign would be on public communication and public education, with the following objectives:

To communicate AMCHAM's concerns over the South African situation
To focus on key positives of the reform processes
To be seen to be prepared to stand up and be counted

As one would expect, the public relations campaign emphasized the heavy use of full-page advertisements in mass media—advertisements that would demand the dismantling of apartheid. The campaign would also include all the other elements of traditional public relations: press conferences, the preparation of speeches for corporate spokespersons, and the publicizing of AMCHAM's politically oriented activities (appendices 8.2 and 8.3).

Unfortunately, like everything else in the amplification process, this campaign was too little, too late. The companies were seen not as dynamic advocates of change and progress, but as timid actors who would do the minimum, only when it was absolutely necessary, and in a manner that would be least offensive to all concerned. They were not seen as leading the charge, but rather as running from behind to catch up with the parade. Furthermore, their motives were largely seen by the body politic as cynical and self-serving—an impression that was reinforced by the companies' own actions.

In launching this public relations campaign, the companies decided that the AMCHAM umbrella would offer the best means for the United States companies to make their point while making no single company vulnerable to the loss of South African government contracts (or to any other form of retribution or punishment by the South African government). Since it was apparent that the planned advertisements would be irritating to the South African government, however, AMCHAM sent a letter to the South African government's cabinet ministers explaining that the campaign's "intention is to communicate, to highlight core issues and, importantly, to help combat the intensifying and adverse dis-investment pressures that we are subject to back here in South Africa and overseas." The companies thus presented their effort apologetically, as the product of the political necessity of defusing public sentiment against the companies and their continued presence in South Africa.

Even as the companies began taking a direct stance against the South African government's apartheid policies, the companies were leaving the country in ever increasing numbers. In October 1986, for example, within weeks of each other, two stalwarts of the Principles program—General Motors and IBM—announced that they were leaving South Africa. Moreover, since these departures were quite at odds with the companies' express support of the Principles program and the companies' equally express determination to continue doing business in South Africa, the departures undercut both the goals of the program and its public credibility.

Following the public relations campaign, its associated advertisements, and activities, the signatory companies' involvement in the public arena became, in fact, more intensified, and it was decided that this involvement should be codified in the Principles. Thus, in November 1986, the fourth amplification was expanded and designated as a new, seventh Sullivan Principle. The companies were expected to:

Use influence [to] support the unrestricted rights of Black businesses to locate in the urban areas of the nation

Influence other companies in South Africa to follow the standards of equal rights principles

Support the freedom of mobility of Black workers to seek employment opportunities wherever they exist, and make possible provisions for adequate housing for families of employees within the proximity of workers' employment

Support the ending of all apartheid laws, practices and customs

Press for a single education system

Use financial and legal resources to assist Blacks, Coloureds and Asians in their efforts to achieve equal access to all health facilities, educational institutions, transportation, housing, beaches, parks and all other accommodations normally reserved for whites

Oppose adherence to all apartheid laws and regulations

Support full and equal participation of Blacks, Coloureds and Asians in the political process

Sullivan saw this expansion—which explicitly included activities that challenged apartheid outside of the workplace and in the wider society—as so important that he called Principle 7 the "fifth amplification."

5. SIXTH AMPLIFICATION: JUNE 1991

An ad hoc committee of the ISU met on 25 June 1991 to consider the future of the organization. At this meeting, Reid Weedon raised the issue of adding an eighth principle to the Sullivan code in a sixth amplification. He believed that the code needed updating in view of the dismantling of statutory apartheid. This new principle would emphasize the concept of Black training and development in the organizational setting, and would codify what the companies were already doing in South Africa.

At the 2 August 1991 meeting of the Ad Hoc Committee, it was decided that Reid Weedon and Roger Crawford, chair of SASA, should draft a revised version of the Principles (exhibit 8, with additions to the Principles in bold type). As a comprehensive revision and a facelift of the Principles, it was to be submitted to the ISU board prior to the fall plenary meeting. It was intended not only to meet the needs of the new South Africa, but to enable the United States companies to be seen in a different, more favorable and constructive light.

Weedon realized that the companies were suffering from "compliance exhaustion" and looking for ways to conclude the Principles program. They were in no mood to seek further expansion of the program and its attendant administrative and financial commitments. He therefore attempted to present this amplification as simply a codification of the activities that the companies were already engaged in. In particular, since he had previously expanded the questionnaire in the light of National Advisory Council recommendations and other reports, he emphasized that the new amplification would require no new reporting procedures.

This argument was somewhat misleading. As we have shown in other parts of the book, the companies' performance was disappointing in the areas of Black workers' training and their promotion to management ranks. For a host of reasons, the companies also had little success in supporting Black businesses through their purchases programs. Therefore, in our view, the companies were not making significant progress in these areas and were unlikely to do so now that there would be less pressure to comply with even the previous "generalized" and "company friendly" monitoring system. The remaining part of this sixth amplification was merely a listing of various activities that the companies were engaged in through their "community out-

Exhibit 8. Memorandum of Understanding

This Sixth Amplification recognizes that by 1986 all Signatory Companies had accomplished the objectives of the first three Principles which applied primarily to the work place. They are:

Principle 1: Non-segregation of the Races in All Eating, Comfort, Locker Room, and Work Facilities

Principle 2: Equal and Fair Employment Practices for All Employees

Principle 3: Equal Pay for All Employees Doing Equal or Comparable Work for the Same Period of Time

In addition, this Amplification recognizes that the laws which constitute apartheid have been rescinded, but there is still much more that companies can do to help in the transformation of South Africa into a non-racial, democratic nation.

The socio-economic needs of the South African society will be accentuated after apartheid. This Sixth Amplification focuses on the present needs which include Principles 4, 5, 6, and 7, and adds Principle 8.

Principle 4: Initiation and Development of Training Programs that will prepare Blacks, Coloureds and Asians in Substantial Numbers for Supervisory, Administrative, Clerical and Technical Jobs.

Each Signator of the Statement of Principles will proceed immediately to:

- Determine employee training needs and capabilities, and identify employees with potential for further advancement.

- Take advantage of existing outside training resources and activities, such as exchange programs, technical colleges, and similar institutions or programs.

- Support the development of outside training facilities, individually or collectively – including technical centers, professional training exposure, correspondence and extension courses, as appropriate, for extensive training outreach.

- Initiative and expand inside training programs and facilities.

- **Implement significant Black, Coloured and Asian advancement in all sectors of the company.**

- **Stimulate economic employment of Blacks, Coloureds and Asians.**

Principle 5: Increasing the Number of Blacks, Coloureds and Asians in Management and Supervisory Positions.

Each Signator of the Statement of Principles will proceed immediately to:

- Identify, actively recruit, train and develop a sufficient and significant number of Blacks, Coloureds and Asians to assure that as quickly as possible there will be appropriate representations of Blacks, Coloureds and Asians in the management group of each company at all levels of operations.

- Establish management development programs for Blacks, Coloureds and Asians, as needed, and improve existing programs and facilities for developing management skills of Blacks, Coloureds and Asians.

Continued on next page

Exhibit 8 — continued

- Identify and channel high management potential Blacks, Coloured and Asian employees into management development programs.

- **Work to get Blacks, Coloureds and Asians into senior management.**

Principle 6: Improving the Quality of Employees' Lives Outside the Work Environment in Such Areas as Housing, Transportation, Schooling, Recreation, and Health Facilities.

Each Signator of the Statement of Principles will proceed immediately to:

- Evaluate existing and/or develop programs, as appropriate, to address the specific needs of Black, Coloured and Asian employees in the areas of housing, health care, transportation and recreation.

- Evaluate methods for utilizing existing, expanded or newly established in-house medical facilities or other medical programs to improve medical care for all Black, Coloured and Asian employees and their dependents.

- Participate in the development of programs that address the educational needs of employees, their dependents, and the local community. Both individual and collective programs should be considered, in addition to technical education, including such activities as literacy education, business training, direct assistance to local schools. contributions and scholarships.

- **Offer AIDS and family planning education and tuberculosis examinations to all employees.**

- Acquaint white supervisors and managers with Black, Coloured and Asian living conditions.

- Increase utilization of and assist in the development of Black, Coloured and Asian owned and operated business enterprises including distributors, suppliers of goods and services, and manufacturers.

- **Implement community welfare programs identified by black, Coloured and Asian grass roots organizations. (added)**

- **Assist community development by lending accountants and managers to service agencies, community groups and government, and help train their personnel.**

- **Enhance conflict mediation skills of Blacks, Coloureds and Asians.**

- **Provide legal education, help to establish land tenure rights in rural areas, provide legal assistance necessary in setting up non-profit housing trusts and small business cooperatives, and develop a Bill of Rights society.**

- **Provide career guidance to students at Black, Coloured and Asian primary and secondary schools.**

Principle 7: Working to Eliminate Customs and Practices Which Impede Social, Economic and Political Justice.

Each Signatory of the Statement of Principles will proceed immediately to:

- Press for a single education system common to all races.

Continued on next page

Exhibit 8 — continued

- Use influence and support the unrestricted rights of Black businesses to locate in the urban areas of the nation.

- Influence other companies in South Africa to follow the standards of equal rights principles.

- Support the freedom of mobility of Black workers, including those from so-called independent homelands, to seek employment opportunities wherever they exist and make possible provisions for adequate housing for families of employees within the proximity of workers' employment.

- Use financial and legal resources to assist Blacks, Coloureds and Asians in their efforts to achieve equal access to all health facilities, educational institutions, transportation, housing, beaches, parks and all other accommodations normally reserved for Whites.

- Oppose adherence to all apartheid practices and customs.

- Support the ending of all apartheid practices and customs.

- Support full and equal participation of Blacks, Coloureds and Asians in the political process.

Principle 8: **Increase the involvement of Blacks, Coloureds and Asians in the development and execution of the Principles Program so that their participation can contribute to their personal development.**

Each Signator of the Statement of Principles will proceed immediately to:

- **Involve Black, Coloured and Asian employees who have contact with grass roots organizations in their communities.**

- **Enable Black, Coloured and Asian employees to have a meaningful role in the selection of organizations and projects and to receive help and financial support.**

- **Involve Black, Coloured and Asian employees directly in providing help to others in the community.**

reach programs." Seen in this light, the "amplification" broke no new ground and did not constitute a substantively new amplification of the Principles.

Although the sixth amplification would have placed no new demands on the companies and reflected, instead, what they were already required to do, it was unclear to the companies whether further amplification of the Principles was either appropriate or necessary. Accordingly, at its 24 September 1991 meeting, ISU's board approved Bill Donovan's suggestion to table consideration of the proposed amplification until the next meeting. At that meeting, held on 3 December 1991, the ISU board rejected any further change in the Principles, thus leaving the fifth amplification in place.

APPENDIX 8.1

SULLIVAN: PHASE 3
THE CONCEPT

The initiative of the Sullivan code has effectively demonstrated the capacity of U.S. owned enterprise in South Africa to establish economically sound and progressive business practices, especially with regard to working conditions, employee amenities, benefits, the advancement of less-privileged employees and the recognition of worker associations and the exercise of social responsibility through projects launched in black communities. There is a little doubt that this record of achievement will be maintained.

In recent times, however, a manifest need has arisen for employer bodies, including the Sullivan signatories to interact even more positively with the socio-economic and political environment in the promotion of reform in South African society. This need is reflected in the more open and forceful expression of aspirations for change among black communities and in heightened pressure on South Africa from legislative and other institutions in the United States and elsewhere. Furthermore, a response to this need is facilitated by a substantially greater readiness on the part of the South African Government to consider and, at least at some levels, to institute policies of reform aimed at lessening economic, social, and political inequality among groups in the society. The Sullivan signatories, having substantially achieved the goals established in the code as formulated hitherto, are therefore faced with a need, an opportunity and a challenge to respond to the new situation, with reasonable expectations of significant results.

This new phase of constructive involvement in change should embody the following principles:

1. The new initiative should be based fully on local South African needs and criteria for action and should be geared to opportunities for change and reform that are apparent in a local analysis of the situation.

2. The formulation of project and program objectives should wherever possible be undertaken in cooperation with black people and their representative organizations which are able to interpret the aspirations and needs in black communities and assist in evaluating results.

3. Full account should be taken of other initiatives for change, and very importantly those initiated by other private sector bodies such as the Urban Foundation and the major employer associations in order to seek to compliment the overall effort and avoid unnecessary duplication.

4. Individual initiatives by signatory firms are commendable in their own right and should continue, but should be accompanied by joint initiatives and, in some cases, by collective cooperation with other private sector agencies, so as to generate the benefits of synergy and a deepened pool of resources.

5. The goals of the new initiative should generally be directed at facilitating socio-economic or political change which independent and critical but responsible observers would accept as significant. Where possible, the programs should simultaneously be aimed at improving the organizational effectiveness of participating firms and the operating environment of business.

6. Included in the scope of (5) above is a wide range of important priority areas, including black education, housing, community facilities, key social services, training, black advancement, wage reform, employment growth, the elimination of segregation in and outside of industry and political-constitutional development. These varied possibilities

cannot all be addressed simultaneously and, therefore, the new initiative should include at its outset a careful rigorous exercise to determine a small number of key priorities within which efforts can be concentrated in order to achieve greatest effect.

7. At least one of the priority areas selected should be a major overarching issue which, if significant change can be encouraged, is likely to constitute an important index of change in the society as a whole, and which as such will facilitate many more consequent changes at other levels. This inevitably means that a major political issue will have to be addressed, possibly involving a well-organized, top-level forum in which key political decision-makers can be involved.

8. In the choice of programs all the specific objectives should be valuable in their own right, but should simultaneously contain multiplier effects so that the improvements achieved will of their own volition generate wider or continuing effects. Programs would, where possible, also contain one or more specific projects which will generate some clear-cut early success in order to have a motivational effect on the rest of the program.

9. The new initiative should not proceed until it can be established by careful assessment that substantial endorsement and commitment from the Sullivan Signatories will be forthcoming.

10. The new initiative should proceed under the guidance of a committee which includes representation of participating companies, black people, relevant participation form the United States and selected professional consultants.

This outline of a new approach should be discussed as widely as possible within the Signatory group, with a view to its refinement for acceptance as basic enabling concept.

APPENDIX 8.2

AMCHAM "FOCUS": CAMPAIGN OUTLINE

OBJECTIVE

- To communicate Amcham's concerns over the South African situation.
- To focus on key positives of the reform processes.
- To be seen to be prepared to stand up and be counted.

ADVERTISING STRATEGY

- Launch programme of regular press advertisements each focusing on issues of current relevance and concern - both positive and negative.
- Theme: "Amcham Focus".
- Media: Full page, black and white spaces in newspapers and magazines.
- Timing: May through December 1986.

PR STRATEGY

- Familiarize US Corporate Council with all aspects of campaign.
- Give advance notice to leading SA business people vis Raymond Ackerman, Chris Ball, Tony Bloom, Fred du Plessis, Gavin Relly, et al.
- Preview campaign strategy with influential Black interests via meetings with, for example: Chris Dhlamina of COSATU, Bishop Desmond Tutu, Chief Minister Buthelezi, and officers of NAFCOC.
- Write to State President and each Cabinet Minister (See Exhibit 3).
- Brief Dr. Mark Burger (an Assistant Cabinet Minister in Pretoria) on intentions of Amcham and campaign.
- Hold press conference for local and overseas press prior to break of campaign. This will call for:
  a) Full press kits containing full rationale.
  b) Nomination of Spokespersons: eg. An American member of the Board of Amcham and Roger Crawford of J and J.
    - These gentlemen would need to be prepared to appear on television.
    - Fully rehearsed.
    - They would also need to be available.

All inquiries to participating member companies would have to be directed to the appointed spokespersons to avoid contradiction or confusion.

APPENDIX 8.3

1st May, 1986
From Amcham to the Cabinet Ministers

Dear Sir,

I write this letter to you on behalf of the member companies of the American Chamber of Commerce in South Africa. We want to share with you the concerns we have about this country and the steps envisaged that, in our view, will lead to a peaceful and worthwhile future for all South Africans.

It is because of these concerns that Amcham is about to embark upon a campaign of communication which focuses on the pressing issues and challenges that face us all. We do this as responsible corporate citizens with a stake in South Africa, with a commitment to its peoples and out of an urgent desire to help identify practical solutions to the problems that beset our society. Put another way, we feel compelled to make a constructively challenging contribution to the process of reform and power-sharing that the State President and the Cabinet have so rightly initiated.

Accordingly, you will shortly be seeing in the press the start of an advertising programme which focuses on these issues and the reform process form the South African experience, involvement and perspectives of Amcham and its member companies. The intention is to communicate, to highlight core issue and, importantly, to help combat the intensifying and adverse dis-investment pressures that we are subjected to back here in South Africa and overseas. Such are these pressures that it is becoming increasingly difficult to run our businesses properly and. moreover, to convincingly justify our existence in South Africa.

A more detailed preview of our campaign plans and intentions have been communicated to Dr. Mark Burger in view of his special role in the area of dis-investment. No doubt Dr. Burger will be conveying such details along the appropriate channels. Nevertheless we thought we should put you in the picture by way of this letter prior to the appearance of our campaign. We should be glad to discuss any aspect of it now or at any time convenient in the future.

Yours sincerely,

O. F. C. LUBKE
PRESIDENT
AMCHAM

ENDNOTES

1   Leon H. Sullivan, press conference, National Press Club, Washington, DC, 31 October 1985.
2   Reid Weedon, "Report on the Signatory Companies to the Sullivan Principles," No. 8 (Cambridge, MA: Arthur D. Little, 1984).
3   Roger Crawford (director, human resources, Johnson & Johnson Ltd.), letter to E. N. Brandt (senior counselor, public affairs, Dow Chemical Company), 21 August 1985.

Chapter 9

European and Other Codes of Conduct for the Companies Operating in South Africa

Both in South Africa and the United States, the Sullivan Principles were the most widely known and recognized code of international conduct. The Principles were not, however, the only code of conduct adopted by companies in South Africa. A number of countries and regions, industry groups, and even individual companies had promulgated their own codes, all of which had some generic, or boilerplate, standards or principles dealing with race-based discrimination in the workplace (equal opportunity, upward mobility, and so on).

These other, non-Sullivan codes varied significantly from one to another, however, and also from the Sullivan Principles, in their details concerning acceptable and proscribed practices. The Principles were, moreover, perhaps the most rigorous in their requirements of any of the codes, not only in the scope of the activities covered, but also—and especially—in the detailed requirements concerning performance, verification, and public reporting. For example, even though the Sullivan Principles do not differ significantly in length from the other codes, the Principles required that an annual report be submitted by each signatory company; the 1980 report form included forty-three questions covering some eighteen pages, with each company being graded on the basis of their answers. Under the discussion of "Remuneration" below, the questions covering that area in the 1980 report form are reproduced to provide the reader a concrete sense of the scope of, and of companies' accountability under, the Sullivan Principles.

Most of the non-Sullivan codes emphasized voluntary compliance and were confined to statements of lofty principles. The underlying assumption was that the participating companies were responsible corporate citizens and that their executives had high moral standards and would not condone such unethical practices as race-based discrimination. Voluntary compliance was therefore seen as the best way to engender proactive cooperation and maximum efforts by the corporations involved. There was nonetheless a contradiction in these codes, a contradiction that the companies were either unaware of or unwilling to accept. To wit, if these companies were, indeed, socially responsible and were led by senior managers who could be counted on ethically to do the right thing, then why should these companies be so adamant in refusing to have their actions validated or verified by independent outside monitors? There was no question that the external, sociopolitical environment in South Africa was hostile toward, and suspicious of, both foreign multinational corporations and large, White-controlled South African companies. Therefore, it would have been in the best interests of these companies and their industries to gain public trust and credibility by having their actions monitored and verified by independent, outside organizations or agencies.

Non–United States companies presented a variety of explanations for not joining the Principles program. There was the natural jealousy of, and reaction against, the program's being "Made in the USA." Companies from different countries and industries felt that the Sullivan Principles were not suited to "their" particular needs. The Principles were too parochial and were written with a bias toward the issues that were important in a United States context. There was also a feeling that companies from different countries and industries could better control the process of compliance if it was handled by each particular group and not by organizations or agencies based in the United States. Admittedly, although most companies felt that the Sullivan Principles went too far and, through the amplifications, were unpredictable in their demands, there were also some companies and countries that felt that the Principles did not go far enough. Nonetheless, from the very start, the most controversial areas of disagreement concerned the issues of independent monitoring, verification, and public disclosure.

It is well nigh impossible to undertake a systematic analysis of all the codes that were promulgated by different companies, industries, and countries. There were far too many, and not all of them equally important or even taken seriously by their own sponsors. Consequently, in this chapter we analyze a cross-section of the codes that were followed by foreign multinational corporations, as well by as some of the largest South African companies, during the height of the anti-apartheid campaigns in South Africa and other parts of the world. The codes are a representative sample in that they illustrate the full range of perspectives on the rights and obligations of the different constituencies and stakeholders who would be affected by the companies' operations. The eight codes we analyze are (with the date of enactment and source of origin in parentheses):

EEC Code of Conduct Regarding South Africa (1977; government)

[British] Code of Conduct for Companies with Interests in South Africa (1974 [supplanted in 1977 by Britain's agreement to follow the EEC code]; government)

Administration and Observance of the Code of Conduct Concerning the Employment Practices of Canadian Companies Operating in South Africa (1986; government)

Australian Code of Conduct (1987; government)

Code of Practices of the Federation of Swedish Industries (1977; International Council of Swedish Industries)

United States Department of State's Principles (1986; government)

Urban Foundation and South African Employers' Consultative Committee on Labor Affairs (SACCOLA), Code of Employment Practice, South Africa (1978; Urban Foundation and SACCOLA)

Barlow Rand Group Code of Employment Practice, South Africa (1978; Barlow Rand Group)

Our analysis of these codes, the complete texts of which appear in appendix 9.1, has been divided into two broad categories: (1) the nature, extent, and scope of various subjects covered in different codes; and (2) the extent to which different codes required independent monitoring, evaluation, and verification of companies' performance under the code (with additional attention to the question of public dissemination of information on companies' performance).

1. SCOPE OF COVERAGE

The primary issues covered in these codes were segregation, remuneration, training, development, social responsibility, trade unions, migratory labor, and efforts to eliminate apartheid. An analysis of the codes indicates that they may well have used the Sullivan Principles as a benchmark; the categories used by the codes paralleled those of the Principles. The differences, when present, were largely in the intensity and breadth of coverage of various issues. Moreover, some topics in the Sullivan Principles were sometimes omitted altogether from the other codes.

Despite their many similarities, the Sullivan Principles differed significantly from the other eight codes in two important areas, both of which carried the scope of the Principles beyond the workplace. The first such area concerned the Principles' requirement that signatory companies take action in the political arena—in opposition to the government and toward the elimination of apartheid. None of the eight codes addressed these issues at all. To be sure, the requirement for political activism was incorporated into the Principles rather late in the game (fourth amplification, November 1984), and one might also argue that most of the so-called political activism by the signatory companies was, at best, symbolic—no more than a public relations campaign that included paid advertising in the mass media. Moreover, as we noted in chapter 8, companies were concerned that they not do anything to expose themselves to economic punishment or retaliation by the South African government, especially through the loss of government contracts. Nevertheless, the signatory companies did eventually take a political stand, which is something other companies (and other codes) steadfastly refused to do. Instead, nonsignatory companies resorted to the traditional and widely held belief among the multinational corporations that they should not become involved in the internal, political affairs of a host country.

We should note that such noninterference remains the prevailing dogma among multinational corporations when faced, for example, with human rights issues in countries as diverse as China, Indonesia, Nigeria, and Turkey, to name a few. In standing by this policy, the MNCs are, indeed, not alone. In this new world of global trade and capital flows, even the most powerful among the industrially advanced democratic countries express in muted terms their sense of outrage against human rights violations, thereby balancing their moral indignation against the pressing need of poorer countries to develop economically. The hope is, too, that democratic reforms will emerge in due course with economic growth. Thus, although the United States continues to publish its annual list of countries—for example, China—that have a poor record on human rights, it also commonly exempts such countries from economic sanctions by granting them *most favored nation* (MFN) status for trading with the United States.

The second issue of major difference between the Sullivan Principles and the eight other codes was both less controversial than the requirement for political action and more pervasive in its impact on the South Africa's Blacks. The Sullivan Principles required signatory companies not only to eliminate all forms of discrimination in the workplace, but to endeavor to improve the social infrastructure for Blacks. A central element of this requirement was to oppose the influx control laws, which disrupted the lives of Black families by preventing Black workers from living together with their wives and children (see chapter 8). In addition, signatory companies were evaluated and given higher approval ratings for their work in support of community groups and of agencies providing social services in Black communities. In contrast, to the extent that the other codes focused on conditions beyond the workplace, it was only with regard to the well-being of a company's own workers and their families.

Ironically, it is in this area of social concerns that we most strongly disagree with the thrust of the Principles program. Though initially incorporated into the Principles only through the second amplification in May 1979, improving the social milieu of Blacks was—from the outset—one of the central building blocks of the Principles program. As we have argued in other parts of the book, however, the signatory companies devoted far too many resources to projects aimed at community building—projects that ultimately had little impact just because of the enormity of the task. We believe, moreover, that the United States companies were well aware that their interventions in this area did little to ameliorate the larger, community-based problems. The companies nonetheless continued to pursue these social interventions in order to appease their critics in the United States and to divert attention from their less than stellar progress in areas where the companies had much more control and much better prospects for success; for example, the training of Blacks and their promotion into the supervisory and managerial ranks, and the development of Black economic enterprises through targeted purchasing programs.

In the following sections we provide a comparative analysis of the Sullivan Principles (and amplifications) and the other eight codes. The analysis is by no means exhaustive; it is intended, instead, to provide an overview of how the different codes approached various problem areas and the relative emphasis they gave to each area. Table 9 presents a summary of the topics covered in the eight codes and how they compared to the Sullivan Principles. The shaded areas denote the topics that were similar to those covered in the Principles, whereas the blank areas denote topics that were covered in the Principles but not present in the other codes.

1.1   Segregation (Table 10)

The Sullivan Principles were much stronger than the other codes in addressing segregation; for example, the Principles state that "each Signator will proceed to abolish segregation." Most of the other codes employ less-demanding language. For example, the EEC code stated that "companies should abolish segregation so far as it lays within their own companies," and the Australian code, that "Except where the law of South Africa otherwise requires, companies should integrate . . . ."

Table 9. General Comparison of Sullivan Principles with Other Codes of Conduct for Doing Business in South Africa

	Segregation	Remuneration	Training	Development	Social responsibility	Trade unions	Migratory labor
European Econ. Community	■	■	■	■ *	■	■	■ *
United Kingdom	■	■	■	■	■	■	■
Sweden		■	■	■		■	
Canada	■	■	■		■	■	■
Australia	■	■	■	■	■	■	
U.S. State Department	■	■		■	■	■	
Urban Foundation/SACCOLA	■	■	■	■	■	■	
Barlow Rand Group	■	■	■	■	■	■	

* These two areas were not included in the original 1977 EEC Code but were added to the 1985 version.

Table 10. Summary of Codes: Segregation

Code	Requirements
European Economic Community	Everything possible to be done to desegregate in the factory.
United Kingdom	Aim at nonsegregation, but duplication of facilities if separation required by law.
Sweden	
Canada	Where segregation not completely achieved, employers should do everything possible to abolish any practice of segregation.
Australia	Except when South African law otherwise requires, companies should integrate the workplace, canteen, and recreational, educational, training, and other company-provided facilities.
U.S. State Department	Desegregating the races in each employment facility.
Urban Foundation/SACCOLA	Removal of discrimination in all aspects of employment.
Barlow Rand Group	Work areas to be fully integrated.

1.2 Employment Practices (Table 11)

There was a consensus among the codes on the concept of "equal pay for equal work," a requirement that was first enunciated by the Sullivan Principles. However, the Principles were more forceful in that they required each company to "proceed immediately" to implement the requirement. In contrast, the EEC code set forth the principle of equal pay as simply an abstract moral goal to which no sense of urgency was attached: "The principle of equal opportunities for all employees *ought* to be fully respected . . . and wages *should* be based on a qualitative job evaluation. The same pay scales *should* be applied to the same jobs" (emphasis added).

1.3 Remuneration (Table 12)

The EEC code specifically referred to the cost-of-living data collected and analyzed by the University of South Africa (UNISA), and advocated a minimum wage at the Supplemental Living Level (SLL) for a family of average size (specified as five or six persons). The previous text of the same code also mentioned that "the minimum wage should exceed by at least 50% the minimum living level (MLL) required to satisfy the basic needs of an employee and his family."

Like the EEC code, the Canadian code referred to the UNISA data on the cost of living, with an additional reference to the University of Port Elizabeth's (UPE) Household Subsistence Level (HSL). The code urged companies to "introduce minimum wages which substantially exceed this level."

Table 11. Summary of Codes: Employment Practices

Code	Requirements
European Economic Community	Equal and fair employment practices for all employees.
United Kingdom	Fringe benefits for Blacks. No discrimination in any sphere at work including promotion.
Sweden	Manufacturing should be organized, equipped and managed so that Africans find wider opportunities so as to enter more qualified jobs and consequently obtain higher wages.
Canada	Companies should ensure supervisory and management jobs and those requiring high technical qualifications are open to their Black employees.
Australia	There should be equal application of policies and practices to all employees.
U.S. State Department	Providing equal employment opportunity for all employees without regard to race or ethnic origin.
Urban Foundation/SACCOLA	No discrimination based on race or color in job advancement and fringe benefits
Barlow Rand Group	People will be appointed and promoted solely on the basis of their ability to meet the requirements of the post to be filled.

The Australian code also considered remuneration based on UNISA's Minimum Living Level and UPE's HSL as "inadequate," and aimed at a base payment for staff on entry to employment "no lower than the figure of the UNISA's Supplemented Living Level (SLL) or UPE's Household Effective Level (HEL) for the geographic area where the staff are employed."

Although the EEC, Canadian, and Australian codes had recommendations for remuneration that were similar to that of the Sullivan Principles, a key difference was that the companies were specifically accountable under the Principles but not under the other codes. The Statement of Principles Progress Report submitted every year by each company had six questions concerning remuneration. Each signatory company was required to answer these questions and was awarded points on the basis of their answers (which, in turn, entered into the calculation of each company's rating for the year). Exhibit 9 reproduces the six questions from the 1980 Sullivan Report Form and also includes some typical responses from the 1980s.

Table 12. Summary of Codes: Remuneration

Code	Requirements
European Economic Community	The minimum wage should initially exceed by at least 50 percent the minimum level required to satisfy the basic needs of an employee and his family.
British Code of Practice	Fair wages above Poverty Datum Line and equal pay for equal work. Reduce wage gap.
Sweden	Wage structures should follow the principle of job evaluation, regardless of race, and should be regularly reviewed.
Canadian	Companies should formulate specific guidelines aimed at improving their terms of employment and at implementing the principle of "equal pay for equal work."
Australian	Companies should apply the principle of equal pay for equal work, regardless of race.
U.S. State Department	Assuring that the system is applied to all employees without regard to race or ethnic origin. Establishing a minimum wage and salary structure.
Urban Foundation/SACCOLA	Elimination of discrimination based on race or color.
Barlow Rand Group	At all levels the salaries and wages paid to employees will be competitive in relation to "going rates" in the areas in which the companies of the group operates.

Exhibit 9. Selection from Sullivan Report for Remuneration (1980)

21. Does your pay system pay Blacks, Coloreds, and Asians on the same pay scale as Whites for the same work for the same period of time?

    If "No" to Q. 21:

    21a. What are the reasons for an unequal pay system?   *(Write in)*

_____

22. Please describe in which manner your company establishes that you are indeed paying equally for equal work.

    (Write in) <u>All jobs have been analyzed, evaluated and graded; pay rates are based on those grades.</u>

23. Merely for the purpose of establishing a reasonable comparison, we ask you to refer to the data established early in 1980 either by the Bureau of Market Research, UNISA, or by the Institute for Planning Research, Port Elizabeth. Please select the city/town which is closest to your company's major location(s) and indicate it below, along with the amount of the minimum living level (MLL) or Household Subsistence Level (HSL) established for a family of 5 or 6.

Continued on next page

Exhibit 9—continued

Question 23		Question 24	
City/ Town selected from UNISA or PE forms	Monthly MLL or HSL for Family of 5 or 6	Percent by which your base entry pay exceeds this MLL	Number of Employees currently earning this entry level pay
Johannesburg R 167.73		46% 12	
Rustenburg (Brits) R 148.72		64% 21	

24. By what percent does your current entry level pay surpass the MLL established by UNISA or the HSL established by the University of Port Elizabeth?

Figures used are those produced by UNISA as at end February, 1980.

Please indicate above and write in the column to the right the number of people currently receiving your entry level pay.

Note that the Principles state that your entry level pay needs to be substantially above the minimum.

25. Use Supplement C to establish the average pay increase your employees received in the past twelve months and in the twelve months prior to that period, or, if the method does not appear suitable under your company's circumstances, please define the method used for arriving at these percentages. Note that supplement C is merely a worksheet which need not be submitted with your report.

	Black	White	Colored	Asians
Average pay increase July 1979–June 1980	21.6%	10.1%	26.4%	12.2%
Average pay increase July 1978–June 1979	13.1%	17.3%	27.3%	16.4%

26. What is the amount of your total payroll, including all incentives, bonuses, etc., for all your employees for the period of July, 1979 through June, 1980?

Total Payroll
Past 12 months   R 2,710,913
$3,225,986
Exchange rate: $1.19 = 1 Rand

1.4   Training (Table 13)

The Sullivan Principles envisioned training as a means to large-scale Black advancement. This same rationale was also presented in a number of our other eight representative codes. For example, the Australian code stated that "Company training and development programs should be implemented," and the Barlow Rand Group code, that "Companies will undertake the training and development of employees to improve their work performance and prepare for levels of responsibility commensurate with their ability."

The Urban Foundation code made reference to "Training programs to achieve advancement in technical, administrative, and managerial positions."

Table 13. Summary of Codes: Training

Code	Training
European Economic Community	Development of training programs for Blacks.
United Kingdom	Internal or external training, including artisan skills. Stop usage of White immigrant labor.
Sweden	It is recommended that programs cover the following areas: in-company training; industry-sponsored training centers, etc.; and high school and university-level education.
Canada	Employers should draw up an appropriate range of training schemes of a suitable standard to provide training for their black employees.
Australia	Company training and development programs should be implemented to facilitate equality of employment opportunities at all levels of the company on the same basis and selection criteria.
U.S. State Department	
Urban Foundation/SACCOLA	Training programs or facilities to improve productivity or skills to achieve advancement in technical, administrative, and managerial positions.
Barlow Rand Group	Companies will undertake the training and development of employees to improve their work performance and prepare for levels of responsibility commensurate with their abilities.

1.5   Career Development (Table 14)

The Canadian code was unique (in our sample) in quantifying a goal for the advancement of non-White employees: "The aim should be to fill fifty percent of all supervisory and management positions with employees other than those designated as white persons within a period of time which companies should clearly specify in their employment plans and development programs." The other codes were not specific in their requirements for developing human resources.

1.6   Social Responsibility (Table 15)

The Sullivan Principles required signatories to "improve the quality of employee's lives outside of the work environment." This statement was mirrored in three other codes: those of the State Department, the Australian government, and the Barlow Rand Group. This last code—the only private

Table 14. Summary of the Codes: Career Development

Code	Requirements
European Economic Community	Companies should ensure that supervisory and management jobs and those requiring high technical qualifications are open to their black African employees.*
United Kingdom	Encouragement of training to develop full potential, and nonracial promotion policy.
Sweden	Manufacturing should be organized, equipped, and managed so that Africans find wider opportunities so as to enter more qualified jobs and consequently obtain higher wages.
Canada	The aim should be to fill 50% of all supervisory and management positions with employees other than those designated as White persons within a period of time that the companies should clearly specify.
Australia	Companies should appoint and promote personnel solely on the basis of their qualifications and ability.
U.S. State Department	Increasing by appropriate means the number of persons in managerial, supervisory, administrative, clerical, and technical jobs who are disadvantaged by the apartheid system.
Urban Foundation/SACCOLA	No discrimination in selection, employment, advancement, or promotion of all employees.
Barlow Rand Group	Technical, supervisory, and management training will be provided both from the group's resources and by appropriate outside agencies.

* This provision was not included original EEC code (1977) but was added in the 1985 version.

Table 15. Summary of the Codes: Social Responsibility

Code	Requirements
European Economic Community	Improvement of employees' living conditions at home.
United Kingdom	Fringe benefits to aid home purchase, education, and food.
Sweden	
Canada	Companies should concern themselves with the living conditions of their Black employees and families.
Australia	Companies should concern themselves with the quality of life of their employees and their families.
U.S. State Department	Implementing fair labor practices by recognizing the right to all employees to self-organization and to form, join or assist labor organization.
Urban Foundation/SACCOLA	Taking reasonable steps to improve the quality of employees' lives outside the work environment.
Barlow Rand Group	Companies will concern themselves with the quality of life of employees both at work and outside.

code under review in this chapter—disclosed the scope of the company's corporate responsibility through multiple, albeit nonspecific, references such as "The C.S. Barlow Foundation will continue to provide financial support for education and technical education" and, in reference to compensation and company standards, "The group will neither acquire nor establish any business that depends, for an acceptable financial return, on wages and conditions of service, which are lower than group standards."

1.7   Trade Unions (Table 16)

The Sullivan Principles added trade union rights in the second amplification, stating that Blacks have the right to form, or belong to, registered or unregistered trade unions. The other codes in our sample discussed the issue in more detail. The Urban Foundation code, for example, stated that "Recognition of basic rights of workers of freedom of association, collective negotiation, lawful strikes and protection against victimization."

Table 16. Summary of the Codes: Trade Unions

Code	Requirements
European Economic Community	Companies must recognize the right of the workers to be represented by trade unions.
United Kingdom	Encourage lawful collective bargaining with Blacks. Recognize Black unions where they exist.
Sweden	Swedish industry regards organized labor as a natural feature of industrial life.
Canada	Companies should pay particular attention to Black trade unions and ensure that Black employees are free to form or join the trade union of their choice.
Australia	Employees should be allowed the free choice of membership in representation by industrial organizations.
U.S. State Department	Implementing fair labor practices by recognizing the right of all employees, regardless of racial or other distinctions, to self-organization and to form, join or assist labor organizations, freely and without penalty or reprisal, and recognizing the right to refrain from such activity.
Urban Foundation/SACCOLA	Recognition of basic rights of workers of freedom of association, collective negotiation, lawful strikes and protection against victimization.
Barlow Rand Group	There should be no differences in the rights available to the various races and therefore we would like to see negotiations at industry or national level between employers' organizations and multi-racial unions, rather than Black unions.

1.8   Migratory Labor (Table 17)

The EEC code defined the system of migrant labor as an instrument of apartheid that caused grave social and family problems, and asked companies to ensure "freedom of movement for black African workers and to give them the opportunity to lead a family life." Similarly, the Sullivan Principles (under the heading "employee's care outside the work environment") required the companies to "support changes in influx control laws to provide for the right of Black migrant workers to normal family life."

Both the British and Canadian codes stressed the importance of having families reside together, and the former explicitly referred to the need to provide legal aid to pass offenders.

2.   ENFORCEMENT, VERIFICATION, AND PUBLIC DISCLOSURE (TABLE 18)

The major difference between the Sullivan Principles and the other South African codes was in their accountability structures. As discussed in earlier chapters, the Sullivan Principles imposed mandatory enforcement. Under the majority of the other codes, accountability was lax, and reporting was voluntary. Consider, for example, the following excerpt from the procedure section of the EEC code (as revised in 1985):

Criteria for implementation:

A detailed and fully documented report should be prepared by all companies, which have a controlling interest in a South African company employing black workers.

In other companies where there are European interests, whether significant or not, the European shareholders should make every effort to ensure that the principles of this Code are implemented and that a report is produced.[1]

Content analysis of the language used throughout the text of the EEC code (see appendix 9.1) reveals its voluntary character; for example, "companies *should* ensure," "*should* pay," *should* be prepared," *should* do everything possible" (emphasis added). This type of language is weak and in sharp contrast to that of the Sullivan Principles, where every heading was preceded with "each signatory will proceed immediately to . . ." Thus, the EEC code was, in essence, a recommendation; it resulted in a situation where "the Governments are dependent on the voluntary co-operation of the business community."[2]

Table 17. Summary of Codes: Migratory Labor

Code	Requirements
European Economic Community	Employers have the social responsibility to contribute towards ensuring freedom of movement for Black African workers and giving them the opportunity to lead a family life.*
United Kingdom	Choose locations that permit family-based labor. Legal aid for pass offenders.
Sweden	
Canada	Employers have the social responsibility to contribute towards ensuring freedom of movement for Black workers and giving them the opportunity to lead a family life.
Australia	
U.S. State Department	
Urban Foundation/SACCOLA	
Barlow Rand Group	

* This provision was not included in the original EEC code (1977) but was added in the 1985 revision.

Table 18. Summary of Codes: Requirements Concerning Enforcement, Verification, and Public Disclosure

Code	Enforcement	Verification	Public Disclosure
European Economic Community	Voluntary	National authorities of the country of origin	Mandatory for annual, national, joint reports; recommended public disclosure for companies' reports[a]
United Kingdom[b]	Voluntary	Dep't of Trade	Mandatory
Sweden	Voluntary	Nonspecified	Nonspecified
Canada	Voluntary	Independent administrator	Voluntary
Australia	Voluntary	Independent administrator	Voluntary
U.S. State Department	Mandatory[c]	State Department annually	Annual report with Congress
Urban Foundation/ SACCOLA	Voluntary	Nonspecified	Nonspecified
Barlow Rand Group	Company-sponsored	Nonspecified	Nonspecified

[a] The 1985 revision of the EEC code required that all company and national reports be made public, following the British government and companies' practice.
[b] The British Code of Practice was established in 1974 and was in effect until 1977, when UK adopted the EEC code.
[c] Reporting is mandatory only in order to qualify for U.S. government export assistance.

Soon after the completion of the EEC code's 1985 revision, its voluntary character was defended by B. J. Everett of the United Kingdom's Department of Trade and Industry. He stated: "We believe that the code's credibility depends on a high level of voluntary co-operation and compliance with code standards."[3] The lack of adequate monitoring mechanisms, however, undermined the code's legitimacy in many quarters. Consider this account in the *New African* magazine of February 1979: "The West German firms have been very coy about revealing their progress, though. The giant IG Metal trade union requested information from them but it was refused; to date it seems they are also refusing to give information to the Federal government. What makes the West German subsidiaries' record particularly bad is that there is so little in the EEC code that is forbidden by law in South Africa—there is no law which prevents negotiations with Black trade unions, or prevents equal pay for equal work."[4]

As pointed out by Donald C. Huss of the General Motors European Advisory Group in a report dated 11 October 1977, "the [EEC] code has no legal status so its only value is through moral pressure on firms not respecting it." Furthermore, this same report, which covered the announcement of the EEC code, mentioned that the "nine foreign ministers agreed to study other ways of bringing pressure to South Africa such as a ban on new investments (French, British and German opposition prevented this from being included in the code), blocking of export credits, and a total embargo on the sale of arms."[5]

Although the majority of the South African codes had little in the way of accountability structures, there were some exceptions. The State Department's Principles, for example, required United States companies that owned or controlled South African entities having twenty-five or more employees to implement fair employment practices in order to qualify for United States government export assistance (see appendix 9.1). This code was quite similar to the Sullivan Principles except that the seventh principle—commonly considered the most difficult principle to implement in that it concerned efforts to eliminate laws and customs that impede social, economic, and political justice—was voluntary and not required under the State Department program. For this very reason, the State Department's Principles were not held in high regard by university endowments and pension funds, which discouraged companies from shifting their observance to them from the Sullivan Principles.

Under the British code, there was also some accountability. Unlike the governments of other European countries, the United Kingdom enforced the public disclosure of companies' reports. The specific provision under the reporting clause of the British code states:

In respect of the information requested under the United Kingdom Code of Practice, the then Secretary for Trade announced in the House of Commons on 12 December 1975 that the Government would look for publication of the detailed information only where the British company held 50 percent or more of the equity of the South African company. British companies with a minority shareholding (exceeding 10 per cent of the equity) were encouraged to publish information whenever possible.[6]

For the most part, however, the codes imposed little accountability. Consider the case of the Canadian code (see appendix 9.1). At the time of its sixth report, the Canadian government did not even rate the compliance of the reporting companies because of "the small number of companies reporting under the Code and the small number of non-white employees affected."[7]

Similarly disappointing was the case of the Australian code. Although its text (see appendix 9.1) made clear that "the Code of Conduct will be reviewed on an annual basis, by an independent and impartial Administrator," the provision for dealing with noncomplying businesses—a "notice to the Parliament"—was weak and of uncertain legal significance. Moreover, the administrator of the code released only two reports from 1985 to 1993, the first in March 1987 and the last in May 1989. In 1993 the Investor Responsibility Research Center stated the obvious: "This program now appears to be moribund."[8]

APPENDIX 9.1. CODES OF CONDUCT FOR INTERNATIONAL BUSINESS

1. The European Community Code of Conduct

2. The British Code of Conduct

3. Code of Practice of the Federation of Swedish Industries

4. The Canadian Code of Conduct

5. The Australian Code of Conduct

6. The U.S. State Department's Principles

7. The Urban Foundation & SACCOLA Code of Conduct

8. The Barlow Rand Group Code of Employment Practice

1. The European Community Code of Conduct

This Code is addressed to all companies from the European Community, which have subsidiaries, branches or representatives in South Africa.

The aim of the Code is to make some contribution towards abolishing apartheid. None of the provisions of this Code should be interpreted as leading to discrimination between the various racial communities in South Africa. The dispositions concerning black employees have the sole objective of putting these on an equal footing with the other employees.

1.   Relations within the undertaking

(a)   Companies should ensure that their employees irrespective of racial or other distinction are allowed to choose freely and without any hindrance the type of Organization to represent them.

(b)   Companies should pay particular attention to black trade unions and be prepared to recognize them.

(c)   Companies should be prepared to sign recognition agreements with representative black trade unions within the company and allow collective bargaining, including the signing of collective agreements, in accordance with internationally accepted labor standards.

Employers should regularly and unequivocally inform their employees that consultations and collective bargaining with organizations, which are freely elected and representative of employees are part of company policy.

(d)   Companies should do everything possible to inform their employees within the company of their social and trade union rights. Employers should make every effort to ensure that black African employees are free to form or join the trade union of their choice. Steps should be taken as a matter of course to allow trade union officials to explain to employees the aims of trade unions and the advantages of membership, to distribute trade union documentation and display trade union notices on the company's premises, to have reasonable time off to carry out their union duties without loss of pay and to organize meetings. Employers should encourage trade union members to take part in trade union training programs.

(d)   Companies should do everything to establish a climate of confidence in their relations with their employees and should in particular make available to them the text of the Code of Conduct of the European Communities and inform them, in an appropriate language and in places to which they normally have access, of what the company is doing to implement this Code.

(f)   In companies where works or liaison committees already operate, trade union officials should have representative status on these bodies if employees so wish. The existence of these types of committee should not prejudice the development or status of trade unions or of their representatives.

2.   Migrant labor

(a)   The policy of apartheid leads to the use of migrant labor, which robs the individual of the basic freedom to seek and obtain the job of his choice. It also causes grave social and family problems.

(b)   Employers have the social responsibility to contribute towards ensuring freedom of movement for black African workers and giving them the opportunity to lead a family life.

(c)   Employers should endeavor to alleviate the effects of existing regulations, in particular by facilitating the regular renewal of contracts of employment and making it easier for the families of employees to settle near their companies.

3.   Pay and wage structures

(a)   Companies should assume a special responsibility as regards the pay and conditions of employment of their black African employees. In this context, they should refer to the data of the University of South Africa (UNISA).

They should formulate specific guidelines aimed at improving their terms of employment. Pay based on the "supplemented living level" for an average-sized family must be considered as the absolute minimum necessary. *Nevertheless companies should make every effort to exceed this level when fixing wages. In their reports they should supply the required explanations and, in particular, give an account of their wage scales and the possibilities for progress in this context.

(b)   The principle of equal opportunities for all employees ought to be fully respected. The principle of "equal pay for equal work" means that all jobs should be open to any worker who possesses suitable qualifications, irrespective of racial other distinction, and that wages should be based on a qualitative job evaluation. The same pay scales should be applied to the same jobs.

*In this context it is to be recalled that the previous text of the Code mentioned that the minimum wage should exceed by at least 50% the minimum living level required to satisfy the basic needs of an employee and his family.

4.   Training and promotion of black employees

(a)   The principle of equal pay would, however, be meaningless if black African employees were kept in inferior jobs. Employers should therefore draw up an appropriate range of training schemes of a suitable standard to provide training for their black African employees and reduce the dependence of their companies on immigrant white labor.

(b)   Companies should ensure that supervisory and management jobs and those requiring high technical qualifications are open to their black African employees.

Companies should, if possible, organize occupational training programs for their black employees. Companies should, if possible, help their black employees to take advantage of other educational and occupational training programs outside their places of work. Where required companies should set up or use educational facilities to enable their black employees to benefit from more specialized training.

(c)   Companies should make every effort to eliminate in practice the de facto restrictions based on custom on apprenticeships for black employees. They should ensure that employees of different racial groups can take part in training programs without any form of segregation.

5.   Fringe benefits

(a)   In view of their social responsibilities, companies should concern themselves with the living conditions of their employees and their families.

(b)   For this purpose, company funds could be set aside to provide benefits over and above those currently provided according to South African legislation:

—   providing complete social protection schemes for employees and their families (health, accident and unemployment insurance and old age pensions);

—   ensuring that their employees and their families have the benefit of adequate medical care;

—   in the education of members of their families;

—   involving the accommodation of black African staff and their families, in particular by helping them to buy their own housing;

—   providing transport from home to work and back;

—   providing their employees with assistance in problems they encounter with the authorities over their movement from one place to another, their choice of residence and their employment;

—   providing leisure facilities.

(c)   Companies should support projects, which aim to improve the quality of life of the black communities from which they draw their staff.

6.   Desegregation at places of work

(a)   Employers should do everything possible to abolish any practice of segregation, notably at the workplace, in canteens, in education and training and in sports activities. They should also ensure equal working conditions for all their staff.

(b)   Along with the advancement of their black employees, companies should directly support inter-staff contacts, and help employees from different racial groups to get to know each other better and integrate more fully.

Companies should encourage sporting activities in which employees from different racial groups take part as mixed teams in mixed competitions.

7.   Encouragement of black businesses

As far as they are able, companies should, in the framework of their activities, encourage the setting up and expansion of black businesses by sub-contracting, providing assistance for their black employees to set up their own businesses and preferential, priority treatment in customer-supplier relations.

PROCEDURE

1.   Criteria for implementation

(a)   A detailed and fully documented report should be prepared by all companies, which have a controlling interest in a South African company employing black workers.

(b)   In other companies where there are European interests, whether significant or not, the European shareholders should make every effort to ensure that the principles of this Code are implemented and that a report is produced.

2.   Drafting of reports

(a)   Reports shall be drafted by companies according to the uniform criteria agreed by the European Community countries. These reports shall be sent either to Embassies in South Africa or directly to the national authorities of the country of origin and should be made public by the companies.

(b)   The reports shall cover the period from 1 July of the previous year to 30 June of the current year. They should be sent to the national authorities by the end of September. The authorities will then be responsible for drawing up national reports to be available by the end of March in the following year and submitted to the national parliaments. A summary report will be prepared by the Presidency in-Office of the countries of the Community and presented to the European Parliament and the Economic and Social Committee of the European Community before the summer recess. The national and joint reports will be public.

3.   Coordinating implementation of the Code.

The Member States will consult regularly on the implementation of this Code, in particular through their representatives in South Africa. To this effect, the latter will draw up an annual report which will be taken into account when the summary report is drafted. This annual report will also assess the impact of this Code of Conduct in the economic and social context of South Africa and in particular the views of the relevant trade union and employers' circles concerning its content and implementation.

2. The British Code of Conduct

Code of Conduct for Companies with Interests in South Africa:

Government Guidance to British Companies on the Code of Conduct Adopted by the Governments of the Nine Member States of the European Community on 20 September 1977

1.   At their meeting in Brussels on 20 September 1977 the Foreign Ministers of the Nine Member States of the European Community approved the text of a Code of Conduct for companies with interests in South Africa, which is at Annex 1.

2.   The Government urges United Kingdom companies with interests in South Africa to make every effort to promote the adoption of the policies and practices recommended in the Code of Conduct to the fullest possible extent. It is in the interests of companies themselves that they should maintain the best employment practices in South Africa and be seen to do so. Many United Kingdom companies have already demonstrated their commitment to this policy. In South Africa, and elsewhere, it remains Her Majesty's Government's policy that United Kingdom companies and their affiliates should act in accordance with the laws of the countries within which they operate. In urging adoption of the policies and practices recommended in the Code at Annex 1, including those in Section 1, the Government is not asking companies to act contrary to South African law. These policies and practices are in many respects already incorporated and recommended in other international codes. For example, the OECD

Guidelines for Multinational Enterprises, and the ILO Tripartite Declaration of Principles Concerning Multinational Enterprises and Social Policy. Whilst welcoming the
initiative taken by the Urban Foundation in Johannesburg in conjunction with
employers' organizations in South Africa to adopt an enlightened code of employment
practice, the Government emphasizes that it is the Code of Conduct of the Nine which it
commends for adoption by United kingdom companies.

3.   The new Code replaces the Code of Practice recommended by the Trade and Industry
      Sub-Committee of the House of Commons Select Committee on Expenditure in March
      1974 and subsequently accepted by the Government'.

4.   The new Code covers broadly the same aspects of employment practices in South
      Africa as were dealt with by the earlier Code of Practice but places greater emphasis on
      industrial relations and collective bargaining arrangements (see Section I of the new
      Code).

Reporting

5.   Section 7 of the Code states that parent companies should publish each year a detailed
      and fully documented report on the progress made in applying the Code, and that a
      copy of each report should be submitted to the national Government of the parent
      company concerned.

      [The preceding was presented in the House of Commons on 1 May 1974 by the
      Secretary of State for Trade, Hansard cols. 1156–57; Wages and Conditions of African
      workers Employed by British Firms in South Africa (Cmnd. 5845) published in
      December 1974.]

6.   In respect of the information requested under the United Kingdom Code of Practice, the
      then Secretary of State for Trade announced in the House of Commons on 12 December
      1975 that the Government would look for publication of the detailed information only
      where the British company held 50 percent or more of the equity of the South African
      company. British companies with a minority shareholding (exceeding 10 per cent of the
      equity) were encouraged to publish information whenever possible. As regards the
      request for reports in the new Code, the Government will expect publication of such
      reports in the United Kingdom and submission of a copy to the Government in all cases
      where a parent company holds 50 per cent or more of the equity of a South African
      company. As previously, United Kingdom companies with a minority shareholding will
      be expected to use their influence to seek to have the Code of Conduct put into effect,
      and to publish in the United Kingdom and to submit to Government as much
      information as possible on the policies and practices of their South African affiliates in
      respect of the areas covered in the Code.

7.   As under the earlier United Kingdom Code of Practice, the Government recognizes that
      the provision of detailed reports would not be appropriate where the South African
      affiliate concerned employs less than 20 black Africans, but parent companies are asked
      wherever possible at least to state publicly how many Africans they employ and
      whether their pay and conditions of employment are in line with the Code.

8.   Guidance on the format of reports for those companies to which the full reporting
      arrangements apply is given in Annex 3. The report should state the facts as at 30 June
      each year and should give an account of progress over the previous twelve months. The
      report should be published and a copy sent to the Government not later than 30
      September each year. The report need not form part of the United Kingdom parent
      company's Annual Report, but companies are asked to ensure that a reference to the

public availability of such reports is included in their Annual Report or Chairman's statement.

9. Companies are asked to provide reports relating to the new Code in the format recommended at Annex 3 for the twelve months ending 30 June 1978 onwards.

Explanatory material

10. From time to time the Department of Trade has issued explanatory material about the earlier Code of Practice, for example the booklet *Supplementary Guidance for United Kingdom Companies with Interests in South Africa* issued in January 1975 and the guidance note *Publication by Companies of Information on Employment Practices in South Africa* issued in December 1975. Up to date explanatory guidance relating to the new Code and superseding the earlier publications is provided in Annex 2.

ANNEX 1

1. Relations within the Undertaking

(A) Companies should ensure that all their employees irrespective of racial or other distinction are allowed to choose freely and without any hindrance the type of Organization to represent them.

(B) Employers should regularly and unequivocally inform their employees that consultations and collective bargaining with organizations, which are freely elected and representative of employees are part of company policy.

(C) Should Black African employees decide that their representative body should be in the form of a trade union, the company should accept this decision. Trade unions for Black Africans are not illegal, and companies are free to recognize them, and to negotiate and conclude agreements with them.

(D) Consequently, the companies should allow collective bargaining with organizations freely chosen by the workers to develop in accordance with internationally accepted principles.

(E) Employers should do everything possible to ensure that Black African employees are free to form or to join a trade union. Steps should taken in particular to permit trade union officials to explain to employees the aims of trade unions and the advantages of membership, to distribute trade union documentation and display trade union notices on the company's premises, to have reasonable time off to carry out their union duties without loss of pay and to organize meetings.

(F) Where works or liaison committees already operate, trade union officials should have representative status on these bodies if employees so wish. However, the existence of these types of committee should not prejudice the development or status of trade unions or of their representatives.

2. Migrant Labor

(A) The system of migrant labor is, in South Africa, an instrument of the policy of apartheid which has the effect of preventing the individual from seeking and obtaining a job of his choice: it also causes grave social and family problems.

(B) Employers have the social responsibility to contribute towards ensuring freedom of movement for Black African workers and their families.

(C) In the meantime employers should make it their concern to alleviate as much as possible the effects of the existing system.

3. Pay

Companies should assume a special responsibility as regards the pay and conditions of employment of their Black African employees. They should formulate specific policies aimed at improving their terms of employment. Pay based on the absolute minimum necessary for a family to survive cannot be considered as being sufficient. The minimum wage should initially exceed by at least 50 percent the minimum level required to satisfy the basic needs of an employee and his family.

4. Wage Structure and Black African Advancement

(A)   The principle of 'equal pay for equal pay for equal work' means that all jobs should be open to any worker who possesses suitable qualifications, irrespective of racial or other distinction, and that wages should be based on a qualitative job evaluation.

(B)   The same pay scales should be applied to the same work. The adoption of the principle of equal pay would, however, be meaningless if Black African employees were kept in inferior jobs. Employers should therefore draw up an appropriate range of training schemes of a suitable standard to provide training for their Black African employees, and should reduce their dependence on immigrant white labor.

5. Fringe Benefits

(A)   In view of their social responsibilities, undertakings should concern themselves with the living conditions of their employees and families.

(B)   For this purpose company funds could be set aside for use

- in the housing of Black African personnel and their families.
- in transport from place of residence to place to work and back;
- in providing leisure and health service facilities;
- in providing their employees with assistance in problems they encounter with the authorities over their movement from one place to another, their choice of residence and their employment;
- in pension matters;
- in improving medical services, in adopting programs of insurance against industrial accidents and unemployment, and in other measures of social welfare.

6. Desegregation at Places of Work

In so far as it lies within their own competence, employers should do everything possible to abolish any practice of segregation, notably at the workplace and in canteens, sports activities, education and training. They should ensure equal working conditions for all their staff.

7. Reports on the Implementation of the Code of conduct

(A)   Parent companies to which this Code is addressed should publish each year a detailed and fully documented report on the progress made in applying this Code.

(B)   The number of Black Africans employed in the undertaking should be specified in the report and progress in each of the six areas indicated above should be fully covered.

(C)   The Governments of the Nine will review annually progress made in implementing this Code. To this end a copy of each company's report should be submitted to their national government.

3. Code of Practice of the Federation of Swedish Industries

International attention has been focused on South Africa for many years. The United Nations and many of its member nations individually have tried to influence South African policies.

The International business community has been asked to contribute in these efforts. Substantial efforts are already made by South African industry to improve the situation for its African employees. Swedish industry feels strongly its share of responsibility as a member of the international business community and supports those new tendencies within South African industry, which are in line with the management policies of Swedish industry. Swedish industry is convinced that there are possibilities for substantial economic improvement of Africans in South Africa and that concrete results can and must be achieved within the existing legal and political framework. Although Swedish business interests in South Africa account for only a few thousand employees and thus have only a very limited effect on conditions in South Africa. Swedish industry is prepared to make forceful efforts to improve the situation within its sphere of influence.

All Swedish industrial activities in South Africa are organized as South African companies. Some are wholly owned by Swedish firms, some have Swedish majority interests and others have only a minority interest. Almost all of their employees are South Africans. These companies are governed, of course, by South African law and regulations.

Swedish industry is aware, however, that by setting good examples it can play at least a small role in creating equal opportunities and better living conditions for all races in South Africa. Such steps can, it goes without saying, be more successful when implemented in co-operation with employees of all groups.

Labor-management relations

Although the industrial environment differs greatly from one country to another, Swedish companies operating in South Africa should utilize their international experience, particularly in the field of labor-management relations.

Manufacturing should be organized, equipped and managed so that Africans find wider opportunities so as to enter more qualified jobs and consequently obtain higher wages. Companies with Swedish interests, operating in South Africa, are generally of modest size, highly specialized and capital intensive rather than labor intensive. These factors naturally limit the prospects for extensive programs but nevertheless offer opportunities for individual specialization in technical skills.

Swedish industry regards organized labor as a natural feature of industrial life. In the absence of unions in South Africa effectively representing Africans, companies with Swedish interests should establish and maintain effective channels of communication so that works committees and other responsible representatives of African employees can regularly consult with management on wages and other employment conditions as is already the case among several companies with Swedish interests.

Recent enquiries indicate that, in general, companies with Swedish interest spay their African employees no worse than other industrial companies, although this is in, itself, not an acceptable yardstick of industrial performance. Some companies have, however, recently introduced schemes for acceleration of wage increases.

South Africa has a complex wage rate system with numerous detailed agreements and wage determinations. It would therefore not be practical to draft here a detailed set of recommendations for all Swedish activities in South Africa. It can be stated, though, that wage structures should follow the principle of job evaluation, regardless of race. Furthermore, these structures should be regularly reviewed. Wages that allow satisfactory living standards should be granted to all employees, and wage policies should aim at closing the current economic gap between Africans and Whites.

Employment benefits

Industrial activity in South Africa calls for special consideration of African employees. Long ago companies with Swedish interests introduced and gradually expanded benefit programs designed to improve the well being of Africans. Further development of such programs should be carried out regarding:

— Pension schemes
— Insurance schemes
— Sick pay benefits
— In-company medical services
— Nutritious meals at nominal rates
— Travelling allowances.

Education and training

There is a great need for better education and training among Africans as a prerequisite for advancement into mote skilled jobs. It should therefore be natural for companies in South Africa with Swedish interests to make particular efforts in the field of education and training of Africans. Through the years successful programs have been developed and maintained which can be applied on a broader scale. In addition to such wider implementation of current programs, new projects should also be tried and developed wherever feasible. It is recommended that programs cover the following areas:

1. **In-company training**

   Systematic training of African employees should be an integrated part of all industrial operations.

2. **Industry-sponsored training centers etc.**

   Companies should participate actively in these newly launched schemes, designed to prepare African for more skilled jobs and higher positions.

3. **High school and university-level education**

   Financial support has long been given to higher education of Africans by several companies with Swedish interests. This support should continue.

It is understood that these measures will cost money, and that to be meaningful they must gain the understanding and support of all employee-groups. But it is also strongly felt that Swedish industry must prove by action its sense of equal responsibility for all employees.

Swedish industry believes that industry in South Africa is all-important to that country's economic future and offers the best possible opportunities for advancement of Africans, economically and socially. Industrial investment including investment from abroad is thus regarded as an important factor in paving the way for a better life for Africans in South Africa.

4. The Canadian Code of Conduct
(as last revised in 1986)

General Working Condition

In general, companies should regard the constant improvement of the overall work situation of black employees as an objective having a high priority. They should ensure that employment practices applicable to any group of workers are equally applicable to all workers.

Collective Bargaining

(a) Companies should ensure that their employees are free to organize collective bargaining units of their own choosing that can effectively represent them, and should undertake to engage in collective bargaining with such units in accordance with internationally accepted principles.

(b) Companies, recognizing that the South African Labor Relations Act and Labor Law is now free of provisions that discriminate on the basis of race, should pay particular attention to black trade unions and ensure that black employees are free to form or join the trade union of their choice. They should be prepared to sign recognition agreements with representative black trade unions within the company and allow collective bargaining, including the signing of collective agreements. Employers should regularly and unequivocally inform their employees that consultations and collective bargaining with organizations, which are freely elected and representative of employees are part of company policy.

(c) Companies should as a matter of course allow trade union officials to explain to employees the aims of trade unions and the advantages of membership, to disseminate trade union information material and display trade union notices on the company's premises, to have reasonable time off to carry out their union duties without loss of pay and to organize meetings.

(d) In companies where works or liaison committees already operate, trade union officials should have representative status on these bodies if employees so wish. The existence of these types of committee should not prejudice the development or status of trade unions or of their representatives.

(e) Companies should do everything possible to establish a climate of confidence in their relations with their employees. In this connection it is important that each company ensure that its employees be familiar with the Canadian Code of Conduct and that at regular intervals they can see or have the text of the Code read to them in a language they understand. The company should be prepared to inform its employees what it is doing to implement the Code and should review and discuss with them or their representatives its annual report on the implementation of the Code.

Migrant Labor

(a) The policy of apartheid leads to the use of the migrant labor, which robs the individual of the basic freedom to seek and obtain the job of his choice. It also causes grave social and family problems.

(b) Employers have the social responsibility to contribute towards ensuring freedom of movement for black workers and giving them the opportunity to lead a family life.

(c) Employers should endeavor to alleviate the effects of existing regulations, in particular by facilitating the regular renewal of contracts of employment and making it easier for the families of employees to settle near their workplace.

Wage and Pay Structures

(a) Companies should formulate specific guidelines aimed at improving their terms of employment and at implementing the principle of "equal pay for equal work." The staffing of and remuneration for a position should be based on the qualifications of an individual and not on his or her racial origin. The same pay scales should be applied to the same job.

(b) Companies should also provide remuneration sufficient to assist their black employees in particular to achieve a standard of livings sufficiently above the minimum level required to meet their basic needs. In this context they should refer to the data on living costs regularly collected and analyzed by the University of South Africa (UNISA) and the University of Port Elizabeth (UPE).... Pay based on the 'Supplemented living level for an average-sized family must be considered as the absolute <u>minimum</u> necessary and the Canadian Government strongly urges companies, taking into account the value of work performed in particular industries, to introduce <u>minimum</u> wages which substantially exceed this level at an early stage of their programs for improving the terms of employment of their black employees.

(c) In their continuing review of pay and wage structures, companies should take particular note of the impact of inflation. Annual wage increases should offset the impact of this factor but, if the desired improvement in real wages is to be achieved, it cannot be the only factor to be reflected in the determination of wage increases.

Training and Promotion

(a) The principle of equal pay for equal work would not mean much if black employees were kept in inferior jobs. Implementing the principle of equality of opportunity must also be given a high priority. Employers should therefore draw up an appropriate range of training schemes of a suitable standard to provide training for their black employees.

(b) Companies should ensure supervisory and management jobs and those requiring high technical qualifications are open to their black employees.

The aim should be, as a preliminary objective only towards the ultimate goal of a fair and balanced racial composition of the workforce, to fill fifty percent of all supervisory and management positions with employees other than those designated as white persons within a period of time which companies should clearly specify in their employment plans and development programs.

(c) Companies should, if possible, organize occupational training programs for their black employees and help them to take advantage of other educational and occupational training programs outside their places of work. Where required. companies should set up or use educational facilities to enable their black employees to benefit from more specialized training, and generally should support them and members of their families in their right of access to equal, integrated and universal educational facilities and opportunities.

(d) Companies should make every effort to eliminate in practice any de facto restrictions based on custom on apprenticeships for black employees. They should ensure that employees of different racial groups can take part in training programs without any form of segregation.

(e) In general whether it is a matter of an imbalance in the racial composition of a company's workforce and staff or of such an imbalance at any of the different levels of management and workforce, companies should, in their forward planning, treat the need to correct this situation as a matter of some urgency.

Fringe Benefits

(a) In view of their social responsibilities, companies should concern themselves with the living conditions of their black employees and their families.

(b) For this purpose, company funds could be set aside to provide benefits over and above those currently provided according to South African legislation:

- providing complete social protection schemes for employees and their families (health, accident and unemployment insurance and old age pensions);
- ensuring that their employees and their families have the benefit of adequate medical care:
- assisting in the education of members of their families
- helping them to buy their own housing or to obtain accommodation which enables all workers to live with their families near their workplace:
- providing transport from home to work and back with particular attention to alleviating the difficulties facing those employees who are obliged to commute some distance to the workplace;
- providing their employees with assistance in problems they encounter with the authorities over their movement from one place to another, their choice of residence and other employment;
- providing leisure facilities.

(c) Companies should support community projects which aim to improve the quality of life of the black communities from which they draw their staff.

Race Relations and Desegregation

(a) Where this has not already been completely achieved, employers should do everything possible to abolish any practice of segregation, notably at the workplace, in canteens, in education and training and in sports activities. They should also ensure equal working conditions for all their staff.

(b) Along with the advancement of their black employees, companies should directly support inter-staff contacts, and help employees from different racial groups to get to know each other better and integrate more fully.

(c) Companies should encourage sporting activities in which employees from different racial groups take part in mixed teams in mixed competitions.

Encouragement of Black Businesses

As far as they are able, companies should, in the framework of their activities, encourage the setting up and expansion of black businesses by contributing their expertise, counseling and advice, by sub-contracting, by providing assistance for their black employees to set up their own businesses and by preferential, priority treatment in customer-supplier relations.

Social Justice

By positive constructive and legal means and approaches and in cooperation with other foreign companies and with their South African partners, Canadian companies should use whatever channels of influence are available to them to promote the cause of social justice and the peaceful achievement of necessary social and political changes and reforms.

The revised procedure establishes a reporting system on the adherence of companies to the Code of Conduct, which is reviewed on an annual basis by an impartial and independent Administrator. In conformity with a standard reporting format issued to them for this purpose, all Canadian companies should submit to the administrator annual public reports in sufficient detail to permit assessment of their progress in realizing the objectives of the Code of

Conduct. On the basis of his review and collation of the responses of the companies. the Administrator submits to the Secretary of State for External Affairs an annual report which is subsequently tabled in Parliament.

Although the Code of Conduct is addressed primarily to the employment practices of Canadian companies in South Africa, there may be other Canadian establishments, as is the case with the Canadian Embassy in Pretoria, which employ people locally in South Africa and whose employment practices, accordingly, should conform to the regulations set out in the Code. The Canadian Government invites any Canadian public or private organization, temporarily or permanently located in South Africa and employing local labor there, to comply voluntary with the Code of Conduct.

The Canadian Government will continue to follow closely developments in South Africa and the efforts of companies in regard to the Code of Conduct. Where the process of change and reform make them necessary and appropriate, further amendments to the provisions of the Code will be introduced.

5. The Australian Code of Conduct

1. General

Australian companies with interests in South Africa are expected to extend to non-white employees' terms and conditions no less favorable than those extended to white employees.

2. Desegregation at Places of Work

Except where the law of South Africa otherwise requires, companies should integrate the workplace, canteen, recreational, educational, training and other company-provided facilities.

3. Employment and Industrial Relations Practices

(a) Companies should, as far as is legally possible, ensure that management attitude and practices adopted by their operations in South Africa are consistent with those, which they apply in Australia. In this respect it should be noted that it is unlawful in Australia to discriminate in employment on the grounds of race. In particular, there should be equal application of policies and practices to all employees.

(b) Employees should be allowed the free choice of membership in and representation by industrial organizations. Companies should recognize the lawful development of consultation and collective bargaining processes with trade unions or comparable organizations, which are freely elected, and representative of employees and every effort should be made to inform employees of this policy.

(c) Trade union officials should be permitted access to employees to undertake promotional work and where applicable, be given time off to carry out their union duties without any loss of pay. The display and distribution of trade union notices and documents should be permitted at the workplace.

4. Remuneration

(a) Companies should apply the principle of equal pay for equal work, regardless of race. If equality of remuneration is not already practiced, staged programs should be implemented to ensure that within a given time, the staffing of, and remuneration for, a position are based on an employee's qualifications and capacities and are not influenced by racial origin.

(b) Remuneration based on either the University of South Africa's Minimum Living Level (MLL) or the University of Port Elizabeth's Household Subsistence Level (HSL) is considered inadequate. While companies work towards equality in remuneration, the base payment for staff on entry to employment should be no lower than the figure of the University of South Africa's Supplemented Living Level (SLL) or the University of Port Elizabeth's Household Effective Level (HEL) for the geographic area in which the staff are employed. Social and geographic variables result in a range of figures for the SLL, but for the purposes of this Code average figures for family households in the Cape Peninsula, Johannesburg and Port Elizabeth areas are used in the reporting format. These figures will be periodically updated.

(c) Taking into account the value of work performed in particular industries, the appropriate wage would need to be considerably in excess of the SLL or HEL and in these cases companies should ensure that such a wage is paid.

5. Training and Management

In accordance with the undertaking to apply company policies and practices equally to all employees, companies should appoint and promote personnel solely on the basis of their qualifications and ability.

Company training and development programs should be implemented to facilitate equality of employment opportunities at all levels of the company on the same basis and selection criteria. Specifically, these programs should encourage the movement of non-whites into semi-skilled, skilled, supervisory, managerial and executive positions. Non-white employees with potential for further advancement should be identified and supported to undertake outside training courses or expanded internal training programs.

6. Labor Restrictions

Australian companies should, as far as possible within South African law, act to eliminate, in the work place, racially discriminatory practices which impede the implementation of equality of opportunity, treatment and conditions in employment.

To assist non-white employees to achieve and safeguard their basic rights, employers should provide advice on, and support changes to, pass laws, work permits, job reservation, restricted apprenticeships, restricted family residential requirements, etc., adversely affecting their employees. Companies should assist non-white employees and their families with advice and aid relating to legal matters to avoid infringing freedom of movement and to alleviate the deleterious effects of the migrant labor system.

7. Quality of Life

Australian companies should concern themselves with the quality of life of their employees and their families. Recognizing that this is not inconsistent with their concern for welfare of their workforce. Companies should aim to provide, in an equitable manner, fringe benefits to all workers such as:

(i) Contributory pension and/or provident funds

(ii) Contributory disability insurance

(iii) Contributory unemployment insurance

(iv) Sick leave benefits

(v) Annual leave benefits and

(vi) Contributory medical benefits schemes.

The Australian Government also encourages companies to participate in, and to set aside fund for the development of programs, which address transportation to and from work, health services, housing, and education/especially for the dependents of employees.

It is further recommended that in circumstances where Australian companies require outside services to further their commercial interests, every effort be made by these companies to engage the services of non-white personnel.

8. Monitoring

The performance of Australian companies in terms of their adherence to the Code of Conduct will be reviewed on an annual basis, by an independent and impartial Administrator. The Administrator will work with the companies and appropriately concerned parties in examining compliance with the Code and will review responses to a standard questionnaire, a copy of which is attached at Annex A. Detailed information provided to the Administrator will remain strictly confidential, including between parties involved in the process.

The Administrator will prepare an annual report for submission to Parliament through the Minister for Foreign Affairs indicating the overall level of compliance. Companies will also be encouraged to make public their implementation of the Code.

The Administrator will bring to the attention of companies instances of non-compliance with the Code and will inform the Minister for Foreign Affairs if such instances are not remedied within a reasonable period of time after consultations with non-complying business there is an evident intent to continue with non-compliance with the Code the Minister will report this fact and the notice of the noncompliance to Parliament. In all other cases detailed Information provided by companies to the Administrator will be treated with absolute confidentiality.

The provisions of the Code are framed with a view to South African laws and conditions as presently undergoing. Insofar as these may improve. as it is hoped they will, it may be necessary to amend the Code's provisions. The Australian Government therefore will keep the provision of the Code under continuing review.

6. The U.S. State Department's Principles

[A September 1985 executive order (renewed in 1986) and a section of the Anti-Apartheid Act of 1986 that remains in effect require U.S. companies that own or control entities in South Africa that employ 25 or more people to implement fair employment practices in order to qualify for U.S. government export assistance. The fair employment guidelines outlined in executive order # 12532 and the Anti-Apartheid Act are modeled on the Sullivan principles, except that the seventh principle, on lobbying for change outside the workplace, is voluntary and not required under the State Department program.]

1. Desegregating the races in each employment facility,
2. Providing equal employment opportunity for all employees without regard to race or ethnic origin,
3. Assuring that the pay system is applied to all employees without regard to race or ethnic origin,

4. Establishing a minimum wage and salary structure based on the appropriate local minimum economic level which takes into account the needs of employees and their families,

5. Increasing by appropriate means the number of persons in managerial, supervisory, administrative, clerical and technical jobs who are disadvantaged by the apartheid system for the purpose of significantly increasing their representation in such jobs,

6. Taking reasonable steps to improve the quality of employees' lives outside the work environment with respect to housing, transportation, schooling, recreation and health, and

7. Implementing fair labor practices by recognizing the right of all employees, regardless of racial or other distinctions, to self-organization and to form, join or assist labor organizations, freely and without penalty or reprisal, and recognizing the right to refrain from any such activity.

Any U.S. company that owns or controls an entity in South Africa with 25 or more people must register with the State Department and maintain records of its implementation of the guidelines. Beginning on Feb. 15, 1987, all registered companies were required to report to the State Department annually on their implementation. However, any company that is a "bona fide" Statement of Principles signatory-defined by the State Department as receiving a Category I, II or IIIA rating -may meet the requirements by writing a short letter to the State Department certifying its participation in the Statement of Principles program and reporting its rating for the relevant year. Companies that receive a Category IIIA rating will be given the benefit of the doubt and considered "bona fide" signatories as long as their ratings improve the following year.

The major difference in content between the two sets of principles is that the mandatory State Department principles do not contain all of the amplifications that have been made to the Statement of Principles. The original six Sullivan principles have been amplified four times since they were introduced. The first three amplifications expanded upon the requirements of the six principles by spelling out specific actions that companies should take to implement them. The fourth amplification (Principle VII) was designed to take companies farther in challenging apartheid in the society as a whole, rather than restricting their effort to the workplace. The State Department principles do not require firms to implement the areas described in the fourth amplification, but they do state that U.S. companies covered by the State Department principles "are encouraged to take reasonable measures to extend the scope of their influence on activities outside the workplace."

Under President Reagan's executive order of September 1985, forms are submitted to the State Department Office of Southern African Affairs, which will use them to "determine whether the U.S. national is adhering to the principles." Failure to comply with the requirements results in severe penalties. Unlike the graded ratings for the Statement of Principles program, this determination is made on a pass/fail basis. The Office of Southern African Affairs is required to file an annual report with Congress on the performance of companies that are not signatories to the Statement of Principles. The most recent ratings were provided to IRRC in February 1994 for calendar year 1992. The future of the State Department's Fair Labor Standards program hinges on the April 27, 1994, South African elections. If President Clinton finds that the elections were free and fair, the State Department's program will end, although its final report for the year ended Dec. 31, 1993, will still be published.

7. The Urban Foundation & SACCOLA Code of Conduct

The Urban Foundation and SACCOLA -

- believing that the opportunity for men and women to develop themselves to their fullest potential plays a basic role in the quality of their lives, and

- knowing that free enterprise has a major contribution to make towards improving the quality of life of all people in South Africa, and

- recognizing progress already achieved in the matters dealt with below, recommends the adoption by all members of the private sector of a Code of Employment Practice whereby the subscriber is committed, within the evolving South African legal framework:

1. To strive constantly for the elimination of discrimination based on race or color from all aspects of employment practice

    and to apply this principle in good faith—with due regard to different job categories fairly determined on considerations other than race or color—especially in the following respects:

    1.1   The selection, employment, advancement and promotion of all employees;

    1.2   the remuneration of employees

    1.3   the provision of

    −   pensions, medical aid, leave, sick pay, employee insurance, assistance with housing, and like facilities

    −   physical working conditions and facilities related thereto

    −   training programs or facilities to improve the productivity and skills of employees to enable them to achieve advancement in technical, administrative and managerial positions

    1.4   the recognition of the basic rights of workers of freedom of association, collective negotiation of agreements on conditions of service, the lawful withholding of labor as a result of industrial disputes, and protection against victimization resulting from the exercise of these rights.

2. To promote and maintain, through contact and consultation sound and harmonious relations between employers and all categories of employees,

AND

3. To continue to co-operate with other organizations in the public and the private sectors in promoting

    3.1   the accelerated creation of employment opportunities for the South African population at wage rates aimed at the maintenance of viable living standards;

    3.2   the progressive transition to a system wherein the rates of remuneration paid and any benefits relating to conditions of employment will be such as to render unnecessary any differential subsidy based on race or color.

8. The Barlow Rand Group Code of Employment Practice

This section of the Code sets out the specific policies and practices which managements of group companies undertake to implement

Selection and promotion

Within the limits prescribed by law and by legally enforceable agreements, people will be appointed or promoted solely on the basis of their ability to meet the requirements of the post to be filed, unless group planning considerations dictate otherwise .Group policy will be to promote from within the group and not necessarily from within the company where the vacancy has arise.

Training and development

Companies will undertake the training and development of employees to improve their work performance and prepare them for levels of responsibility commensurate with their abilities. This will ensure that the necessary skills will be available to secure their own and the group's progress.

As many of the group's employees enter its ranks with a minimum of formal education, training in literacy and numeracy will be offered to enable them to form a foundation for the development of their basic skills.

Technical, supervisory and management training will be provided both from the group's resources and by appropriate outside agencies.

As part of its corporate responsibility of augmenting the flow of skilled manpower in Southern Africa, the C.S. Barlow Foundation will continue to provide financial support for education and particularly technical education.

Remuneration

Employees will be remunerated on a non-discriminatory basis and performance, the demands of the job and experience will be the main criteria for determine salaries and wages.

At all levels the salaries and wages paid to employees will be competitive in relation to "going rates" in the areas in which the companies of the group operate. Where these rates do not provide a reasonable living standard, company rates will be fixed at a higher level.

Within the constraints of business viability, companies will meet the group's commitment, made by the Chairman of the group in his 1977 statement to shareholders, to ". . . improving the quality of life of the least privileged sections of our work force by ensuring that their earning rise at a rate materially higher than their living costs".

All permanent and migratory employees will qualify for paid annual leave, the duration of such leave being governed by length of service, seniority and statutory provisions.

The group will neither acquire nor establish any business that depends for an acceptable financial return on wages and conditions of service, which are lower than group standards.

Retirement benefits and redundancy

Every permanent employee will qualify to belong either to a pension or provident fund to which the Employer Company will contribute. Supplementary retirement benefits will be provided for employees with a minimum of 10 years' continuous group service if they have not been members of funds for the full period of their employment.

Companies will endeavor to provide continuity of employment. If at any tine retrenchment becomes unavoidable, every effort will be made to place redundant employees within the group. If placements cannot be made, the hardships suffered by the employees concerned may be mitigated by ex gratia payments. The quantum of payments will be governed by length of service within the group, the adequacy or otherwise of pension fund redundancy benefits and the quality of service rendered.

Negotiating rights

In his 1977 statements to shareholders the Chairman of the group observed that " The basic requirement is that there should be no difference in the rights available to the various races and therefore we would like to see negotiations at industry or national level between employers' organizations and multi-racial unions, rather than black unions, with supplementary negotiation on domestic issues at plant level between management and multi-racial committees."

It is certain that there will be changes in negotiating rights. Pending these changes companies of the group will be prepared to consult and negotiate with unregistered unions provided such unions are so constituted that they would satisfy the Industrial Conciliation Act's requirement for union registration, can demonstrate that the majority of the employees concerned wish to be represented by them, and accept that companies must continue to abide by the laws and agreements to which they are subject.

The group believes that irrespective of whether unions are recognized or not, liaison committees will continue to play an important part in in-company consultation and negotiation. The effectiveness of committees will be enhanced by the training of its members and demands, requests and suggestions will be fairly and promptly dealt with.

Integration of facilities

Work areas will be fully integrated. The groups' policy is to move positively towards the integration of other facilities but it recognizes that legal constraints and social attitudes will influence the rate of change.

Quality of life

Companies will concern themselves with the quality of life of employees within and outside the working environment. This involves a general awareness of employees' needs and aspirations and a willingness to help them to achieve a satisfying life.

Specifically, companies will assist employees under certain circumstances to acquire or improve homes. Where employees live in group hostels, companies will strive to achieve acceptable and continually improving standards of accommodation.

In regard to the education of the dependants of employees, companies will provide financial assistance when it is feasible and necessary to do so.

CONCLUSION

Changes in laws and regulations governing employment of all race groups in South Africa and in society's attitudes towards employment practices are occurring at a rapid pace and are likely to accelerate in the future. The group will examine on an on-going basis the laws and attitudes that affect employment practice, and will review the Code constantly so that it represents the most enlightened practice attainable in the circumstances prevailing at any time.

Parts of the code relate specifically to the situation in South Africa, Where most of the companies of the group are located. However, all companies of the group are committed to the basic principles underlying the Code, namely equitable treatment of employees and the elimination of discrimination.

ENDNOTES

1 Community Firms in South Africa, "Code of Conduct for Companies from the European Community with Subsidiaries, Branches or Representation in South Africa," *Bulletin EC* 11–1985.

2 Federal Republic of Germany, "Report on the Application of the European Code of Conduct for Companies with Subsidiaries, Branches or Representation in South Africa," Fall 1977.

3 U.K. Department of Trade and Industry, letter to British companies operating in the U.S. at the time of its 1985 revision, 18 November 1985.

4 "Code Ignored," *New African*, February 1979.

5 Donald C. Huss (General Motors European Advisory Council), excerpt from the report "EEC Code of Conduct regarding South Africa," 11 October 1977.

6 United Kingdom, "Code of Conduct for Companies with Interests in South Africa, Government Guidance to British Companies on the Code of Conduct Adopted by the Governments of the Nine Member States of the European Community" (London: Her Majesty's Stationary Office, 1978).

7 IRRC, "International Business in South Africa 1992," (Washington, DC: IRRC, 1992).

8 IRRC, "International Business in South Africa 1993," (Washington, DC: IRRC, 1993).

Chapter 10

Corporate Compliance with the Sullivan Principles
Evaluation of the Overall Performance of United States
Companies in South Africa

The working of the Sullivan Principles in South Africa can be analyzed along two dimensions. The first relates to the Principles themselves: their content; their evolution and modification; their underlying rationale and social and moral import; and the goals they were designed to achieve. These questions were central in motivating us to write this book. In the current chapter, however, we focus on the second dimension of the working of the Principles. To wit, we consider the manner in which the Sullivan Principles were operationalized and implemented in South Africa. In particular, we examine the criteria by which projects were selected and managed, and the standards and processes that were created for monitoring and evaluating performance. We also attempt to evaluate operational efficiency, the achievement of goals (as measured by the auditing and monitoring instruments used in the process), and the impact the companies' efforts when seen from the perspectives of the recipient groups.

The operation of the Sullivan Principles during the eighteen years of the program was not always smooth. It could hardly have been otherwise, especially in view of the Principles' unprecedented character, the intense and emotionally charged sociopolitical environment, and the large measure of distrust between the corporations and their critics. One should also note that the United States companies were operating under the public spotlight of the Sullivan Principles, whereas their major competitors—both South African companies and other foreign multinational corporations operating in South Africa—were not burdened with similar requirements. Although many of these other companies adopted some guidelines and practices modeled after the Sullivan Principles (see chapter 9), the absence of a mandatory requirement for compliance and verification often produced a large gap between the rhetoric of the companies' public claims and the reality of what they were doing.

1.   OPERATIONALIZING AND IMPLEMENTING THE SULLIVAN PRINCIPLES: THE EMPHASIS ON RATINGS

At one level, it would appear that the entire compliance process was driven by the "ratings game." According to the signatory companies' South African managers we interviewed for this study, there was never any doubt that the United States headquarters would be content only with the highest annual ratings under the Sullivan Principles. "Some top officers wanted the highest rating for moral reasons," according to Christianne Duval, an officer of Reader's Digest South Africa, "but all needed the highest rating for business reasons." Since the ratings were used by United States pension and endowment funds, as well as by church groups tracking the situation in South Africa, they were crucially important. The pressure exerted on the signatory companies by activist groups in the United States was also a major factor in shaping the industry response. A major criterion for selecting a project under the Principles program was its potential to contribute to a higher rating; the inherent worth of a project was secondary.

There were some companies, however, that stood out because of the moral leadership of top management. For example, David R. Clare, the CEO of Johnson & Johnson, was known for his ethical leadership in the United States business community. In a 4 February 1987 address at the Massachusetts Institute of Technology, he relied primarily on moral reasons to justify his company's remaining in South Africa. This pervasive moral perspective—and its extension to a company's South African operations and the injustices of apartheid—is also apparent in the detailed memorandum (exhibit 10) from a top Johnson & Johnson officer in the United States headquarters to the company's South African subsidiary in 1979 (early in the Principles program), and in a telex sent by a top Johnson & Johnson official, F. Robert Kniffin, to South Africa in the following year:

> Jim Burke would like us to identify the top five or so companies who have done the best job in attracting blacks capable of development and instituting management development programs for their advancement. We can discuss during my visit, but I wanted to alert you beforehand. The purpose is to see what specific programs and techniques we might adopt from the most successful companies.[1]

Exhibit 10. Foster Memorandum on Suggested Corporate Activities and Programs in South Africa

The following are selected suggestions for attainable programs that might be instituted by us in South Africa as part of our efforts to implement the Sullivan Principles. The list, while hardly exhaustive, has been gleaned from materials in our offices and from a pre-distribution copy of the minutes of the latest meeting of signatory companies (attached).

* Signatory companies to deposit R50,000 to R100,000 in the African Bank or in the New Republic Bank at the competitive time-deposit rates and/or to support the NAFCOC student bursary program.

* Signatory companies to contact the branch or regional NAFCOC office, volunteer to provide consultancy services for three small businesses, and specify the volunteers to be available on a continuous basis for at least one year. This commitment is described as requiring approximately 24 man-hours per month. Note: The Norton Company's consultancy program is describes as "ideal" in that it involves two employees working full time as consultant to Colored-and Black-owned businesses.

* Signatory companies to volunteer management personnel for training activities at local universities of NAFCOC Educational Seminars. This commitment is described as requiring approximately 10 man-hours per month.

* The Adopt-A-School program. A detailed description of this effort is in the process of being completed. As the name implies, the sense of the program is that signatory companies contribute funds and consultancy services to support a school. In some instances support may involve reconstruction or rehabilitation of an existing facility, supplying educational materials, etc. A brief description of the program notes that participating companies are being asked to agree to a five-year commitment at an average annual financial contribution rate of $5,000 to $6,000.

The following are samples of other signatory companies' activities programs in South Africa:

American Cyanamid

Bill Elliot is extremely involved in forming an educational pilot program in South Africa, and has encouraged Johnson and Johnson to get in touch with him if we are interested in joining his efforts. He has just returned from South Africa and results of his research show education of blacks is the most important priority (housing is high on the list too). His pilot program should be ready by June 1980. He is developing an educational system to train Bantu teachers to eventually train others. The product of current Bantu education does not result in skilled or trainable people. There is a 150,000 shortage of black teachers. The goal of his program would be to turn out blacks who can go on to a university, a technical field or join the workforce.

Eastman Kodak

Has donated $125,000 to "Project PACE" (Advanced Community Education) to build schools in Soweto (other companies have also contributed). Also gives a $15,000 scholarship (an on-going program) to a deserving black to study in the U.S. (through the International Institute for Education). $10,000 has been given to the Management Government Training Institute, to train blacks for advancement.

Continued on next page

Exhibit 10, continued

Colgate-Palmolive

Involved in community projects, i.e. Adopt-A-School, set up "Colgate Games" (track programs in black towns), take employees to the seashore (camp-like program) and gives financial assistance to black employees wishing to purchase a home.

3-M

Provides financial assistance to black employees for secondary school and university education (55 employees received aid in 1979). Also have an educational center for black employees (for literacy and management training), interest-free loans, employee recreational and social programs (for all employees), multi-racial soccer team and contributed $50,000 plus operating costs towards a $4 million high school in Soweto.

Pfizer

Involved in a Adopt-A-School program in the area where they have a manufacturing plant. Also give a four-year scholarship to blacks to study agriculture at the university, have a literacy training program for black employees and send students to a training center.

Warner-Lambert

Company has for the past two years authorized their South African company to spend, on a charge-back basis to the U.S. parent, $7,500 for educational programs for W-L employees. The company plans to do the same in 1980.

SmithKline

Has two major programs. Provides education assistance to blacks, such as school fees and books, and provides housing assistance, i.e. loans for improvements and repairs.

Merck

Help employees to finance homes, have scholarship programs for black students attending Fort Hare University and provide free books and other material to children of black employees.

Control Data

Are involved with terminal and computer-based programs in education, provide scholarships and have set up training centers for blacks.

American Hospital Supply

Has an employee committee, whereby blacks meet with management on working conditions. Also have a school program, providing scholarships and books for families of black employees.

Arthur Swartz, managing director of Beckman Instruments in South Africa during much of the period that the Sullivan Principles were in effect, recalls that his superiors in the United States carefully monitored the subsidiary's progress in the Principles program: "South Africa got much more of top management's time because of the continued pressure from groups in the U.S.," and "The rating was everything and low ratings meant that your job might be in jeopardy." Christianne Duval of Reader's Digest recalls that the Otis Elevator Company actually sent an officer from the headquarters in

Chicago to manage the Sullivan program in South Africa after the company received a low rating. Moreover, the previous Sullivan manager at Otis lost his position in the company—a move that sent reverberations throughout the South African management of the signatory companies.

Senior corporate officers from the United States, both as members of committees for the Principles program and as executives representing their companies, continued to travel to South Africa; the ratings assigned by Arthur D. Little for implementing the Principles were too important to be left completely to subordinates. Indeed, if any managers of the South African offices of United States companies had any doubt about the concerns of the top managers in the United States, that doubt was removed by observing the constant parade of company officers from the United States visiting their South African subsidiaries. Many of these same officers were also deeply involved in the Sullivan program itself. For example, a little over a year and a half after the Principles were announced, a nine-member group of United States company officers charged to advise Sullivan—a group then called the Industry Steering Committee—visited South Africa for discussions. Upon returning to the United States on 26 August 1978, the group issued a press release announcing that it had met with over fifty major leaders in South Africa—of all ethnic and racial groups—in government, academia, church, and business. The discussions had centered on two areas: (1) the Sullivan Principles and their implementation in, and impact on, South Africa, and (2) the position and activities of United States groups critical of United States investment in South Africa.[2]

The membership of the committee, which indicates the strength of corporate interest in the Principles program, was impressive not only for the range of important companies represented, but also because of the senior managers who were present in the group: James W. Rawlings, chairman (vice chairman, Union Carbide Africa and Middle East, Inc.), Paul R. Gibson, vice chairman (president, Envirotech International), J. Wayne Fredericks (executive director, international government affairs, Ford Motor Company), Roderick J. Ironside (director, personal and industrial relations, General Motors South Africa), Sal G. Marzullo (manager, public affairs field services, Mobil Oil Corporation), Robert J. McCabe (director, treasurer's office administration section, General Motors Corporation), John E. Purcell (regional director, Asia and Africa, Goodyear International Corporation), Charles E. Taylor (program manager, IBM Corporation), and Edgar K. Yucel (assistant general counsel, Minnesota Mining and Manufacturing Company).

2.   ANALYSIS OF AGGREGATE DATA PERFORMANCE

The analysis of signatory companies' performance data has been derived from seventeen annual reports of the Sullivan program—covering the period 1977 to 1993. Our findings are summarized in tables 19 to 28.[3] This information has been grouped in four categories. The first category (tables 19 to 20) describes the industry representation of the signatory companies, some salient characteristics of individual companies, and the changes in group representation over time. The second category (table 21) provides information about the aggregate contributions of the signatory companies from year to year. The third category of data (tables 22 to 24) details signatories' contributions in supporting different areas of community activities. The final category (tables 25 to 28) deals with the changes in workforce composition and the mobility of Blacks, Coloreds, and Asians in various occupational and managerial ranks.

2.1   Industry Profile of Signatory Companies

In 1978 there were 177 operational units representing 105 companies across various industries reporting as Sullivan signatories in South Africa (table 19).[4] In the following year, the number of units increased to 240. By 1986 the Principles program included over 180 signatory companies (and many more units), the highest in the program's history. Starting in 1986, however, there was a precipitous decline in the number of signatory companies. The highest rate of disinvestment took place between from 1986 to 1988, during which period 97 companies (52 companies in 1987 alone) left South Africa. From 1978 to 1986, less than 30 percent of the signatory companies received a top rating. However, the percentage consistently improved, and between 1989 and 1993 over 70 percent of the signatory companies received top ratings.

We have classified the signatory companies as falling in thirteen industry groups. The pattern of divestiture shows that exit rates were far higher in certain industries (for example, financial industries) and lower in others (for example, pharmaceutical and health-care companies, and chemical/allied products).

The data show that in the early years of the Principles program, a majority of signatory companies employed more than 1000 workers in South Africa (table 20). Unfortunately, these companies also displayed a higher rate of exit. The result was that by 1990, companies employing more than 1000 workers represented less than 7 percent of the signatory companies. The most severe drop in total employment by the signatories occurred during

Table 19. Representation by Industry Group

Period	Year	Reporting Units	1[a]	2	3	4	5	6	7	8	9	10	11	12	13
1	1977	0	0	0	0	0	0	0	0	0	0	0	0	0	0
2	1978	177	12	32	2	0	1	8	25	3	0	8	3	5	0
3	1979	240	11	24	0	0	1	7	17	3	15	9	2	7	3
4	1980	136	10	24	3	0	1	8	9	6	27	0	4	5	4
5	1981	131	8	20	3	0	0	8	10	8	29	0	5	7	3
6	1982	120	11	20	4	1	2	8	10	7	18	4	3	7	5
7	1983	125	10	19	5	0	2	9	11	7	19	2	4	6	5
8	1984	116	13	22	4	0	3	10	10	8	12	4	3	7	3
9	1985	146	15	20	3	8	1	13	10	5	0	8	5	7	5
10	1986	129	15	20	4	6	2	9	11	7	0	9	3	9	5
11	1987	97	18	18	3	9	4	16	9	6	0	5	3	7	0
12	1988	80	15	19	8	10	6	16	1	6	0	8	4	8	0
13	1989	64	17	19	5	13	5	20	9	5	0	2	4	3	0
14	1990	59	22	19	3	14	5	20	7	3	0	0	3	3	0
15	1991	54	22	19	4	11	6	20	7	4	4	0	4	0	0
16	1992	52	23	19	4	12	6	19	8	4	4	2	0	0	0
17	1993	53	23	21	4	9	6	17	9	4	4	4	0	0	0

[a] Industry classifications:
1. Pharmaceutical/Health Care
2. Consumer Goods/Food Products/Distribution
3. Petroleum Products
4. Construction/Engineering/Building Materials
5. Agricultural Equipment/Farm/Forestry
6. Chemical/Allied Products
7. Industrial Equipment and Supplies/Equipment Installation, Service, and Maintenance/ Materials Manufacture
8. Automotive, Motor Trades, and Related
9. Other
10. Services (for example, advertising, publishing)
11. Mining and Quarrying
12. Computers, Data Processing/Electronics
13. Financial Industries (for example, insurance. real estate, banking, travel)

the periods 1981 to 1983 and 1986 to 1989. In the first period the drop was 16,958 employees; in the second, 35,340 employees.

2.2 Financial Contributions by the Signatory Companies

The magnitude and disposition of the signatory companies' financial contributions to comply with the Sullivan Principles are described in table 21. Our data show that from 1978 to 1993, average financial contributions per signatory company increased from ZAR 38,914 to ZAR 1,865,300 (almost 50-fold). During the same period, average contributions per signatory-company employee increased from ZAR 61 to ZAR 5,919 (almost 100-fold).

Table 20. Employee Distribution by Firm Size, by Percentage of Total Employees

				Firm Size			
Period	Year	Total Employees	N<25	N>24 N<101	N>100 N<501	N>500 N<1001	N>1000
1	1977	38,061	N/A	N/A	N/A	N/A	N/A
2	1978	51,488	0	9	30	13	47
3	1979	55,671	0	1	20	19	59
4	1980	71,572	0	3	9	22	66
5	1981	83,133	0	2	17	18	63
6	1982	69,013	0	3	20	19	58
7	1983	66,175	0	3	20	20	57
8	1984	64,724	0	2	22	18	57
9	1985	62,356	0	3	22	23	52
10	1986	62,376	8	23	44	13	12
11	1987	43,865	9	26	39	17	9
12	1988	33,451	3	28	42	18	9
13	1989	27,036	2	28	45	14	11
14	1990	21,072	0	32	46	15	7
15	1991	17,693	0	31	48	15	6
16	1992	16,837	0	32	47	15	6
17	1993	15,758	0	35	47	12	6

Although there was a regular—and in the later years, quite precipitous—decline in the number of signatory companies remaining in South Africa, total expenditures not only remained stable, but continued to increase every year. For example, between 1981 and 1993, the last year of the official report on signatories' activities, the number of signatory companies declined from 101 to 50 (over 50 percent), but total expenditures increased from ZAR 9 million to ZAR 93 million (100-fold).

Even during the peak period of divestment—when some of the United States companies with the largest operations in South Africa (in terms of both employees and financial resources)—were leaving the country, total corporate contributions under the Sullivan program continued to increase. For example, during the period from 1986 to 1993, the number of reporting companies dropped by more than half (from 110 to 50), but average contributions per signatory company more than compensated for the lost resources and increased by a factor of 3.5, from just over ZAR 510,000 to just below ZAR 1.9 million. Similarly, average contributions per employee increased 6-fold, from ZAR 901 to ZAR 5,919.

2.3 Developing Black-Owned Businesses: A Vision without Results

Discretionary purchases from BCA companies increased continuously through 1993. On a per-employee basis between 1983 and 1993, purchases increased from ZAR 136 per employee to about ZAR 3,744 per employee. Although this increase is significant, the purchases from BCA companies nevertheless represented a tiny fraction of the companies' total revenues or economic activity in South Africa. For example, in 1993 the signatory companies spent over ZAR 93 million in community-related activities but managed to spend only ZAR 59 million on purchases from BCA companies. This poor performance did not bode well for the growth of Black-owned enterprises in South Africa. The poor performance of signatory companies in this area elicited intense criticism from their critics. Sullivan himself expressed frustration over the difficulty of persuading United States companies to help the growth of Black-owned business through corporate purchasing policies. The signatory companies conceded that BCA purchases had not grown to desirable levels. However, they attributed this lack of growth to the paucity of Black-owned businesses capable of supplying requisite products rather than to the companies' lack of effort in encouraging and developing such enterprises.

Since at least some of the signatory companies did want to encourage the development of Black-owned businesses, it is not immediately apparent why the results were so unimpressive. The answer lies, in part, in the specific dynamics (and misfirings) of Task Group 7—later to be called the Community Economic Development Task Force—whose mission was "to support existing and to develop new non-white businesses in South Africa."[5] The eleven representatives serving on this task group were senior- and middle-level managers, each from a different United States company. According to the minutes of the task group, "it was accepted that the U.S. Task Group should continue to act as a sounding board and communicator for the South African Task Group and that it should review their recommendations before passing them on to Dr. Sullivan. The U.S. Task Group was not in a position to develop meaningful objectives and must depend on the South African Task Group to fulfill this function."

The South African counterpart of Task Group 7 was formed in early 1979 and included in its membership not only members from the signatory companies, but also prominent representatives of Black community. In September 1979, the counterpart task group sent to the United States group a twelve-point action plan for community and economic development. With some minor changes, the United States task group approved this plan on 16 October 1979 and sent it on the Sullivan for his endorsement. Sullivan subsequently urged all signatory companies to implement the plan (see exhibit 11).

As it turned out, very few of the signatory companies adopted the action plan for South Africa—a cause of serious concern on the part of Task Group 7 since the Principles program thereby ran the risk of losing credibility

Table 21. Contributions of Reporting Signatories

Period	Year	Total Employees	Reporting Signatories (No.)	Total Contributions (ZARs in 1000s)	Ave. Contrib..Per Signatory (ZARs in 1000s)	Ave. Contrib. Per Employee (ZARs)
1	1977	38,061	78	N/A	N/A	N/A
2	1978	51,488	81	3,152	39	61
3	1979	55,671	97	2,784	29	50
4	1980	71,572	100	6,408	64	82
5	1981	83,133	101	8,939	89	108
6	1982	69,013	93	15,224	164	221
7	1983	66,175	99	10,547	107	159
8	1984	64,724	98	14,885	152	230
9	1985	62,656	112	38,942	348	622
10	1986	62,376	110	56,230	511	901
11	1987	43,865	88	67,828	771	1,546
12	1988	33,451	70	63,824	912	1,908
13	1989	27,036	59	83,034	1,407	3,071
14	1990	21,072	54	65,400	1,211	3,104
15	1991	17,693	51	73,992	1,451	4,182
16	1992	16,837	49	82,580	1,685	4,905
17	1993	15,758	50	93,265	1,865	5,919

Exhibit 11. Recommendations of the South African Counterpart Task Group: 12-Step Action Plan

OBJECTIVE:	To contribute towards the economic welfare of all the people of South Africa by assisting in the development of Black, Colored, and Asian enterprises including suppliers of good and services and manufacturers.	

PROGRAMME	ACTION STEPS	RESOURCE REQUIREMENT
	1) Signatory companies to become Associate members of NAFCOC	1) Up to R500/year based on company size
Linkage Phase	2) Signatory companies to deposit R50,000 to R100, 000in the African Bank or in the New Republic Bank at competitive time deposit rates and/or to support the NAFCOC student Bursary Programme	2) R50,000 to R100,000 competitive return, minimum risk investment of R100,000 or R1000 per student bursary assistance.
	3) Signatory Companies' Executives in S.A. to contact the NAFCOC national executive and establish a working relationship at regional and branch office levels to encourage "involvement" by subordinates	3) No major requirements
Involvement Phase	4) Signatory Companies to conduct a tour of their facilities for NAFCOC branch officials familiar with products and services locally available in order to evaluate potential supply opportunities	4) No major requirements
	5) Signatory Companies to visit local manufacturing facilities of Black, Colored, & Asian businessmen to evaluate supply opportunities and assess "needs"	5) No major requirements

	6) Signatory Companies to contact one of the following Universities to assess opportunities for support of business development programmes by company:
	    U. of the North
	    U. of South Africa (UNISA)
	    U. of Potchesfstroom
	    U. of Stellenbosch
	    U. of Witwatersrand	

Joint Action	7) Signatory Companies to select 5 products for supply by Black, Colored and Asian community and forward	

Continued on next page

Exhibit 11, continued

	requests for tender to small businesses and local NAFCOC branch. Typical products now manufactured or supplied by Black businessmen are: furniture, coffins, work clothes, school uniforms, cane work, candle making, stationery, printing, panel beating (auto body work), dry cleaning, spinning, brick making, and welding.	
	8) Signatory Companies to send list of 5 products to the NAFCOC Exec. Director for use in a "finders" column in the NAFCOC journal	8) Small fee for advertising
	9) Signatory Companies to contact the branch or regional NAFCOC office. Volunteer to provide consultancy services for 3 small business, and specify the volunteers to be available on a continuous basis for at least 1 year.	9) Approximately 24 man hours/month
	10) Or, alternately, Signatory Companies to volunteer management personnel for training activities at local universities or NAFCOC Educational Seminars.	10) Approximately 24 man hours/month
	11) Signatory Companies as Associate Members of NAFCOC to support (NAFCOC) efforts to eliminate bureaucratic red-tape and the lifting of commercial discrimination.	11) General Management Support
Assessment	12) Signatory Companies to periodically assess results, costs and benefits of their own Action Plan and to take necessary corrective action.	12) Management's time

The Task Group on Periodic Reporting and Community Economic Development (Task Group VII), with Dr. Sullivan's endorsement, now urges that each Signatory Company consider the adoption of the 12 Step Action Plan developed by the South African Counterpart Task Group.

in non-White communities. In an effort to secure better cooperation, Task Group 7 recommended in November 1980 that membership in the National African Chamber of Commerce (the first of the twelve steps in the action plan) be made mandatory and duly graded by Reid Weedon of ADL in his annual review. Sullivan agreed, and companies were subsequently graded on whether they had become members of NAFCOC. The projects listed in the action plan were also to be used as points of reference when it came to grading companies for their efforts to encourage Black-owned businesses.[6] Nonetheless, though the action plan continued to be actively discussed (within both the task groups and the companies themselves), there is little evidence that the plan was ever aggressively implemented by United States companies.

2.4   Contributions to Community Activities

The disposition of signatories' contributions to the Principles program had two major components: educational assistance for non-employees, and community development (tables 22 to 24) Of the two, the community-development component consistently received a larger portion of the total contributions. In 1978 the total contributions for community development amounted to just over ZAR 2 million, which by 1993 increased to ZAR 51 million. Similarly, educational assistance to non-employees increased from ZAR 1 million to ZAR 42 million during the same period. However, the contributions of companies to community development—when measured by reference to employee-days—showed greater variability and, indeed, fell significantly from 1986, when it was at a high of 52 thousand employee-days, to 1993, by which time it was only 31 thousand (a reduction of 40 percent).

2.5   Changes in Work Force Composition and BCA Mobility

The racial composition of the workforce showed only marginal improvement over the eighteen years of the Principles program (table 25). To put it differently, despite eighteen years of effort, the number of BCAs employed by the signatory companies, and, by implication, by the formal economic sector of South Africa, did not show any appreciable change. There was, however, one area of improvement: the percentage of Whites managed by BCAs, which increased from an initial 2.5 percent in 1983 to 15 percent in 1993. Nevertheless, data from other sources also indicate that BCA supervisors generally held entry-level supervisory positions. There is also another reason to interpret these statistics somewhat cautiously. Because most firms in the manufacturing and petroleum industries, which were among the largest United States employers, had divested their holdings in South Africa by the late 1980s, the composition of the signatory group became increasingly skewed toward smaller companies, thereby reducing the ratio of White employees being supervised by BCAs.

Table 22. Contributions of Signatories to the Community-at-Large

Period	Year	Total Educational Assistance Non-Employees (ZARs in 1000s)	Total Contribution Community Development (ZARs in 1000s)	Total Monetary Contribution (ZARs in 1000s)	Discretionary Purchases from BCAs (ZARs in 1000s)
1	1977	N/A	N/A	N/A	N/A
2	1978	1,042	2,110	3,152	N/A
3	1979	1,336	1,448	2,784	N/A
4	1980	3,516	2,892	6,408	N/A
5	1981	4,139	4,800	8,939	N/A
6	1982	4,091	11,133	15,224	N/A
7	1983	5,259	5,288	10,547	9,000
8	1984	7,012	7,873	14,885	11,000
9	1985	13,327	25,615	38,942	16,000
10	1986	24,736	31,494	56,230	22,000
11	1987	31,054	36,774	67,828	27,000
12	1988	28,376	35,448	63,824	45,000
13	1989	37,512	45,522	83,034	40,000
14	1990	29,705	35,695	65,400	44,000
15	1991	33,173	40,819	73,992	40,000
16	1992	38,366	44,214	82,580	58,000
17	1993	42,265	51,000	93,265	59,000

Table 23. Distribution of Contributions to Community Development, by Percentage of Expenditures

A. 1978–88 (Report Nos. 2–12)

Period/Report No.	Total ZARs (in 1000s)	Education	Housing	Health/Welfare	Recreation	Various
1978/2	3,152	33.06	.64	34.32	1.35	30.62
1979/3 (6 months)	2,783	48.00	14.90	10.67	6.10	20.31
1980/4	2,892	0	47.75	14.51	18.27	19.45
1981/5 (est.)	4,850	0	30.50	28.80	22.68	20.61
1982/6	11,133	0	10.37	69.05	9.54	11.02
1983/7	5,287	0	33.45	22.42	17.69	22.42
1984/8	7,872	0	29.62	31.01	18.73	31.10
1985/9	25,614	0	14.56	15.93	26.80	42.69
1986/10	31,493	12.12	27.60	38.20	10.44	11.63
1987/11	37,774	8.64	25.53	39.58	0	26.24
1988/12	35,448	9.19	21.37	23.22	0	28.72

B. 1989–93 (Report Nos. 13–17)

Period/Report No.	Total ZARs (in 1000s)	Supp./Devel. of BCA Enterprises	Housing	Land/Ownership Residential Segregation/Removals	Health Care	Development of BCA Leadership	Political Rights Activities	Civic Activities	Social Segregation	Other
1989/13	45,522	30.72	9.70	4.54	16.09	6.89	7.41	14.59	3.67	6.33
1990/14	36,695	24.04	11.92	4.86	21.83	7.19	6.15	13.77	0	10.23
1991/15	40,819	24.07	11.85	2.09	22.04	6.07	6.59	13.04	0	14.23
1992/16	44,214	26.79	14.66	2.19	18.25	7.60	5.13	11.79	0	13.59
1993/17	51,000	31.80	10.80	2.00	17.80	7.01	5.23	12.36	0	12.74

Table 24. Contributions to Community Development (Employee-Days)

A. 1982–85 (Report Nos. 6–9)

Period/ Report No.	Employee-Days	Housing (%)	Health/ Welfare/ Civic (%)	Recreation (%)	Various (%)
1982/6	7,355	11.69	26.78	51.71	9.80
1983/7	7,926	18.00	42.41	28.99	10.58
1984/8	9,143	20.68	47.33	20.78	11.19
1985/9	46,938	9.72	15.21	25.55	43.51

B. 1986–88 (Report Nos. 10–12)

Period/ Report No.	Employee-Days	Housing (%)	Health/ Welfare (%)	Civic/ Recreation (%)	Assistance to Social Programs (%)	Assistance to BCA Business (%)	Other (%)
1986/10	51,772	14.45	18.97	22.84	10.49	33.24	0
1987/11	29,375	15.35	28.24	22.80	0	33.60	0
1988/12	31,477	17.31	21.28	24.85	0	36.546	17.40

C. 1989–93 (Report Nos. 13–17)

Period/ Report No.	Employee-Days	Support/ Development of BCA enterprises (%)	Housing (%)	Land/ Ownership Residential Segregation/ Removals (%)	Health Care (%)	Civic Activities (%)	Other (%)
1989/13	32,999	30.11	17.18	0	21.87	30.83	0
1990/14	26,580	21.24	13.45	0	26.04	18.24	21.02
1991/15	27,997	22.34	13.16	0	31.22	14.04	19.23
1992/16	34,182	23.11	10.74	0	27.26	13.69	25.24
1993/17	30,908	26.25	10.96	0	29.32	17.79	14.74

Table 25. Racial Composition of Work Force

Year/Period	Total Employees	BCAs (%)	White (%)	Whites (%) Managed by BCAs
1977/1	38,061	56	44	N/A
1978/2	51,488	56	44	N/A
1979/3	55,671	57	43	N/A
1980/4	78,572	63	37	N/A
1981/5	83,133	65	35	N/A
1982/6	69,013	64	36	N/A
1983/7	66,175	63	37	N/A
1984/8	64,724	63	37	2.5
1985/9	62,656	60	40	3.1
1986/10	62,376	60	40	3.5
1987/11	43,865	62	38	4.9
1988/12	33,451	61	39	6.2
1989/13	27,036	62	38	6.4
1990/14	21,072	63	37	8.5
1991/15	17,693	60	40	9.8
1992/16	16,837	59	41	10.5
1993/17	15,758	59	41	12.0
				15.0

The dispersion of BCA employees among various occupational classifications is described in table 26. The data show that BCAs accounted for unskilled and semiskilled workers. The proportion of BCAs in higher occupational classifications (table 27) showed, from the early years through 1993, different rates of progress: supervisors, from 26 to 60 percent; professionals, from 6 to 37 percent; sales personnel, from 13 to 20 percent; and managers, from 3 to 16 percent. However, this data, too, must be interpreted cautiously because of the exit of many large employers from South Africa during the 1986–88 period, which created an upward bias in the number of BCA employees in higher-occupational categories among the remaining companies. The same cautionary note applies to any effort to interpret the increasing number of BCAs in managerial careers.

The signatory companies' efforts in attracting more BCAs to fill vacancies are shown in table 28. The data present a generally mixed picture. The proportion of BCAs filling all jobs declined from 71 percent in 1981 to 57 percent in 1993, and for sales personnel, from 45 percent in 1984 to 29 percent in 1993. However, in the other three categories, there were increases: supervisors, from 42 percent in 1982 to 73 percent in 1993; professionals, from 28 percent in 1984 to 51 percent in 1993; and managers, from 10 percent in 1981 to 31 percent in 1993.

Table 26. Distribution of BCA Workers among Various Skill Levels, by Percentages

Year/Period	Unskilled	Semiskilled	Skilled	Supervisor	Clerical	Professional	Sales	Manager
1977/1	N/A	N/A	N/A	N/A	N/A	N/A	N/A	N/A
1978/2	N/A	N/A	N/A	26	35	6	13	3
1979/3	N/A	N/A	N/A	27	34	6	14	3
1980/4	99	95	35	19	38	9	18	3
1981/5	99	N/A	51	37	35	10	27	3
1982/6	99	N/A	46	34	39	11	35	3
1983/7	99	N/A	45	35	38	13	36	4
1984/8	99	N/A	49	39	40	15	37	5
1985/9	99	N/A	47	40	39	15	29	5
1986/10	99	97	50	40	41	17	20	8
1987/11	99	97	51	44	39	21	21	8
1988/12	99	95	54	53	40	25	20	10
1989/13	99	95	58	58	42	31	20	12
1990/14	99	95	59	59	43	35	21	13
1991/15	99	95	60	56	43	35	21	13
1992/16	100	95	61	58	42	35	23	14
1993/17	100	95	60	60	42	37	20	16

Table 27. Racial Composition of Work Force in Managerial Careers. by Percentages

Year/ Report No.	Level 1[a]	Level 2[b]	Level 3[c]	BCAs in Managerial Posts
1981/5	N/A	N/A	N/A	3
1982/6	N/A	N/A	N/A	3
1983/7	N/A	N/A	N/A	4
1984/8	N/A	N/A	N/A	5
1985/9	N/A	N/A	N/A	5
1986/10	N/A	N/A	N/A	8
1987/11	N/A	N/A	N/A	8
1988/12	N/A	N/A	N/A	10
1989/13	N/A	N/A	N/A	12
1990/14	N/A	N/A	N/A	13
1991/15	N/A	N/A	N/A	13
1992/16	3	12	19	14
1993/17	5	14	23	16

Note: Data for years previous to 1981 could not be located.

[a] The highest level of management, including managing directors and in-company directors.
[b] Managers report to the managing director and coordinate the activities of one or more departments through subordinate managers.
[c] Managers plan, direct, and coordinate department activities through subordinate supervisors, identified here as level 3 managers.

3. IMPACT OF THE REPORTING SYSTEM ON THE IMPLEMENTATION AND EFFECTIVENESS OF THE SULLIVAN PRINCIPLES

The framework of the performance evaluation and reporting system—as designed and implemented by Reid Weedon of Arthur D. Little—was presented in chapter 4. In this chapter, we focus our attention on the implementation of the system and the impact that it had on

- the way companies executed their policies and programs to achieve the best possible ratings under the monitoring system (and therefore their performance under the Principles)

- the selection, location, and management of projects

- the shift in emphasis and activities of various NGOs in their efforts to secure funding from the United States companies

- the improvement in the economic and sociopolitical conditions in the recipient communities, and the extent to which community expectations, dependence on aid, and self-reliance (or lack thereof) might have been affected by the infusion of funds from the United States companies

- the public reporting of United States companies' performance, and the public perceptions thereby created of the role of these companies under apartheid

Table 28. Distribution of Job Vacancies Filled by BCAs, by Percentages

Year/ Period	Total Employees	Percent BCA	Manager	Supervisor	Professional	Sales	All Jobs
1977/1	38,061	56	N/A	N/A	N/A	N/A	N/A
1978/2	51,488	56	N/A	N/A	N/A	N/A	N/A
1979/3	55,671	57	N/A	N/A	N/A	N/A	N/A
1980/4	78,572	63	N/A	N/A	N/A	N/A	N/A
1981/5	83,133	65	10	42	N/A	N/A	71
1982/6	69,013	64	6	49	N/A	N/A	71
1983/7	66,175	63	6	49	N/A	N/A	74
1984/8	64,724	63	15	49	28	45	67
1985/9	62,656	60	14	41	22	32	61
1986/10	62,376	60	20	52	28	25	66
1987/11	43,865	62	24	60	36	24	67
1988/12	33,451	61	23	61	38	23	58
1989/13	27,036	62	27	68	47	20	62
1990/14	21,072	63	20	63	40	23	63
1991/15	17,693	60	27	60	45	30	61
1992/16	16,837	59	35	70	52	28	58
1993/17	15,758	59	31	73	51	29	57

3.1   An Assessment of the Reporting System

Arthur D. Little's Weedon faced a difficult task in developing processes for converting the Sullivan Principles into operational practices. He confronted a similar challenge in creating standards for evaluating and publicly reporting the compliance efforts and performance by the signatory companies. There were no precedents to follow. For example, the reporting measures of the European Community's code were voluntary, nonstandardized, and left entirely to the discretion of the companies involved. Consequently, the company reports were either unavailable or contained little substantive information.

The Principles' reporting system was designed to be flexible in order to accommodate the evolving requirements and scope of the Principles and also in order to facilitate the presentation and assessment of qualitative data. This design, however, made the final reports difficult to compare from one year to another. There were other methodological problems with regard to data collection and reporting. The qualitative or descriptive data were selected without any apparent predefined criteria, and were primarily intended to provide illustrative examples rather than to suggest either the impact of the activities reported or the extent to which the signatory companies pursued them. It was, indeed, impossible even to determine whether the qualitative data selected by Weedon for inclusion in the reports was, in fact, "illustrative"; the complete set of the companies' qualitative comments were not made public or even made available to research scholars for further analysis and examination.

Another significant problem was that the reported data could not be verified for accuracy. The reports submitted by publicly held signatories were, to be sure, reviewed by the companies' outside accounting firms. However, that review was limited to five items: total payroll; total employment by race; vacancies; lowest-paid-employee pay compared to the MLL/HSL (minimum living level or household subsistence level for a family of five or six members); and total expenditures for education, community development, and social justice programs. Items that were qualitative in nature—such as desegregation, equality of benefits, and projects described on the reporting form—were not independently verified by the auditors or by any other outside sources.

Quite apart from the possibility of intentional distortions by the companies, this system left considerable room for individual interpretation and hence inconsistency. Even under conditions of conventional reporting of financial data—a far better defined framework than companies' reporting under the Principles—companies have a certain latitude in reporting various sources of income and expenditure, which makes comparative analysis difficult and leaves the data open to differing interpretations. There was, moreover, no provision for A. D. Little to evaluate independently the veracity of company reports; hence one could judge neither the accuracy of the reporting (were they "padded"?) nor the extent to which all firms interpreted and reported similar expenditures in a similar manner. Although one can accept the rationale for not duplicating the audit process, it would have been desirable for A. D. Little to audit a representative sample either of the expenditures under various categories or of individual company reports in order ensure their authenticity and consistency. In any case, Weedon's reporting system demanded in many cases only that companies check off whether they have been active in a given area. Consequently, companies were strongly motivated to spread their activities over many areas, which typically led to fragmented efforts and ineffective interventions. Moreover, the annual reporting basis led many companies to make short-term commitments rather than more enduring investments in social-responsibility projects.

Even in the areas in which companies' efforts were quantified in terms of expenditures, the reporting system emphasized inputs to the process—the amount of expenditures in each of a wide array of categories—rather than outcomes. Consequently, companies often "threw money" at projects rather than engaging in careful planning, implementation, and evaluation; companies' rating points came from the donations they made rather than being based on the effectiveness of their projects. This approach was especially common during the early years of the Principles program, when pressure to perform was the greatest. Moreover, the annual reporting period of the monitoring process exacerbated the problem; companies had to spend their target amounts quickly in order to be able to report that they had met their yearly objectives. The monitoring system, as we argued earlier, was therefore one in which success was measured by "bean counting" rather than by impact. In our opinion, this emphasis was a fatal flaw that undermined the entire enterprise of monitoring the companies and ensuring their implementation of the Principles.

3.2   Consultation with Employees

As part of the monitoring process, the companies were obligated both to inform employees of the categories for reporting and to review the implementation of the Principles with employee groups. Nonetheless, although some companies established formal procedures for involving employees in decision making, our interviews with employee representatives from different signatory companies indicated that rank-and-file employees generally felt that they were not consulted adequately. Some employees also were resentful that the entire monitoring system was run by White management consultants from a United States firm (Arthur D. Little) and that Black-owned firms, either from the United States or elsewhere, were not employed for that purpose. The exclusion of Black firms from taking part in the monitoring process made the consultations (such as they were) with employees appear to be no more than paternalistic, gratuitous gestures by the signatory companies.

3.3   Consultations with Community Representatives

Another criticism leveled against the United States companies was that local community representatives (that is, both the providers and the beneficiaries of the services funded by the signatory companies) were not allowed to participate in decisions concerning project selection and funding, either at the level of the individual companies or at that of the entire group of signatory companies. Corporate executives and ADL's Weedon have rejected this criticism, however, asserting that they constantly sought the advice and counsel of various NGOs that had expertise in the relevant areas.

It would have been difficult, in our judgment, to give NGOs a formal role in the decision-making process; each company had both its own decision-making structure and, based on its geographical area of operations and the products and services it produced, its own preferences for projects. Also, NGOs had no central, parent organization, and there was no viable basis for creating a system that would be broadly representative of all NGOs. Finally, different types of NGOs had their own priorities, which did not always mesh with those of other NGOs or those of the companies involved. Nevertheless discussions between the authors and NGO representatives in South Africa revealed a fairly broad level of discontent with United States companies. The representatives suggested that the companies were predominantly interested in doling out funds for the largest possible number of projects, thus covering the maximum number of categories under the Principles' reporting system and securing, in turn, a high performance rating.

ENDNOTES

1 F. R. Kniffin (Johnson & Johnson, New Brunswick, NJ), telex to Howard Cook (Johnson & Johnson, South Africa), 12 May 1980.
2 Industry Steering Committee, press statement, 26 August 1978.
3 The discussion in this section is based on a composite of various annual reports and a review of the reporting nature of the "core" findings. No attempt is made to profile details of reporting changes and reporting format that necessarily occurred in response to changed circumstances from one year to another.

4 Before one can discuss the tables in this study, a clarification of the terms is necessary. References to reporting units refer to a reporting unit of a company or one of its several business units. An individual signatory company may have more than one reporting unit, each one separately submitting compliance reports under the Principles program. Hence, the number of signatory companies in a given period may not be the same as the number of reporting units in the same period.

5 Minutes of the meeting of Task Group 7, 21 April 1983.

6 James W. Rawlings (vice president, Union Carbide Africa and Middle East, Inc.), letter to All Members of the Periodic Reporting and Community Development Task Group, 23 October 1979. Also, minutes of the Periodic Reporting and Community Economic Development Task Group of 6 November and 30 December 1980.

PART III

CONFLICTING FORCES
The Shaping of Corporate Performance

Chapter 11

The Comprehensive Anti-Apartheid Act of 1986
The Role of the United States Government and the Congress

The third of October 1986 was a momentous day in the history of the United States and also in the presidency of Ronald Reagan, one of the most popular United States presidents at home and abroad: both houses of Congress voted by significant majorities to override President Reagan's veto and thereby enact into law the Comprehensive Anti-Apartheid Act (CAAA) of 1986 (H.R. 4868). The law was intended to express strong United States opposition to the apartheid regime of the White-controlled minority government of South Africa. In addition to imposing economic and trade sanctions on that country, the law sought to bring worldwide political and economic pressure on South Africa's government with a view to creating a democratic, nonracial society there.

The United States Congress has historically deferred to presidents by giving them the widest possible latitude in conducting foreign policy. The override of CAAA was, indeed, the first time since 1973 that Congress had overridden a presidential veto in the area of foreign policy.[1] For President Reagan, opposition to CAAA was an avowedly "principled" stand against a widely held preference. Though fully aware that his position would be rejected, he was convinced that history would vindicate him. He had taken just such a principled stand before—when he had defied world opinion and strong public support at home to have the United States vote against the enactment of a World Health Organization (WHO) International Code of Marketing of Breast-Milk Substitutes. As discussed in chapter 3, this code was designed to curb marketing and promotion activities in the sale of infant formula products. Although inherently safe when used properly, the products were often used improperly and unnecessarily in economically poor nations, thereby contributing to infant mortality and exacerbating already severe economic deprivation.[2] In the case of both CAAA and the Infant Formula Code, the administration felt that any sanctions-related strategy would face serious enforcement problems, be contrary to the economic goals of the United

States, give a competitive advantage to businesses from other countries, and potentially undermine larger foreign policy goals of the United States.

Whatever the apparent strength of the above arguments, similar ones could be used to justify the diametrically opposite position. To wit, why should a president defy public opinion on behalf of a law that, though not doing much good, would not do much harm, either. The law may have been imperfect, but so were the alternatives advocated by the Reagan administration and its conservative business and political allies in the United States. The administration's stance had not received strong political support even from its political allies abroad (with the exception of the United Kingdom).[3] Reactions of other countries ranged from lukewarm to outright opposition. Many nations already had sanctions in place against South Africa. For example, the Arab states, with the exception of Iran, had sanctions against exporting oil to South Africa since 1963; Norway had stopped export credit in 1976; Canada had removed its commercial consuls in 1977; Sweden had restrictions on investment and ownership in South Africa since 1979; ships registered in Denmark were banned from transporting oil to South Africa beginning in 1984, the same year that Denmark ended investment in South Africa and began to limit its imports from that nation.[4]

The United Nations had also been active on the South Africa question for several years. Dating back to 1962, the UN General Assembly called for voluntary sanctions against South Africa. Additional measures were passed over the years, leading up to the designation of 1982 as the "International Year of Mobilization for Sanctions in South Africa." In 1993 the Security Council stepped up pressure by passing voluntary sanctions against the sale of military goods. Although strong in rhetoric, the actions called for were only voluntary and not binding (even so, both the United States and Great Britain withheld their support of the sanctions).[5] The Eminent Persons Group (EPG) on South Africa—the members of which were drawn from throughout the British Commonwealth—was also outspoken on American policy (and policy, in general) regarding South Africa. Jeffery Gayner, representing the EPG during the 1986 Senate hearings on CAAA, suggested that existing policy created no motivation for the South African government to act, and that the lack of any immediate threat of sanctions may have actually supported a stance of no action: "It's already the case that [the absence of sanctions] and Pretoria's belief that they need not be feared defer change."[6]

In the economic arena, many large United States corporations had already started withdrawing from their operations and investments in South Africa in response to public pressure in the United States and a deteriorating political and economic climate in South Africa. Even so, these corporations remained strong opponents of economic sanctions. It could be argued, too, that President's Reagan's stance showed his reflexively pro-business, pro-free-market stance. Furthermore, when these biases combined with his visceral antagonism toward the Evil Empire of Communism, his choice of policy options became all too apparent. Unfortunately for the administration and for Reagan, the United States companies abandoned their ideological stance when it no longer made economic sense.[7]

An analysis of the events both prior and subsequent to the enactment of CAAA provides strong evidence of a sea change in the public mood. There was strong sentiment for adhering to moral and ethical values in society's actions even when adherence to those principles might seem irrational, economically unjustifiable, and harmful to other important policy goals. This stance brings out the dichotomy in the American psyche or character, which is pragmatic in seeking solutions to societal problems but nevertheless has a strong ethical foundation—a combination that may lead to actions that are contrary to self-interest and that can be justified only on the basis of moral principles.

1.   UNITED STATES POLICY TOWARD SOUTH AFRICA

The United States government's policy toward South Africa during the Reagan era can best be understood in terms of three factors: (1) broad foreign policy concerns and strategic issues pertaining to the entire region of sub-Saharan Africa; (2) tactical aspects of responding to specific domestic and international concerns relating to South Africa; and (3) the ideological mindset that prevailed in the Reagan White House and the influence of the ultraconservative wing of the Republican Party during the Reagan administration.

1.1   Foreign Policy Considerations

The Reagan administration, strongly supported by the State Department, viewed South Africa as a key player in combating Communism and Soviet influence in sub-Saharan South Africa. This concern was heightened by border conflicts and leftist uprisings in Angola and Mozambique, by the emergence of socialist-dominated regimes in Zambia, by the strong influence of the Communist Party in the ranks of the African National Congress, and by the alleged training ANC troops in the Soviet Union, Zambia, Cuba, and Libya (among other countries). In light of these issues, many believed that a posture congenial to the South African government was necessary.

The Reagan administration formulated its policy on South Africa and apartheid within the context of the above concerns. This broader perspective and the associated foreign policy agenda were consistently raised by State Department and other witnesses in hearings in both the House and the Senate in support of a more proactive and less punitive policy stance toward South Africa.[8] A punitive stance toward South Africa, it was argued, would make it difficult for the United States government to mediate peace in the region and to reduce armed conflict among various warring nations.[9]

1.2   "Constructive Engagement"

The foreign-policy posture adopted by the Reagan administration and the State Department put severe limits on the administration's ability to fashion strategic options and tactics that would meet the general public's concerns about apartheid and South Africa. The administration had to develop a modus operandi that would communicate the United States government's support for the goals, if not actions, of those who sought political freedom and economic and social justice for the Black people of South Africa. At the same time, the United States government could not be seen to be so hostile toward the South African government as to drive it toward greater belligerence or even recklessness. This strategy of maintaining a "delicate balance" between the two widely divergent and almost irreconcilable goals came to be known as *constructive engagement,* a term coined by the assistant secretary of state, Chester A. Crocker, who made it the cornerstone of his—and the Reagan administration's—policy for sub-Saharan Africa.

Constructive engagement can best be described as a nonpunitive policy aimed at social and economic reform. The underlying premise was that the United States could use its friendship with other countries to move them toward such reform. The administration described the policy as the best and perhaps the only rational option that would lead to the desired ends advocated by anti-apartheid advocates in the United States and abroad. Nonetheless, constructive engagement was not conceived as a policy aimed specifically at the apartheid issue in South Africa. The policy was intended, instead, to be regional in scope. Crocker's fundamental objective for this policy of constructive engagement was "to foster a regional climate conducive to compromise and accommodation in both Southern and South Africa."[10] From Crocker's perspective, which became the administration's perspective, South Africa was simply one of many countries that needed to be understood within the regional sociopolitical and national-security perspective. In an August 1981 speech, Crocker emphasized that "we cannot and will not permit our hand to be forced to align ourselves with one side or another in disputes." He went on to explain that "the Reagan Administration has no intention of destabilizing South Africa in order to curry favor elsewhere. Neither will we align ourselves with apartheid policies that are abhorrent to our own multi-racial democracy."[11] The administration's arguments could best be summarized as follows:

- Bipartisan support in Congress and a united political front were needed to make substantial progress toward achieving political and economic freedoms for all the people of South Africa.

- The opponents of the administration's policy had distorted the true meaning and substance of constructive engagement.

- The historical track record of economic sanctions was not good.

- There were many avenues open for diplomacy between the United States and South Africa. The United States government should employ all of these avenues rather than focus on a narrower and highly dubious approach of economic sanctions that could both undermine relations between the two countries and jeopardize larger foreign policy interests of the United States in sub-Saharan Africa.

- The United States government should promote more United States economic activity in South Africa, not less.

- Punishing South Africa through sanctions would have a negative impact that would result in a restricted negotiating position.

Important segments of both political parties in Congress, however, were losing confidence in the administration's position regarding South Africa. By the middle of 1986, Congress believed it needed to do something. Even Richard Lugar—the chairman of the Senate Foreign Relations Committee who had encouraged Reagan's 1985 executive order imposing limited sanctions on South Africa but had, along with other senators such as Nancy Kassebaum and Robert Dole, delayed congressional action on the 1985 version of CAAA—was unwilling to take on the role of buffer between the Senate and the White House. Though well recognizing that "a premium should be placed on the American Government speaking with one voice,"[12] the voice of the Reagan administration was seen as no longer effective.[13]

To the South African government, constructive engagement reflected the Reagan administration's sympathetic understanding of that country's political and socioeconomic problems; it presented the prospect of a "deliberate and structured" transition toward political and economic integration, a transition that would be manageable without causing extreme social unrest and violence. Constructive engagement would enable reform to proceed under South Africa's control and at that country's chosen pace (that is, at the pace preferred by South Africa's president P. W. Botha). The perception was that the United States supported and encouraged reform, but did not intend to force it by bullying the South African government. The fundamental *assumption* underlying this strategy—and what was continually asserted by the supporters of constructive engagement—was that Botha's government not only recognized that reform of apartheid was inevitable, but was committed to pursuing it. What Botha meant by *reform,* however, was not clear. If he intended to dismantle apartheid, he never said so.

1.3   The Reagan Administration's Mindset and Ideological Blinders

President Reagan's political and ideological perspective took shape during the darkest days of the Cold War. To him, there was no evil greater than the Communist evil, and the Soviet Union was an Evil Empire that must be contained, if not destroyed, at all costs. Reagan was therefore willing to live with a smaller evil—South Africa's White-minority government—if it would help to contain the greater evil of Communism.

Unfortunately, the Reagan administration's arguments in support of constructive engagement were undermined by the administration's own actions and lack of progress toward political reforms in South Africa. Not only had the Botha administration made little progress toward reform, but in his now infamous address, the "Rubicon Speech," President Botha had backtracked from his earlier promises for democratic reforms and restated his hard-line position of "reforms" at a pace to be determined by "his" government.[14] Chester Crocker's immediate response (the next day, in a speech before the Commonwealth Club) was to suggest that discussion was not enough from Botha; it was time for action. Interestingly, though, Crocker went on to state that he believed there was some good buried within the political smoke screen of the speech and that the United States should continue to work with South Africa and not withdraw from that country.[15]

Progress was equally lacking on other important issues in the sub-Saharan region; for example, Namibian independence, excursions by the South African military into neighboring states (allegedly in pursuit of ANC terrorists), and South Africa's support of the guerilla movement in Angola. The Reagan administration was also unwilling to expend significant resources—in terms of economic and political aid to the disenfranchised Black majority of South Africa—in putting constructive engagement into practice. The United States government's actions were seen more as symbolic rhetoric than as a serious commitment. Thus, over time, constructive engagement came to be discredited and to be understood as a cynical means of undercutting both anti-apartheid sentiment and anti-apartheid activists in the United States.[16]

Although the administration purported to communicate and work with all factions in South Africa, its primary focus was on the Botha government. There was little direct engagement between the White House and Black South African reform groups. In the April 1985 hearings of House Committee on Foreign Affairs, Chester Crocker was chastised for just that lack of engagement with Black South African constituencies. Congressman Howard E. Wolpe challenged Crocker by suggesting that the administration did not seek—and had, in fact, squandered—opportunities to meet with Black South African leaders. He cited a 1985 example; namely, when ANC leader Oliver Tambo was in the United States, no ranking administration official made any attempt to meet with him. Wolpe also noted that Congress essentially forced President Reagan to meet with Archbishop Desmond Tutu.[17] In his 1986 statement during Senate hearings, Senator William Roth criticized the administration's minimal involvement with Black leaders in South Africa and argued that the United States, contrary to the assertions of the Reagan administration, has not actually "been constructively engaged with all parties in South Africa."[18]

2. THE NATIONAL DELIBERATIONS LEADING TO THE PASSAGE OF CAAA

United States policy toward South Africa evolved over the course of several presidential administrations. The emergence of support for CAAA must therefore be viewed in the context of global developments relating to South Africa, and the political orientations of several successive presidential administrations. Moreover, the enactment of CAAA itself was the product of extended and often rancorous debate at all levels of the legislative and executive branches. Lobbying was also intense, as was coverage by the mass media.

Shorn of its racial overtones, the economic context of apartheid in South Africa was little different from the economic conditions of many other countries the world over. The labor of one group is coercively expropriated by, and for the benefit of, another group—typically either the majority or a group possessing the political or military means of subjugation. For example, India has been engaged for centuries in such egregious conduct under its "caste system," in which members of higher castes have routinely appropriated for themselves the economic and social benefits of an economic system that forces members of lower castes to perform menial jobs and live in abject poverty. Similar subjugation of minorities is blatantly practiced in various countries of Africa, the Middle East, and Latin America.

Why, then, did the world choose to treat South Africa differently? There are many answers. First, South Africa proclaimed itself to be a civilized, democratic country that aspired to be a member of the family of Western nations. South Africa also wanted to be seen and treated differently than the "barbaric" backward countries of southern Africa that surrounded it. The problem was that Western countries, which were willing to turn a blind eye toward apartheidlike discrimination in "backward" countries, were equally unwilling to countenance such conduct from a country that professed to be one of them. Second, most industrially advanced countries, with the exception of Japan, were increasingly becoming multi-ethnic and secular; in this context, the racism of the apartheid system was contrary to these countries' express public values. Third, the United States had a long tradition of anti-racism—despite its less than perfect record of combating racism within its own borders. The enactment of civil rights laws in the 1960s added further momentum to the drive to eliminate racism. Fourth, the Black population in the United States had taken up the apartheid issue as its cause célèbre and as a litmus test for candidates seeking elective office.

The first well-defined policy toward South Africa emerged under President Jimmy Carter. The Carter administration had made human rights the centerpiece of its foreign policy. Consequently, it was less tolerant of the apartheid activities of South Africa. As Senator Richard Lugar noted, "the Carter Administration publicly attacked South Africa for its racist policies and attempted to separate the U. S. from it."[19] Carter used Vice President Walter Mondale, Secretary of State Cyrus Vance, and the United States ambassador to the United Nations, Andrew Young, to carry the administration's message to South Africa. It was also during the Carter administration that the House of Representatives began to show interest in legislative sanctions.[20] Mondale exerted intense pressure on the South African government and did not mince words in his discussions with the South African leadership: "The U. S. would not intervene to save South Africa from the consequences of its policies. Our paths will converge and our policies will come into conflict."[21]

The Carter administration's policy and its activities were criticized by the South African government, which also dismissed the policy as simply tough talk and no action. The Reagan administration subsequently rejected Carter's policy—in substantial part, according to Senator Lugar, because the Reagan administration believed that Carter had underestimated the threat of Communism in Southern Africa.[22] Chester Crocker, Reagan's assistant secretary of state for Africa, strongly criticized Carter's South African policy on similar grounds, suggesting that "Carter's malaise over Cubans in Africa was driven in part by a critical and anxious chorus in foreign policy journals, think tanks, Congressional hearings and media commentary."[23]

The Reagan administration's initial policies represented a distinct shift in that the administration took a more conciliatory, rather than confrontational, stance toward South Africa. There was a rapid dismantling of the sanctions imposed during the Carter years; for example, early in his presidency, Reagan lifted United States restrictions on trade with South Africa. In 1981, sales of medical supplies were allowed. In 1982, this relaxation of trade was extended to the sale of nonmilitary goods to military and police organizations in South Africa. Also in 1982, the United States started supporting International Monetary Fund (IMF) loans to South Africa. From the perspective of South Africa's government, it was an auspicious start to what came to be known as constructive engagement. However, from the perspective of anti-apartheid activists, the Reagan administration had reneged on the United States' commitment to oppose apartheid and had taken a large step backward toward business as usual.

The Reagan administration adamantly followed its policy of constructive engagement in the face of both increasing opposition from a bipartisan Congress and widespread public sentiment against that policy. It was only much later—1985—that the administration sought to stiffen its resolve against the South African government through a more stringent and restrictive measure in the form of Executive Order 12532 (appendix 11.1). This belated measure was, however, generally perceived as a feeble and manipulative attempt to persuade the Congress not to pass CAAA.

2.1   Policy Debate and Deliberations: The White House and the Congress

From the very start, the debate between the administration (primarily the Department of State) and Congress was based on their very different interpretations of the results of the United States policy toward South Africa. Where the administration saw progress (albeit slow), Congress saw decline. Where the administration saw a need to support economic development as the means to an end, Congress saw direct United States support of economic growth as support of the Botha government and its hostility toward reform. Congressional reaction to the State Department policy can be summarized as follows:

- Bipartisan support for the administration's policy was necessary but not forthcoming because of serious disagreements both as to the content of the policy and the reasons and data provided by the administration for pursuing its policy.

- Constructive engagement had not, after five years, yielded measurable results. On the contrary, the administration's policies had weakened restrictions on South Africa.

- The United States had acted to weaken United Nations sanctions against South Africa and had thereby appeared to opponents of apartheid as an ally of the Botha government.

- Contrary to its assertions, the administration had not used "quiet diplomacy" in getting South Africa to move toward political and economic reform.

- For fear of alienating the Botha government, the United States government had not been evenhanded in dealing with that government's domestic opponents. Thus, the Reagan administration unwittingly played into the hands of the Botha government and was seen to be indifferent to the concerns of the Black population of South Africa.

2.2   Congressional Action: Early Interest

On the issue of South Africa, the administration and Congress were clearly at odds. Although limited partisan support for the administration's policy existed in both houses of Congress, it was too small a constituency to influence or contain the drive toward sanctions. Reflecting the higher proportion of Democrats in the House than in the Senate, support for legislative sanctions was more pronounced in the House. Stephen J. Solarz (chairman of the House's Subcommittee on South Africa), William H. Gray (an active member of the Congressional Black Caucus), and Howard E. Wolpe (Solarz's successor as chairman of the House's Subcommittee on South Africa)—all in the House of Representatives—were among the early supporters of sanctions. The emerging sentiment of the House became clear in a 1984 letter to the South African ambassador that, in effect, threatened legislative action if immediate steps were not taken to dismantle his government's apartheid policies (a complete text of the letter, together with the names of all the signatories, is presented in appendix 11.2). The letter, which was signed by thirty members of the House, stated, among other things, that:

- The signatories of the letter were, for the most part, politically conservative and recognized the importance and strategic value of South Africa. It was for these very reasons that the signatories could not condone policies of apartheid, which they believed would adversely affect South Africa's long-term interests and impair the United States' ability to deal with South Africa in a constructive manner.

- The signatories looked with alarm on the escalating violence in South Africa and on the lack of progress by the South African government in moving toward "real" human rights reforms.

- The signatories were inclined to support the Reagan administration's policy of constructive engagement only as long as "real steps toward complete equality for all South Africans [were] ongoing." But if constructive engagement became "an excuse for maintaining the unacceptable status quo," that policy would "engender no meaningful support among American policy-makers."

The letter went on to state that the United States Congress would take immediate steps to change its policies toward the South African government unless meaningful changes were not forthcoming. A central demand was for "an immediate end to the violence in South Africa accompanied by a demonstrated sense of urgency about ending apartheid." The letter concluded by stating that if the suggested actions were not forthcoming, the Congress would recommend that the United States curtail new American investment in South Africa and organize international diplomatic sanctions against South Africa.

2.3   Public-Interest Groups

The House debate was often contentious, lacked clarity as to what policies would or would not work, and was subjected to intense lobbying by groups covering the entire spectrum of political ideology, economic stakes, and moral fervor. However, with the exception of a handful of groups that were either ultraconservative or promoting free markets, most groups advocated some sort of sanctions against South Africa's White-controlled government. Testimony from various hearings in both the House and the Senate found almost universal condemnation of apartheid and of the discriminatory actions of the South African government. Table 29 summarizes the positions of selected public-interest groups.

The most conspicuous and ardent advocates of economic sanctions were representatives of religious groups. The National Council of Churches and its program agency, the Interfaith Center on Corporate Responsibility, coordinated the efforts of the United States groups. The National Council of Churches (led by Rev. Willis Logan) and the United Church of Christ (led by Avery D. Post) were generally in support of broad sanctions. Rev. John T. Walker, bishop of the Episcopal Church of Washington, DC, was a proponent of limited, targeted sanctions aimed at specific acts of inequality and at specific solutions. The predominant theme coming from these religious groups was a peaceful solution to apartheid and the rejection of violence and radical interventions. Although the groups differed concerning the scope, specificity, and intensity of the sanctions they advocated, the general position was that the United States government needed to take more forceful action and that its current policies were ineffective and unacceptable.

In South Africa, Archbishop Desmond Tutu was outspoken in his unhappiness with the United States' policy of diplomacy and viewed the Reagan administration's position as soft and as sympathetic to the Botha government. Tutu made his position clear in an article in the *New York Times*, stating that "we are suffering already. To end it, we will support sanctions, even if we have to take on additional suffering." He went on to state that "we do not want apartheid made comfortable, we want it eliminated."[24] It was much the same point that Stephen Biko had made nine years earlier: "The argument is often made that loss of foreign investment would hurt blacks most. It would undoubtedly hurt blacks in the short run, because many of them would stand to lose their jobs, but it should be understood in Europe and

Table 29. Public-Interest Positions on Sanctions

Affiliation	Representative	General Action	Position on Sanctions
AFL-CIO	Thomas Donahue	supports Black trade unions constructive engagement does not work	supports tough sanctions
International Confederation of Free Trade Unions	(in Donahue testimony)	supports Black SA trade unions	supports tough sanctions
National Council of Churches	Rev. Willis Logan	wants peaceful change majority rule	supports sanctions
South Africa Federation	John H. Chettle	well-being for all South Africans employees/Blacks would suffer from sanctions	does NOT support sanctions
TRANSAFRICA	Randall Robinson	U.S. policy must change Black right to vote restoration of rights to land constructive engagement does not work without intervention, violence will increase people of South Africa are desperate	supports sanction
Heritage Foundation	Mark Huber (report)	does not support Sullivan critical of Sullivan reporting system	supports constructive engagement
	Jeffrey B. Gayner	critical of "forced" Sullivan sanctions will not motivate SA govt. sanctions will hurt Blacks in SA	does NOT support sanctions
Eminent Persons Group	group report	concern about Communist force within ANC British Commonwealth observer group	supports graduated, targeted sanctions
Desmond Tutu		Black South Africans have suffered already and will accept more if something comes of it	supports sanctions if they will make a difference
Zulu tribe	Gatsha Buthelezi	sanctions will hurt govt. but will also hurt the Blacks in SA	does NOT support sanctions

Affiliation	Representative	General Action	Position on Sanctions
U.S. colleges and universities	group communication	letter to Dole on sanctions, with 95 signatures	supports sanctions
Investor Responsibility Research Center	David Hauck	economic sanctions will not affect SA	supports noneconomic sanctions
Carnegie Endowment for International Peace	Pauline H. Baker	constructive engagement has failed White House needs to reconsider its position and policy	supports sanctions for political and psychological impact economic impact less important
Episcopal Church, Wash., D.C.	Rev. John T. Walker	"neither constructive nor engaging" sanctions not thought through issues are citizenship and right to vote	supports focused sanctions
United Church of Christ, Wash., DC	Avery D. Post		supports sanctions
National Committee to Restore Internal Security	Robert Morris	ANC is radical and dangerous current policy is working	does NOT support sanctions
National Education Association	John DeMars	philosophically opposed to apartheid supports totally equal economic and political system	supports sanctions
Leon Sullivan			supports sanctions

North America that foreign investment supports the present economic system and thus indirectly the present system of political injustice. We blacks are therefore not interested in foreign investment. If Washington wants to contribute to the development of a just society in Africa, it must discourage investment in South Africa. We blacks are perfectly willing to suffer the consequences. We are quite accustomed to suffering."[25]

Labor unions in the United States were also active in the anti-apartheid movement and provided support for the Black unions of South Africa. The principal organizations speaking for the organized workers were the AFL-CIO and the International Confederation of Free Trade Unions (ICFTU). Both organizations supported aid programs intended to assist Black South Africans in establishing and maintaining their own unions in South Africa—specifically by providing training and education programs for the leaders and members of South African trade unions. The AFL-CIO and the ICFTU also advocated sanctions against South Africa.

A wide array of other organizations also provided testimony in favor of sanctions: Transafrica, the National Education Association, the Carnegie Endowment for International Peace, the Investor Responsibility Research Center, and the Eminent Persons Group. The Eminent Persons Group was in favor of a graduated and targeted sanctions program, and the IRRC was primarily in favor of non-economic sanctions. The Carnegie Endowment for International Peace viewed the economic impact of sanctions as less powerful than the political and psychological message the sanctions would send both to the Botha government and to Black South Africans. Additional support for sanctions came from a group of college and university presidents, approximately one hundred of whom expressed their support of sanctions through a series of efforts, including a jointly signed communication to Senator Robert Dole expressing their views and asking for his support.[26]

Support for sanctions was not universal, however. In South Africa the principal opponent of sanctions was the Zulu tribal chief, Gatsha Buthelezi. In the United States, support for constructive engagement came primarily from conservative groups (for example, the Heritage Foundation and the National Committee to Restore Internal Security [NCRIS]) and the business community. NCRIS believed that sanctions would open up an opportunity for ANC to take power and, with its majority control, to impose radical and dangerous policy. The Heritage Foundation was concerned that sanctions would have little effect on the government, open the door for Communist influence, and negatively affect Black South Africans. The Heritage Foundation was also critical of the Sullivan Principles themselves—specifically their reporting practices and the problematic sense of voluntarism associated with corporate compliance with the Principles.

2.4 Congressional Debates: The Final Stretch

By the time congressional deliberations started in earnest in the latter part of 1985, it was apparent that the public mood had swung strongly toward a more forceful demonstration of the country's sentiment against South Africa's apartheid regime. It was also clear that the administration's policy of constructive engagement had few supporters in the public-at-large and among influential groups representing widely divergent segments of public opinion.

2.4.1 Sanctions Debate: The House of Representatives

Although there was general agreement that something needed to be done, the debate quickly turned toward what specifically to do. In the House, a powerful voice in favor of sanctions was that of the Congressional Black Caucus. The chairman of the Black Caucus, William Gray (Democrat; Pennsylvania) was an early supporter of congressional action with respect to South Africa and later played a major force in the drafting of CAAA.[27]

Members of the House rushed to take a place on the sanctions bandwagon, which presented the opportunity to ally themselves with a popular cause that would stand them in good stead with their constituents. Consequently, a large number of bills were introduced. With minor differences, they were similar in scope and were intended primarily as a means of jockeying for position—a negotiating ploy—in the shaping of the final bill. Table 30 provides a brief description of representative bills.

Table 30. Related Bills Proposed in Congress

HR 1986: Denies loans to business in SA (Coyners)
HR 632: SA Human Rights Act of 1985 (Roemer)
HR 1812: Bans SA honorary consulates in U.S. (Lowry)
HR 1133: Bans sales of nuclear technology to SA (Rangel)
HR 1135: Prohibits importing of coal & uranium from SA (Rangel)
HR 1357: Prohibits employee stock funds to invest in SA (Hayes)
HR 1358: SA Political Sanctions Act of 1985; severs relations with SA if apartheid not abolished within 2 years of bill's passage
(Roth, MacDonald, Dodd) 1985: Restricts SA flights from using U.S. airports
S 2636: Bans investments and loans and bans landing rights (Kassebaum)
S 2498: (Kennedy-Weicker)

An alternative to the above bills was proposed by Mark R. Siljander (Republican; Michigan) and supported by Henry Hyde, Toby Roth, and Gerald Solomon (all Republicans, from Illinois, Wisconsin, and New York, respectively). This Siljander bill had two major components: it called for

(1) a congressional commission to monitor anti-apartheid activity in South Africa for a three-year period, and to report to Congress on a semiannual basis, and (2) mandatory adherence to the Sullivan Principles for any United States company employing more than twenty persons in South Africa. A similar bill was proposed by Robert Walker (Republican; Pennsylvania). Both of these bills, however, failed to gain any significant support. It would have been difficult, if not impossible, to monitor and enforce compliance with such bills. Second, the bills addressed only part of the issue. Anti-apartheid sentiment by that time had gone far beyond economic policy; adherence to the Sullivan Principles was therefore considered by critics of apartheid to be an insufficient response.

2.4.2   Sanctions Debate: The Senate

Early Senate attention to the sanctions issue was generated by Richard G. Lugar (chair, Senate Foreign Relations Committee) and Nancy L. Kassebaum (chair, Senate Foreign Relations Committee's Subcommittee on Africa). Kassebaum, although initially not in favor of sanctions, expressed the need for a review of White House policy. Senator Lugar played a central role at this stage by helping to build a compromise position between the Senate and the White House on the apartheid issue. Lugar himself was in agreement with the White House policy to the extent that he believed United States businesses should remain in South Africa. He also believed, however, that it was Congress, not the president, that should set the country's policy toward South Africa.[28] Even so, Lugar ultimately intervened on behalf of the White House after both houses of Congress passed the Anti-Apartheid Act of 1985 (H.R. 1460): he was instrumental in negotiating the president's executive order (E.O. 12532) of November 1985, which was a compromise between White House and congressional sentiments (and which, in effect, superseded the Anti-Apartheid Act of 1985, which had not yet been submitted to President Reagan for his signature).

Fundamentally, Reagan's executive order represented a stopgap arrangement: though including some of the sanctions that would have been imposed under the anti-apartheid bill supported by Congress, the order also had some obvious limitations. First, unless reinstated by the president, an executive order is in effect only for a one-year period. Second, the restrictions in the executive order were less stringent and narrower in scope than those called for in the anti-apartheid bill. Third, with the exception of two small aid increases (up to $8 million in scholarship funding and up to $1.5 million in human rights funds), the executive order did not provide for any additional aid in support of social development in South Africa.

Given the gap between the pending legislation and Reagan's executive order, it is appropriate to question why Congress did not proceed with submitting the 1985 anti-apartheid act to President Reagan for him to sign into law. The obvious answer is that Reagan, under no uncertain terms, made clear that he would veto any legislation that included sanctions against South Africa. It is doubtful that bipartisan support was sufficiently strong in 1985 to override a presidential veto.

3. COMPREHENSIVE ANTI-APARTHEID ACT OF 1986: THE LAW

On 3 October 1986, with the passage of the Comprehensive Anti-Apartheid Act of 1986 (H.R. 4868), the United States Congress sent a powerful message to South Africa and the rest of the world. Two months earlier, the bill had easily passed both houses of Congress, but, as expected, it was vetoed by President Reagan (on September 26; see appendix 11.3). By overriding that veto, both houses then showed their commitment to sanctions as a means of addressing apartheid in South Africa.

The Comprehensive Anti-Apartheid Act of 1986 comprised three basic sections:

- Specification of sanctions and policy components

- Reporting and procedural elements

- Specific conditions under which, and only under which, the president was empowered to lift the sanctions

The major policy elements of CAAA included severe, punitive restrictions and prohibitions, which were supplemented by a variety of social and economic measures on behalf of South Africa's Black population. The restrictions and prohibitions included the following:[29]

- No air traffic between the United States and South Africa, including a restriction of landing rights in the United States for South African carriers and the prohibition of United States carriers flying to South Africa.

- No new investment in South Africa by United States firms, with the explicit exception of loans to Black-owned ventures. United States firms' expenses earmarked for compliance with the Sullivan Principles were excluded.

- No loans to the South Africa government, with an exception for certain lending in the areas of humanitarian funds, including provisions for housing and education.

- No importation of goods produced, grown, or otherwise brokered by organizations owned, controlled, or supported by the South African government.

- No importation of Krugerrands.

- Termination of bilateral tax treaty with South Africa.

- Suspension of United States support to encourage trade with South Africa.

- No exportation of computers, nuclear products, oil, and weapons and munitions to South Africa.

- Requirement that fair labor practices (as defined by the Sullivan Principles) be implemented by United States companies with employees in South Africa.

- Requirement that the White House provide an annual status report and recommendations for additional action if deemed necessary.

Simply ending the oppressive treatment of Black South Africans was not the only objective of the legislation. The bill contained supplementary components aimed at beginning the process of reparation: assistance projects specifically intended to benefit those who were adversely affected by apartheid's restrictions and violations. The main areas addressed were education and scholarships, legal assistance (with regard to human rights, in particular), banking assistance (for Black business enterprises), housing, and famine relief. A common argument against sanctions was the damage it would do to commerce in South Africa and consequently to the economic plight of Black South Africans. It was this problem that—through support for education, commerce, and social well-being—the assistance programs were designed to address.

CAAA included reporting requirements for the purpose of monitoring the legislation's impact. Specific reporting responsibility was designated in the following areas:

- Communist Party activity in South Africa

- Violations of a United Nations arms embargo

- Import, export, and banking activity

- ANC compliance

- Assistance to disadvantaged South Africans

The bill further called for the White House actively to encourage other countries to adopt restrictions similar to those specified in CAAA. The administration was required to report annually to Congress on the status of, and progress in, the five areas indicated above, including an evaluation of any progress that would justify repeal of the sanctions (see next paragraph).

CAAA was not intended to exist indefinitely. The power to repeal the law rested in the hands of the president. Five conditions were established that, when and if they were all satisfied, would authorize termination of the act:

- The release of Nelson Mandela and all other political prisoners
- The repeal of the South African State of Emergency and the release of all persons detained under such an order
- The repeal of South Africa's bans on political parties
- The repeal of Group Areas and Population Registration Acts
- Good-faith negotiations with members of the Black majority

As we shall see, the provisions for termination did not provide a clearcut set of measures for identifying the appropriate conditions to repeal CAAA. Significant differences of opinion existed and were debated between Congress and the White House in relation to President George Bush's 1991 repeal of CAAA (see chapter 15 for a discussion of the circumstances and debate surrounding Bush's lifting of the sanctions).

3.1 The Presidential Veto

As expected, on 26 September 1986 the Comprehensive Anti-Apartheid Act of 1986 was returned to Congress by President Reagan with a veto letter (appendix 11.3). The administration did not accept punitive sanctions and severe economic restrictions as a solution to the apartheid problems in South Africa.

President Reagan also responded to the sentiment behind the legislation with a commitment to extend Executive Order 12532 for another year and to toughen some of the restrictions imposed in the earlier, preexisting executive order of 1985. The tone of Reagan's response represented a softening of the administration's hitherto uncompromising resolve and a move toward a middle ground. However, the letter and the commitments it included were not enough to satisfy congressional demands. There was still a significant gap between Reagan's commitment to sanctions and the terms of CAAA, and it was a gap that could not be bridged.

3.2 The Veto Override

The reaction to Reagan's veto was predictable and anticipated. The override vote in the House, with its Democratic majority, was 313 in favor of an override, with 83 opposed. Even in the Senate, with its Republican majority, the vote was 78 in favor of, and 21 opposed to, the override. In both cases, the vote to override was well over the two-thirds majority required. It was a long and somewhat difficult path, but Congress and most of the constituencies represented in congressional testimony got what they wanted, with the minor qualification that the sanctions against South Africa were too strong for some and too weak for others. The final bill that went to the president was nonetheless representative enough of the many bills introduced or proposed to secure a positive override vote.

Even so, the override may not have succeeded but for the occurrence of a few key events. First, the situation in South Africa was getting worse. Second, President Reagan, in a July speech on South Africa, although still denouncing apartheid, looked favorably on the action that the Botha government was taking to change its policies, and seemed to be recognizing the government for its achievement. These perceptions were inconsistent with those of many South Africans and others around the world who were following the apartheid issue. Desmond Tutu quickly denounced Reagan's view. Both Democratic and Republican members thus had little choice but to contemplate the unusual and difficult step of taking some control of foreign policy from the administration through the passage of legislation; namely, CAAA. Third, though Senator Lugar had, in 1985, brokered a deal to give the White House some additional time to pursue its policy toward South Africa, he was not willing to do so again in 1986. Lugar firmly believed that it was up to the Congress to set policy and became one of three significant Senate voices in support of the override—the other two being Senators Kassebaum and Dole. Three of the most influential members of the Senate thus took positions in strong opposition to the White House.

3.3 Reagan's Stance of Principled Opposition

The Reagan administration may have claimed to be standing on principle in opposing CAAA on ideological and moral grounds, but the facts demonstrate otherwise. The administration's moral and principle-based arguments were ambiguous and untenable, and its actions had clearly failed to promote its express goals, either in support of peaceful alternatives or in providing economic aid to Black South Africans. Nor did the administration succeed in eliciting a more positive response from the belligerent and recalcitrant South African government.

Reagan was an insular president who was unfamiliar with, and uninterested in, the complex nature of international business and global geopolitical issues. Surrounded by advisors who strongly supported his anti-Communist commitment, he was content to let them formulate policies that in the end would undermine—within the international arena—the very values in which he so fervently believed: democratic institutions, private enterprise, and individual responsibility. Taken in by his own rhetoric of individual freedom under a system of free markets and private enterprise, he then equated the latter system with the interests of big business and large corporations. Indeed, it was just the apparent linkage between individual values and free enterprise, on the one hand, and the interests of large multinational corporations, on the other, that provided Reagan with the necessary rationale to justify accommodating the interests of highly undemocratic and repressive foreign governments (a dynamic that also may have been at work in the Iran-Contra affair).

In our judgment, the fundamental problem—whether from a humanitarian, political, or economic perspective—was that United States policy under the Reagan administration, was "neither constructive nor engaging."[30] For example, in 1985 United States aid to South Africa amounted to only $20 million dollars, or approximately eighty cents per Black person in South Africa, the target group for such aid. For comparative purposes, during the same year, Israel and Egypt received in excess of $6 billion, Turkey $739 million, and El Salvador $435.7 million.[31] The point is not that the countries cited did not deserve aid but that, both in absolute and relative terms, United States aid to South Africa was trivial.

In the end, a highly moralistic president lost the high moral ground—and even his ability to lead the American public—when he advocated policies and programs that tended to undermine the struggle for individual freedom and democratic values in South Africa. Furthermore, just like the American business community, he failed to justify his position on ethical and moral grounds in a situation that cried for a moral stance, thereby causing a serious erosion to his moral authority to lead the American people.

APPENDIX 11.1

Executive Order (12532)

Prohibiting Trade and Certain Other Transactions Involving South Africa

By the authority vested in me as President by the Constitution and laws of the United States of America, including the International Emergency Economic Powers Act (50 U.S.C. 1701 et seq.), the National Emergencies Act (50 U.S.C. 1601 et. seq.), the Foreign Assistance Act (22 U.S.C. 2151 et seq.), the United Nations Participation Act (22 U.S.C. 287), the Arms Export Control Act (22 U.S.C. 2751 et seq.), The Export Administration Act (50 U.S.C. App. 2401 et seq.), the Atomic Energy Act (42 U.S.C. 2011 et seq.), the Foreign Service Act (22 U.S.C. 3901 et seq.), the Federal Advisory Committee Act (5 U.S.C. App. I), Section 301 of Title 3 of the United States Code, and considering the measures which the United Nations Security Council has decided on or recommended in Security Council Resolutions No. 418 of November 4, 1977, No. 558 of December 13, 1984, and No. 569 of July 26, 1985, and considering that the policy and practice of apartheid are repugnant to the moral and political values of democratic and free societies and run counter to united Sates policies to promote democratic governments throughout the world and respect for human rights, and the policy of the United States to influence peaceful change in South Africa, as well as the threat posed to United States interests by recent events in that country,

I, **Ronald Reagan**, President of the United States of America find that the policies and actions of the Government of South Africa constitute an unusual and extraordinary threat to the foreign policy and economy of the United States and hereby declare a national emergency to deal with that threat:

Section 1.

Except as otherwise provided in this section, the following transactions are prohibited effective October 11, 1985:

(a) The making or approval of any loans by financial institutions in the United States to the Government of South Africa or to entities owned or controlled by that Government. This prohibition shall enter into force on November 11, 1985. It shall not apply to (i) any loan or extension of credit for any educational, housing, or health facility which is available to all persons on a nondiscriminatory basis and which is located in a geographic area accessible to all population groups without any legal or administrative restrictions; or (ii) any loan or extension of credit for which an agreement is entered into before the date of this Order.

The Secretary of the Treasury is hereby authorized to promulgate such rules and regulations as may be necessary to carry out this subsection. The initial rules and regulations shall be issued within sixty days. The Secretary of the Treasury may, in consultation with the Secretary of State, permit exceptions to this prohibition only if the Secretary of the Treasury determines that the loan or extension of credit improve the welfare or expand the economic opportunities of persons in South Africa disadvantaged by the apartheid system, provided that no exception may be made for any apartheid enforcing entity.

(b) All exports of computers, computer software, or goods or technology intended to service computers to or for use by any of the following entities of the Government of South Africa:

    (1)   The military;

    (2)   The police;

    (3)   The prison system;

(4) The national security agencies;

(5) ARMSCOR [Arms Corporation of South Africa] and it's subsidiaries or the weapons research activities of the Council for Scientific and Industrial Research;

(6) The administering authorities for the black passbook and similar controls;

(7) Any apartheid enforcing agency;

(8) Any local or regional government or "homeland" entity which performs any function of any entity described in paragraphs (1) through (7).

The Secretary of Commerce is hereby authorized to promulgate such rules and regulations as may be necessary to carry out this subsection and to implement a system of end use verification to ensure that any computers exported directly or indirectly to South Africa will not be used by any entity set forth in this subsection.

(c) (1) Issuance of any license for the export to South Africa of goods or technology which are to be used in a nuclear production or utilization facility, or which, in the judgement of the Secretary of State, are likely to be diverted for use in such a facility; any authorization to engage, directly or indirectly, in the production of any special nuclear material in South Africa; any license for the export to South Africa of component parts or other items or substances especially relevant from the standpoint of export control because of their significance for nuclear transport purposes; and any approval of retransfers to South Africa of any goods, technology, special nuclear material, components, items or substances described in this section. The Secretaries of State, Energy, Commerce, and Treasury are hereby authorized to take such actions as may be necessary to carry out this subsection.

(2) Nothing in this section shall preclude assistance for International Atomic Energy Agency safeguards or IAEA programs generally available to its member states, or for technical programs for the purpose of reducing proliferation risks such as for reducing the use of highly enriched uranium and activities envisaged by Section 223 of the Nuclear Waste Policy Act (42 U.S.C. 10203) or for exports which the Secretary of State determines are necessary for humanitarian reasons to protect the public health and safety.

(d) The import into the United States of any arms, ammunition, military vehicles produced in South Africa or of any manufacturing data for such articles. The Secretaries of State, Treasury, and Defense are hereby authorized to take such actions as may be necessary to carry out this subsection.

Section 2.

(a) The majority of United States firms in South Africa have voluntarily adhered to fair labor principles which have benefited those in South Africa who have been disadvantaged by the apartheid system. It is the policy of the United States to encourage strongly all United States firms in South Africa to follow this commendable example.

(b) Accordingly, no department or agency of the United States may intercede after December 31, 1985, with any foreign government regarding the export marketing activity in any country of any national of the United States employing more than 25 individuals in South Africa who does not adhere to the principles stated in subsection (c) with respect to that national's operations in South Africa. The Secretary of State shall promulgate regulations to further define the employers that will be subject to the requirements of this subsection and procedures to ensure that such nationals may register that they have adhered to the principles.

(c) The principles referred to in subsection (b) are as follows:

(1) Desegregating the races in each employment facility;

(2) Providing equal employment opportunities for all employees without regard to race or ethnic origin

(3) Assuring that the pay system is applied to all employees without regard to race or ethnic origin;

(4) Establishing a minimum wage and salary structure based on the appropriate local minimum economic level which takes into account the needs of employees and their families;

(5) Increasing by appropriate means, the number of persons in managerial, supervisory, administrative, clerical, and technical jobs who are disadvantaged by the apartheid system for the purpose of significantly increasing their representation in such jobs;

(6) Taking reasonable steps to improve the quality of employees' lives outside the work environment with respect to housing, transportation, schooling, recreation, and health;

(7) Implementing fair labor practices by recognizing the right of all employees, regardless of racial or other distinctions, to self-organization and to form, join, or assist labor organizations, freely and without penalty or reprisal, and recognizing the right to refrain from any such activity.

(d) United States nationals referred to in subsection (b) are encouraged to take reasonable measures to extend the scope of their activities outside the workplace, by measures such as supporting the right of all businesses, regardless of the racial character of their owners or employees, to locate in urban areas, by influencing other companies in South Africa to follow the standards specified in subsection (c) and by supporting the freedom of mobility of all workers, regardless of race, to seek employment opportunities wherever the exist, and by making provision for adequate housing for families of employees within the proximity of the employee's place of work.

Section 3.

The Secretary of State and the head of any other department or agency of the United States carrying out activities in South Africa shall promptly take, to the extent permitted by law, the necessary steps to ensure that the labor practices described in section (2) (c) are applied to their South African employees.

Section 4.

The Secretary of State and the head of any other department or agency of the United States carrying out activities in South Africa shall, to the maximum extent practicable and to the extent permitted by law, in procuring goods or services in South Africa, make affirmative efforts to assist business enterprises having more than 50 percent beneficial ownership by persons in South Africa disadvantaged by the apartheid system.

Section 5.

(a) The Secretary of State and the United States Trade Representative are directed to consult with other parties to the General Agreement on Tariffs and Trade with a view toward adopting a prohibition on the import of Krugerrands.

(b) The Secretary of Treasury is directed to conduct a study to be completed within sixty days regarding the feasibility of minting and issuing gold coins with a view toward expeditiously seeking legislative authority to accomplish the goal of issuing such coins.

Section 6.

In carrying out their respective functions and responsibilities under this Order, the Secretary of the Treasury and the Secretary of Commerce shall consult with the Secretary of

State. Each such Secretary shall consult, as appropriate, with other government agencies and private persons.

Section 7.

The Secretary of State shall establish, pursuant to appropriate legal authority, an Advisory Committee on South Africa to provide recommendations on measures to encourage peaceful change in South Africa. The Advisory Committee shall provide its initial report within twelve months.

Section 8.

The Secretary of State is directed to take the steps necessary pursuant to the Foreign Assistance Act and related legislation to (a) increase the amount of internal scholarships provided to South Africans disadvantaged by the apartheid system up to $8 million from funds made available for Fiscal; Year 1986, and (b) increase the amount allocated for South Africa from funds made available for fiscal Year 1986 in the Human Rights Fund up to $1.5 million. At least one-third of the latter amount shall be used for legal assistance for South Africans. Appropriate increases in the amounts made available for these purposes will be considered in future fiscal years.

Section 9.

This order is intended to express and implement the foreign policy of the United States. It is not intended to create any right or benefit, substantive or procedural, enforceable at law by a party against the United States, its agencies, its officers, or any person.

APPENDIX 11.2

Congress of the United States
House of Representatives
Washington, DC 20515

December 4, 1984

The Honorable Bernardus G. Fourie, Ambassador
Extraordinary and Plenipotentiary
Office of the Embassy of the Republic of South Africa
Washington, DC 20008

Dear Ambassador Fourie:

Events of recent weeks in South Africa have raised serious questions about your government's willingness to move more progressively and aggressively toward real human rights reforms. With this letter we wish to make clear that we view the violence in your country and the questions raised by it with alarm. Furthermore, we want you to know that we are prepared to pursue policy changes relative to South Africa's relationships with the United States if the situation does not improve.

We are, for the most part, politically conservative and as conservatives recognize all too well the importance and the strategic value of South Africa. We understand the need for stability both within the internal affairs of your country and your external relationships with the United States. But precisely because we do feel strongly about our mutual interests, we cannot condone policies of apartheid which we believe weaken your long-term interests and certainly our ability to deal with you in a constructive manner.

The Reagan Administration has dealt with your nation on the basis of "constructive engagement". That policy merits our support as long as real steps toward complete equality for all South Africans are ongoing. If "constructive engagement" becomes in your view an excuse for maintaining the unacceptable status quo, it will quickly become an approach that can engender no meaningful support among American policy-makers.

We are looking for an immediate end to the violence in South Africa accompanied by a demonstrated sense of urgency about ending apartheid. If such actions are not forthcoming, we are prepared to recommend that the U.S. government take the following two steps:

1) Curtail new American investments in South Africa unless certain economic and civil rights guarantees for all persons are in place.

2) Organize international diplomatic and economic sanctions against South Africa.

In closing, let us reiterate our strong view that an end to apartheid is instrumental to the maintenance and the growth of the relationship between South Africa and the United States. We wish to be able to endorse policies that produce stronger ties between our two nations. But the reality of apartheid and the violence used to keep it in place make it likely that our relations will deteriorate. Those obstacles to a constructive alliance must be ended.

Sincerely,

Vin Weber, M.C.	Mike DeWine, M.C.
Dan Coats, M.C.	Nancy Johnson, M.C.
Bill Goodling, M.C.	Frank Wolf, M.C.
John Hiler, M.C.	Mickey Edwards, M.C.
Richard Armey, M.C.	Lynn Martin, M.C.

Bob Walker, M.C.
Robert Dorran, M.C.
Benjamin Gilman, M.C.
George Gekas, M.C.
Barbara Vucanovich, M.C.
Robert Lagomarino, M.C.
Connie Mack, M.C.
Newt Gingrich, M.C.
Tom Bliley, M.C.
Bill Dannemeyer, M.C.
Bob Livingston, M.C.
Duncan Hunter, M.C.
Jim Courter, M.C.
Bill McCollum, M.C.

Tom Lewis, M.C.
Bobbi Fiedler, M.C.
Steve Gunderson, M.C.
Chalmers Wylie, M.C.
Mark Siliander, M.C.
Ed Szchau, M.C.
Tom Ridge, M.C.
Bill Thomas, M.C.
Bill Clinger, M. C.
Rod Chandler, M.C. (no signature)
John Rowland, M.C.

APPENDIX 11.3

I am returning herewith without my approval H.R. 4868, the Comprehensive Anti-Apartheid Act of 1986. Title III of this bill would seriously impede the prospects for a peaceful end to apartheid and the establishment of a free and open society for all in South Africa.

This administration has no quarrel with the declared purpose of this measure. Indeed, we share that purpose: To send a clear signal to the South African Government that the American people view with abhorrence its codified system of racial segregation. Apartheid is an affront to human rights and human dignity. Normal and friendly relations cannot exist between the United States and South Africa until it becomes a dead policy. Americans are of one mind and one heart on this issue.

But while we vigorously support the purpose of this legislation, declaring economic warfare against the people of South Africa would be destructive not only of their efforts to peacefully end apartheid, but also of the opportunity to replace it with a free society.

The sweeping and punitive sanctions adopted by the Congress are targeted directly at the labor-intensive industries upon which the victimized peoples of South Africa depend for their very survival. Black workers—the first victims of apartheid –would become the first victims of American sanctions.

Banning the import of sugar, for example, would threaten the livelihood of 23,000 black farmers. Banning the import of natural resources is a sanction targeted directly at the mining industries of South Africa, upon which more than half a million black laborers depend for their livelihood.

By prohibiting the importation of food and agricultural products, the measure would invite retaliation by South Africa, which since June has purchased over 160,000 tons of wheat from the United States. Denying basic foodstuffs to South Africa—much of which go to feed the black population—will only lead to privation, unrest, and violence. It will not advance the goals of peaceful change.

Are we truly helping the black people of South Africa—the lifelong victims of apartheid—when we throw them out of work and leave them and their families jobless and hungry in those segregated townships? Or are we simply assuming a moral posture at the expense of the people in whose name we presume to act?

This, then, is the first and foremost reason I cannot support this legislation. Punitive economic sanctions would contribute directly and measurably to the misery of people who already have suffered enough. Using America's power to deepen the economic crisis in this tortured country is not the way to reconciliation and peace. Black South Africans recognize that they would pay with their lives for the deprivation, chaos, and violence that would follow an economic collapse. That is why millions of blacks and numerous black leaders in South Africa are as firm in their opposition to sanctions as in their abhorrence of apartheid.

The imposition of punitive sanctions would also deliver a devastating blow to the neighboring states in southern Africa that depend on Pretoria for transportation, energy, markets, and food. An estimated million-and-a-half foreign workers, legal and illegal, now live in South Africa. The number of people, women and children especially, outside South Africa who are dependent upon the remittances of these workers for their survival has been estimated to be over five million. Do we truly wish to b directly responsible for increased suffering, and perhaps starvation, in southern Africa? Do we truly wish our action to be the rational Pretoria invokes for expelling these workers? De we truly wish to trigger a cycle of economic sanctions and counter sanctions that end up crippling the economy of South Africa and devastating the economies of the frontline states? What sense does it make to send aid to those impoverished countries with one hand while squeezing their economies with the other?

Disrupting the South African economy and creating more unemployment will only fuel the tragic cycle of violence and repression that has gripped that troubled country. Black unemployment in South Africa in some areas is over 50 percent—and adding to it will create more anger, more violence, and more competition among blacks struggling to survive. It will not improve prospects for negotiations.

Another feature of the bill would require the Administration to publicly identify within six months any and all nations that have chosen not to join us in observing the UN arms embargo against South Africa, "with a view to terminating United States military assistance to those countries". But the United States will not revert to a single-minded policy of isolationism, with its vast and unforeseen effects on our international security relationships, that would be dictated by the unilateral decisions of our allies. No single issue, no matter how important, can be allowed to override in this way all other considerations in our foreign policy. Our military relationships must continue to be based upon a comprehensive assessment of our national defense needs and the security of the West.

Not only does this legislation contain sweeping punitive sanctions that would injure most the very people we seek to help, the legislation discards our economic leverage, constricts our diplomatic freedom, and ties the hands of the President of the United States in dealing with a gathering crisis in a critical subcontinent where the Soviet Bloc—with its mounting investment of men and arms—clearly sees historic opportunity. Therefore, I am also vetoing the bill because it contains provisions that infringe on the President's prerogative to articulate the foreign policy of the United States.

There are, however, several features of the measure that the Administration supports. Title II of the bill, for example, mandates affirmative measures to eliminate apartheid and provide assistance to its victims, including support for black participation in business enterprises as owners, managers, and professionals. It authorizes the President to take steps for the purpose of assisting firms to fight apartheid and extend equal opportunity to blacks in investment, management, and employment. The bill also contains a number of other useful and realistic provisions, such as those calling upon the African National Congress (ANC) to reexamine its Communist ties mandating a report on the activities of the Communist Party in South Africa and the extent to which it has infiltrated South African political organizations. Still other portions of the bill call upon the ANC to condemn the practice of "neck-lacing" and terrorism and to state affirmatively that it will support a free and democratic post-apartheid South Africa. These provisions, as well as many others in the bill, reflect the agreement of the Congress and the Administration on important aspects of an overall anti-apartheid policy.

The Administration has been—and remains—prepared to work with the Congress to devise measures that manifest the American people's united opposition to apartheid—without injuring its victims. We remain ready to work with the Congress in framing measures that—like the 1962 U.S. embargo of military sales and the carefully targeted sanctions of my own Executive order of 1985—keep the United States at arms distance from the South African regime, while keeping America's beneficent influence at work bringing about constructive change within that troubled society and nation.

It remains my hope that the United States can work with its European allies to fashion a flexible and coordinated policy—consistent with their recent actions—for constructive change inside South Africa. I believe we should support their measures with similar executive actions of our own, and I will work with the Congress toward that goal. It remains my hope that, once again, Republicans and Democrats can come together on the common ground that, after all, we both share: An unyielding opposition both to the unacceptable doctrine of apartheid as well as the unacceptable alternative of Marxist tyranny—backed by the firm determination that the future of South Africa and southern Africa will belong to the free. To achieve that, we must stay and build, not cut and run.

That the Americans should recoil at what their television screens bring them from South Africa—the violence, the repression, the terror—speaks well of us as a people. But the historic crisis in South Africa is not one from which the leading nation of the West can turn its back and walk away. For the outcome of that crisis has too great a bearing upon the future of Africa, the future of NATO, the future of the West.

Throughout the postwar era, we Americans have succeeded when we left our partisan differences at the water's edge—and persevered; as we did in the rebuilding of Europe and Japan, as we are doing today in El Salvador. We have failed when we permitted our exasperation and anger and impatience at present conditions to persuade us to forfeit the future to the enemies of freedom.

Let us not forget our purpose. It is not to damage or destroy an economy, but to help the black majority of South Africa and southern Africa enjoy a greater share of the material blessings and bounties their labor has helped to produce—as they secure as well their legitimate political rights. That is why sweeping punitive sanctions are the wrong course to follow, and increased American and Western involvement—by firms that are breaking down apartheid by providing equal opportunity for the victims of official discrimination—is the right course to pursue.

Our goal is a democratic system in which the rights of majorities, minorities, and individuals are protected by a bill of rights and firm constitutional guarantees.

Ronald Reagan
The White House, September 26, 1986

Source: Congressional Record, No. 132, House 8648, Monday, September 29, 1986.

ENDNOTES

1 President Richard M. Nixon, in 1973, was overridden on the "War Powers Resolution." See Stephen R. Weissman, *A Culture of Deference* (New York: Basic Books, 1995), 164–77. Pages 173–77 are of special interest.

2 S. Prakash Sethi, *Multinational Corporations and the Impact of Public Advocacy on Corporate Strategy: Nestle and the Infant Formula Controversy* (Boston: Kluwer Academic Publishers, 1994). See especially chapter 12. The United States position with regard to its negative vote in the case of WHO-sponsored Infant Formula Code was expressed by Elliott Abrams, who was then the newly appointed assistant secretary of state for international affairs, and a conservative hard-liner. He stated:

> After very careful consideration of this issue at all levels of the administration and with several agencies, we have determined that the U.S. delegation to the World Health Assembly must cast a negative vote on the draft code of Marketing of Breast-milk Substitutes. . . . This has been a very difficult and highly emotional issue in the United States, and in arriving at our decision, we have tried to take into consideration the positive and negative aspects of the draft code in the context of our own social, constitutional and legal systems.

> The code causes us serious problems—both on constitutional and legal grounds and on economic/commercial grounds. . . . Fundamentally, it would be hypocritical for the U.S. to vote in favor of a code that we could and or would not wish to implement here. We, therefore, could not recommend its implementation to others.

Ibid., 211.

3 Brenda M. Branaman, *Sanctions against South Africa: Activities of the 99th Congress—Report no. 87–200 F.* (Washington, DC: U.S. Government Printing Office, 1977).

4 Janice Love, *The U.S. Anti-Apartheid Movement: Local Activism in Global Politics* (New York, Praeger Books, 1985).

5 Ibid.

6 Senate Committee on Foreign Relations, *Situation in South Africa. Hearing before the Committee on Foreign Relations*, 99th Congress, 2nd sess., 22–24 and 29 July 1986.

7 It should be noted that business corporations followed a similar strategy in the case of the infant formula controversy. During the vote on WHO code, efforts were made to meet the conditions laid out by the United States representatives so that a negative vote could be avoided and that the United States would at least abstain from casting a vote. From all indications, the negotiations were all but satisfactorily concluded when the United States delegates received instructions from Washington to cast a negative vote. The story was broken by the columnist Jack Anderson:

> On May 1, Meese, Allen and two other members of Reagan's inner circle, Lyn Nofziger and Martin Anderson, sat down to discuss the developments in Geneva. Foggy Bottom officials learned from a National Security staffer that the four White House aides "have met and concluded that the U.S. should cast a negative vote on the WHO infant formula code" and that they "are not prepared to abstain even if the [U.S.] conditions are met.

> What happened was that American formula makers like Bristol-Myers, Abbott Laboratories and American Home Products, had lobbied the administration against the code. They were joined by the Grocery Manufacturers of America, which feared the code might be applied to other baby foods despite assurances to the contrary.

> The pressure from the companies apparently swayed the White House. U.S. officials in Geneva were put on hold.

Quoted in Sethi, *Multinational Corporations*, 212. And yet, soon after the code was passed, and following Nestle's lead, American companies announced that they, too, would abide by the WHO code in developing countries.

8 Sanford J. Unger and Peter Vale, "South Africa: Why Constructive Engagement Failed," *Foreign Affairs* 64 (1985): 234–58.

9 George P. Schultz, testimony, *Situation in South Africa: Hearing before the Senate Committee on Foreign Relations*, 99th Congress, 2d sess., 23 July 1986, 80.

10 Chester A. Crocker, *High Noon in Southern Africa* (New York: W. W. Norton, 1992), 75. See also Oliver F. Williams, *The Apartheid Crisis* (San Francisco: Harper & Row, 1986).

11 Crocker, *High Noon in Southern Africa*, 75.

12 Richard G. Lugar, testimony, *Situation in South Africa: Hearing before the Senate Committee on Foreign Relations*, 99th Congress, 2d sess., 29 July 1986, 22–24.

13 See Weissman, *A Culture of Deference*.

14 Chester A. Crocker, *State Department Bulletin* 85 (October 1985): 4–7. Les de Villiers, *In Sight of Surrender* (Westport, CT: Praeger, 1995), 85–91. Crocker's article is a transcript of a speech he delivered the day after the Rubicon Speech.

15 Crocker, *State Department Bulletin*.

16 In his 1992 book, *High Noon in Southern Africa*, Crocker offers his own defense of constructive engagement and points to the independence of Namibia and also to the settlement of the Angolan civil war as evidence that "constructive engagement" had been a successful policy. It should be noted, however, that Namibian independence and the settlement of the Angolan Civil War both came about long after the passage of CAAA.

17 Chester A. Crocker, testimony before the House Committee on Foreign Affairs, 17 April 1985, 136–38.

18 Senator William V. Roth, testimony, *Situation in South Africa: Hearing before the Senate Committee on Foreign Relations*, 99th Congress, 2d sess., 22–24 and 29 July 1986.

19 Senator Richard Lugar, "Promoting True Democracy in South Africa," in S. Prakash Sethi, ed., *The South African Quagmire* (Cambridge, MA: Ballinger, 1987).

20 Weissman, *A Culture of Deference*, 170.

21 Robert Kinloch Massie, *Loosing the Bonds: The United States and South Africa in the Apartheid Years* (New York: Doubleday, 1997), 412.

22 Lugar, "Promoting True Democracy in South Africa."

23 Crocker, *High Noon in Southern Africa*, 53.

24 Desmond Tutu, "Sanctions vs. Apartheid," *New York Times*, 16 June 1986.

25 Stephen Biko, in Massie, *Loosing the Bonds*, 420–21.

26 Letter to Robert Dole, 7 July 1986, presented in testimony, *Situation in South Africa: Hearing before the Senate Committee on Foreign Relations*, 99th Congress, 2d sess., 22–24 and 29 July 1986.

27 David Hauck, M. Voorhes, and G. Goldberg, "Two Decades of Debate: The Controversy over U.S. Companies in South Africa" (Washington, DC: IRRC, 1983), 29–59.

28 Weissman. *A Culture of Deference*.

29 Pauline Baker, *The United States and South Africa: The Reagan Years* (New York: Ford Foundation, 1989).

30 Sethi, *The South African Quagmire*, 12.

31 Ibid., 17.

Chapter 12

The Anti-Apartheid Movement and Its Impact on United States Companies to Withdraw from South Africa

The strategic thrust of the anti-apartheid movement in the United States was to force United States companies to disinvest in South Africa and to cease doing any business in that country. This strategy had widespread support among the anti-apartheid groups in the United States, and it was also supported by a vast majority of Black South Africans. As companies began to adopt the strategy of divestment, critics pointed out its defects, only to be largely ignored.

Data on direct foreign investments indicated that United States investments in South Africa amounted to less than 10 percent of total foreign investments in that country. Thus, the withdrawal of United States investments would make no little or no tangible difference unless other major investing nations—in particular, England, Germany, and Japan—could be induced to follow suit. Divestment on the part of the United States companies would also involve a sale of their assets at fire-sale prices to local partners or other South African investors. The acquiring companies would become inherently more profitable by buying these assets on the cheap. Being South African companies, they would also be required to sell their products to the South African military and police. Furthermore, the companies would not necessarily be inclined to undertake policies that would help their South African workers along the lines of the Sullivan Principles. And last but not least, any market share lost by the United States companies would be taken over by other foreign competitors—especially Japan, Germany, and England, which were determined to continue doing business in South Africa.

The magnitude of withdrawal and its projected impact was, that is, far less than what the companies alleged and what anti-apartheid critics claimed. A number of companies maintained their contacts with the acquiring firms by supplying parts and technical support services, and through other forms of strategic alliances. Some companies also had buy-back agreements that entitled them to re-enter the South African market. A more insidious form of alliance included supplying their local partners through the companies' foreign, non–United States affiliates. This strategy allowed the foreign affiliates to keep running the companies' South African operations in disguise, while keeping the critics in the United States at bay by claiming that the companies had indeed withdrawn from South Africa. As demonstrated by our analysis of divestments (reported elsewhere in the book), the combination of sham transactions, concealed tie-in and buy-back arrangements, and use of third-party channels of distribution considerably reduced whatever real or alleged impact such withdrawals could have had in South Africa. Similarly, all available evidence indicates that the South African operations of other non–United States multinationals were not adversely affected by their non-compliance with the Sullivan Principles.

Corporate critics—both in the United States and in South Africa—were well aware of corporate practices to circumvent the impact of divestments (although the actual magnitude of these practices was uncertain at the time). The practices did, indeed, both anger and frustrate critics, who were nonetheless unable to take or even suggest any effective countermeasures. With very few exceptions, the United States companies were unwilling to disclose publicly the terms of their withdrawal, leading to the inescapable conclusion that the number of companies with "clean" withdrawals made up a small fraction of all those companies that had claimed to withdraw from South Africa.

We suspect that the critics of the United States companies were also unwilling to be more vociferous in their exposure of offending companies because it would have revealed the hollowness of their so-called victories. As things stood, and without muddying the waters with complexities of fact, divestiture strategy had a high emotional and moral content. It was simple and lent itself to easy sloganeering. To wit, how can one profit from the sale of products in a country whose government was inherently immoral and was in serious violation of human rights? Moreover, those who argued for such a strategy had little to suffer from its adverse economic consequences, which were invariably borne by others.

Critics of the divestiture strategy also argued that if the anti-apartheid movement's objective was to discourage foreign investments in South Africa, they should boycott the Japanese, British, and German products in the United States, thus discouraging those companies from doing business in South Africa. However, it was apparent that any efforts by anti-apartheid groups to mobilize American consumers against Japanese VCRs and television sets and German cameras and cars would have little impact. Therefore, rather than taking a more rational approach to goal achievement, the strategy of withdrawal became an end in itself; its ultimate effect was irrelevant.

The anti-apartheid movement primarily used three types of activities against companies doing business in South Africa: (1) shareholder resolutions urging United States companies to divest from South Africa, (2) sale of offending companies' stock as a protest against their investments and operations in South Africa, and (3) restrictions on the sale of these companies' products to city and state governments in the United States.

1. SHAREHOLDER RESOLUTIONS

Ever since 1970, when the Securities and Exchange Commission (SEC) decided that shareholders should be allowed to submit public-interest resolutions for vote at companies' annual meetings, the role of United States companies in South Africa was consistently the subject of such resolutions. A majority of these shareholder resolutions were organized by the Interfaith Center on Corporate Responsibility, an organization affiliated, as we noted earlier, with mainstream Protestant churches and also with religious orders and dioceses of the Catholic Church.

It should be noted here that the primary objective of these resolutions was not to force the companies to change their policies toward South Africa, although the language of the resolutions might indicate such a purpose. In fact, very few shareholder resolutions succeed without the support of the corporation's management. The primary purpose, therefore, was to focus media attention on corporate conduct, increase public awareness of issues that would otherwise be neglected, and potentially embarrass the corporations themselves. These resolutions also sometimes had the effect of portraying corporations as unethical and therefore as unworthy of public trust and support—a stance that was destined to make corporate managers both uncomfortable and angry.

The ritual character of these resolutions was best captured in the following quotation from an article in the *New Yorker:*

> Every spring, at many of the annual meetings of large American corporations, disaffected minority shareholders ritualistically proffer resolutions which, after solemn and often heated debate, are thumpingly turned down by proxy votes that management had comfortably stashed away all along. . . . Large corporations manage, as a rule, to take their perennial haranguers more or less in stride, but lately they have found it increasingly hard to ignore the importunities of the people who care, or profess to care,

about South Africa, and the collective pressure of these people is privately being referred to nowadays in business and financial circles as the "hassle factor."[1]

1.1   South Africa-Related Shareholder Resolutions

One of the first church-sponsored shareholder resolutions was directed at General Motors Corporation. It asked GM to cease its manufacturing operations in South Africa. This resolution received minimal support but generated considerable publicity. It was the first time that GM's management had been exposed to such criticism on an issue that the company had hitherto not considered terribly important in business terms. Thus, despite its lack of sufficient votes, the resolution succeeded in raising GM management's level of consciousness about the issue. Even more importantly, the novelty of the tactic and the aggressiveness with which it was pursued turned the resolution into a media event and lent considerable credibility to ICCR and its executive director, Tim Smith. As it turned out, this shareholder resolution, originated by the Episcopal Church and coordinated by the ICCR, was presented at the first board meeting attended by Sullivan. And much to the dismay of Tim Smith, it was Sullivan who, in creating what came to be known as the Sullivan Principles, offered the first serious challenge to ICCR's strategy of seeking corporate withdrawal from South Africa.

Typical of this approach of seeking corporate withdrawal was an exchange of letters between ICCR's Tim Smith and GM's CEO Tom Murphy. For example, in one letter dated 14 August 1978, Smith took issue with GM's contingency plans in South Africa; he assigned to them an insidious motive and rhetorically asked, "The real issue is GM's role in South Africa and whether it is a force of progress or assisting apartheid."[2] ICCR pursued this approach with vigor and barraged GM's management with letters, phone calls, and public announcements demanding that the company provide ICCR with justifications for, and explanations of, its activities in South Africa. From the very beginning, ICCR's posture was that of an accuser demanding an accounting from GM; ICCR insisted on being treated by GM as an adversary worthy of respect and not as some fringe group that management could ignore with impunity.

1.2   South Africa-Related Shareholder Resolutions, 1986–92

The peak period for the shareholder resolutions was 1986–89. Just prior to this period—in 1985—Ford Motor Company, after years of struggle to find both profit and social progress in South Africa, sold its business to

Anglo American Corporation of South Africa. Ford's withdrawal, coupled with those of other companies, encouraged the emergence of new types of shareholder resolutions calling from sweeping changes in the United States companies' activities in South Africa.[3] Accordingly, during the 1986 proxy season, the roles and responsibilities of the American companies in South Africa were the principal targets of shareholder resolutions. These resolutions accounted for more than half of all shareholder resolutions that came up for a vote that year. At some companies, the resolutions received relatively strong support from the shareholders, at least when compared to other shareholder resolutions that were opposed by the company's management.

In 1987 the number of South Africa-related shareholder resolutions reached a peak of 156, an increase of 148 percent over the previous year. Of the 156 resolutions, 90 were brought to vote, of which 87 resolutions received enough support for resubmission to the annual meeting in the following year. This intense shareholder activity came at a time when President P. W. Botha's regime, appearing to turn its back on the reforms it had hinted at in 1985–86, took a hard-line stance to protect its mandate among White South Africans. For the first time, the predominance of shareholder resolutions in 1987 was clearly in favor of complete withdrawal.

From 1987 to 1989 the South African government initiated a number of mild reforms that were aimed at abolishing some of the more obnoxious elements of apartheid, both at places of work and in the communities where the majority of South African Blacks lived. However, these reforms left largely intact the foundations of the apartheid system designed to maintain the White hegemony in South Africa. Political repression was maintained through a nationwide state of emergency. During this period, the number of shareholder resolutions that came up for a vote increased very slightly, from 90 in 1987 to 93 in 1989.

The political situation began to change radically in South Africa in the early part of 1990. For example, in February 1990 South Africa's new president, F. W. de Klerk, released Nelson Mandela from prison; removed the ban on ANC, on other anti-apartheid organizations, and on individual activists; and committed the government to initiating discussions with ANC and others about a new constitution. By the middle of 1991, the South African government had repealed most of the key components of the apartheid system. The changes in political climate had a significant impact on shareholder activism; the number of shareholder resolutions dropped from 93 in 1989, to 89 in 1990, 68 in 1991, and 40 in 1992 (figure 2).

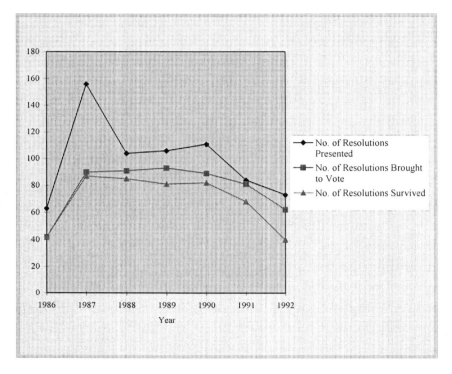

Source: "How Institutions Voted on Social Responsibility Shareholder Resolutions in the 1986–1992 Proxy Seasons," Investor Responsibility Research Center (Helen E. Booth, 1986; Heidi J. Welsh, 1987; Rebecca A. Williams, 1988; Max A. Keller, 1989; Krista M. Johnson, 1990).

Figure 2. Social Responsibility Shareholder Resolutions (1986–92)

1.3   Types of South Africa-Related Shareholder Resolutions

An analysis of South Africa-related shareholder resolutions indicates that corporate critics focused on five broad categories of actions to be undertaken by United States companies operating in South Africa (figure 3): (1) to withdraw from, or cut ties with, South Africa; (2) to end or prohibit sales to South Africa's security agencies; (3) to become signatories to the Sullivan Principles; (4) to disclose more details of the companies' operations in South Africa; and (5) to prohibit loans to South Africa's agencies, to state-owned or -controlled companies, and to private-sector corporations.

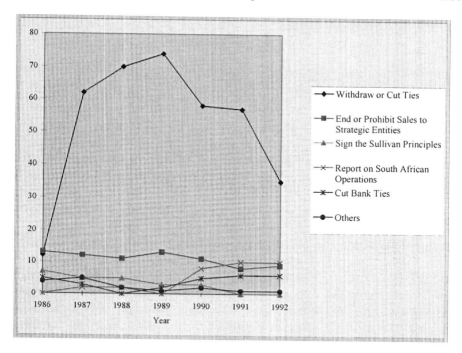

Source: "How Institutions Voted on Social Responsibility Shareholder Resolutions in the 1986–1992 Proxy Seasons," Investor Responsibility Research Center (Helen E. Booth, 1986; Heidi J. Welsh, 1987; Rebecca A. Williams, 1988; Max A. Keller, 1989; Krista M. Johnson, 1990).

Figure 3. Types of Shareholder Resolutions Brought to Vote (1986–92)

1.3.1 Withdraw from, or Cut Ties with, South Africa

The resolutions for companies to withdraw from, or cut ties with, South Africa were perhaps the most stringent in their requirements and far-reaching in their demands. They asked the companies to refrain from new investments or business relations in South Africa, or to develop plans for the parent company and its subsidiaries that would expeditiously terminate all such existing relationships in South Africa. This type of resolution became more widespread in 1987 and subsequent years. Three developments may have accelerated the pace at which they were introduced. First, there was already an exodus of American companies from South Africa, which gave credence to the activists' demands. Second, in 1987 Sullivan abandoned his campaign to encourage companies to abide by the Sullivan Principles and called, instead, for the complete withdrawal of foreign companies. Third, the passage of the Comprehensive Anti-Apartheid Act of 1986, which prohibited the introduction of new American investment into South Africa, created further pressure on United States companies operating in South Africa.[4]

1.3.2   End or Prohibit Sales to Security Agencies

Resolutions to end or prohibit sales to South Africa's security agencies were prevalent in the early days of the anti-apartheid movement, even when the demands of the activists were modest. Their popularity waned somewhat starting in 1986, when the anti-apartheid movement opted for a more aggressive strategy. Nevertheless, these resolutions continued to be introduced against certain companies that had strategic importance for South Africa. The resolutions asked the companies to ensure that their products in South Africa were not available to those agencies of the South African government—that is, the police and military—that furthered the goals of apartheid and were the enforcement agencies of the South African government. A representative example of such a resolution was presented to Chevron, a major producer of petroleum products in South Africa (Chevron and Texaco each owned 50 percent of Caltex, a South African multinational corporation). The resolution asked Chevron's board of directors to adopt a policy to "terminate forthwith the sales of petroleum and petroleum products to any entity of the South African military, police and any of their agencies or instrumentalities" until the South African government "officially commits itself to the termination of apartheid and takes meaningful steps to achieve political and legal equality for the black majority population."[5]

1.3.3   Become a Signatory of the Sullivan Principles

Resolutions for companies to become signatories of, and to comply with, the Sullivan Principles were more prevalent during the early period of the shareholder-resolution activity, especially for the more moderate elements of the anti-apartheid movement. These resolutions were often part of omnibus resolutions that called for endorsing the Sullivan Principles but also for eventual withdrawal if no progress was being made toward the abolition of apartheid. Such a resolution was introduced, for example, by the shareholders of the Timken Corporation.[6]

1.3.4   Cut Bank Ties

Resolutions to cut bank ties were quite common in the early stages of the anti-apartheid movement. They were, indeed, the early forerunners of the shareholder-resolution approach. Aimed at the major United States banks, these resolutions asked them to refrain from providing banking services and making loans to South Africa. Typical of this type of resolution was the one presented to Chase Manhattan Bank. It asked the bank to hold no account of any public or private entity in South Africa, and to provide no other correspondent banking services, such as transmission of funds, for such entities.[7]

1.3.5 Report on South African Operations.

Resolutions calling for companies to issue reports on their South African operations—often including the taxes paid to the South African government—were also common in the early stages of the anti-apartheid campaign. These resolutions became less frequent when a large number of companies became signatories to the Sullivan Principles. However, there was a minor resurgence in this type of shareholder resolution toward the end of the anti-apartheid campaign. It would appear that, although anti-apartheid activists and their shareholder supporters were still determined to bring about a complete break in the United States companies' commercial relations with South Africa, they were also adamant about making companies report on their operations in South Africa. For example, a 1992 resolution presented to Abbott Laboratories, a pharmaceutical company, asked the company to report on (1) taxes paid to the South African government in the last three years, profits remitted to the United States, and the amount contributed to social programs in South Africa; (2) contingency plans for divestment, including negotiations with workers and recognition of unions by the purchasers; (3) actions taken and funds expended for lobbying against divestment in the last three years; and (4) an accounting of business lost in the United States through selective contracting legislation and divestitures.[8]

2. SALE OF STOCK IN COMPANIES DOING BUSINESS IN SOUTH AFRICA

The second element of the anti-apartheid movement against United States companies doing business in South Africa was to demand that institutional investors sell their stock in companies doing business with or in South Africa. The rationale was that this institutional pressure would be more effective than any efforts by individual shareholders; because institutions often held large blocs of a corporation's stock, they were expected to be taken more seriously than individual investors by a corporation's management. This strategy, in our opinion, was similar in concept and approach to that of shareholder resolutions. Likewise, it was also more important for its symbolism than for its real impact. Even a simple analysis of the strategy— urging pension funds and institutions to divest their stock in companies that did business in South Africa—would indicate its very limited economic potential in affecting corporate behavior.

The number of funds and institutions that agreed to divest was very small compared to the total number of such funds. The divestment activity was confined almost entirely to public institutions whose trustees were willing to advocate a socially responsible position and thereby, at least in theory, subordinate their fiduciary duty. To the best of our knowledge, there was not a single instance in which these trustees sought a vote of their shareholders or beneficiaries about their actions.

The actual amounts divested were also extremely small, both in terms of the total holdings of the funds and in terms of the total number of outstanding corporate shares.

It should be apparent that divestment did not directly involve the corporations; the divested shares were simply bought by individuals or groups that found the selling price attractive.

Total trades involved in such institutional divestments constituted an extremely small part of the average daily trading volumes of the companies' stocks; since the institutional sellers wanted to avoid any potential financial loss, they made every effort not to disrupt the market by dumping large blocs of stock of any particular company. Thus, a change of ownership of such small magnitude was almost invisible from the perspective of corporate decision making. The real value of the stock sale (or the announcement thereof) was to generate publicity about, and public awareness of, corporate activities that the institutions considered unethical and inappropriate.

2.1   Rationale for Divestment by Academic Institutions

The primary source of data for our analysis of divestment by academic institutions was a study conducted by the Investor Responsibility Research Center in 1989.[9] IRRC canvassed 164 colleges and universities regarding their policies on investments related to South Africa. Of the 164 institutions, 93 responded. It is not clear whether the institutions that failed to respond had no policy with regard to South African investments or did not chose to respond for other reasons. Therefore, the findings of this survey, as well as our conclusions, cannot be said to represent all academic institutions or those that had policies concerning investments in companies with operations in South Africa. Nevertheless, the institutions responding to the survey included many of the best known and largest academic institutions (in terms of both endowments and enrollments). We can thus consider the findings of the survey[10] to be quite significant and indicative of the views of the academic institutions of higher learning in the United States.

Of the 93 institutions that responded to the IRRC survey, 77 institutions had some type of policy concerning South Africa. There were 36 institutions whose policies prohibited them from owning any stock in companies that had direct investments in South Africa. Another 40 institutions had different types of partial divestment policies. The one remaining institution prohibited only "new" or "additional" investments in companies doing business in or with South Africa.

Of the total $15.0 billion held in the investment portfolios of the responding institutions, approximately 13 percent was not covered by the institutions' divestment policies. For example, several schools indicated that their bond holdings or commingled funds were excluded from such policies.

A sizable number of the reporting institutions had also begun applying their divestment policies to their holdings in foreign companies.

Only one institution reported that its divestment policy extended not only to companies with direct investments in South Africa, but also to companies that operated in South Africa solely through distributors, licensees, or other non-equity arrangements.

The IRRC survey also reported that 1985 marked the peak of divestment activity, with 32 schools either adopting new investment policies or substantially revising old ones. The number of schools reporting divestment-policy activity dropped each year—falling to 29 in 1986, 14 in 1987, 8 in 1988, and 3 through June 1989.[11] IRRC attributed this decline to the success of the anti-apartheid activists in forcing United States companies to withdraw from South Africa. Curiously enough, IRRC also attributed the decline in the divestment policies of academic institutions to a diminution of student campaigns and demonstrations against South Africa. It was suggested that the South African government's policy of censoring information on that country's repressive and other apartheid-related policies deprived American students of the necessary information to devise responsive strategies.[12]

In this section we report our own analysis of the IRRC data. The analysis is intended to shed further light on the types of rationales used by different institutions to explain their divestment policies. Even within the context of adopting specific policies such as partial or total divestment, academic institutions used a wide variety of justifications and articulated their rationales at some length and in ways that reflected the schools' value orientations, histories, faculties, and student bodies. A summary of a selected sample of these policy statements is provided in appendix 12.1. Our analysis is based on thirty institutions that divested $5 million or more of their stock holdings in companies doing business in South Africa (table 31 and figure 4).

2.1.1   Group 1: Institutions with Total Divestment Policy

A policy of complete divestiture of all companies with equity links to South Africa was adopted by 16 institutions from our group of 30 schools, or 53 percent of the sample. The amounts of holdings divested within this group vary from the University of California's $3.1 billion[13]—which exceeded the combined amount divested by all other United States colleges and universities to that date—to Ohio State University's $6.4 million.

In the case of the University of California's total divestment policy, it is worth mentioning the role played by Governor George Deukmejian. The governor took the initiative in drafting the policy, which was approved by the university's Board of Regents on a 13 to 9 vote even though the university's own president, Dr. David P. Gardner, firmly opposed it. There were also repeated warnings from the University of California treasurer, Herbert Gordon, who stated that the "divestiture would cost more than $100 million in commissions and other expenses."[14]

The political repression and violence in South Africa, coupled with the student demonstrations on college campuses in the United States, were influential in moving many institutions toward a policy of total divestment. For example, Columbia University's trustees mentioned the "recent developments in South Africa" to justify their policy of total divestment "in an orderly way" and "with appropriate exceptions" (appendix 12.1). This policy made Columbia University the first Ivy League institution to choose divestment to protest South Africa's apartheid.[15] However, as the chairman of the board of trustees, Samuel L. Higgenbottom, stated in announcing the new policy, "We are in the fortunate position of having only a small fraction of endowment in companies doing business in South Africa, and so we can divest without imposing a heavy penalty . . . on our faculty, students and staff."[16] However, the trustees' statement purposely ignored any reference to the three-week sit-in by hundreds of Columbia students, who blocked a building on the Morningside Heights campus, attracting national attention.[17]

The group of schools with total divestment policies included two—Colgate University and Bryn Mawr College—that had adopted the June 1987 deadline that Sullivan had proposed for complete divestment "unless the structures of apartheid have been dismantled by that time."[18] The group also included numerous schools that had originally adopted a policy of partial divestment but later opted for total divestment because of the lack of progess in abolishing apartheid in South Africa. For example, in changing its policy, the Vassar College board of trustees "determined that the current situation in South Africa cannot be interpreted as representing any significant progress to the end of apartheid and agreed that the college should divest of all remaining stocks in companies with operations in South Africa by October 10, 1988."[19] In the case of the University of Rochester, its board

Table 31. Partial List of Universities and Their Amounts of Divestment

Institution	Amount Of Divestment
Univ. of California (1)	3.10 billion
Harvard (2)	230 million
Michigan	51 million
Cornell	42 million
Columbia	37 million
Vassar College	33.9 million
Univ. of Rochester	33 million
Univ. of Cincinnati	33 million
Brown	31.2 million
Mount Holyoke	22 million
Yale	17 million
Syracuse	16 million
Notre Dame	15 million
Queen's	15 million
Carnegie Mellon	14.7 million
Oberlin College	14.6 million
State Univ. of New York (3)	14.6 million
Middlebury College	12 million
Wesleyan	10.5 million
Univ. of Wisconsin	10.2 million
Haverford College	10 million
Univ. of North Carolina at Chapel Hill	8.8 million
Colgate	7.5 million
Northwestern	7.6 million
Stanford	7.6 million
Bryn Mawr College	7 million
Ohio State	6.4 million
Princeton	5.2 million
Univ. of Delaware	4.5 million
Williams College	4.6 million

Sources: Jennifer D. Kibbe, "Divestment on Campus: Issues and Implementation," IRRC, November 1989; (1) Anne C. Roark, "UC to Sell Investments with Links to South Africa," *Los Angeles Times*, 19 July 1986; (2) David E. Sanger, "South Africa Stock Sale by Harvard," *New York Times*, 15 February 1985; (3) "South African Divestment Voted by State University Trustees," *New York Times*, 25 September 1985.

of trustees declared that a partial divestment policy was "offensive to many, for it has been interpreted as a sign of approval and support of the policies of the government of South Africa."[20] Similar sentiments were echoed on behalf of Syracuse University and the Universities of Cincinnati and North Carolina at Chapel Hill.[21]

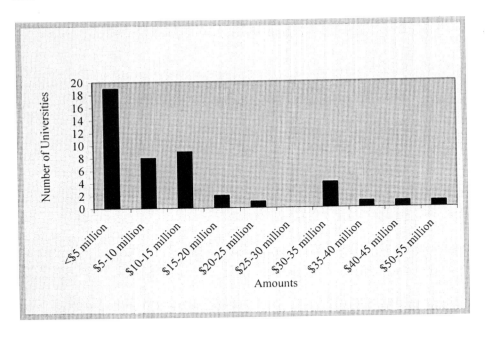

Sources: Jennifer D. Kibbe, "Divestment on Campus: Issues and Implementation," IRRC, November 1989; Anne C. Roark, "UC To Sell Investments With Links To South Africa," *Los Angeles Times*, 19 July 1986; David E. Sanger, "South Africa Stock Sale by Harvard," *New York Times*, 15 February 1985; "South African Divestment voted by State University Trustees," *New York Times*, 25 September 1985.

Figure 4. Extent of Divestment by Companies Doing Business in South Africa

2.1.2   Group 2: Institutions with Partial Divestment Policy

The thirteen schools with partial divestment policies—43 percent of our sample—divested holdings ranging from $230 million to $4.6 million. The foremost institution in this group was Harvard University. Harvard sold its entire holdings in Baker International Corporation, an Orange, California, maker of pipeline and mining equipment. This action was prompted by the company's refusal to give the university information showing that it adhered to "reasonable ethical standards."[22] In commenting upon the sale of the stock—the first time that the university had sold any South African holdings from its portfolio—Harvard's president, Derek C. Bok, stated, "We simply reached a point were we decided that no further persuasion or efforts to vote on shareholder resolutions had a reasonable chance of success."[23] At about the same time as Harvard announced its decision, and for similar reasons,

Stanford voted to sell its holdings in Motorola, which continued to sell its communications equipment to the South African military and police. In making the announcement, Stanford's president, Donald Kennedy, stated that as "as a responsible investor we will not succeed unless we demonstrate that we are, under the right circumstances, willing to employ divestiture as a last resort."[24]

Most universities opting for partial or selective divestment considered a company's observance of the Sullivan Principles as a precondition for continuing to hold the stock of a company doing business in South Africa. For example, Cornell University's policy stated that "the university should strengthen its policy of partial divestment" by divesting its current holdings and making no investments in "companies that fail to merit rating of 'making good progress' or 'making progress' [under the Sullivan rating system] . . . or that fail to demonstrate equivalent behavior."[25] Brown University's divestment policy included the option of keeping its investments in companies whose performance in South Africa was rated in February 1988 as falling into category I ("making good progress") of the Sullivan program's evaluation system. Similarly, Yale University eliminated an option in its earlier policy whereby it would accept into its portfolio those companies that proved "equivalency to the Sullivan Principles" even though not formally participating in the Principles program. The policy statement of the University of Notre Dame stated that "Notre Dame will not invest in any company doing business in South Africa that has not signed the Statement of Principles." Princeton University's criteria called for the exclusion from the university's portfolio of any company with "a demonstrated unwillingness to sign the Sullivan Principles, repeated failure to achieve a satisfactory rating under the principles or otherwise to meet the standards they establish."[26]

2.2   Disagreement and Debate on Divestment Policies of the Universities and Colleges, and Reactions of the Business Community

The adoption of divestment policies at most universities was highly contentious. In addition to conflicting values, there were debates on the mission of the university and on how and where an academic institution might take a position on the social, political, and moral issues of the day. Critics argued that rather than standing on high moral ground, these institutions were being inconsistent and selective in expressing their moral outrage; they were sacrificing their principles because it was politically expedient to placate radical student groups and to be "politically correct." There were also many others, however, who argued that in response to a very serious violation of human rights, divestment was appropriate. The debate on all sides was emotionally charged and passionate. An added element was the uncertain reaction of the corporations that were the target of these restrictions; in many cases, these very same corporations were among the universities' primary benefactors in financial and other means of support.

A clear example of corporate displeasure is provided by Johnson & Johnson's reaction to the divestment actions at Rutgers University. Corporate officials sent an angry letter expressing their resentment at being portrayed as "immoral" for continuing its operations in South Africa.[27] Shortly after Rutgers announced its decision to divest itself of stock in all companies doing business in South Africa, Johnson & Johnson's chairman, James E. Burke, resigned from the university's fund-raising campaign, stating that "the action of Rutgers in the disposition of stock of companies doing business in South Africa has rendered him ineffective because the campaign will be asking for funds from many companies whose stock is being disposed by the university."[28] This action was taken even though Rutgers had not owned any stock in Johnson & Johnson. Another example of this confrontational approach was that of FMC, a Chicago manufacturer of food-processing equipment. In ending its grants to at least six schools, the company stated, "If our corporation isn't good enough for you, you aren't good enough for our corporation."[29]

In contrast to FMC and Johnson & Johnson, IBM continued its support to Rutgers even though the company was affected by the university's disinvestment policy. Just after Rutgers sold more than eighteen thousand shares of IBM with a value of $2.3 million, a spokesperson for the company noted that though "the university's divestment policy has nothing to do with our support for colleges, . . . we are always sorry to lose an IBM stockholder, particularly when it is based on what it may be an incorrect perception of our involvement in South Africa."[30] Similar nonpunitive responses came from Xerox Corporation and General Motors. A GM spokesman, when asked about the company's plans to cut financial aid based on a college's divestment strategies, stated that they were "two entirely separate issues."[31]

Some corporate executives accused the universities of "hypocrisy for shedding company stocks while keeping a hand out for donations from the same corporations." Critics of apartheid, however, viewed this stance as a "kind of blackmail which drastically jeopardizes universities' academic freedom."[32] The gravity of the issue is illustrated by the following commentary from the *Wall Street Journal:* "Although the extent of corporate moves is still unclear, the stakes involved are huge. U.S. companies gave $1.57 billion to some 3,000 colleges and universities in 1984–1985, according to the Council on Finance Aid to Higher Education in New York. And many of the biggest, most generous givers are big-name concerns with high-profile units in South Africa."[33]

The decision to divest was equally contentious within the universities. It was most notable and vocal among the institutions that had a high profile in terms of ethical values. For example, at Notre Dame, the two extreme positions (those seeing it as a "step forward" versus those who considered the vote as a "sellout") persisted even after the university's board of trustees voted on 9 May 1986 to continue the university's policy of "selective investment" in United States companies with operations in South Africa. The board authorized divestment if United States companies in South Africa were found to be "not influencing the dismantling of apartheid" or if "there is further deterioration of conditions of South Africa."[34] Father van Rensburg, a Catholic priest from South Africa who was studying at Notre Dame on a university scholarship and undertook a water-only fast in anticipation of the trustees' vote, argued: "Three people were shot this weekend in South Africa. Is three deaths a deterioration? If the board says not, then Black deaths come cheaply. . . . Is one death a deterioration? Ten deaths? A hundred deaths?"[35] In contrast to Rensberg's position, Notre Dame's president, Holy Cross Father Theodore M. Hesburgh, considered the updating of the South African investment policy to be "a significant step forward and a beefing up of its pressure for social change."[36]

3. STATE AND LOCAL SANCTIONS AGAINST UNITED STATES COMPANIES OPERATING IN SOUTH AFRICA

The third main strategy of the anti-apartheid movement was to enlist the support of state and local governmental bodies in exerting pressure on United States companies to discontinue their operations in South Africa. According to an IRRC survey, 168 state, city, county, and regional authorities responded that they had some form of policy restricting their business dealings with United States companies doing business in South Africa. The types of policies and restrictions included:

- Divestment of all holdings from companies doing business in South Africa.

- Partial divestment, based on a variety of criteria, including the company's observance of the Statement of Principles, or the ratings received.

- Barring banking and financial institutions that had business interests in South Africa from doing business with the local agency.

- Selective purchasing laws banning contracts to companies doing business in South Africa.

- "Shell-free zones," which initially referred to the boycott of products of the Shell Oil Company because of its presence in South Africa. The term came to be used more broadly to include laws that prohibited localities from buying products of companies doing business in South Africa.

- Ban on purchasing goods made in South Africa.

This "local option" policy raised serious constitutional issues and was seen by some as local interference in foreign policy and thus violative of the United States Constitution. The supporters of the policy argued that it was an expression of local choice and freedom to use local tax money without federal interference. For political and strategic reasons, United States companies chose not to litigate the issue in the courts. The only case to come before a court was that of the City of Baltimore in 1989: Maryland's highest court held that the City of Baltimore had the right to pass a statute that withdrew its investments in companies doing business in South Africa.[37]

It is beyond the scope of this book to address the legal and constitutional issues, which remain largely unresolved.[38] More recently, a federal judge in Massachusetts invalidated a Massachusetts law that "largely bars the state government from doing business with companies that trade with Myanmar [formerly known as Burma]." In rejecting the state's argument, the judge held that "State interests, no matter how noble, do not trump the Federal Government's exclusive foreign affairs power." The judge also held that the Maryland decision did not apply because in that case, "the city [Baltimore] was seeking only to modify its own investment practices. . . . Baltimore did not seek to influence individuals or companies in their private commercial activities."[39]

In the present case, we shall therefore focus our attention on the economic rationale and effectiveness of this strategy in terms of changing United States' companies' policies and practices in South Africa. In our opinion, the economic argument for such a strategy was not convincing. We believe it is similar to those of the previous two strategies of shareholder resolutions and of divestiture by universities and public pension funds. That is, although the strategy had a symbolic value and, when widely followed, could harm one or more individual companies, its practical effect was, at best, symbolic. When all the hoopla is ignored, the number of local bodies having a restrictive policy on South Africa was quite small compared to the number of such bodies in the United States. Moreover, in many cases, such policies were poorly implemented and enforced.

Figure 5 analyzes the types of policies enforced by 168 localities (states, cities, counties, and regional authorities). The localities are grouped by the number of policies passed, ranging from one policy (89 localities, or 53 percent of the sample) to five policies (2 localities, or 1 percent of the sample). The details of each locality's policies are provided in appendix 12.2.

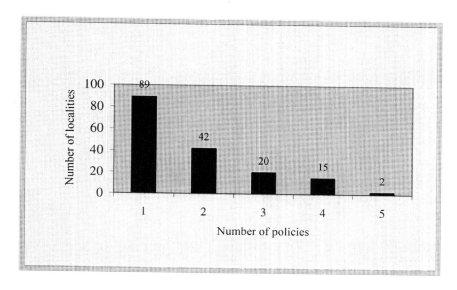

Source: "A Guide To American State and Local Laws on South Africa," William F. Moses, IRRC, 1993.

Figure 5. Number of South Africa-Related Laws and Policies Enacted by U.S. Localities

Figure 6 covers the extent of the divestment policies enacted by the ten largest cities in the United States. Philadelphia had the largest number of policies in force (five): divestment and bank restriction policies were put into effect in June 1982, followed seven years later by selective purchasing, "Shell-free zone," and a ban on goods produced in South Africa.

4. SOME CONCLUDING REMARKS

Our analysis of the strategies and tactics of the anti-apartheid movement leads us to several conclusions. It is apparent anti-apartheid activists, and notably the groups associated with ICCR, were convinced that the only way to abolish apartheid was to get the American companies to withdraw from South Africa. For this purpose, it did not matter that such a withdrawal would not eliminate the use by other companies of the facilities that the American companies left behind. What mattered, instead, was the symbolic value of the withdrawal. It would make a statement and demonstrate a moral stand not only on the part of the United States companies, but also on the part of the United States of America (the nation, not the government).

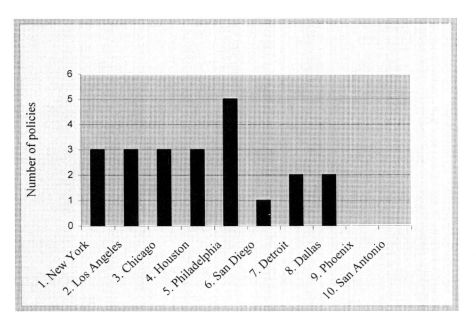

Source: "A Guide To American State and Local Laws on South Africa," William F. Moses, IRRC, 1993.

Figure 6. Number of South Africa-Related Laws and Policies Enacted by the 10 Largest Cities in the U.S.

Equally important, though not explicitly admitted, was that this strategy would help ICCR and its supporters stake out the organization's claim to the moral high ground, and also establish ICCR's reputation for having the clout to make corporations "toe the line." It is for this reason that, although Tim Smith and ICCR did not openly oppose the Sullivan Principles at the time of their initiation, they did not hide their anger and disgust at the maneuver, either. They saw Sullivan as an unwitting tool of the companies. For example, in a letter to Sullivan, Tim Smith chastises him for not being more aggressive in his dealings with GM: "We are particularly concerned about the fact that GM continues to supply vehicles to the South African military or police, thus undercutting the U.S. arms embargo. Have you asked GM to pledge to end all sales, directly or indirectly to the South African military? Is there any way that you can insure that GM applies such a standard to its sales?"[40] Another example of public disdain by some anti-apartheid activists could be seen in a pamphlet distributed by the Africa Fund, "U.S. Business in South Africa: Voices For Withdrawal," which is reproduced in exhibit 12.

The withdrawal of United States companies from South Africa was undoubtedly influenced by the activities of ICCR and other groups. It is

Exhibit 12. Perspectives No. 1–78: "U.S. Business in South Africa: Voices for Withdrawal"

The role of foreign corporations in South Africa has become a matter of increasing debate since the spread of mass rebellion throughout that country in the summer of 1976. The death in detention of Steve Biko, founder of the Black Consciousness Movement, in September, 1977, and a subsequent wave of government bannings and arrests added new urgency to the issue.

The South African government recognizes that continuing economic support, particularly from Europe and the United States, is essential for its survival. It is spending millions of dollars on public relations campaigns urging investors to put their dollars into this profitable paradise. At the same time it has charged people advocating the withdrawal or foreign investment from South Africa with the crime of "terrorism" an offense punishable by a minimum sentence of five years imprisonments and a maximum sentence of death.

In November, 1977, the Polaroid Corporation announced its withdrawal from South Africa in a statement which was perceived as an admission that the company no longer believed its own earlier contention that U.S. business could play a positive role in eliminating apartheid. Other corporations, however, continue to insist that this is true, despite the evidence of increasing repression – more than 700 people were known to be in detention at the end of 1977 – and despite such comments as those of Donald Sole, South African Ambassador to the US.

In an interview published in Princeton University's The Forerunner Magazine on February 27, 1978, Sole was asked what role US might play in bringing about political change in South Africa. He responded, "I do not think that they play any role in what you refer to as 'elimination of apartheid.' . . . They cannot play any role *whatsoever* in the institution of Black majority rule. . . . Foreign investment can change standards of living, can improve society and things of that kind, but it will not change political patterns."

While no major elected US official has yet called for withdrawal, a 1978 report of the Senate Subcommittee on African Affairs noted that "Collectively, US corporations operating in South Africa have made no significant impact on either relaxing apartheid or in establishing company policies which would offer a limited but nevertheless important model or multinational responsibility. Rather, the net effect of American investment has been to strengthen the economic and military self-sufficiency of South Africa's apartheid regime..." The report recommended various actions designed to discourage investment.

In an indication of growing public support for some form of government action, Harris public opinion poll released in December, 1977, showed that 42% of those Americans polled favored preventing any new investment in South Africa, compared with 33% against.

The following is a small sampling of the voices of those who have come to believe that investment in South Africa is no longer – if it ever was – defensible. There are many different speakers, but they are united by their belief that what is needed in South Africa is the total abolition of apartheid.

Source: The Africa Fund, 305 E. 46th St., New York, N.Y. 10017

clear, too, that the resolutions, the "hassle factor," and "confrontation fatigue" also played a role in getting corporations to walk away from South Africa. Nonetheless, we believe that the deteriorating economic situation and political uncertainties were instrumental in persuading many United States corporations to withdraw from South Africa. This impression is reinforced by the observation that the United States companies' withdrawals were concentrated in those industries that were particularly vulnerable to poor economic conditions; for example, the automobile industry. Companies in other industries—for example, the pharmaceutical industry—chose to resist similar pressures from the anti-apartheid groups and continued their operations in South Africa. Moreover, health-care companies not only remained but were seldom hassled by activists, who apparently were concerned that their products be available.

The strategies and tactics of the anti-apartheid movement played an important part in increasing both public and management awareness of the South Africa issue. In our view, however, such activities and the awareness they created had little impact on achieving the ultimate goal; namely to put sufficient pressure on the South African government to force it to abolish apartheid. The impact, that is, was marginal and diversionary. Apartheid was, to be sure, eliminated, and South Africa did achieve a nonracial democracy. However, it would be the height of self-delusion to assign to the anti-apartheid strategies anything but a cameo role that kept the audience occupied while the principal characters were getting ready to enter the stage.

We believe—and our analysis in this book gives ample supporting evidence—that it was the political unrest in South Africa, coupled with the end of the Cold War, Communism, and the Soviet Union, that made South Africa's White-dominated government all but untenable. It was the huge costs of maintaining internal security—while at the same time being the pariah of industrialized world to which South Africans aspired to belong—that caused the de Klerk government to come to terms with the new reality. Although the financial sanctions initiated in 1985 had some influence on the White leadership, it is highly doubtful that the activists would have been anything but a peripheral inconvenience if the Cold War had continued and Washington and Moscow were still aggressively seeking for increased influence in sub-Saharan Africa.

APPENDIX 12.1. Investment Policies of Selected United States Academic Institutions Pertaining to Companies with Operations in South Africa

Columbia University adopted a total divestment policy on 7 October 1985 that included the recommendations submitted to the board on 28 August by the Ad Hoc Committee Regarding Companies with Operations in South Africa:

In view of recent developments in South Africa, [the committee's recommends] divestment of the approximately $39 million of common stock of American corporations with operations in South Africa; such divestment to be accomplished in an orderly manner over a period not to exceed two years. The trustees should consider appropriate exceptions, such as news media companies, that will not detract in substance from a policy of total divestment.

Harvard University operated under a selective divestment policy since 1985, which the university reaffirmed it in December 1988. An excerpt of the policy reads as follows:

[The university] would not continue to hold stock in companies that persist, after adequate dialogue with the university, in selling significant quantities of an important good or service used in the direct enforcement of apartheid by any agency of the South African government, regardless of the company's record of employment practices. In addition, the university will carefully review companies that sell goods of strategic importance to the South African government, with the expectation that a company will be willing and able to achieve the highest Sullivan rating and to demonstrate that its presence results in more good than harm within South Africa. Final decisions on the portfolio status of such companies will be made on a case-by-case basis. In addition, the university will dispose of stock when it becomes clear that there is not likelihood the company will provide essential information requested on company policy or practice in South Africa, including sales information. Sale of stock may also occur if in the university's judgement the company has failed in substantial ways to adhere to reasonable ethical standards (including progressive employment and social policies), following extensive efforts to persuade the firm to change its policies.

The University of Notre Dame Du Lac, revising a 1978 policy, adopted a partial divestment policy on 25 October 1985 (amended on 9 May 1986 and 26 October 1989), which consisted of several points:

(1) Notre Dame will not invest in any company, lending institution or government if such an investment would support the policy of apartheid. Such support would include, but not be limited to, selling goods or services to the South African police, military or government. (2) Notre Dame will not invest in any company doing business in South Africa that has not signed the Statement of Principles. In addition, companies will be judged on the intensity of their support to the Statement of Principles and the proposals of the American Chamber of Commerce in South Africa. (3) International companies will be judged on the country of origin's guidelines or sanctions and on any formal code of conduct. It is expected that such guidelines and codes of conduct will, at a minimum, support the provisions of the Statement of Principles. (4) Notre Dame will not invest in any banks that makes loans directly or indirectly to the South African government or its agencies. (5) Notre Dame will not invest in any banks or other institutions that engage in the sale or trading of South African krugerrands.

Yale University followed a revised partial divestment policy, first adopted on 2 November 1985. The policy stated:

The university will hold in its endowment only those shares of companies which: (1) Subscribe to the Fourth Amplification of the Sullivan Principles or their equivalent. . . . (2) Receive one of the two highest Sullivan ratings or demonstrate equivalent behavior. (3) Either publicly demonstrate that they are actively working for the dismantlement of apartheid, or have a plan for the orderly withdrawal of South Africa. Actively working for the dismantlement of apartheid would be evidenced, for example, by joining the U.S. Corporate Council on South Africa. . . . Yale will . . . divest itself of those companies, in an orderly fashion consistent with fiduciary responsibility, which do not satisfy these conditions by June 30, 1986. In addition, new investments by Yale will be confined to signatory companies with one of the two highest Sullivan ratings.

The University of Michigan adopted a partial divestment policy on 14 April 1983. The resolution stated:

[T]he board hereby directs the vice president and chief financial officer to take prudent action to replace equity investments in any organizations operating in the Republic of South Africa with alternate investments . . . [and] to make no further investments in shares of corporate stocks and other equities of organizations operating in the Republic of South Africa. . . . Notwithstanding the foregoing, this resolution shall not operate to cause the divestiture or to prevent the acquisition by the university of: (1) Investments in corporations headquartered in Michigan or which employ substantial numbers of employees in Michigan, provided that dividends derived from that proportion of such corporation's earnings attributable to their South Africa operations shall be devoted by the university to programs intended to promote educational opportunities related to South Africa. (2) Investments in the University of Michigan Buy-Write program. (3) [Gifts] . . . maintained in a specifically invested account at the suggestion of the donor. It is further resolved that the vice president and chief financial officer shall initiate appropriate efforts to encourage corporations in which the university owns stock or other equities to withdraw from the Republic of South Africa.

APPENDIX 12.2. South Africa-Related Laws and Policies at the State and Local Levels

Name of Locality	Divestment	Partial Divestment	Bank Restriction	Selective Purchasing	Shell-Free Zone	South African Goods Ban
Alameda County, Calif.		*	*	*		*
Alameda/Contra Costa Transit Dist., Calif.			*	*		*
Alexandria, Va.		*	*			
Amherst, Mass.	*					
Ann Arbor, Mich.	*					*
Arkansas		*				
Atlanta, Ga.			*			
Atlantic City, N.J.	*		*			
Austin, Tex.	*		*	*	*	*
Baltimore, Md.	*		*			*
Bay Area Rapid Transit, Calif.				*		
Bergen, N.J.			*			
Berkeley, Calif.			*	*	*	*
Birmingham, Ala.	*		*	*		
Boston, Mass.			*	*	*	*
Boulder, Colo.			*			
California	*		*			
Chapel Hill, N.C.			*	*		*
Charleston, N.C.				*		
Charlottesville, Va.		*		*		
Chesapeake, Va.			*	*		
Chicago, Ill.			*	*		*
Cincinnati, Ohio			*			
Cleveland, Ohio			*			
College Park, Md.			*			*
Columbus, Ohio			*			
Connecticut	*					

Name of Locality	Divestment	Partial Divestment	Bank Restriction	Selective Purchasing	Shell-Free Zone	South African Goods Ban
Dade County, Fla.						*
Dade, Fla.			*	*		
Dallas, Tex.						*
Dallas/Ft. Worth Int'l Airport, Tex.		*		*		
Davis, Calif.			*			
Dayton, Ohio			*			
De Kalb County, Ga.		*				
Des Moines, Iowa		*				
Detroit, Mich.			*			
Durham, N.C.			*	*		
East Lansing, Mich.			*	*		
East Palo Alto, Calif.			*	*	*	
Fairmont, W. Va.			*	*		
Ford Collins, Colo.			*	*		*
Fort Wayne, Ind.			*	*		*
Fort Worth, Tex.		*	*	*		
Freeport, N.Y.			*			
Fresno, Calif.			*	*		
Fulton, Ga.			*			
Gary, Ind.			*			
Grand Rapids, Mich.			*			*
Harrisburg, Pa.			*	*		*
Hartford, Conn.				*		
Hawaii	*					
Hayward, Calif.				*		
Hennepin County, Minn.				*		
Hennepin, Minn.			*			
Houston, Tex.			*	*		*
Howard County, Md.			*	*		*

Name of Locality	Divestment	Partial Divestment	Bank Restriction	Selective Purchasing	Shell-Free Zone	South African Goods Ban
Howard, Md.			*			
Hudson County, N.J.				*		
Illinois						*
Iowa		*	*			
Jersey City, N.J.			*	*		*
Kansas		*				
Kansas City, Kan.				*		
Kansas City, Mo.			*	*		*
Kentucky	*					
King, Wash.			*			*
Lexington-Fayette Urban City, Government, Ky.				*		
Lincoln, Neb.			*			
Long Beach, Calif.			*			
Los Angeles Metropolitan Transit Authority, Calif.		*				
Los Angeles, Calif.			*	*		*
Louisiana			*			
Madison, Wis.				*		
Maine	*		*			
Maryland	*		*	*		*
Massachusetts	*		*	*		*
Md.-Nat'l Cap. Park & Planning Comm., Md.		*	*			
Md.-Nat'l Cap. Park & Planning Comm., Mo.				*		
Metropolitan Atlanta Rapid Transit Authority, Ga.		*				*
Metropolitan Transportation Authority, N.Y.			*			
Miami, Fla.			*			
Michigan	*		*			*
Minneapolis, Minn.			*	*		
Minnesota		*				
Missouri	*		*			

Name of Locality	Divestment	Partial Divestment	Bank Restriction	Selective Purchasing	Shell-Free Zone	South African Goods Ban
Monmouth County, N.J.						*
Monmouth, N.J.						
Monroe County, N.Y.			*			
Monroe, N.Y.			*	*		*
Montgomery, Md.			*			
Mount Vernon, N.Y.			*			
Municipality of Metropolitan Seattle, Wash.						
Nebraska	*					*
New Castle, Del.			*			
New Haven, Conn.				*	*	*
New Jersey	*		*	*		
New Orleans, La.	*		*	*		*
New York, N.Y.	*		*	*		
Newark, N.J.	*		*			
Newton, Mass.	*		*			
Niagara Falls, N.Y.			*			
North Carolina	*	*		*		*
Oakland, Calif.	*	*	*	*		*
Oklahoma			*			
Omaha, Neb.	*		*			
Opa-Locka, Fla.	*		*	*		*
Orange, N.J.				*		
Orlando, Fla.						
Palo Alto, Calif.		*	*			
Pasadena, Calif.				*		
Pennsylvania	*					
Philadelphia, Pa.	*		*	*	*	*
Pittsburg, Pa.			*	*		
Port Authority of New York & New Jersey	*	*	*			*

Name of Locality	Divestment	Partial Divestment	Bank Restriction	Selective Purchasing	Shell-Free Zone	South African Goods Ban
Portsmouth, Va.		*				*
Prince George's County, Md.				*		*
Prince George's, Md.			*			
Rahway, N.J.			*			
Raleigh, N.C.			*	*		*
Ramsey, Minn.			*			
Rhode Island	*					
Richmond, Calif.	*			*		*
Richmond, Va.			*	*		
Rochester, N.Y.	*		*	*		*
Rockland, N.Y.			*	*		
Sacramento, Calif.	*		*	*		*
Saint Louis, Mo.			*			
Saint Paul, Minn.			*			
San Diego, Calif.				*		
San Francisco County, Calif.				*		*
San Francisco, Calif.	*		*	*		*
Santa Barbara County, Calif.			*			
Santa Barbara, Calif.			*			
Santa Clara, Calif.			*			
Santa Cruz County, Calif.				*	*	
Santa Cruz, Calif.			*	*	*	
Santa Monica, Calif.		*	*	*	*	
Seattle, Wash.	*		*	*	*	
Solano County, Calif.				*		
Solano, Calif.			*			
Sonoma County, Calif.				*		*
Sonoma, Calif.			*			
St. Louis, Mo.	*					

Name of Locality	Divestment	Partial Divestment	Bank Restriction	Selective Purchasing	Shell-Free Zone	South African Goods Ban
St. Paul, Minn.	*					
St. Petersburg, Fla.		*				
Stockton, Calif.	*		*			*
Syracuse, N.Y.	*		*			
Takoma Park, Md.					*	
Tallahasse, Fla.	*		*	*		*
Tampa, Fla.	*		*			
Tennessee	*		*			
Texas		*				
Toledo, Ohio						
Tompkins, N.Y.			*	*		
Topeka, Kan.			*			
Vermont	*		*			
Virgin Island	*					
Virginia	*					
Washington, D.C.			*	*		
Watertown, Mass.			*	*		
Watsonville, Calif.			*	*	*	
West Hollywood, Calif.				*		
West Virginia	*					
Westchester, N.Y.			*	*		
Wilmington, Del.			*			
Youngstown, Ohio			*			*
Ypsilanti, Mich.		*				

Source: "A Guide To American State and Local Laws on South Africa," William F. Moses, IRRC, 1993.

ENDNOTES

1 *New Yorker*, "Annals of International Trade: A Very Emotive Subject," 14 May 1979.
2 Tim Smith (director, ICCR), letter to T. A. Murphy (CEO, General Motors), 14 August 1978.
3 *Business Week*, "South Africa—The Screws are Tightening on U. S. Companies," 11 February 1985.
4 IRRC, "How Institutions Voted on Social Policy Shareholders Resolutions in the 1992 Proxy Season" (Washington, DC: IRRC, 1992), 88.
5 Helen E. Booth, "How Institutions Voted on Social Policy Shareholders Resolutions in the 1986 Proxy Season" (Washington, DC: IRRC, 1986), 55.
6 Ibid., 67.
7 Ibid., 54.
8 IRRC, "How Institutions Voted on Social Policy Shareholders Resolutions in the 1992 Proxy Season" (Washington, DC: IRRC, 1992), 93–94.
9 Jennifer D. Kibbe, "Divestment on Campus" (Washington, DC: IRRC, 1989).
10 IRRC, "IRRC Finds Declining College Divestment Activity," *IRRC South African Reporter* 8, 4 (1989): 75–76.
11 Ibid.
12 Ibid.
13 Anne C. Roark, "UC to Sell Investments with Links to South Africa," *Los Angeles Times*, 19 July 1986.
14 Ibid.
15 Robert D. McFadden, "Columbia Plans to Sell by '87 Stock Linked to South Africa," *New York Times*, 18 October 1985.
16 Christoper A. Coons, "The Responses of Colleges and Universities to Calls for Divestment" (Washington, DC: IRRC, 1986), 65–66.
17 McFadden, "Columbia Plans to Sell by '87 Stock Linked To South Africa," *New York Times*, 8 October 1985.
18 Kibbe, "Divestment on Campus."
19 As stated by Eilleen Shaw, financial analyst at Vassar College, and reported in Kibbe, "Divestment on Campus," 64.
20 Ibid., 58.
21 Ibid., 40, 52, 61.
22 David E. Sanger, "South Africa Stock Sale by Harvard," *New York Times*, 15 February 1985.
23 Ibid.
24 Ibid.
25 Kibbe, "Divestment on Campus," 43.
26 Ibid.
27 Patricia McCormick, "J & J Gives Rutgers Professors Its Side of Divestment Debate," *New Brunswick Home News*, 22 September 1985.
28 Ibid.
29 Dennis Kneale, "Firms Tied to South Africa Strike at Colleges That Sell Their Stock," *Wall Street Journal*, 10 January 1986.
30 Patricia McCormick, "Divestment Costs Rutgers J & J Chief," *New Brunswick Home News*, 24 September 1985.
31 Kneale, "Firms Tied to South Africa."
32 Ibid.

33 Ibid.

34 "Notre Dame to Continue Investment in South Africa," *Times Review*, 15 May 1986.

35 Ibid.

36 Robert J. McClory, "Notre Dame Divestment Divides School," *NCR*, May 1986. A co-author of this volume, Oliver Williams, served on the Board of Trustees Committee on South Africa.

37 William F. Moses, "A Guide to American State and Local Laws on South Africa" (Washington, DC: IRRC, 1993).

38 Grace A. Jubinsky, "State and Municipal Governments React against South African Apartheid: An Assessment of the Constitutionality of the Divestment Campaign," *University of Cincinnati Law Review* 54 (1985): 543–78; Peter J. Spiro, "State and Local Anti-South African Action As an Intrusion Upon the Federal Power in Foreign Affairs," *Villanova Law Review* 72 (1986): 813–60; Kevin P. Lewis, "Dealing with South Africa: The Constitutionality of State and Local Divestment Legislation," *Tulane Law Review* 67 (1987): 469–517; H. N. Fenton, III, "State and Local Anti-Apartheid Laws: Misplaced Response to a Flawed National Policy on South Africa, " *N.Y.U. Journal of International Law and Policy* 19 (1987): 883–919; A. L. McCardle, "In Defense of State and Local Government Anti-Apartheid Measures: Infusing Democratic Values into Foreign Policy Making," *Temple Law Review* 52 (1989): 813–47.

39 Carey Goldberg, "Limiting a State's Sphere of Influence," *New York Times*, 15 November 1998.

40 Tim Smith (director, ICCR), letter to Leon H. Sullivan, 6 July 1977.

PART IV

THE END GAME
The Drive toward Divestment and Exit

Chapter 13

Stampeding toward the Exit
Withdrawal of United States Companies from South Africa

From 1977 to 1982 the number of United States companies that became signatories of the Sullivan Principles continued to expand rapidly, reaching a high point of 146 companies in 1982.[1] There was a perceptible decline from 1983 to 1986, and the decline was precipitous from 1987 onwards. In 1993, the last year before South Africa freed itself from apartheid and its White-minority government, there were only 50 signatory companies left in South Africa. Clearly, during this period there were forces at work whose combined effect was to erode the arguments in support both of the Sullivan Principles and of United States companies' continuing their operations in South Africa.

United States companies had consistently argued that support for economic sanctions against South Africa was based on faulty economic and political reasoning and on a poor reading of history. It was suggested that economic sanctions very rarely, if ever, had the political impact they aimed for, and that they invariably affected adversely the very groups the sanctions were intended to protect. Moreover, United States companies were the leaders in bringing about socioeconomic changes in South Africa. This leverage would be lost if the companies were to withdraw from South Africa; they would be replaced by South African companies and multinational corporations from other countries who were less inclined to pursue the goals set forth in the Principles. The United States companies would also be abandoning their high moral ground by leaving behind employees who depended on the companies for their livelihoods and who would be condemned to a life of unemployment and abject poverty. The companies would, moreover, be seen as yielding to unreasonable and unjustifiable pressure from "irresponsible" outsiders who had their own political agendas, thus opening the door to similar pressures in the future.

All of the above arguments had some merit, especially in the early stages of the anti-apartheid movement. In the final analysis, economic sanctions merely raise the cost of doing business; they are seldom a total or even a significant deterrent to a country's political agenda if the regime in power is determined to absorb such costs. There are very few historical examples of successful economic sanctions, even when backed with the threat of strong military action. In the case of South Africa, the question of applying military force was never contemplated, and the support for economic sanctions among other industrialized nations with sizable investments in South Africa rarely went beyond moral platitudes and empty rhetoric.[2]

Meritorious or not, all of the arguments against economic sanctions and in favor of remaining in South Africa came to naught as companies fell over each other in their rush to exit the country in the latter half of the 1980s. In doing so, the companies communicated lessons to the anti-apartheid movement that were, in fact, directly contrary to the ones they had intended:

- Political and social agendas are more likely to be swayed in the public arena by moral and emotional arguments than by economic arguments alone.

- Economic arguments have low credibility when (1) they are advanced by groups for which the arguments appear to be self-serving, (2) their intended beneficiaries are unwilling or unable to openly support them, and (3) the actions of those promulgating such arguments are incongruent with their public posture.

Business organizations have ignored these lessons—much to their disadvantage—in other instances, and South Africa was no exception. Tragically, the United States companies also reinforced the impression that economic organizations, despite their huge economic advantage against their opponents, were more vulnerable to economic pressures and would all too easily abandon their "principled stand" when confronted with economic costs.

Conversely, there is a lesson here that corporate critics learned well and remembered well. They saw that the United States corporations with operations in South Africa were unwilling to use moral arguments to defend their position even when those moral arguments were justified. Moreover, the corporations were seen as willing to abandon long-term economic and political principles and interests when confronted with short-term economic and political costs.

1.   THE RATIONALE FOR WITHDRAWAL FROM SOUTH AFRICA

In announcing their withdrawal from South Africa, United States companies offered a variety of reasons for doing so. Our objective here is to compare the justifications offered in those announcements with the previously stated positions of the companies for staying in South Africa and for their adherence to, and support of, the Sullivan Principles.

Included in our analysis are 76 of the 250 companies that left South Africa from 1984 to 1991 (with the largest number of withdrawals taking place from 1985 to 1987).[3] The data for the companies' withdrawal and the year of their withdrawal is presented in appendix 13.1. We included only those companies whose statements for withdrawal were made public and could be procured through major national and international newspapers, business publications, and other archival data sources. When company press releases were not available, we used the explanations credited to the firms in news stories and editorial comments from the same media sources.

The 76 companies included in our sample are not a scientifically selected random sample of the companies that left South Africa during the period under review. Nevertheless, we believe that these companies provide a substantive and dependable sample both of the departing companies and of the entire set of United States companies with operations in South Africa. The sample comprises firms that came from both signatory and nonsignatory companies. The signatory companies included in our sample constituted 63 percent of the total number of signatory companies in South Africa during 1986, one of the peak years for membership in the Sullivan program.[4] Another indication of the robustness of our sample is that it includes six of the seven largest United States employers that left South Africa: General Motors (4,307 employees), Coca-Cola (4,288), Mobil (3,182), RJR Nabisco (2,772), Goodyear Tire (2,471), and IBM (1,600).[5]

A content analysis of the company press releases, news reports, and editorials[6] shows that 62 of the companies in our sample, or 82 percent, presented a single reason for withdrawing from South Africa. These reasons fell into five general categories. The remaining 14 companies, or 18 percent of the sample, offered multiple reasons to explain their withdrawal. Summary data for the first group of companies is presented in figure 7 and exhibit 13, and for the second group of companies in figure 8 and exhibit 14.

The five reasons cited by the single-reason companies were:

1. Deterioration of the economic and business climate in South Africa
2. Reaction to the campaign by anti-apartheid activists and to shareholder resolutions against doing business in South Africa
3. Opposition to apartheid
4. Response to the selective purchasing laws (both state and local) in the United States
5. Disinvestment as part of a worldwide realignment strategy that included South African operations

The companies that offered multiple reasons can be categorized into six groups:

Group A: companies citing both economic and political reasons for withdrawing from South Africa

Group B: companies citing both their declining profitability in South Africa and the increasingly militant campaign against American involvement in that country

Group C: companies citing the increased uncertainty in South Africa's economic situation and the selective purchasing laws in the United States

Goup D: companies citing decreased profitability and increasing stockholder disapproval

Group E: companies describing withdrawal as part of a restructuring program and as an effort to reduce interest expenses

Group F: companies citing growing societal pressure in the United States and also the disproportionate amount of management time required to oversee the South African situation

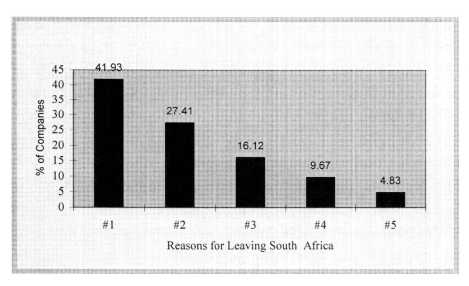

Reason 1: 26 companies
Reason 2: 17 companies
Reason 3: 10 companies
Reason 4: 6 companies
Reason 5: 3 companies

Total: 62 companies

Figure 7. U.S. Companies' Reasons for Leaving South Africa

Exhibit 13. Companies with Single-Reason Explanation for Withdrawing from South Africa

Economic and Business Climate in South Africa

American Home Products (1989)	Foote, Cone & Belding (1990)	National-Standard Corp. (1990)
BBDO (1985)	General Electric Co. (1986)	Oak Industries (1985)
Black & Decker (1987)	Honeywell (1986)	Pepsico Inc. (1987)
CPC International (1987)	Johnson Controls Inc. (1986)	Phillips Petroleum (1986)
Citicorp (1987)	Kraft Inc. (1986)	Playtex (1986)
Emhart Corp. (1987)	Marriott Corp. (1986)	Rohm & Haas (1986)
Exxon (1986)	Merck & Co. (1988)	Tambrands Inc. (1987)
Federal-Mogul Corp. (1988)	Mobil (1989)	Tidwell Industries (1985)
FMC Corp. (1987)	Motorola (1985)	USX Corp. (1989)

Shareholder Pressure and Anti-Apartheid Activists

American Express (1985)	Diamond Shamrock (1986)	Stanley Works (1986)
AMR Corporation (1985)	Dow Chemical (1988)	St. Paul Cos. Inc. (1989)
Avery International (1989)	Ford Motor Corp. (1988)	Tenneco Inc. (1990)
Boeing (1984)	Phibro-Salomon (1985)	Westin Hotel (1988)
Cigna Corp. (1987)	RJR Nabisco Inc. (1990)	Westinghouse Electric (1987)
Cooper (1986)	SPS Technologies (1986)	

Opposition to Apartheid

Apple Computer (1985)	Hewlett-Packard ((1989)	Warner Communications (1987)
Borg-Warner (1987)	Kodak (1988)	Xerox Corporation (1987)
Coca-Cola (1986)	McGraw-Hill (1987)	
Dun & Bradstreet (1987)		

State and Local Purchasing Laws

Allied-Signal (1987)	Eaton Corp. (1986)	General Foods (1985)
Ashland Oil (1986)	Fluor Corp. (1987)	Lockheed (1988)

Part of Global Strategy

City Investing (1985)	Scovill (1986)	Sentry Corp. (1987)

Exhibit 14. Companies with Multiple-Reason Explanation for Withdrawing from South Africa

Group A

General Motors (1986)	Revlon (1986)	Goodyear Tire & Rubber (1989)
IBM (1987)	Bausch & Lomb (1988)	Tambrands (1987)
Proctor & Gamble (1986)		

Group B

Blue Bell (1985)	Perkin-Helmer (1985)

Group C: Bell & Howell (1986)

Group D: Sara Lee Corp. (1986)

Group E: Newmont Mining (1986)

Group F: Norton Co. (1987)

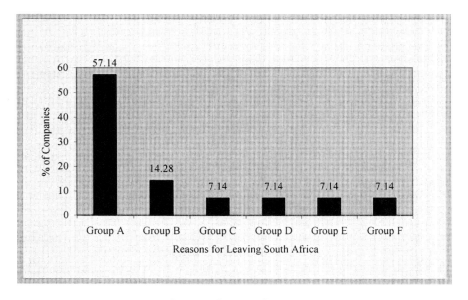

Group A: 8 companies
Group B: 2 companies
Group C: 1 company
Group D: 1 company
Group E: 1 company
Group F: 1 company

Total: 14 companies

Figure 8. U.S. Companies Leaving South Africa Citing More Than One Reason

1.1 Reason 1: Deterioration of the Economic and Business Climate in South Africa

The largest number of companies cited South Africa's deteriorating economic and business climate as the reason for withdrawing from that country. The twenty-seven companies in this group—36 percent of all of the companies in our survey, and 43 percent of the companies offering a single reason for their withdrawal from South Africa—were not concentrated in any particular industry but were spread across the spectrum of United States companies operating in South Africa: advertising and communications, banking and financial services, consumer products, lodging, oil and petroleum products, metals and machine tools, and pharmaceuticals, among others. It would therefore seem that this first reason provided a generic, all-purpose explanation even though there were variations on this theme of economic deterioration that enabled one company to differentiate its reason for leaving from that of other companies.

Typical of this approach was the statement of Citicorp when it withdrew from South Africa in 1987. The announcement stated that Citicorp will "sell its wholly owned South African subsidiary because of growing constraints on the unit's business operations. The subsidiary, Citibank NA Ltd., will be sold to the First National Bank of Southern Africa, Ltd., for SAR130 million, or US$ 38.2 million." Citicorp also stated that its current outstanding loans to South African borrowers, in the amount of $700 million, would not be affected and that those loans would be carried on the Citicorp's books.[7] Citicorp was the last United States banking company with a direct investment in South Africa. Two other United States banking companies, Chase Manhattan and the NCNB Corporation, closed their South African operations in 1985 and 1986, respectively. According to the published press reports:

> The Citicorp sale follows mounting public criticism of the company's presence in South Africa. A minority of shareholders called for the withdrawal. Until recently the bank had argued that maintaining a presence in South Africa would accomplish more toward combating official racial separation policies and providing leverage for change than would a pull-out.[8]

The Citicorp spokesperson, however, termed the sale a "management, business decision," insisting that the sale was a "response to increasing constraints on doing business in South Africa. . . . We've always listened to the opinion of shareholders, but the pressures and any business impact they might have had were not substantial. They were not a key factor in the decision."[9]

Alison Cooper, a research analyst with the Investor Responsibility Research Center, offered a contrary view. "It's surprising to see their turnaround. They have been among the outspoken leaders who said they will stay in [South Africa]." Cooper conceded, however, that deteriorating economic and business conditions may have been a "big factor in the Citicorp move." It is also worth noting, however, that "nearly 14% of the shareholders recently supported a stockholder proposal for withdrawal."[10] Furthermore, Citicorp was not completely withdrawing from South Africa; in the process of that withdrawal, the company set up licensing arrangements and other types of indirect links to South Africa, thereby allowing it to retain, in effect, a presence there despite its nominal exit.

In the withdrawal announcement of USX Corporation, the oil and steel concern, the company emphasized that its decision was primarily motivated by business factors and was "part of its continuing restructuring." The company admitted to receiving a shareholder resolution to this effect but stated that the resolution was withdrawn after negotiations for a sale of its South African assets were underway.[11]

Other companies included in this group presented similar explanations, albeit with minor variations. BBDO, a major advertising agency, noted in its exit statement that "financial losses from the South African subsidiary were the primary reason for its decision. . . . This is not intended as a political statement," according to Allen Rosenshine, president and chief executive officer of the agency. The company nevertheless intended to continue serving both its major account in South Africa (namely, Gillette) and other clients through local partners and "through an associate relationship with the newly independent South African operations."[12] In plain language, what this announcement meant was that the United States parent managed to stay in South Africa through the process of creating an "independent agency" and establishing an "associate relationship" with that agency.

In the advertising and communications group, another major agency that chose to leave South Africa was Foote, Cone & Belding Communications, Inc., which left South Africa only one month after it had signed the Sullivan Principles. The agency had owned a 24 percent stake in Lindsay Smithers-FCB, one of the five largest agencies in South Africa, since 1975. "We wanted to affirm that even though we only own 24 percent, we are doing the right thing," said Vance Webb, a spokesperson for the agency.[13] During this same period, however, the agency also stood a good chance of winning the Jamaica Tourist Board advertising account. "The tourist board was concerned with FCB's ties with a South African agency in light of that country's apartheid policy. . . . An FCB official confirmed that the agency had been for the last 18 months reassessing its role in South Africa, noting what were described as 'whole range of complications.'"[14]

Another company whose withdrawal was closely linked to protecting or gaining business elsewhere, notwithstanding its prior commitment to South Africa, was Marriott Corporation. As reported in the *Washington Post,* a company spokesperson explained the pullout in terms of "business and economic reasons related to the unsettled political situation there."[15] However, the very same article revealed that the company was concerned about losing an important account:

> The food service and lodging giant disclosed its [withdrawal] plans in a letter to the president of the State University of New York at Binghamton, where the administration planned a referendum to decide whether to renew a Marriott food service contract in light of the South African operation.[16]

There were three major oil companies in this group: Mobil, Exxon, and Phillips Petroleum. Mobil was a leading company in following the Sullivan Principles, and one of its senior executives, Sal Marzullo, served the longest term as president of the Industry Support Unit. And yet, ironically, Mobil divested from South Africa by selling its operations to Gencor mining company, which "has a reputation among blacks as a harsh employer." Mobil withdrew, indeed, despite its repeated statements to the contrary in the preceding months, statements in which the company publicly reaffirmed its commitment to remain in South Africa and its determination to help improve both the quality and quantity of programs supporting the South African Black community. Mobil's chairman, Allen Murray, indicated that his company "was pressured into leaving [South Africa] by the Rangel Amendment," a law that prevented United States companies from deducting taxes paid to South Africa. "We had to weigh business considerations." Needless to say, Mobil's withdrawal was viewed by United States activists, who believed disinvestment was a sure way to fight apartheid, as a "surrender" and a triumph for their cause. Tim Smith of the Interfaith Center on Corporate Responsibility considered Caltex to be the center's next target. "Caltex is very vulnerable" as the last United States oil company in South Africa, but arguments similar to those advanced by Mobil—even coupled with threats by ICCR—proved unpersuasive. Caltex's CEO, James Kinnear, stated that his concern for the company's 476 employees was paramount. He added that "Walking away is not the right way to fight apartheid."[17]

In the case of Exxon, the company first tried to sell its South African operations to local parties. However, when that effort failed, the company decided to sell to "an independent trust established to continue business and pursue social responsibility and employee support programs."[18] General Electric also chose a similar path in its withdrawal by selling its South African operations to a group of local employees. However, GE also said that "the decision to negotiate with the employees reflected business considerations and was not politically motivated."[19]

Some other examples of statements from companies in this category present variations on the above themes. International Playtex, Inc., said that "it sold its South African operation to local management. The selloff was for purely business reasons. . . . The 400 to 450 employees in South Africa will retain their jobs."[20] Honeywell, unlike Playtex, maintained business links with its South African operations after it withdrew from that country. Honeywell asserted that its decision to withdraw reflected an assessment of the "total business environment in that country."[21]

Although both Pepsico and Motorola cited the poor business climate as their primary reason for leaving South Africa, they, like many other notable companies, maintained ties with their South African subsidiaries after their withdrawal.[22] According to IRRC, there were more than 175 American companies that had similarly maintained a non-equity interest in South Africa in the form of contracts, licenses, franchisees, or other arrangements.[23] The retention of licensing and distribution agreements by many United States firms departing South Africa, however, gave rise to further controversy. These arrangements prompted many anti-apartheid activists to attack the companies for what they called "sham disinvestments," and the activists vowed to continue their campaigns against the companies.[24]

1.2   Reason 2: Reaction to the Campaign By Anti-Apartheid Activists And to Shareholder Resolutions against Doing Business in South Africa

Companies falling into this group included, among others, Cigna Corporation, Cooper Industries Inc., Dow Chemical, Ford Motor Company, Merck & Co., and Westin Hotels. Dow Chemical said that it was "forced to leave because it could no longer resist public pressure to do so."[25] Merck, another pharmaceuticals company, left in 1989, one year after Dow Chemical. Notwithstanding the withdrawal of Dow Chemical and Merck, a number of other companies in the pharmaceuticals industry, including Eli Lilly, Johnson & Johnson, Pfizer, Schering-Plough and Warner Lambert, continued to operate in South Africa. These companies stated that they would remain in South Africa because they believed that their doing so would help the Black cause.[26]

A number of companies yielded to shareholder pressure in extricating themselves from South Africa (though they generally refused to acknowledge such pressure). Typical of this group were American Express, AMR, Boeing, Phibro-Salomon, RJR Nabisco, Tenneco, and Westinghouse Electric. Their withdrawal statements invariably followed either disclosure in the media of strong shareholder resolutions, or announcements or threats of stock sales by major public pension funds, charitable organizations, or university endowments. These pressures were often mentioned by financial analysts. For example, in the case of Philbro-Salomon, an industry analyst said that "concern about the divestment campaign was a major reason for the company's action,"[27] citing the Smithsonian Institute and other such organizations that had recently sold their stock in Phibro-Salomon. Corporate critics were also not deceived by the nominal withdrawal of ownership that nevertheless maintained the company's business activity in South Africa. Jennifer Davis, the executive director of the American Committee on Africa, stated: "As a victory, it's tremendous. But it's a funny sort of situa-

tion. What does it mean—that there is not going to be South African operations but there is going to be South African ownership?"[28]

1.3   Reason 3: Opposition to Apartheid

In 1985 Apple Computer became the first company to explain its decision to leave South Africa as being motivated by "the apartheid situation in
that country."[29] In the same *Washington Post* article, however, Jennifer
Davis of the American Committee on Africa stated that about twenty companies had closed or sold their South African interests and that the "pressure
here is starting to take its toll." David Hauck, who monitored South African
investments for the Investor Responsibility Research Center, said that "the
companies are very close-lipped about this. Generally, they say they don't
want to leave and they regret it, but their subs [subcontractors] aren't making
any money down there."[30]

Two other companies from this group, Coca-Cola and Borg-Warner, are
illustrative of the group that followed an opportunistic course of action by
having their cake and eating it, too. Although they joined the anti-apartheid
bandwagon, they also took steps both to protect their current market share
and to safeguard their future interests. In the case of Coca-Cola, the company's announcement of its withdrawal stated that "the sale is a statement of
our opposition to apartheid."[31] However, the announcement was made only a
few weeks after the Atlanta-based Southern Christian Leadership Conference, a powerful anti-apartheid organization, threatened Coca-Cola with a
national boycott.[32] Coca-Cola sold its bottling plants in South Africa, closed
its syrup plant, and built a new one in neighboring Swaziland. The company
continued to sell syrup to the South African bottlers (some of which were
Black owned) and to capture its very substantial share of the soft drink market in that country.

The case of Kodak was quite different. The company decided to "go all
the way"[33] in its disinvestment, which included halting South African sales
of its entire product line. Tim Smith of ICCR considered this move "a very
important precedent. We have said the other moves were commendable, but
they were really first steps. Kodak has completed the total package all at
once."[34]

1.4   Reason 4: Withdrawal in Response of State and Local Purchasing Laws

For companies that depended on state and local agencies for significant amounts of business, state and local purchasing laws were a source of very significant pressure to leave South Africa. Indeed, when it came to risking business in the United States versus staying in South Africa, it was "no contest." As Mark Fabiani, legal adviser to the mayor of Los Angeles, Thomas Bradley, boasted, "we've hit them where it hurts, in the bottom line."[35] A number of companies included in this group—for example, Ashland Oil, Allied-Signal, and Fluor Corporation—lost important municipal contracts at least in part because of the objections raised by local officials the companies' continuing ties to South Africa.

1.5   Reason 5: Disinvestment as Part of a Global Strategy That Included South African Operations

City Investing, Scovill, and the Sentry Corporation were among the group of companies that left South Africa alleging that divestment was part of their global restructuring strategy. The Sentry Corporation, an insurance company, insisted at the time of its withdrawal that "the move was not politically motivated, Sentry Corporation having decided to dispose of all its operations outside U.S. in order to concentrate on the home market."[36]

1.6   Companies with Multiple Explanations for Withdrawal from South Africa

The companies offering multiple explanations for their divestiture included some of the largest and most highly respected United States companies operating in South Africa (exhibit 14). However, the explanations for their withdrawal, as well as the rationales behind those explanations, were not dissimilar to the ones offered by companies who provided only a single reason. For example, on 20 October 1986 General Motors' chairman Roger Smith, in announcing the company's departure from South Africa, noted that the "the ongoing recession in that country, along with the lack of progress [in eliminating apartheid], has made operating in the South African environment increasingly difficult."[37] The company also indicated that it had been losing market share and sales during the previous years. Just one day after General Motors' move, John F. Akers, IBM's chairman, announced his

company's withdrawal, citing "deteriorating business and political conditions."[38]

In response to such departures, some anti-apartheid activists were disappointed; for example, Richard Knight, head of corporate research at the
American Committee on Africa, said that "It's not doing what we want,
which is to cut off the technology."[39] Other activists were delighted because
the departures were an obvious blow to the Reagan administration's policy
of constructive engagement, which had been encouraging multinational
companies to remain active in South Africa.

IBM had long been one of the most ardent corporate supporters not only
of constructive engagement, but also of the Principles program. However,
IBM had never endorsed the last amplification prior to its withdrawal;
namely, the one calling on signatory companies to support anti-apartheid
civil disobedience. In the words of IBM's chairman Akers, "We are not in
the business of conducting socially responsible action. We are in business to
conduct business."[40]

2.   SOME CONCLUDING REMARKS

United States corporations, including some of the largest and most highly
respected ones, initially defined their rationale for staying in South Africa in
terms of broadly defined enlightened self-interest; that is, as an expression of
good corporate citizenship. They were also determined to uphold their
responsibility toward multiple stakeholders, including workers and consumers in South Africa. Furthermore, the companies viewed their decision to
remain in South Africa as an important element in defense of private enterprise, which they perceived as a positive force of social change. This stance
was buttressed by substantial historical evidence and economic and political
logic that economic sanctions were rarely effective, especially against a
determined government and when imposed for an extended period of time.

It was apparent to the corporations—even, it seems, when they made
their initial decision to remain in South Africa—that their decisions to do so
would necessarily involve some economic costs. In most cases, South Africa
represented a small amount of business in the context a company's overall
global operations and was unlikely to have any substantial impact on a company's financial performance.

Except for sheer nuisance value (through publicity in the mass media),
the activists' means of attacking the corporations—shareholder resolutions
and threats of boycotts—were not especially effective or persuasive from an
economic perspective. Given the highly liquid nature of financial markets, a

stock divestment by one institution would be picked up by other individuals or institutions for which such investments provided superior returns. One only need consider companies producing alcoholic beverages, tobacco, and armaments, which have continued to flourish and find eager buyers of their stocks, when the price was right, even in the face of harsh criticism from the companies' critics.

And yet, when it came to confronting the consequences of their decisions, most of these companies were all too willing to abdicate their responsibilities to their workers, as well as their economic rationale, their clear-headed perception that their continuing presence in South Africa was making a difference, and their defense of free enterprise as a force of social change. In other words, leaders of large corporations were all too often driven by short-term economic considerations. They also seemed to lack the staying power of their adversaries, whether South African or American. And notwithstanding their rhetoric, they were all too often willing to abandon their long-term social and political interests—an abandonment that may eventually seriously and adversely impact the legitimacy and credibility of corporate America, in general, and the growth and survival of their companies, in particular.

Clearly, problems related to South Africa consumed an inordinate amount of management time. However, this explanation begs the question rather than answers it. To wit, why did the management of these companies assume that their stance would be acceptable to their critics and would not cause them undue pain or discomfort? The case of South Africa was not the first time that critics had opposed corporate actions in one or more social arenas and for a variety of corporate sins of omission and commission. Nor have these corporations been reluctant to engage in political lobbying and in mass media public relations in defense of their corporate self-interest (albeit often disguised as the public interest).[41] Nevertheless, when real issues of economic, ethical, and political substance were involved, and when vital corporate and public interests were at stake, corporate actions fell sadly short of corporate rhetoric. To be sure, the arguments of corporate critics were not without some merit, but it is not clear that business leaders ever viewed those arguments as compelling or persuasive. It seems that the most of the corporations simply responded meekly to the pressure—a worrisome trend.[42]

APPENDIX 13.1. Years That Companies Withdrew from South Africa

	1984	1985	1986	1987	1988	1989	1990
Allied-Signal				*			
American Express		*					
American Home Products Corp.						*	
Apple Computer		*					
Ashland Oil Inc.			*				
Avery International						*	
Bausch & Lomb					*		
BBDO		*					
Bell & Howell			*				
Black & Decker				*			
Blue Bell		*					
Boeing	*						
Borg-Wagner			*				
Cigna Corp.				*			
Coca-Cola			*				
Cooper Industries			*				
CPC International				*			
Citicorp				*			
City Investing		*					
Diamond Shamrock Corp.			*				
Dow Chemical Corp.					*		
Dun & Bradstreet				*			
Eaton Corporation			*				
Emhart Corp.				*			
Exxon			*				
Federal-Mogul Corp.					*		
Fluor				*			
FMC Corp.				*			
Foote, Cone & Belding							*
Ford Motor Corp.					*		
General Electric Co.		*					
General Foods		*					
General Motors			*				
Goodyear Tire & Rubber						*	
Hewlett-Packard					*		
Honeywell			*				
IBM				*			
Johnson Controls Inc.			*				
Kentucky Fried Chicken				*			
Kodak					*		
Kraft Inc.			*				
Lockheed			*				
Marriott Corp.				*			
McGraw-Hill					*		
Merck & Co.						*	

	1984	1985	1986	1987	1988	1989	1990
Mobil						*	
Motorola		*					
National-Standard Corp.							*
Newton Mining			*				
Norton Co.				*			
Oak Industries.			*				
RJR Nabisco							*
Pepsico Inc.				*			
Perkin-Helmer			*				
Phibro-Salomon			*				
Phillips Petroleum			*				
Playtex			*				
Procter & Gamble			*				
Revlon			*				
Rohm & Haas			*				
Sare Lee Corporation			*				
Scovill			*				
The Sentry Corp.		*					
SPS Technologies			*				
Stanley Works			*				
The St. Paul Cos. Inc						*	
Tambrands Inc.				*			
Tenneco Inc.							*
Tidwell Industries		*					
USX Corp.						*	
Warner Communications				*			
Westin Hotel					*		
Westinghouse Electric				*			
Xerox Corp.				*			

ENDNOTES

1 Data compiled from 1982–93 Annual Reports of the Sullivan signatory companies.
2 Gary Clyde Hufbauer, Jeffrey J. Schott, and Kimberly Ann Elliot, "Economic Sanctions Reconsidered," 2d ed. (Washington, DC: Institute for International Economics, 1990); Jose I. Fernandez, "Dismantling Apartheid: Counterproductive Effects of Continuing Economic Sanctions," *Law and Policy in International Business* 22, 3 (1991): 577–601; Merle Lipton, "Sanctions and South Africa: The Dynamics of Economic Isolation," Special Report No. 1119, *The Economist* Intelligence Unit (London: *The Economist*, 1988); IRRC, "International Business in South Africa 1993" (Washington, DC: IRRC, 1993)
3 Data compiled from IRRC, "U.S. Business in South Africa 1991" (Washington, DC: IRRC, 1991), Appendixes O and P.
4 Data compiled from the 1977–93 Annual Reports on the Sullivan signatory companies.
5 Dennis Kneale, "Sullivan's Tougher Principles," *Wall Street Journal*, 1 July 1986.

6 The primary sources used for press releases, news reports, and editorials were the *New York Times*, *Washington Post*, *Wall Street Journal*, and various news services, e.g., Reuters, Associated Press, and the Xinhua General Overseas News Service. In addition, a variety of other sources was used, either as original sources or as secondary sources and for corroboration. These sources included the *Financial Times*, *Business Week*, and various newspapers and periodicals from South Africa, among others.

7 James R. Kraus, "Citicorp to Sell South African Subsidiary; Business Constraints Led to Move, Company Says," *American Banker*, 17 June 1987.

8 Ibid.

9 Ibid.

10 Ibid.

11 "USX Out of South Africa," Associated Press, 9 October 1989.

12 Richard W. Stevenson, "BBDO Unit in South Africa Sold," *New York Times*, 21 August 1985.

13 Ibid.

14 "On Marketing," *Chicago Tribune*, 5 February 1990.

15 "Marriott to Sell South African Airline Caterer," *Washington Post*, 23 January 1986.

16 Ibid.

17 Frederick H. Katayama, "Did Mobil Help or Hurt Apartheid? Mobil Sells South African Operations to Gencor, Which Has a Reputation As a Harsh Employer," *Fortune*, 5 June 1989.

18 "Exxon Sells Interests in South Africa Firms," *Chicago Tribune*, 31 December 1986.

19 William Hall, "GE May Sell its South African Interests to Local Employees," *Financial Times* (London), 14 November 1985.

20 "Playtex Out of South Africa," *Chicago Tribune*, 27 November 1986.

21 "Two More U.S. Firms Quit Racist South Africa," Xinhua General Overseas News Service, 5 December 1986.

22 Christine Winter, "Motorola Sells Last South African Operation," *Chicago Tribune*, 9 October 1985; Anthony Ramirez, "Pepsico out of South Africa Following Failure of Bottler," *New York Times*, 12 April 1990.

23 Anthony Ramirez, "Pepsico Out of South Africa."

24 "Two More Firms Quit Racist South Africa," Xinhua General Overseas News Service.

25 "Merck Out of South Africa; Growth Stifled by U.S. Law," Reuter Textline, 6 January 1988.

26 Ibid.

27 Nicholas D. Kristof, "Phibro to Pull out of South Africa," *New York Times*, 22 August 1985.

28 Ibid.

29 Michael Isikoff and Peter Behr, "U.S. Business Debates S. Africa Ties; Companies Sell Off Operations; Cut Back Sales to Pretoria," *Washington Post*, 25 August 1985.

30 Ibid.

31 John Gorman, "Coke Quitting South Africa, Black and White Investors Buying Interests," *Chicago Tribune*, 18 September 1986.

32 "Coca-Cola Co. to Withdraw from South Africa," Xinhua General Overseas News Service, 18 September 1986.

33 Randolf Picht, "Kodak: 'We Went All The Way' with South African Disinvestment," Associated Press, 19 November 1986.

34 Ibid.

35 Michael Isikoff, "Local Boycotts Power Pullouts By U.S. Business: Firms Hesitate to Risk Contracts For Small South African Revenue," *Washington Post*, 17 November 1986.
36 Reuter Textline, *Financial Mail*, 15 May 1987.
37 "GM Leaving South Africa; Money-Loser Being Sold to Management Group," *Chicago Tribune*, 21 October 1986.
38 Barnaby J. Feder, "I.B.M. is Shedding South Africa; Pressure is Cited," *New York Times*, 22 October 1986.
39 Ibid.
40 Ibid.
41 S. Prakash Sethi and Paul Steidlmeier, eds., *Up Against the Corporate Wall: Corporations and Social Issues of the Nineties*, 6th ed., (Englewood Cliffs, NJ: Prentice-Hall, 1997). See also the earlier editions of this book (1971, 1974, 1977, and 1991); S. Prakash Sethi, *Advocacy Advertising and Large Corporations* (Lexington, MA: Lexington Books, 1976); and S, Prakash Sethi, *Multinational Corporations and the Impact of Public Advocacy on Corporate Strategy: Nestle and the Infant Formula Controversy* (Boston: Kluwer Academic Publishers, 1994).
42 What we are arguing for here is a clear statement for departing from (or staying in) South Africa based on moral and ethical grounds. There were some notable exceptions to the general lack of use of moral language by business leaders. For example, on 4 February 1987 David Clare, CEO of Johnson & Johnson, delivered a widely discussed paper at the Massachusetts Institute of Technology. In presenting a case for staying in South Africa based on ethical reasons, he cites some of the arguments made by one of the authors of this volume (Williams) in the then recently published book, *The Apartheid Crisis*.

Chapter 14

Repeal of the Comprehensive Anti-Apartheid Act of 1986

On 19 July 1991, President Bush issued Executive Order 12769 repealing the Comprehensive Anti-Apartheid Act of 1986 (CAAA). Bush stated that "the Government of South Africa has taken all the steps specified in Section 311(a) and Title III Section 501(c) and 504(b) of the act" (exhibit 15). Although other, more limited, sanctions remained in place, this action marked a major shift, both legally and philosophically, in the United States relationship with South Africa. CAAA stipulated five conditions that had to be met before sanctions were lifted:

1. The release of Nelson Mandela and all other political prisoners
2. The repeal of the South African state of emergency and the release of all persons detained under it
3. The repeal of the ban (in South Africa) of political parties
4. The repeal of Group Areas and Population Registration Acts
5. Good-faith negotiations with members of the Black majority

In the years leading up to the enactment of CAAA, a battle had been fought over what to do in South Africa. Consequently, several narrowly defined sanctions were passed before there was sufficient support for something as far reaching as CAAA. By the time President Bush moved to repeal the law, the debate had turned from what sanctions to impose, if any, to whether the act was making a difference, and whether, or to what degree, the terms of the law had been met. The South African government had made some progress toward dismantling apartheid. That government, at least officially, no longer banned the existence of political parties. It had released many political prisoners, including ANC deputy president, Nelson Mandela. It had also lifted the national state of emergency and repealed the Separate Amenities Act. It had

Exhibit 15. Executive Order Terminating U.S. Sanctions against South Africa

Executive Order
No. 12769 of July 10, 1991

Implementation of Section 311(a) of the Comprehensive Anti-Apartheid Act.
56 F.R. 31855

By the authority vested in me as President by the Constitution and the laws of the United States of American, including the Comprehensive Anti-Apartheid Act of 1986 (Public Law 99-440), as amended ("the Act"), and section 301 of title 3 of the United States Code, and having concluded that the Government of South Africa has taken all of the steps specified in section311(a) of the Act, and ,therefore, that title III and sections 501(c) and 504(b) of the Act have terminated, it is hereby ordered as follows:

Section 1. *Implementation of Section 311(a) of the Act.* All affected executive departments and agencies shall immediately take all steps necessary, consistent with the Constitution, to implement the termination of those sanctions which were imposed by title III and sections(c) and 504(b) of the Act.

Section 2. *Status of Prior Executive Order,* Except as superseded by section 1 of this order, Executive Order No. 12571[1] of October 27, 1986." Implementation of this order, the Inter-Agency Coordinating Committee established by section 12 of that order shall monitor the termination of those sanctions which were imposed by the title III and sections 501(a) and 504(b) of the Act.

Section 3. *Actions Taken and Proceedings Pending.* This order shall not affect any action taken or proceeding pending and not finally concluded or determined on the effective date of this order, or any action or proceeding based on any act committed prior to the effective date of this order, or any rights and duties that matured or penalties that were incurred prior to the effective date of this order.

Section 4. Revocation. Executive Order No. 12532[2] of September 9, 1985, and Executive Order No. 12535[3] of October 1, 1985, which lapsed on September 9, 1987, pursuant to the provisions of sections 1622(d) and 1701 of title 50 of the United States Code are hereby revoked.

Section 5. Effective Date. This order shall be effective immediately.

THE WHITE HOUSE
7-10-91

1. 22 U.S.C.A. §5111 nt.
2. 50 U.S.C.A. §1701 nt.
3. 50 U.S.C.A. §1701 nt.

introduced legislation that would eventually bring down the three pillars of apartheid: the Group Areas Act, the Lands Act, and the Population Registration Act. The Bush administration was of the opinion that with these changes, the only remaining unmet conditions to lifting the sanctions under the CAAA were the release of all political prisoners and the return of exiles.

In repealing CAAA, the Bush administration and its Republican allies in Congress worked from a literal interpretation of the terms of the law. When asked whether he had any reservations on removing the sanctions and whether it would undermine the progress that had been made so far, Bush asserted that CAAA did not give him any flexibility in removing the sanctions. The administration's public posture, however, was designed to appeal to broad sections of the public. He did not imply that apartheid had been abolished or that the United States could relax its concern for South Africa. Instead, he asserted that significant progress had been made, enough to warrant removing the CAAA-imposed sanctions.

He also responded to criticism from those who believed that all five conditions of the CAAA had not been met: "I happen to think it's the right thing to do. I believe that this will result in more progress toward racial equality instead of less, and certainly, in more economic opportunity rather than less. So the time has come to do it."[1] Bush justified his repeal of CAAA by stating:

> President de Klerk has repealed the legislative pillars of apartheid and opened up the political arena to prepare the way for constitutional negotiations, and I really firmly believe that this progress is irreversible. The CAAA anticipated the benefit of lifting these sanctions as a means of encouraging the Government of South Africa and the people of South Africa to continue the progress that has been made in eliminating apartheid.[2]

Even with the removal of CAAA-related sanctions, several other separately legislated American sanctions remained in force. These included limitations on South Africa's borrowing from the International Monetary Fund and the Export-Import Bank, a ban on all exports to South Africa's military and police, a mandatory UN arms embargo on South Africa, and a ban on all intelligence sharing. Bush acknowledged that the United States position remained steadfast in that racial prejudice (apartheid) was unacceptable and that the United States was committed to bringing an end such repugnant practices. The president said that the United States would use all available means to encourage the establishment of a nonracial, multiparty democracy in South Africa. In a move supportive of those affected by apartheid, Bush authorized a doubling of United States assistance to Black South Africans (to $80 million), to be used for housing, economic development, and education programs. Herman J. Cohen, assistant secretary of state for African affairs, added his hope that the lifting of sanctions by the federal government would also spur colleges, universities, states, and local governments to rescind their restrictions concerning companies doing business in or with South Africa. These restrictions, in their own way, were as damaging as those required under CAAA.[3]

President Bush personally called Nelson Mandela to inform him of his intention to repeal CAAA. Mandela was not in favor of Bush's decision and felt that it was too much, too soon. Echoing this same view were top Democratic leaders, the Congressional Black Caucus, and the National Association for the Advancement of Colored People. Those in opposition disputed the State Department's assessment that all political prisoners had been released. This time, though, the balance—both of the argument and of public sentiment—had shifted in the administration's favor: the opposition in Congress was not sufficiently strong to attempt an override of the president's decision. Interestingly, the cast of characters involved in the debate on the repeal of CAAA was quite similar to that involved in its enactment in 1986. Furthermore, the arguments advanced for and against the repeal covered the same ground, although there was some softening of the positions on both sides.

1.   THE BUSH ADMINISTRATION

Assistant Secretary of State Cohen testified in support of the administration's position before the House Committee on Foreign Affairs (13 July 1991). He argued that in the eighteen months preceding Bush's lifting of sanctions, South Africa had made considerable progress toward achieving CAAA's objectives. He stated that CAAA recognized that "once the transition process got well underway, renewed external contracts, trade, and communication would play a vital role in encouraging continued progress and laying a sound economic basis for renewed growth in post-apartheid South Africa." Cohen also argued that "the language, structure, and legislative history of the Act show that the possibility of lifting sanctions was intended as an incentive for the South African Government to create the conditions for good faith negotiations, not as a reward to be withheld until the apartheid system had been completely eliminated."[4]

Cohen's testimony provides a concise review of the administration's perspective on South Africa's satisfaction of the five conditions of the CAAA:[5]

– "The first condition in section 311(a) of the CAAA required the South African Government to release from prison Nelson Mandela and all persons persecuted for their political beliefs or detained unduly without trial. This standard is consistent with the criteria we have long applied in our annual human rights reports." Mr. Cohen stated that the United States Embassy in Pretoria had completed an exhaustive review of persons incarcerated by the South African government and concluded that no prisoner or detainee who met the criteria of section 311(a) was being held.

- The second condition required the South African government to repeal the state of emergency and to release all emergency detainees. This condition had been met in 1990. The detainees had been freed, as confirmed by the South African Human Rights Commission.
- The third condition required the South African government to remove its ban on democratic political parties and to permit South Africans of all races to form political parties, express political opinions, and otherwise participate in the political process. This ban had been eliminated in 1990. The assertion by some that this third condition required that Black South Africans be given the right to vote was not a condition of CAAA.
- The fourth condition required the South African government to repeal the Population Registration Act and Group Areas Act, and to institute no other measures with the same purpose. The government had repealed the two laws in June 1991. The transitional measures contained in the repeal legislation were limited solely to maintain the existing constitution until a new constitution was adopted. The population register was frozen as of the date of repeal of the act; no racial information would be entered for newborns or added for other persons in the future. Similarly, the residential-standards provisions adopted in connection with the repeal of the Group Areas Act were zoning rules (not unlike those that exist throughout the United States) that expressly prohibited racial discrimination.
- The fifth condition required that the South African government agree to enter into good-faith negotiations, subject to no preconditions, with truly representative members of the Black majority. Cohen stated that the government had so agreed. Although critics challenged whether the government would conduct the negotiations in good faith, the United States government was firmly convinced that President de Klerk and his government were committed to achieving nonracial democracy in South Africa. Knowing that there could be no turning back to the policies of apartheid and White privilege, they would approach the coming negotiations in good faith and with the full intention that they succeed.

Cohen also commented on the view emanating from Congress and some public groups that lifting sanctions was premature. "Many of you have expressed concern that the lifting of sanctions will take the pressure off the South African Government to move forward with constitutional talks. But the clock cannot be turned back. Sanctions have played a role in encouraging the South African government to move ahead with reforms, and the irreversible process of dismantling apartheid is now underway. The termination of sanctions does not lessen our commitment to support the creation of nonracial democracy in South Africa. We are supporting the negotiating process through a balanced policy of frequent contacts with all parties."[6]

Given the sensitivity of the issue and the potential for disagreement, Cohen specifically addressed the question of whether all political prisoners had been released: "Essentially, did they release all persons persecuted for their political beliefs or detained unduly without trial?"[7] To determine if the terms of CAAA had been met, the embassy in Pretoria had studied over 5,691 files to see what the prisoners had been sentenced for and what they had been convicted of. It was found that all those who had not yet been released had been convicted of violent crimes against persons or property, and did not fit the definition of political prisoner as expressed in the statute. Of those who were still in prison, Cohen said, "The government [of South Africa] thinks they are not qualified under their definition, and the ANC or the Human Rights Commission thinks they are qualified. We do not think we should adjudicate between the ANC and the government. We must follow our own definition."[8]

2.   UNITED STATES CONGRESS

By the time the sanctions were lifted, active concern in the issue of sanctions had considerably diminished. The interests of many in Congress had moved on to other, more pressing issues. As might be expected, however, there were still pockets of especially concerned senators and representatives, including those involved in the Congressional Black Caucus. Other critics on Capitol Hill were uncertain as to what Bush's decision to lift sanctions would mean in the near term. For example, Democratic Representative Maxine Waters of California expressed the view that regardless of United States sanctions, the minority government of South Africa had a long way to go before achieving a nonracial democracy. Other supporters of CAAA in 1986, including Democratic Senators Kennedy of Massachusetts and Paul Simon of Illinois, argued that its repeal was coming too soon. Doubt was expressed concerning the opportunity to realize economic gain by removing the sanctions, which appeared to be a significant part of the Republican justification for supporting the administration's position.

2.1   House of Representatives: Opposition to Repeal

In the House, attention focused on understanding the degree to which the terms of CAAA had been satisfied. Many of those who believed very strongly in the United States' responsibility in and for South Africa remained unconvinced. Most vocal in reaction to Bush's 1991 repeal were the Democrats Ronald Dellums of California, Julian Dixon of California, Mervyn M. Dymally of California, William Gray III of Pennsylvania, Kweisi Mfume of Maryland, and Howard Wolpe of Michigan, and the Republicans Dan

Burton of Indiana and Toby Roth of Wisconsin. This group strongly corresponded to the one that had propelled the legislative activity that led to the enactment of CAAA in 1986.

On 31 July 1991, in the wake of President Bush's executive order of 10 July to lift sanctions against South Africa, the House's Committee on International Relations, Subcommittee on International Economic Policy and Trade, and Subcommittee on Africa held hearings. Chair Mervyn Dymally reiterated in his opening remarks the sentiments he expressed during hearings in April: "Indeed, there have been some changes in South Africa. However, the government is moving at a slow pace in implementing announced reforms, and many obstacles remain before a climate conducive to formal negotiations and, ultimately, a nonracial democracy can occur. Despite the release of Mr. Mandela, the South African Government has failed to release all persons persecuted for their political beliefs or detained unduly without trial."[9] Dymally noted that the administration's widely anticipated action had raised an international outcry among the anti-apartheid and prodemocracy groups, which disputed the administration's assessment that the South African government had complied with all of the conditions. These groups felt that despite the repeal of several anti-apartheid laws and the modification of the Internal Security Act, the conditions had, at best, been only partially met, and that the government had failed to comply with the letter and spirit of the law.[10]

In arguing that CAAA's conditions had not yet been met, Dymally identified South African laws that were still in effect; for example, the Internal Security Act No. 74, which allowed administrative detention without trial or charge, and the Public Safety Amendment Act of 1986, which authorized powers almost identical to those authorized under the 1986 state of emergency. Further, Black South Africans did not have the right to express political opinions or participate in the political process. Dymally stated that "it is inconceivable that, at such a critical juncture in the negotiating process, in the face of such strong opposition from the ANC and other pro-democracy groups, and in the wake of such staggering levels of violence that the U.S. could, in good conscience, consider lifting sanctions."[11]

Another critic of the Bush administration, Kweisi Mfume, believed that CAAA's conditions had been met only if one used an exceedingly narrow and limited definition—one that had been tailored to the specific purpose of repealing the law. He believed that the South African government had "been careful to adhere to the minimal criteria for lifting sanctions. Many of the steps the government has taken are not uniform, and they appear to be all over the map in selecting what apartheid statutes will remain and which ones will indeed go."[12]

Howard Wolpe, who had been instrumental in the creation and passage of CAAA, challenged the administration's claim that the conditions required for repeal—especially the one concerning the ban on political parties—had been met. Assistant Secretary of State Cohen insisted that all political exiles who wanted to come back could do so, and those not accused of committing any crime would not be imprisoned. Wolpe argued, however, that political exiles were yet to be indemnified and were still prohibited from free political participation because of the threat of arrest on their return.

In addition to the written testimony he submitted, Ron Dellums argued that CAAA's conditions had not been met; lifting sanctions was not only wrong, but illegal. Dellums supported keeping CAAA in place and recommended, moreover, that the threat of further sanctions be used to keep pressure on the South African government, especially if it were to retreat from its commitment to good-faith negotiations. Finally, on the positive side, Dellums argued that a robust aid package would support and encourage a nonracial, democratic South Africa.[13]

In Dellums's view the de Klerk regime had displayed limited or no compliance with the five conditions established by Congress. He argued:

1. Mandela had been freed from prison, but he and 23 million other Black South Africans were still deprived of full citizenship, voting rights, equal economic opportunity, and justice in the land of their birth.
2. The 1986 state of emergency had been repealed, but the regime could still declare "unrest areas" within which it exercised virtually unbridled power.
3. Despite the removal of the ban on political parties, Blacks had not been given the freedom, economic means, or media access to compete openly in the political process.
4. The repeal of the Land Act allowed Blacks to purchase land anywhere in the country, but the repeal neither provided for the return of confiscated land nor compensated the nearly four million Blacks who were forcibly removed from their property when the Land Act was in effect.
5. No formal process had been established for good-faith negotiations with representative members of the Black majority. Such negotiations would require that Blacks be fully empowered to participate as equals, that political exiles be allowed safe return, and that Blacks be free to elect their own leaders. "The de Klerk regime cannot be both a participant in and referee of this process without causing grave damage to the integrity of the process itself.[14]

Representative Julian Dixon questioned what Congress should do—now that the sanctions had been lifted. He suggested that Congress should at least continue to monitor the South African situation. "The President should formally report to Congress on a quarterly basis concerning the political prisoners, and progress that has been made toward democracy in a nonracial, democratic system in South Africa."[15]

2.1.1 Special Focus: House Congressional Black Caucus

Although unhappy with Bush's action, members of the Black Caucus felt that there was probably little they could do beyond speaking out in opposition to the repeal. The chairman of the House Congressional Black Caucus, Ronald Dellums, opposed the initiation of a court challenge to the administration's decision. Instead, he indicated that he would explore the possibility of creating a group to continue monitoring the situation in South Africa; if the negotiations broke down, the group would be in a position to demand that Congress revisit the need for sanctions. The Black Caucus felt that the president's action was tantamount to rewarding South Africa's President de Klerk and his government for what everyone agreed were significant steps toward reform—but steps that fell short of satisfying the five conditions established in 1986 by CAAA.[16]

2.1.2 In Support of the Repeal

In support of repealing CAAA, a ranking Republican leader, Dan Burton, argued that the "South African Government has proven its good faith and its desire to negotiate a fair constitution. It is time for the ANC to prove it is serious about democracy. It is time for the ANC to disassociate itself from the Communist Party. It is time for the ANC to endorse free market principles. It is time for the ANC to renounce its links to Fidel Castro, Muammar Quaddafi, and Yasser Arafat, for these associations speak volumes about ANC itself."[17] Burton, as a powerful and outspoken Republican voice, was attempting to shift responsibility for the atrocities and the current conditions in South Africa from the government to ANC. Responding to critics of the Bush administration, Burton also argued that the time had come to move past the issue of apartheid and to address, instead, the future of South Africa *after* apartheid. He recommended, for example, an emphasis on measures to stimulate the South African economy. He felt that Americans needed to start looking for positive ways to help the people of South Africa meet the challenges of the future, a process that could not begin until the sanctions were repealed.

Congressman Toby Roth also agreed with President Bush's decision to end the sanctions. It was Black South Africans, not the White majority and their government, who had borne the brunt of those sanctions; when American and other businesses were forced out, the people who lost their jobs were Blacks. Ending the sanctions, in his view, would pave the way for an economic revitalization, which would help South Africa's Blacks work their way back to the economic position they had before the sanctions had been imposed. As was the case in 1986, Republican concern appeared to be oriented more toward economic issues than toward those of human rights.

2.2   Senate

The Democratic Senators Paul Simon of Illinois, Ted Kennedy of Massachusetts, Alan Cranston of California, and Paul Sarbanes of Maryland were among the original sponsors of CAAA in 1986. Now, in 1991, they met with Assistant Secretary Cohen, urging him to advise President Bush to refrain from lifting the sanctions. These senators, like others, contended that by lifting sanctions, the administration would lose its leverage over the South African government to create a nonracial, democratic society. In a Senate speech on 10 June 1991, Senator Kennedy cited the following factors as evidence of South Africa's continuing noncompliance: failure to release all political prisoners; failure to allow forty thousand political exiles to return with full immunity; and failure to repeal all security laws, coupled with the enactment of new legislation that, in place of the repealed Group Areas Act, imposed new restrictions on Blacks. The only condition that had been fully met, in Kennedy's opinion, was the repeal of the state of emergency and the release of everyone imprisoned under it.[18] Senator Paul Simon urged the Bush administration to hold the line on sanctions. He suggested that the Senate might consider a "gesture" in lieu of the president's executive order.

Kennedy joined Representatives Dellums and Waters in supporting the president's decision to leave in place sanctions that existed outside of CAAA, including an arms embargo and a ban on United States support through IMF and Export-Import Bank loans. Though Kennedy also welcomed Bush's decision to recommend the 100 percent increase to $80 million in the level of United States aid to South African Blacks, Dellums dismissed the president's recommendation as gratuitous.

Democratic Senator John Glenn of Ohio, chairman of the Senate Governmental Affairs Committee, echoed the sentiments of lawmakers from both chambers and suggested that Bush searched for and found technical compliance with CAAA in an effort to support his long-held opposition to economic sanctions. Glenn said he preferred to see the United States gradually phase out sanctions in direct relation to progress toward reform in South Africa, thus keeping pressure on the White minority government.

The ranking minority member of the Senate Foreign Relations Subcommittee on African Affairs, Republican Senator Nancy Kassenbaum of Kansas, supported the president's decision to lift sanctions and agreed that the arms embargo and IMF sanctions should remain in place. Her position reflected a general view that lifting all sanctions, specifically those outside of the CAAA, was not warranted until a more representative constitutional process was in place in South Africa.

3. THE PERSPECTIVE OF THE PUBLIC-INTEREST GROUPS

Elected officials were not the only voices speaking out on the president's decision to lift sanctions. Public-interest groups from different perspectives were equally vociferous in expressing their opinions on President Bush's July 10 executive order. These voices came forward in the media, public forums, and congressional hearings. Here, too, many of the names and faces were the same as those who had been active during the push to enact sanctions in the early 1980s.

Randall Robinson, executive director of TransAfrica, urged Congress to maintain sanctions not only because the five conditions of CAAA had not been met, but also because it was still too early to judge the progress of reform. He believed that there was not enough evidence that the de Klerk government was prepared to facilitate the creation of a nonracial democracy in South Africa, thus justifying the removal of sanctions. Robinson denounced the White House action as a "disgrace" that would impede the progress toward nonracial democracy in South Africa.[19]

Many other witnesses attended the congressional hearings to support the maintenance of sanctions until there was greater evidence of change. Witnesses included the Reverend Joan Campbell, National Council of the Churches of Christ in the United States; Jennifer Davis, executive director, the Africa Fund; Mathew Phosa, African National Congress, Legal Department; and Gay McDougall, director, Southern Africa Project, Lawyers' Committee for Civil Rights Under Law. They all generally agreed that none of CAAA's five conditions had been met, and that the sanctions should remain in place until profound and irreversible change was achieved.

John G. Healey, executive director, Amnesty International, testified on the human rights situation on South Africa: "Recent revelations have shown that the South African government has been using significant amounts of money from clandestine funds to finance and ferment unrest. At the same time, the government has attempted to distance itself from apartheid's history of brutal oppression by waging a huge public relations campaign aimed at promulgating a carefully crafted international image of reform. However, despite this glowing reputation which the government currently enjoys with the U.S. Administration, the truth is that very serious human rights abuses are still being committed under the auspices of the South African authorities."[20]

Amnesty International had the following recommendations to make to members of Congress and the South African government:

- Put an end to incommunicado detention and allow detainees not only prompt access to legal counsel, but communication with their family and access to independent medical examination

- Speedily complete the review of all cases in political prisons

- Put an end to extraditial execution and account for the deaths and detention which are continuing to occur

- Instruct judicial authorities to investigate thoroughly any allegations of human rights abuses (including those relating to extradition), and to bring the perpetrators to justice[21]

Additional testimony was provided by Meg Voorhes, director, South Africa Review Service, Investor Responsibility Research Center. Voorhes argued that the repeal of sanctions would have little impact in persuading companies to invest in South Africa; state and local laws within the United States would still restrict contracts with companies that do business in South Africa. "Unlike the CAAA, state and local sanctions policies do not usually specify time tables or conditions for their repeal, or if they do, they use broad formulations that allow them to be applied until apartheid has ended, or until all South Africans have equal voting rights. State and local laws were often adopted after constituent coalitions of antiapartheid activists, black Americans, church leaders, students, and unions lobbied for them, and state and local governments will probably hesitate to reverse them until they receive a go-ahead from their constituent interests. So far, many of the leaders of these constituencies believe President Bush reacted too soon in lifting the Federal sanctions."[22]

Voorhes listed other factors that would influence corporate America's decisions on whether or how to do business in post-sanctions South Africa:

- Reestablishment of IMF borrowing privileges for South Africa

- Assurances that South Africa was able to resolve its political problems peacefully, without the violence or instability that could threaten the country's assets or citizens

- Assurances that the policies of the future government would not choke economic growth and hem in business with regulation and red tape

- Assurances that the rules for businesses operating within the country would not change constantly[23]

The Heritage Foundation, as would be expected, responded to the repeal by suggesting that, at best, the effect of sanctions had been modest. Also, the foundation considered events outside the sanctions initiative (for example, the waning of the Cold War and the collapse of Communism) to have had much more impact than the sanctions on the prospects for change in South Africa.

Representative Dan Burton presented reports from the group Peaceful Progress in South Africa in support of his testimony at the hearings. This group, which included both Americans and South Africans, shared a long-standing distaste for apartheid and a strong conviction that disinvestment and sanctions had been ineffective—even counterproductive—in the effort to eliminate apartheid.[24] The group felt that "most of the laws making up the structure of apartheid had been repealed before the advent of sanctions in 1986. To the extent that the CAAA had any effect it was negative, weakening the Progressive Federal Party, strengthening candidates of the reactionary Conservative Party, and slowing down the reform process. The so-called anti-apartheid act almost gave apartheid a new lease on life."[25] It was the position of this group that delays in negotiations stemmed from additional preconditions originating with ANC. The group also believed that keeping sanctions in place in order to enforce objectives outside of the CAAA was tantamount to "moving the goal posts."

4.   REACTIONS IN SOUTH AFRICA

4.1   The South African Government

In his article "De Klerk's Victory," Christopher Wren wrote that "with the lifting of American economic sanctions against South Africa today, President F. W. de Klerk has received the most significant foreign endorsement yet of his contention that the dismantling of apartheid that he began last year will not be reversed. Yet the pressure is being relaxed on Pretoria when black South Africans still have no vote and no power in a government that remains white-dominated, a contradiction that the African National Congress and other proponents of continued sanctions were quick to point out today."[26]

President de Klerk, in his statement on the United States action, stressed that Blacks would benefit from an expanding economy unfettered by sanctions. "The removal of these sanctions will contribute to the revival of our economy to the benefit of all South Africans, especially those disadvantaged South Africans who have borne the brunt of sanctions, including many of the unemployed."[27] Again, the issue was being positioned as an economic one—and not as one involving politics or human rights.

Meanwhile, South African Foreign Minister Pik Botha expressed his government's "sincere appreciation" of President Bush's action. Describing the effects of repealed trade sanctions as mainly "psychological," Botha described the move as "a momentous decision" that would pave the way for other governments, particularly in Africa, to end all sanctions and close an "era with tremendously harmful effects on the growth of the South African economy."[28]

4.2   The African National Congress (ANC)

The ANC did not feel that there had been enough change in South Africa to warrant the lifting of sanctions. During a European tour in June 1990, and again in response to a call from President Bush giving notice of his intent to lift the sanctions, Nelson Mandela argued that it was not yet time to do so. Chris Hani, leader of the military wing of ANC, shared Mandela's view and feared that lifting sanctions would send a message that would cause Blacks in South Africa to feel that they were again being left to fend for themselves. Sanctions were viewed by ANC as a crucial indicator of political support while the organization pushed the South African government toward the adoption of a democratic constitution. As stated by Cyril Ramaphosa, the new secretary general of ANC, "progress should be judged not only by fine words but by actual deeds, and such progress cannot be determined by the South African Government nor accepted on its word alone."[29]

4.3   Other South African Organizations

The ANC was not the only nongovernment group speaking out in South Africa. The more radical Pan-Africanist Congress called Bush's announcement "a sugar-coated poison tablet" and stated that it would press for other sanctions to continue "until all vestiges of white racist minority rule have been removed and the masses of our people have placed in power a government which truly represents them."[30] The South African Council of Churches, which was aligned with the ANC, also criticized the American action. "Unfortunately, the struggle is not over yet and we fear that the premature lifting of sanctions will mean that one of the major incentives motivating the South African Government to change, will be lost,"[31] said the council's secretary general, Frank Chicane.

Chief Mangosuthu Gatsha Buthelezi, the chief minister of the Zulu homeland, took a position opposed to that of many Black South Africans. He had remained opposed to sanctions during the entire period that CAAA was in place. At its repeal he reiterated his position that sanctions had succeeded only in causing economic devastation among Black South Africans and that sanctions should have been abolished much earlier.

ENDNOTES

1 *New York Times*, 11 July 1991, A10.
2 Ibid.
3 Thomas L Friedman, "Bush Lifts a Ban on Economic Ties to South Africa," *New York Times*, 11 July 1991, A1.
4 House Committee on Foreign Affairs, *The Termination of Economic Sanctions against South Africa*, joint hearing before the Subcommittees on International Economic Policy and Trade, and on Africa, 102d Congress, 1st sess., 31 July 1991, 17 [hereinafter 31 July 1991 Hearing]. This hearing specifically concerned the termination of economic sanctions against South Africa.
5 Ibid., 19–20.
6 Ibid., 22.
7 Ibid., 34.
8 Ibid.
9 House Committee on Foreign Affairs, joint hearing before the Subcommittees on International Economic Policy and Trade, and on Africa. 102d Congress, 1st sess., 30 April 1991, 1 [hereinafter 30 April 1991 Hearing].
10 31 July 1991 Hearing, 1.
11 30 April 1991 Hearing, 2–3.
12 Ibid., 8.
13 Ibid., 44.
14 31 July 1991 Hearing, 136–38.
15 Ibid., p. 13.
16 Bureau of National Affairs Daily Report for Executives, 11 July 1991.
17 31 July 1991 Hearing, 5.
18 *Boston Globe*, 10 July 1991.
19 31 July 1991 Hearing, 123–24.
20 Ibid., 76.
21 Ibid., 85–86.
22 Ibid., 98.
23 Ibid., 103–4.
24 Ibid., 48.
25 Ibid.
26 *New York Times*, 11 July 1991, A10.
27 Ibid.
28 Ibid.
29 Ibid.
30 Ibid.
31 Ibid.

Chapter 15

The Rocky Road to Post-Apartheid South Africa
The Sullivan Principles without Sullivan

By the end of 1986 both Leon Sullivan and the Principles program had reached a crossroad. The proportion of United States corporations participating in the program was at a peak. Despite this success, however, it was not clear that the program had significantly influenced the political agenda to secure a democratic South Africa. Moreover, by this same time, the anti-apartheid movement had escalated to a point where economic issues had been pushed aside and political issues had gained ascendancy. And Sullivan himself had argued all along that his larger agenda was the abolition of the apartheid regime of South Africa, and that economic issues and the Principles program were but a means to that end. In this context, he was becoming increasingly frustrated with the Principles program and with its lack of impact in the political realm.

1.   SULLIVAN ISSUES AN ULTIMATUM

On 7 May 1985 Sullivan announced in an article in the *Philadelphia Inquirer* that "if apartheid has not, in fact, ended legally and actually as a system within the next 24 months, there should be a total U.S. economic embargo against South Africa, including the withdrawal of all U.S. companies, to be followed, I hope, by other nations."[1] In speaking to a plenary meeting of the signatories a month later (12 June), Sullivan stated that he had not consulted with anyone other than his wife prior to issuing the statement. He also indicated that his hope was that the South African government would move to dismantle the pillars of apartheid within the next two years and thus spare him his threatened departure. He went on to say that although he still held out hope for some sign of the dismantling of apartheid, "This may be our last meeting of this kind, but everyone should be proud of how much we have done since we started the journey."

From the perspective of the signatory companies, Sullivan's willingness to abandon his own program was a major blow that could seriously undermine their credibility in the eyes of the public. His departure would also erode the legitimacy of their approach as having a positive impact on the dismantling of apartheid in South Africa. The companies therefore mobilized a major effort designed to persuade Sullivan to stay with the program. A Black Caucus group collected over two hundred thousand signatures urging him to remain. The program's Industry Support Unit proposed that Sullivan should undertake a major tour of South Africa. Such a trip would include visits to various projects undertaken by the signatory companies, and meetings with major political and business leaders, including Chief Buthelezi, Bishop Tutu, and Dr. Michael Rosholt, chair of Barlow Rand. As the advance party for the tour, Daniel Purnell (a Sullivan aide and administrator of the Principles program) and Scott Campbell (an officer of Kellogg Corporation) traveled to South Africa from April 17 to May 2 to plan every detail of Sullivan's visit. Unfortunately, all this planning was of no avail: on 14 May 1987, and after much haggling, the South African consulate informed Sullivan that he would not be granted a visa for a May trip but that he could come in July. Such an act of idiocy and capriciousness was typical of the South African government. The government made strenuous efforts to persuade world opinion that it was making progress toward becoming a more open society. At the same time, it also demonstrated its defiance through actions and gestures whose primary value was in expressing its contempt for the same world opinion.

Sal Marzullo and others, both within and outside of the ISU, valiantly tried to persuade Sullivan to extend his deadline until 30 July 1987. Sullivan would have none of it. On 3 June 1987 he announced his decision to leave the program. On the same day, he issued a five-page press release extolling the progress that had been made under the Principles program for the past ten years. He went on to say:

> Somewhere, somehow, it must be said, as loudly and clearly, and as firmly as possible, that what is happening in South Africa to Black people is immoral, and it is wrong, and it must be brought to an end. It is clear that the South African government does not intend to end apartheid on its own. Since the recent elections, the government has become more defiant to further change. Therefore, something must be done now to dramatize the issue before America and before the world.

Sullivan's critics were elated that he finally saw the wisdom of their position of complete disinvestment. In an extensive on-the-record personal interview with the authors, however, Sullivan presented a more complex picture. What Sullivan had in common with most anti-apartheid activists was his concern for the poor and the disenfranchised—in this case, the Blacks of South Africa. Where Sullivan differed from most activists was in the goals he was seeking in that country. Sullivan always thought that a single-minded focus on political rights was too narrow a vision. From his days as a civil rights activist in the United States, Sullivan believed that the goals of political rights and a better economic future worked in tandem. The elimination of political apartheid without overcoming economic apartheid was not acceptable.

2. THE PRINCIPLES PROGRAM AFTER SULLIVAN

In the real world, the signatory companies had no option but to continue with the program. By this time, over 125 companies were spending tens of millions of dollars on various activities under the Principles' umbrella. The local programs thereby supported had become integral parts of Black communities in South Africa. These local programs also provided a vital economic lifeline to a variety of anti-apartheid, prodemocracy groups in South Africa. Although many of these groups advocated economic sanctions against South Africa, they also depended on the United States companies' support to sustain the local programs and other activities, which ranged from community-building efforts to legal representation of Blacks in South African courts.

Echoing these concerns, a *Washington Post* editorial stated, "The economy is an instrument of white control, but it is also an instrument of black progress. . . . The code remains too valuable to South Africa's blacks to abandon summarily. The firms now thinking of continuing 'the Sullivan Principles without Sullivan' seem to us to be on the right track."[2] In a similar vein, Sal G. Marzullo of Mobil, who was chairman of the board of directors of the Industry Support Unit, wrote a letter to one of the co-authors of this book (Williams) outlining a possible new organizational structure for the signatory companies—and urging Williams to consider joining the redesigned organization. The 30 June 1987 letter stated, in part:

> We shall continue to carry out the Statement of Principles and are reorganizing to better do so in the future. One of the possibilities we foresee is the creation of a small Board of Overseers to the Statement of Principles. . . . The Board of Overseers would be a three to five person group

that would be a consultative body to us, examining what we are doing; visiting South Africa; and working with us to keep the Principles relevant. It would be independent of us, yet act as an advisory body to us. Would you consider joining such a group if we form one? I would appreciate your thinking on this.[3]

The decision to be made, in the mind of this co-author, was whether joining this board of overseers would be in the best interests of Black South Africans. Williams had known and admired Leon Sullivan for a number of years. Sullivan had written a highly complementary endorsement to Williams's book on South Africa, published in 1986.[4] Sullivan and Williams had disagreed, however, on whether Sullivan should leave the Principles program, and it was uncertain how Sullivan would react if Williams took an active role in the post-Sullivan program. To Williams's pleasant surprise, Sullivan strongly encouraged him to join the board and to keep the companies' "feet to the fire." Sullivan echoed similar sentiments in a letter to Sal Marzullo several years later. On 17 May 1989, Sullivan wrote: "It is very important that American based members of the Industry Support Unit, representing American companies still remaining in South Africa, maintain a vital role in providing continuing direction to these efforts."[5]

In any event, Williams agreed to join the endeavor, and on 23 September 1988, a press release (exhibit 16) announced the new National Advisory Council. Between June 1987 and the time of that announcement, the program had been run by the Industry Support Unit, which had seven board members—from Mobil, Colgate-Palmolive, Caltex, Deere, Eli Lilly, Squibb, and Control Data.

The new council involved a radical departure from the existing monitoring system in two important respects. Although Arthur D. Little would continue to verify the companies' own audits of expenditures under the Principles program, Weedon's authority in the evaluation of those activities was scaled back significantly. In addition, the council would have no authority over monitoring activities. Instead, the key emphasis in the work of the National Advisory Council was on the word *advisory.* The primary activity of the council would be to travel to South Africa each year for a ten- to fourteen-day period, and to assess how the Principles program could be made more effective in the effort to dismantle apartheid. During these trips, members of the group would interview major leaders of all sectors of South African society, visit projects funded by the companies, visit company sites and talk to employees, and tour the Black townships. The council would have not any administrative staff or support services. Instead, all logistical support was to be provided by the signatory companies' organizations. The members of the council would submit a list of the persons they wished to

Exhibit 16. Industry Support Unit, Inc. Press Release

S.G. Marzullo, Chairman of the Industry Support Unit, Inc. Signatory Companies to the Statement of Principles, a consortium of American companies still operating in South Africa, announced today the formation of a National Advisory Council.

The Council, a wholly independent body, will provide guidance, assistance and, where appropriate, criticism to the companies as they work toward the removal of laws sustaining apartheid and toward black social and economic empowerment. The Council consists of: Father Oliver F. Williams, C.S.C., Associate Provost of the University of Notre Dame; Melvin B. Miller, Partner, Fitch Miller & Tourse and Trustee, Boston University; and Bishop Richard Laymon Fisher, Presiding Bishop of the Ninth Episcopal District of the African Methodist Episcopal Zion Church.

The National Advisory Council is:

Wholly independent.

The role of the council is to transmit opinion and advice and when necessary constructively criticize—not to evaluate or monitor. Reid Weedon of Arthur D. Little, Inc. continues to retain his independence and remains the evaluator.

The Council presents new opportunities for going forward and is a vehicle for companies to maximize their efforts to eliminate apartheid in South Africa.

---

meet and locations they wanted to examine. At the end of each trip, the council would submit a report to the signatory membership.

The practical impact of this arrangement was a further watering down of an already flawed "independent" monitoring system. The new council's advisory role, coupled with its limited scope and reporting commitments, rendered moot the issue of comprehensive monitoring, objective evaluation, and follow-up. The companies seemed to have recognized, morever, that the character of the Sullivan principles' implementation had fundamentally changed. Although the companies that remained in South Africa were expected to continue with their activities under the Principles program, their role as change agents had become marginalized in the context of the external sociopolitical environment. There was a realization that the Sullivan Principles were no larger a driving force in the companies' justifications for staying in South Africa. Instead, the companies were, in effect, holding the fort until external political events took over and provided the companies with a graceful exit from the formal structure of the Principles program.

3.   THE REORGANIZATION OF THE INDUSTRY SUPPORT UNIT

By 1987, rapid changes, both in public sentiment and in the political situation in South Africa, seemed to have broken the spirit and resolve of the signatory companies. The departure of United States companies from South Africa was gathering momentum. During the three-year period from 1986 to 1989, more than two hundred companies left South Africa, severely eroding not only the Principles program's support base, but also its financial resources. Of all these departures, perhaps the most surprising was that of Mobil, which was announced on 28 April 1989 by Allen Murray, the corporation's CEO. He cited the Rangel Amendment, passed in late 1988, which disallowed foreign tax credits for the income earned by United States companies in South Africa, as one of the major contributing factors—the proverbial "last straw." He stated that the business was simply not producing sufficient return to justify staying in South Africa.

In both symbolic and real terms, Mobil's departure was a fatal blow to the Principles organization. ISU's president, Sal Marzullo, was himself a vice president of Mobil. To large segments of the United States public and to the political establishment in Washington, he was the "public face and de facto voice" of the signatory companies. With the departure of Mobil from South Africa, his effectiveness as the voice of the United States companies was severely undermined. Frustrated and demoralized, he took early retirement from Mobil.

The reduction in the Principle program's financial resources required the development of a less expensive and more efficient operation. The cost of monitoring by Arthur D. Little was, by itself, about $250 thousand each year. There were also other administrative costs that needed to be paid. Consequently, in October 1989, the ISU board asked Thomas Grooms of Deere and Company to convene a committee to draft recommendations for a new ISU structure. At the November 1989 plenary meeting of the ISU, the "Grooms Committee" presented its recommendations, which were then sent to the fifty-seven CEOs of the remaining signatory companies. Of the thirty-six CEOs who voted, all approved the reorganization. The ISU board took formal action on the reorganization at its 18 January 1990 meeting.

Despite the effort to forge a new, streamlined organization, the changes were, in fact, modest. The major difference was the appointment of Sal Marzullo as the paid, part-time administrator of the program. By this time—after retiring from Mobil—Marzullo had moved to Marco Island, Florida, from where he directed ISU until it was disbanded in 1994. William Dunning, a senior officer of Caltex, was named the new chairman of ISU. Dan Purnell, who had been the administrator under Sullivan, also continued as a consultant, but at a considerably reduced fee. The full text of the press release announcing the reorganization is included here as exhibit 17.

Exhibit 17. Statement on Reorganization of the ISU

As a result of six month's of intensive discussions by U.S. Signatory Companies and their South African Subsidiaries and subsequent meetings with the National Advisory Council and Mr. D. Reid Weedon of Arthur D. Little, Inc., Signatory Companies to the Statement of Principles voted the following:

I.   To support the Statement of Principles by reaffirming the following Mission Statement:

a. To work together through the Principles to strengthen the forces for change in South Africa and to help eliminate laws, regulations, customs and attitudes that impede the attainment of political, economic and social justice for all South Africans.

II.   To continue Signatory Company association with Arthur D. Little, Inc., continuing an independent evaluation of company performance in South Africa through the submission of an annual report.

III. To strengthen cooperation, communication and liaison with the South Africa Signatory Association and to help it broaden its relationships with the South African non-white communities.

IV.   To maintain a continuing association with all business and non-business groups in the U.S. and elsewhere, including South Africa, seeking to bring about peaceful change in South Africa and the complete elimination of apartheid in that country.

V.   To utilize the experience and expertise of former ISU Chairman Sal Marzullo and Consultant Dan Purnell who have been involved with the Company effort with Dr. Leon Sullivan since the formulation of the Principles in 1976.

The National Advisory Council, a wholly independent body, will provide guidance, assistance and, where appropriate, criticism to the companies as they work toward the removal of laws sustaining apartheid and toward black social and economic empowerment.

The Council consists of: Fr. Oliver F. Williams, C.S.C., Associate Provost, University of Notre Dame; Melvin D. Miller, Partner, Fitch Miller & Tourse and Trustee, Boston University; Bishop Richard Laymon Fisher, Presiding Bishop of the Ninth Episcopal District of the African Methodist Episcopal Zion church; and Professor Edwin S. Munger, Professor of Political Geography, California Institute of Technology, Emeritus and President, Cape of Good Hope Foundation.

VI.   To retain and strengthen the National Advisory Council. To invigorate its activity and increase its direct involvement with the Industry Support Unit, and with the Signatory Companies in their Plenary Meetings.

VII. To retain the Industry Support Unit, Inc. and its Board of Directors as the policy and fund-raising arm of the Signatory Companies.

VIII. To eliminate the Industry Advisory Council and increase the number of Plenary Sessions allowing greater participation by individual companies.

IX.   To work with local, regional, and national groups involved in the pursuit of social justice for all South Africans. To support financially and with human resources, those groups committed to a peaceful elimination of apartheid and the creation of a non-racial democratic South Africa.

Continued on next page

Exhibit 17—continued

INDUSTRY SUPPORT UNIT, INC. BOARD OF DIRECTORS:

Edgar G. Davis	– Eli Lilly & Company
Williams C. Dunning	– Caltex Petroleum Corporation
George A. Franklin	– Kellogg Company
Thomas L. Grooms	– Deere & Company
George J. Schroll	– Consultant, Colgate-Palmolive Company
Linwood W. Tindall	– Squibb Corporation

NATIONAL ADVISORY COUNCIL:

Fr. Oliver F. Williams, C.S.C.
Associate Provost, University of Notre Dame

Melvin B. Miller, Partner, Fitch Miller & Tourse
And Trustee, Boston University

Bishop Richard Laymon Fisher – Presiding Bishop of the Ninth Episcopal District of the African Methodist Episcopal Zion Church

Professor Edwin S. Munger – Professor of Political Geography, California Institute of Technology, Emeritus and President, Cape of Good Hope Foundation.

EVALUATOR:

D. Reid Weedon, Jr. – Senior Vice President, Arthur D. Little, Inc.

ADMINISTRATOR:

Sal G. Marzullo – President, QuinMar Associates, Inc.

4. CHANGES IN THE POLITICAL AND SOCIAL ORDER IN SOUTH AFRICA

The miracle that Leon Sullivan had hoped would occur before his May 1987 deadline—and thus avoid his departure from the program—actually occurred several years thereafter. Between 1989 and 1993, the dismantling of statutory apartheid and the preparations for a free democratic South Africa took place at such a rapid pace that even the most rabid optimists were amazed. It all began when P. W. Botha had a mild stroke on 18 January 1989. After a brief period of rest, the state president announced that he would resign as the leader of the National Party but retain his role as president until the next election, in 1990. Wilhelm de Klerk, a longtime leader in National Party affairs, was elected in a narrow victory (69 to 81) to head the party. He was known as being a conservative and was not expected to do anything but maintain the status quo. Helen Suzman, a prophetic voice in Parliament for years, stated the consensus view: "I can't see him removing the foundation stones of apartheid." It turned out that Helen, who was almost always right in such matters, was wrong in this case.

Under intense pressure from his own party, Botha resigned as president on 14 August 1989, and de Klerk was sworn in as acting president. In the elections, held on 6 September 1989, the National Party, championing a fresh vision beyond Botha, won as expected. There was, however, a decided shift to the more liberal Democratic Party, indicating that the great majority of Whites (National Party and Democratic Party) wanted change. And change they got! Within months, Walter Sisulu and all the remaining Rivonia trial prisoners (except Mandela) were released. In November 1989 the Separate Amenities Act, the law that mandated segregation in most public places, was dropped. On 2 February 1990, in his address opening the Parliament, de Klerk shocked even the ANC by announcing his agenda to have "a totally new and just constitutional dispensation in which every inhabitant will enjoy equal rights." He also lifted the ban on ANC and SACP, and ended all restrictions on UDF, COSATU, and thirty-one other organizations. Finally, he announced that Nelson Mandela would be released without any conditions. As promised, Mandela was freed nine days later, on 11 February 1990.

Unbeknown to each other, both of the book's co-authors were in South Africa during this period. Williams was in Durban with the National Advisory Council; on the day of Mandela's projected release, he was watching the unfolding event on television with Archbishop Denis Hurley, an outspoken opponent of apartheid for over fifty years. After a several-hour delay in releasing Mandela, Hurley said to Williams, "I don't believe the National Party will ever release Mandela. It just won't happen." In a few minutes, it did happen. Like many, Hurley was in disbelief, for he knew this event marked the beginning of the end of White political domination.

Sethi was in Cape Town, where he saw not only the release of Mandela, but heard his first public speech to the nation. It was a momentous and indescribable moment. In Sethi's experience it compared to another historic event that he witnessed as a teenager: in 1945, when India achieved its independence from England and became a free nation.

In February 1991 de Klerk canceled the Population Registration Act, the cornerstone of apartheid. This act had required that every child born in South Africa be registered in one ethnic group, with appropriate documentation. Without this act, there was no statutory apartheid.

In December 1991, under the leadership of Mandela and de Klerk, the National Party, ANC, and other major political parties met together to discuss a new constitution. These negotiations were known as the Congress for Democratic South Africa (CODESA). While there were many bumps in the road, slowly but surely progress was made. In the face of a Conservative Party challenge to his negotiating stance, de Klerk called for a referendum (Whites only), declaring that he would resign his office if he lost. When the

ballots were counted for the 17 March 1992 referendum, de Klerk had gar-
nered two-thirds of the vote.

In February 1993 the government and the ANC announced that after the
first election, a government of national unity—comprising both ANC and
National Party leaders—would serve for five years. In March 1993 a new
round of negotiations opened with CODESA II; three months later, in June,
it was announced that South Africa's first democratic election would take
place in April 1994. In that election, which took place on 26, 27, and 28
April, ANC received 63.7 percent of the vote; National Party, 20.6 percent;
Inkatha Freedom Party, 9.1 percent; and other parties, 6.6 percent. One of
the co-authors (Williams) was sent by the United States Department of State
to be part of the United Nations monitoring team. It was clearly a free and
fair election. Given the many obstacles, it was indeed close to a miracle!

5.   ISU AND THE FUTURE OF THE SULLIVAN
PRINCIPLES

The rapidity and enormity of changes in South Africa from 1989 to 1991
created a large measure of uncertainty as to the likely path that ISU should
take in the future. Some of the United States companies were arguing for a
quick termination of the Principles program, especially in view of President
Bush's repeal of CAAA on 10 July 1991. The National Advisory Council
(including one co-author: Williams) argued for a new focus for the Principles program, one that would stress training Black managers and upgrading
Blacks in preparation for the post-apartheid South Africa. A number of anti-
apartheid organizations, including church groups, trade unions, and the
IRRC, were arguing, however, for a new code of investment that would
replace the Principles program.

At its 24 September 1991 meeting, the ISU board decided to stay the
course and continue the full Principles program. This decision was based on
a number of considerations, including: the law still required United States
companies to report on their activities either to the State Department or to
the Principles program; endowment and pension funds still required the
ADL ratings; and other groups were waiting in the wings to put their codes
in place in South Africa should the Principles program be terminated. The
board decided to send a letter detailing its decisions and the rationale
(exhibit 18) to each signatory company CEO and ISU representative.

Exhibit 18. ISU Board Letter Urging Continued Participation in Principles Program
September 1991

Dear Signatory Company:

The recent lifting of the CAAA sanctions, while welcome, has only served to underscore the complexity and protracted nature of South Africa's movement toward a non-racial democratic society. As has been said on many occasions, there is a long and troubling period ahead of us as developments in South Africa take place with sudden rapidity. Moments of accomplishment will give way to moments of trauma and uncertainty. Yet we must continue what we have become so much a part of during our past fifteen years—advocates for continued peaceful and significant change leading to a non-racial democracy.

To those companies long involved with the change process in South Africa, we continue to urge perseverance. A few people have felt that now is the time to withdraw from our organized effort. The Industry Support Unit has met, and continues to meet, to look at all its options and to prepare for a continuous and strong US company presence in South Africa. Toward that end we would remind all of our member companies, endorsers, and friends, that now is not the time to drop out but rather to further develop our cohesion and organized efforts.

It is necessary to point out the following:

— Company reporting requirements in the United States remain law and are in effect, notwithstanding the removal of the CAAA legislation. Companies are required to report through the ISU to A.D. Little or directly to the Department of State. Most universities, endowment funds, and pension funds still use the A.D. Little report in evaluating their fiduciary policy on companies operating in South Africa.

— Our collective action is stronger than any individual company effort, as we continue to move toward our goals of attaining social justice in South Africa. Critics of U.S. business will find it easier to attack individual companies than to attack a well-organized group of companies with a track record and organization better geared to response and concerted action.

State and local legislation continues to provide punitive prohibitions against doing business with U.S. companies operating in South Africa.

At the most recent meeting of a special ISU ad hoc committee, the following unanimous consensus was developed:

— Now is not the time to end the organized phase of the Statement of Principles. Indeed its existence at this time may be more critical than ever.

— No time frames or goals for future disbanding should be set at this time, but a continuing review process should be maintained.

— We need, as companies, to continue our programs particularly in respect to the advancement of BCA's in our South African companies.

— We need to increase BCA participation in CSR programs by increased concentration on existing programs and policies for advancement.

There will be continued discussion and direct company involvement in any movement toward any future plan. It is obvious that politically it is too soon to think about disbanding ISU or to replace our collective action with individual company action which will not be as efficient.

Very truly yours,

W.C. Dunning
Chairman
Industry Support Unit

6.   ANC WORRIES ABOUT ECONOMIC
APARTHEID: THE NOTRE DAME MEETINGS

During this entire period, the members of the advisory council continued with their annual visits to South Africa. While in South Africa in March 1991, the council received an invitation to visit "top officers" of ANC in their Johannesburg headquarters. The agenda for the meeting was not provided, but the invitation was readily accepted by the council members. The 1991 council team visiting South Africa comprised Melvin B. Miller, Esq., of Fitch, Wyley, Richlin & Tourse; Ned Munger of the California Institute of Technology; and Father Oliver F. Williams, C.S.C., associate provost of the University of Notre Dame and co-author of this book. Accompanying the advisory council on its 1991 visit was the retired Colgate-Palmolive executive George Schroll. The council always had one person who planned the logistics and scheduled the numerous meetings; Schroll served this roll in 1991. It was, in fact, through Schroll that the ANC invitation had been extended at all. Colgate-Palmolive had long employed a midlevel ANC official in its South African plant, and Schroll had himself been a senior Colgate-Palmolive executive with responsibility for South Africa. It was through that role that Schroll had come to know this ANC official, Cleo Nsibande, and Colgate-Palmolive had kept abreast of ANC concerns during the apartheid era. And it was Cleo Nsibande who had relayed the invitation to the members of the advisory council.

The council, accompanied by George Schroll and Sal Marzullo (who happened to be in town), arrived at ANC headquarters at the appointed hour. The group was met by Thabo Mbeki, head of ANC's Department of International Affairs; Stan Mabizela, deputy head of the same department; Walter Sissulu; and several other key members of ANC. The visitors were informed that Nelson Mandela was in the adjoining office talking to his lawyer about the legal problems of his wife, Winnie, but that he would join them later. (Recall that Mandela had been released from prison only a year before, and that his wife was embroiled in a court case in which she was accused of murdering a young bodyguard.) In any event, Mandela did join the group late in the meeting and indicated that Mbeki was speaking in his behalf.

Thabo Mbeki opened the meeting by stating that the nightmare scenario for ANC was that it would win the first election in which everyone in South Africa could vote, but that it would then face conditions of anarchy because of an official employment rate that exceeded 30 percent (and was actually much higher). "Gentlemen," he implored, "we need your help in attracting new U.S. investment to South Africa, especially new investment that will create jobs and/or increase our exports to other nations."[6]

It was a surprising turn of events. The group members were stunned. They had expected to hear more pleas for the withdrawal of United States multinational corporations in an effort to increase the pressure on Whites at the negotiating table. The more radical anti-apartheid activists—for example, Randall Robinson (executive director of the United States anti-apartheid group TransAfrica) and Tim Smith of the ICCR—were continuing their demands for total divestiture from South Africa. Although Mandela had spoken for the need of a mixed economy when he had met with 150 corporate executives at New York's World Trade Center in June 1990, there had, as yet, been no direct call by ANC for new foreign investments in South Africa.

As it turned out, Mbeki's goal at the meeting was to charge the advisory council with communicating to the United States business community that ANC would strongly support new foreign investments as soon as the new government was in place. In the wide-ranging discussion that followed, the council members advised the Mbeki team that indirect messages like the one suggested by the ANC would simply not suffice to overcome the current hostility toward such moves by anti-apartheid groups in the United States. The council bluntly stated that the time for indirect messages had long since passed and that ANC must send a forthright and unequivocal signal indicating its change of direction on such a major issue. Finally, after much discussion, the advisory council agreed to hold a meeting at the University of Notre Dame, one at which United States corporate leaders could hear Mbeki and other ANC leaders make their case for new investment. It was further agreed that the planning for this meeting would commence when and only when ANC sent an official letter to the advisory council requesting such a meeting. The requisite letter was delivered to the advisory council in August 1991, at which point it began planning a meeting for the coming October.

A committee to organize the meeting was quickly formed. It was co-chaired by George Schroll of Colgate-Palmolive and Father Oliver Williams, C.S.C., of Notre Dame. The ten-person committee included Donald R. Keough, president and chief operating officer of the Coca-Cola Company; C. Joseph La Bonté, president and chief operating officer of Reebok International; Ralph Larsen, chairman and chief executive officer of Johnson & Johnson; and Reuben Mark, president, chairman, and chief executive officer of Colgate-Palmolive Company. Symbolically, the membership of this organizing committee demonstrated corporate America's high level of interest in the meeting.

Invitations to the "Notre Dame meeting" did, indeed, receive a highly positive response from the corporate community. Nonetheless, the number of corporations that sent representatives was small in comparison to the more than 250 major United States companies that had been operating in South Africa in the early 1980s. A number of companies chose not to attend and were conspicuous by their absence. Some of these companies had previously withdrawn from South Africa and did not see any point in attending such a meeting. Other companies had not been sympathetic to the Principles program and, moreover, did not view the ANC as a friend of private enterprise. Still other companies were United States subsidiaries of foreign multinationals that had not subscribed to the Principles.

The structure and organization of the meeting had the trappings of a "staged event," at which all activities, including the cast of characters and their order of appearance, would be carefully choreographed. The avowed purpose of the meeting was for the ANC to confer with corporate America, with the specific goal of encouraging new United States investments in their country. The ANC would also be keeping in mind how the meeting would be perceived by its constituents back home in South Africa.

The total budget of the conference was estimated at $75 thousand, an amount easily raised by the participating companies. The advisory council undertook to pay for the travel-related expenses of the ANC delegation, including round-trip airfares between South Africa and the United States. The ANC party was to consist of ten members. ANC requested, moreover, that other Black groups, namely PAC and AZAPO, be invited to send one or two representatives each. ANC also asked the planning committee not to invite Inkatha; the antagonism between ANC and Inkatha was ongoing. Mbeki argued, too, that part of the reason for such a conference was to educate Black South Africans about the new economic realities. A highly pro-ANC atmosphere—with no Inkatha presence—would therefore, he argued, be very conducive to the ANC's economic and political agenda.

Though otherwise supporting the meeting and its goals, some participants and others were surprised and disconcerted that the two cochairs of the meeting would so readily agree to exclude Inkatha and therefore Buthelezi from such important deliberations about the economic future of South Africa. Recall that it was Buthelezi who had constantly argued for greater foreign investment in South Africa. Indeed, his support for such investment had been one of the major sources of conflict between ANC and Inkatha. As it turned out, Buthelezi was incensed that his party, Inkatha, was not invited to the conference, and he so informed the two cochairs, Schroll and Williams, both of whom he knew well. The matter became a cause célèbre in South Africa, was widely covered in the press there, and was ultimately so divisive that the meeting itself was in jeopardy.[7] The cochairs made a strong plea to ANC to reconsider its position. Less than ten days before the start of the 6 October meeting, the ANC sent a fax to Schroll and Williams. It read, in part:

Regarding the Conference in Notre Dame, I wish to report as follows: Members of the ANC (including Thabo) who are attending it say that this conference was meant to bring together American Business Executives and the ANC only. The attendance of the PAC and AZAPO has come about because the ANC wants them to be present as they are members of the South African Patriotic Front. Inkatha rejected the Patriotic Front.

However, the ANC says that if there is a feeling that the Conference must be "an open one" the ANC has no objection to that. They further say that its being opened must not be a move in order to admit only Inkatha; it must be opened to all parties and organizations like the National Party, the Democratic Party, Inkatha, the Conservative Party, COSATU, etc.; and finally, the ANC says that this should be conveyed to the organizers who invited the ANC. Secondly, the ANC will be glad to discuss this with the host or Organizing Committee.

7. THE 1991 NOTRE DAME MEETING: DIVESTMENT AND NEW INVESTMENT/ A STUDY IN MISCALCULATION

On 1 October 1991 an historic announcement, jointly released by the ANC headquarters at Shell House in Johannesburg and by the University of Notre Dame in the United States, heralded "a landmark conference" at Notre Dame: "Officials of the African National Congress (ANC) will meet with the U.S. government representatives and executives of more than 40 major U.S. corporations, and a small group of academic scholars who were actively involved in the South African issue, to discuss for the first time a policy for investment in post-apartheid South Africa."[8]

The meeting opened on the afternoon of Sunday, 6 October, with addresses by the State Department's Herman Cohen and ANC's Thabo Mbeki (who was later elected deputy president of South Africa in 1994, and president in 1999). The two-day meeting was attended by over 120 invited participants: United States business leaders; ANC leaders, including three (Trevor Manuel, Penwell Maduna, and Mbeki) who were appointed to the Republic of South Africa cabinet in 1994; Inkatha leaders, including one (Sipo Mzimella) who was appointed to the cabinet in that same year; AZAPO leaders; and PAC officials. The tone of the meeting was best captured by headlines in the *Washington Post*—"An Uncertain Reentry into South Africa: U.S. Companies Fear Sanctions, Possibility of Nationalization"[9]—and *Business Week*—"The ANC to U.S. Investors: On Your Mark, Get Set . . . Not Just Yet."[10]

8.   ANC'S NEW ECONOMIC POLICY

Thabo Mbeki reiterated at the Notre Dame meeting in October what he had stated in South Africa during his earlier meeting with the advisory council. The backdrop for his discussion was Mandela's famous statement at his Rivonia trial: "The ANC has never at any period in its history advocated a revolutionary change in the economic structure of the country nor has it, to the best of my recollection, ever condemned capitalism." Following this same thread, Mbeki noted, "Now is the time to begin making preparations for entry or reentry into South Africa. It is important to us that South Africa is on the agenda of the U.S. corporate world. We are looking for new investment."[11] Mbeki went on to say that the goal was to shape a more equitable economy for South Africa and that, whereas nationalization was once thought to be the most effective means to that end, it was not thought to be so anymore. A way must be found to change the situation where 20 percent of the people own 87 percent of the land and 90 percent of the businesses. The best way, Mbeki said, was to have rapid economic growth with new international investment and some sort of affirmative-action programs to train Black managers and develop a more equitable distribution of wealth. Now was the time for United States companies to start planning for such investment.

Although making a strong plea for new United States investments, Mbeki was also clear that it was not yet time to lift the remaining sanctions that continued to affect United States corporate activity in South Africa. That is, even after President Bush repealed CAAA in July 1991, there remained (in October 1991, the time of the Notre Dame meeting) 142 state and local governments that had restrictions or prohibitions in place concerning doing business in South Africa. These legal obstacles, a serious deterrent to new investment, were perceived by ANC as a major bargaining chip in its negotiations with the leaders of the White majority over a new constitution.

Had Mbeki's presentation on new investment been the final word on the matter, the Notre Dame meeting would have ended on a high note. United States investors would have seen that South Africa was a safe place to put their money and to secure a good return. As it turned out, however, the Monday morning session (Mbeki spoke Sunday evening) featured Trevor Manuel, secretary of the ANC Department of Economic Planning. Although he would later prove to be a most successful cabinet official, at the Notre Dame meeting Manuel demonstrated his poor understanding of investors by threatening to politicize investment. He suggested that ANC might reward those firms that had left South Africa and penalize those firms that had remained there in opposition to ANC's call to disinvest. His remarks seemed to resonate with those of the other seven members of the ANC delegation, and thus left a decided chill on the discussion of new investment. Moreover, the ANC delegates at this session had such a poor understanding of international finance that many business leaders in attendance were wondering why they had bothered to come to Notre Dame.

The deliberations that followed made it clear that the ANC leadership had no realistic sense of how potential investors were likely to view South Africa. The ANC seemed to believe that investment could be turned on and off like a faucet, and that once the ANC was in power, new international investment would flow like a river after a spring thaw. Sadly for the post-apartheid South Africa, that belief proved to be a serious miscalculation.

At one point in the meeting, the discord between the United States corporate attendees and the ANC delegates was so open and divisive that the meeting almost collapsed, with the two sides going home more suspicious of each other's motives than they had been before. The ANC delegates exhibited almost total ignorance of the working of the international flow of investments. They were also, to put it mildly, lacking in social niceties, were dismissive of the United States delegates, and acted as if they were dealing with supplicants seeking their favor for the privilege of investing in South Africa.

Mbeki, who was involved in other discussions during the Manuel session, heard about the near meltdown just before his scheduled departure for Germany just after noon. He immediately met with several ANC delegates and instructed them to rectify the situation. Manuel was subsequently quoted widely in the press as strongly denying that there was "any threat on our part" since that would be "counter to the spirit with which we've entered into negotiations" with the government.[12] In spite of Manuel's attempt to pacify his critics (even if they had accepted his retraction), there was still a fear that these future leaders of South Africa did not understand that both new and continuing investment in emerging economies depended on financial, not social, considerations. Interjecting the notion of "rewards" and "penalties" for following or rejecting ANC advice had a chilling effect for years to come.

South Africa was soon to learn the hard lesson of international investment. To wit, these investments flow where they find best opportunities and financial rewards that are commensurate with acceptable financial risks. The ANC could not count on "conscience-based" investments when its own moral stance had itself become intertwined with the realities of gaining and maintaining political power. Furthermore, South Africa desperately needed capital that could employ large numbers of unskilled and poorly skilled workers. The country could not, however, compete for such capital against countries in the Asia-Pacific region that had highly disciplined and motivated labor forces, coupled with stable, pro-business political climates. Countries in the Asia-Pacific region also had well-established track records of attracting foreign investment, and the transportation networks and other infrastructure required to ensure timely and dependable movement of manufactured goods to the consumer markets in Europe and the United States. Economic growth and job creation follow only the unyielding rules of the market place. After five years of ANC leadership, there has consequently been only modest new investment in South Africa. The rate of job creation has, in fact, been negative, and employment remains in the 30 to 40 percent range.[13] Even the charismatic leadership and talented statesmanship of Nelson Mandela have been incapable of making a significant difference.

Thus, rather than having "all" the bargaining chips, the ANC delegates had, in fact, very few that would entice foreign capital requiring a high labor-to-capital ratio. It is not clear to these authors whether this lesson has been fully learned by the South African government, even nearly a decade after the Notre Dame meeting. Although South Africa has followed a strict regime of conservative fiscal and monetary policies, it has yet to demonstrate improved efficiencies in domestic competition, a broad commitment to opening its markets to foreign competition, or a determination to make its labor more competitive—not only within a domestic context, but also, and more importantly, within an international context.

In the end, the Notre Dame meeting did not completely achieve the ANC's avowed goals of establishing a friendlier tone and of building new bridges between ANC-led South Africa and the United States business community. To some extent, however, the meeting did achieve its goal of providing economic education to the future rulers of South Africa.

9.   A NEW CODE OF CONDUCT?

From 1991 to 1994 there was much ferment among activist groups to create a new code of conduct for the post-apartheid South Africa. From the activists' viewpoint the issue of monitoring the conduct of United States companies remained far from settled. The activists wanted to remain the moral arbiters of corporate conduct even when the original reasons for instituting a code had become moot. South Africa was on its way to creating a truly democratic and freely elected government, which would—and should, by every right—decide for itself on the rules of conduct governing the private sector's economic activities. To assert otherwise would be a case of extreme arrogance.

It was from just this perspective of opposing any new code that, on 27 April 1992, Sal Marzullo sent a memorandum to the ISU' s board of directors and the National Advisory Council blasting the activities recently reported in the March 1992 *IRRC South Africa Reporter.*[14] The article, "South Africans See Need for Corporate Code," discussed several movements toward code development. Marzullo noted in his memo that the success of the Sullivan code was based on its being devised with the participation of business and on its being voluntary. He summarized what many business leaders were thinking with respect to such new codes, and also indicated that his patience, like that of others in the business community, was wearing thin.

> The old familiar cast of characters—for example, the IRRC, ICCR, and ACOA—was involved in this movement for a new code of corporate conduct, and each was seeking to ensure its own future. What they foresaw was that South Africa's transformation into a multiracial democracy threatened to deprive them of an issue that had, for years, been providing their bread and butter. What better way to maintain their position than by allying themselves with the trade union movement in devising (and monitoring) a code of conduct for business. Indeed, once successful in South Africa, the code be expanded internationally, ensuring not just the groups' continuing existence, but their worldwide growth.

In May 1992, in preparation for a meeting with a consortium of colleges and universities on the South Africa issue, Marzullo forwarded the three members of the National Advisory Council the "official position of the ISU" on codes. There were two key points: (1) the ISU would not cooperate with any external monitoring group or person who is not acceptable to the signatory companies, and (2) the ISU would not accept a special code of conduct for American companies operating in South Africa.

On 20 October 1993 Leon Sullivan reversed his June 1987 position and urged United States companies to return to South Africa. He went on to suggest that the tenets of the Principles program, as well as other codes, be enacted into law in the new South Africa; that all companies be monitored for their compliance; and that Americans be kept apprised of each company's social performance. On 30 March 1994 Sullivan followed up on his 1993 position by establishing the Post-Apartheid Corporate Social Responsibility Leadership Council. This council attempted to encourage state legislatures to require United States multinationals operating in South Africa to adhere to a code and to submit annual reports outlining their social-responsibility activities.

Sullivan was out of sync, however, with the new political environment in South Africa. Before his endeavor got very far, Sullivan was explicitly asked by top ANC officials to cease and desist. The ANC was persuaded that South Africa was in desperate need of new investment and that the country was competing against a number of emerging nations for such investment. Any code that applied only to investors in South Africa would be a deterrent to the much needed new capital. Even so, ICCR filed resolutions in 1994 at sixteen companies asking them to endorse the South African Council of Church's (SACC) new code for business in South Africa; the code had been adopted in July 1993 and was the fruit of earlier cooperation between SACC, ANC, and COSATU. The SACC code (exhibit 19) was quite general. Although it required companies to cooperate with monitors, it had no monitoring mechanism. Most of the companies responded by indicating that their policies were already in accord with the SACC code. No company ever publicly endorsed the code and, perhaps because of the South African government's lack of interest, the code received little attention.

10.   THE FINAL DAYS OF THE PRINCIPLES PROGRAM

Almost from the hour that President F. W. de Klerk delivered his 2 February 1990 opening address to Parliament—an address that clipped, if not cut, the wings of apartheid—various United States companies started clamoring to end the Principles program. This effort was understandable in view of the persistently deteriorating economic conditions in South Africa. Few companies were making a profit, and others were showing a loss. Under such circumstances, spending the equivalent of 12 percent of a company's payroll on social spending (as required under the Principles program) was a punishing economic burden and left little incentive to expand operations in South Africa. Fortunately, wiser minds prevailed. One of those was George J. Schroll, who served as a consultant on South African affairs for the Colgate-Palmolive Company during the last ten years of the Principles program. On 5 December 1990, in the face of pressure from some companies to curtail the program, Schroll wrote a long memorandum to the ISU board and National Advisory Council arguing that "we must stay the course." He argued that the commitment to Sullivan's original goals must continue:

> The opponents of the continuing presence of corporate America in South Africa are many. Some, if not most, are motivated by legitimate concerns with the elimination of wrongs and the establishment of a just society in that country. Many others, however, are more concerned with advancing their own political agendas or are giving vent to long nurtured hatreds of

Exhibit 19. SACC Code of Conduct

Equal Opportunity: Companies should insure that their operations are free from discrimination based on race, sex, religion, political opinion or physical handicap, and implement affirmative action programs designed to protect the equal rights and treatment of the historically disadvantaged.

1. **Training and Education:** Companies should develop and implement training and education programs to increase the productive capacities of their South African employees in consultation with the trade union movement.
2. **Workers' Rights:** Companies should recognize representative unions and uphold their employees' rights to organize openly, bargain collectively, picket peacefully and strike without intimidation or harassment.
3. **Working and Living Conditions:** Companies should maintain a safe and healthy work environment and strive to ensure that the working and living conditions they provide accord with relevant international conventions.
4. **Job Creation and Security:** Companies should strive to maintain productive employment opportunities and create new jobs for South Africans.
5. **Community Relations:** Companies should share information about their practices and projected plans with communities affected by their operations, and develop social responsibility programs in ongoing consultation with representative bodies in these communities.
6. **Consumer Protection:** Companies should inform consumers of any possible dangers associated with their products and cooperate with consumer protection and broader community organizations to develop and uphold appropriate product safety and quality standards.
7. **Environmental Protection:** Companies should utilize environmentally sound practices and technologies, disclose how and in what amounts they dispose of their waste products, and seek to minimize hazardous waste.
8. **Empowerment of Black Businesses:** Companies should strive to improve the development of black-owned South African businesses by purchasing from and sub-contracting to such firms.
9. **Implementation:** Companies should cooperate with monitors establish to implement these standards by disclosing relevant information on a timely fashion.

---

the free enterprise system and the large international corporations which have developed under this system. These opponents, both the sincere and the hypocritical, are not ready to end their efforts in seeking disinvestment of what we know to be our legitimate and socially responsible presence in South Africa. We must stay the course.

At the ISU board meeting of 8 July 1992, it was decided to form a committee "to establish a plan to conclude the organization of companies subscribing to the Statement of Principles for South Africa, when the proper time arrives." One of the co-authors (Williams) served on that committee, which was chaired by Bill Dunning of Caltex. The Dunning committee met and prepared a report, which the board discussed at its 3 November meeting.

The only controversial issue was when—not if—to terminate the Principles program. Various people were consulted. Assistant Secretary of State

Herman Cohen and key members of the Senate Foreign Relations Committee advised continuing the program for "the near future" in order to avoid attacks by critics. A meeting in London—organized by Bill Dunning, chair of ISU—with leaders of the European Community code yielded similar advice. A key concern of many of the United States companies was that, should the Principles program terminate prematurely, there would be a vacuum, and a new code and monitoring system would be forced on business.

At the ISU's 3 November 1992 board meeting, a "white paper" on the termination of the Principles program was approved and sent to all ISU members for discussion at the 24 November plenary meeting. The "white paper" offered three possible triggers that would signal that the program had met its goals and thus that it should be terminated. Since the board could not achieve a consensus position, each of the three possible triggers was presented with its pros and cons (see exhibit 20).

The ISU membership ultimately agreed to stay the course while continually monitoring events. In March 1993 CODESA II was reported to be going well; South Africa's first democratic election was expected to be announced soon (and was, in June). With these circumstances in mind, the ISU board met on 26 May 1993 and made its recommendations, which were approved by the entire board: in effect, the ISU should terminate its operations, along with all reporting and evaluation of social-program activities, upon the successful completion of a nonracial, free, fair, and democratic election in South Africa. Since the Principles program was founded by the CEOs of the member companies, all CEOs were sent a ballot on 1 September 1993 and asked to express their approval or disapproval of the proposal. The proposal was approved.

On 24 September 1993 Nelson Mandela addressed the United Nations Anti-Apartheid Committee and announced that all sanctions should be lifted except for the arms embargo, which should be lifted only after the new government was in place. Lifting the other sanctions was of little immediate consequence, however. Selective purchasing ordinances were still in place in 30 states, 109 cities, and 39 counties, and many companies feared that these ordinances would be replaced with mandated codes of conduct. There was consequently little movement on investment in South Africa at that time. On 27 September 1993, the United States assistant secretary of state for African affairs, George Moose, in speaking to a conference on United States Investment in the new South Africa, said that the Clinton administration was opposed to replacing state and local sanctions with legally mandated codes of conduct. The Clinton administration's position followed that of ANC as set forth in its Platform for Foreign Investment—which was itself discussed at that same conference by Trevor Manuel, head of the ANC Economic

<u>*Exhibit 20.* Alternative Conditions for Terminating the Principles Program</u>

The Board agreed that the organization was not created to be permanent. It was agreed that since the achievement of goals should be the determining factor, setting a time limit on the life of the organization was not an appropriate alternative nor a wise strategy. The major issue for discussion was the determination of when the goals and objectives of the organization would be met.

After lengthy discussions by the Board and its invited guests, it was not possible to arrive at a consensus on specific events that would signal the organization that its goals had been achieved. It was determined to continue monitoring events and to delay making that decision at this time. It was decided to share with you our discussions. Key events considered and the discussions regarding the events follows:

1. <u>The establishment of an interim government in South Africa.</u>

The African National Congress (ANC) has stated that with the establishment of an interim government it (the ANC) will call for a lifting of all sanctions against South Africa except for the arms and oil embargo. It is also expected that the ANC will ultimately call for the renewal of foreign investment in South Africa.

PROS: As the ANC is the leading spokesman for the liberation movement, it is expected that there will be a worldwide positive response to lifting sanctions and serious consideration on new investment and trading in South Africa on the part of potential investors and traders. The economy in South Africa is suffering a serious downturn and is considered a major threat to the peaceful transition toward a non-racial democratic government. As such, the continuance of the stringent requirements of the Statement of Principles could be seen as a deterrent to new trading and investment in South Africa and as an indicator that American business has no confidence in the Interim Government.

CONS: The establishment of an Interim Government is an important step toward true democracy in South Africa but does not fully satisfy the requirements of our objectives. Blacks could continue to be denied the franchise and the Interim Government might not be truly representative. The Statement of Principles is an anti-apartheid organization that pre-dated the impositions of sanctions and should not judge its conduct on the lifting of sanctions alone. The U.S. Government mandated reporting may remain in effect for some time, forcing our membership to report to the U.S. State Department, thereby opening the door for continued government intervention in private business activities and permitting these activities to be made a matter of public record. Further, those who have opposed the Principles and criticized its anti-apartheid objectives as a shield against sanctions, could now feel justified in such criticism and could be encouraged to establish a new code of principles, demanding concurrence by U.S. business.

2. <u>Repeal of U.S. Government mandated reporting requirement.</u>

As you know, under existing law American corporations doing business in South Africa must file a report of their corporate responsibility activities either to the Signatory Association or to the U.S. State Department. Current discussions with the State Department and U.S. Senators of both political parties indicate that when the Interim Government is formed and the ANC calls for the end of sanctions, action will be taken by the Congress to repeal this legislation. (Note: The final position of President-elect Clinton, in this regard, remained unclear).

PROS: While we have never agreed with government mandated sanctions against Business, such sanctions have represented the will and concern of many constituencies or stakeholders in the U.S. The repeal of this legislation will indicate that the U.S. supports

Continued on next page

Exhibit 20—continued

> the Interim Government, the wishes of the liberation movement and the desire in South Africa to increase trade and investment with U.S. business. As the leading organization representing U.S. business in South Africa, for us to continue requiring reporting of activities could be interpreted that we do not agree with this position unless traders and investors are prepared to abide by the Statement of Principles, report to us its activities and be rated on these activities. Such a condition could be a deterrent to new trading and investment in South Africa at a time when all concerned parties are taking an opposite view and when the condition of the economy represents a threat to achieving the goals of our organization.

CONS: The Statement of Principles was founded as an anti-apartheid organization. Our founding pre-dates sanctions and our future should not be guided by the lifting of sanctions. The establishment of an Interim Government is an important step towards democracy but Blacks continue to be disenfranchised and are not fully represented in government. Our critics have long questioned the sincerity of the moral position of the ISU and to end our organized activities at this time could lead to a heightening of criticism against U.S. business in South Africa and encourage the critics to fill the vacuum with an independent code of conduct demanding our compliance.

3. The accomplishment of a free, non-racial election in South Africa.

One of the key functions of the Interim Government is to establish conditions and procedures for a free, non-racial election. It has not yet been determined whether such an election would be for a constituent assembly or for parliamentary representation.

PROS: The Key to any definition of democracy is that the political body be chosen by the people. In South Africa's situation this would be a free, non-racial election. The accomplishment of such elections mean the completion of the final goal of our organization, i.e., to assist in the establishment, through peaceful means, of a non-racial, democratic government in South Africa. At this time, the ISU - Statement of Principles should end its organized activities. The organization will have proven to its critics that we were sincere in our stated objectives and that we now consider it more appropriate to conduct our corporate social responsibility programs, either independently or collectively, "on the ground" in South Africa, as we do in other countries throughout the world.

CONS: The arguments for ending our organized activities when the interim government is formed (see 1 above) or when the U.S. Government repeals the mandated reporting requirements (see 2 above) are the key arguments against waiting until there is a free, non-racial democratic election in South Africa. Additionally, there is no assurance that such an election will be all inclusive, as there may well be major population groups who boycott the election or who may participate and be unprepared to accept the results, such as in Angola. Here again, we should accept such an election as a key step towards democracy but take no final action until we can be assured that the election truly achieves the organization's objectives.

Planning Department. (Manuel had come a long way since the historic Notre Dame meeting in October 1991.) After discussion and debate in the United States Congress, the ANC position prevailed: no code of conduct would be legislatively imposed on United States businesses operating in South Africa. On 23 November 1993, President Bill Clinton signed the South Africa Democratic Transition Support Act (H.R. 225), which eliminated all federal sanctions and enabled South Africa to borrow once again from the IMF and World Bank.

Two weeks later, on 5 December 1993, the seventeenth and final report for the Principles program was issued by Arthur D. Little, Inc. Of the fifty signatory companies remaining in the program, thirty-six received the highest rating (category I), twelve received a rating of "Making Progress Based on Full Reporting" (category II), and three received a rating of having "Passed Basic Requirements" (category III). The final report stated what was a deeply held conviction by most of the signatory companies: "No one would claim that the Statement of Principles ended apartheid. However, few would fail to recognize the important role which the Signatory Companies played. Although never employing more than 1 percent of the economically employed in South Africa, the Signatories as a group set the pace for corporate social responsibility."[15]

The final meeting of the ISU Board was held on 26 May 1994, a month after the successful election in South Africa. Roger Crawford, chair of SASA, was asked to come to New York and present the consensus position of the SASA members on how to dispose of the residual income balance of the ISU (about $268 thousand, or ZAR 1 million). It was recommended by SASA and approved by the board that the money be administered by the South African Institute of Race Relations to fund scholarships for Black South Africans. The final press release by the Principles program announced this gift on 17 August 1994 (exhibit 21). The final sentence of the press release is a fitting end to this program and presents a great challenge, one that is still ongoing: "The ability of the new South African government to overcome the legacy of apartheid is now contingent upon the economic development of all the South African people."

Exhibit 21. Final Press Release of Principles Program

U.S. Signatory Companies Donate R 1,000,000 to South Africa Scholarship Fund

August 17, 1994

Johannesburg, South Africa . . . The group of American companies known as the U.S. Signatory Companies that worked for many years to end the apartheid system in South Africa today donated 1 Million Rand to the South Africa Institute of Race Relations to fund scholarships for black South Africans,.

The American companies, signatories to the Statement of Principles for South Africa, contributed a grant of R 1,000,000 to establish the United States Signatories Education Fund. Its dual purpose is to provide educational opportunities at local universities and technical colleges to black students who would not otherwise receive them, and to assist in developing the local technical and professional workforce that is essential for the economic growth of the new South Africa.

Continued on next page

Exhibit 21—continued

U.S. companies doing business in South Africa formed the U.S. Signatory Association in 1977 to help end apartheid and establish a non-racial democratic society in South Africa. At its peak, the organization had 112 member companies.

Through their South African subsidiaries, these companies met a rigorous standard of conduct in the workplace that ensured equal pay, equal rights and equal opportunity for all their workers, regardless of race. They also initiated, funded and participated in many social, economic and political development programs at the local level. Since 1977, the Signatory Companies invested more than R 1 Billion, towards these initiatives.

With the successful completion of a free, fair and democratic national election in South Africa, the U.S. Signatory Companies voted to disband. Noting that the stated objectives of the organization have been realized, its former chairman, William D. Donovan, said that the ability of the new South African government to overcome the legacy of apartheid is now contingent upon the economic development of all the South African people.

ENDNOTES

1 *Philadelphia Inquirer*, 7 May 1985.
2 "Without Sullivan," *Washington Post*, 5 June 1987.
3 Sal G. Marzullo (chairman, Industry Support Unit, Inc.), letter to Oliver F. Williams, 30 June 1987.
4 Oliver F. Williams, *The Apartheid Crisis* (San Francisco: Harper & Row, 1986).
5 Leon H. Sullivan (pastor-emeritus, Zion Baptist Church of Philadelphia), letter to Sal G. Marzullo (vice president, international governmental relations, Mobil Oil), 17 May 1989.
6 From the notes of Oliver Williams, member of the Advisory Council to the Principles program and co-author of this volume.
7 Somehow the event was leaked to the press and widely covered in South Africa. See Simon Barber, "ANC in U.S. Row Over Inkatha," *Business Day*, 17 September 1991.
8 Available from the University of Notre Dame, Public Relations and Information, Notre Dame, IN 46556.
9 Steven Mufson, "An Uncertain Reentry into South Africa," *Washington Post*, 13 October 1991.
10 Julia Flynn Siler, "The ANC to U.S. Investors: On Your Mark, Get Set . . . Not Yet," *Business Week*, 21 October 1991.
11 From the unpublished address by Thabo Mbeki given at the University of Notre Dame, 6 October 1991.
12 Simon Barber, "ANC's Two Faces Baffle Investors," *Sunday Times* (London), 13 October 1991.
13 See Lawrence Schlemmer and Charisse Levitz, *Unemployment in South Africa* (Johannesburg: South African Institute of Race Relations, 1998).
14 William Moses, "S. Africans See Need for Corporate Code," *IRRC South Africa Reporter*, March 1992, 18–20.

15 To be sure, some have another perspective. In the "Final Report of the Truth and Reconciliation Commission of South Africa" (issued on 29 October 1998), there is one reference to the Statement of Principles Program. In volume 4, chapter 2, paragraph 83, in a discussion of the costs and benefits of apartheid for international business, there is the following. "For others, depressed African wages simply boosted profits to very high levels. Many foreign-owned companies probably fell into the latter category. The fact that they were able to improve wages and working conditions appreciably after being embarrassed by international campaigns to adopt the Sullivan Code (See the submission by the Anti-Apartheid Movement) suggests that they had previously enjoyed substantially high profits at the expense of poorly-paid African labour."

PART V

EPILOGUE
Lessons Learned and Unlearned

Chapter 16

Assessment of the Sullivan Principles As a Role Model for Developing International Codes of Conduct
Lessons Learned and Unlearned

The promulgation of the Sullivan Principles was a watershed event in a drive that had been gathering momentum—primarily in the United States, but also in many other industrialized countries of the world—for enhancing the responsibility of multinational corporations.[1] This drive was a reflection of the worldwide operations of such corporations, coupled with a concern for the worldwide consequences of how those operations were conducted. In its most basic form, the notion of enhanced responsibility has three components:

- MNCs must deal with all of their stakeholders, and not merely stockholders, in a fair and equitable manner. This concern has special relevance when the operations of MNCs involve developing countries or poor people (anywhere); that is, involve those who lack the necessary economic and political power to bargain with MNCs on more equitable terms.

- MNCs must act as positive and proactive agents of change through the use of their enormous economic power—even, when necessary, against the express wishes or prevailing customs of host countries. The goal is to protect and foster basic human rights and democratic values that are the foundation both of MNC's economic strength and of their prosperity in their home countries.

- MNCs must not consider enhanced responsibility and the actions thereby required either as discretionary or as a necessary inconvenience (for example, simply as a cost of doing business). Instead, the standards of enhanced responsibility must be treated as *de minimus* standards of behavior, compliance with which must be mandatory, transparent, and subject to external validation.

The above assertions are no longer controversial and are accepted by important leaders (within both the corporate community and its various external constituencies) and by the public-at-large. When the Sullivan Prin-

ciples were first enunciated, however, large segments of the business community in the United States (and to a lesser extent, in the industrialized
nations of Western Europe) regarded the notion of corporate social responsibility with suspicion or hostility. It was something to be contained like a
virus; though one could not always avoid it, one should try to eliminate it
and also take every precaution to prevent it from spreading.

Viewed in this context, the Sullivan Principles represented the crucial
turning point in the then-ongoing debate about societal expectations for corporate conduct; the Sullivan Principles marked the beginning of a new era,
one in which corporate social responsibility was no longer controversial, but
an accepted norm. The Principles affirmed, moreover, the need for a new
paradigm that required corporations to assume some, if not all, of the
responsibility for the second-order effects, or unintended consequences, of
their actions on segments of society not directly involved in the corporations' activities. That is, it was no longer a question of whether corporations,
as important social institutions, should be responsible for the community's
well-being or for the negative externalities that corporations create as a consequence of their normal business operations. Instead, the locus of debate
permanently shifted to how and to what extent corporations should be held
accountable for the societal impact of their business operations—whether
those consequences are direct or indirect, intended and unintended, or affect
those who are involved in corporate operations or those who are not.

The circumstances and the chain of events in the creation and implementation of the Sullivan Principles have provided us with an excellent
opportunity to examine three interrelated phenomena: the process of transformation of business-society relations, the expanding societal expectations
for corporations, and the changes in corporate responses to meeting those
expectations. These phenomena have been discussed and analyzed in considerable detail in the preceding chapters of this book. In this chapter, we
build on our foregoing results concerning the Principles' creation and
implementation. Our emphasis here is not on the past, however, but on the
future (though in so doing, we will also develop a better sense of what could
have been). There is much to be learned both from the events leading up to
and following the enactment of the Principles, and from the process by
which they were revised, expanded, implemented, and monitored over a
period of eighteen years. As our first step here, we will be assessing the success of the Principles in "achieving their intended goals," both as they were
initially articulated and as they were subsequently modified—in response not
just to changing circumstances, but also to the demands of making the Principles operational in the concrete world of corporate operations. We will
then move on to examine the implications of the Principles program concerning the possibilities and limitations of extralegal, voluntary codes of

conduct, especially in relation to large multinational corporations and their overseas operations (both in general and with a particular focus on operations in developing and poorer nations). That is, as we move into the next millennium, what lessons should be drawn for corporations (and their stakeholders) as they confront the dual challenges of a global economy and of ever changing societal expectations?

1.   CREATION OF THE SULLIVAN PRINCIPLES

The Sullivan Principles arose from a unique set of circumstances that led to certain strengths in their implementation—strengths that had a positive impact, in turn, on the success of the Principles program. These same circumstances, however, also encumbered the Principles with certain constraints that ultimately weakened them through both the dilution of their credibility and the diminution of their potential social impact. Among the strengths in the creation of the Principles were external circumstances and corporate dynamics, both in general and within each industrial group. External circumstances were related to

- the inherently indefensible character of apartheid, which was both morally repugnant and political illegitimate (in relation to what is understood as the American political process)

- the widespread public antagonism in the United States and other parts of the world toward the White-controlled political regime of South Africa

- a widely held belief that corporations were receiving economic benefits through their cooperation, either directly or indirectly, with that political regime

The creation of the Principles also benefited from the economic and sociopolitical dynamics of companies with operations in South Africa, and especially of those that became the founding signatories of the Principles program.

- These corporations were invariably large United States-based multinational corporations that prided themselves in being "responsible" economic institutions and for whom "reputation" and "public trust" were important assets that must be protected—the loss of which could result in more intrusive governmental regulation and oversight, and a deterioration in consumer patronage and market franchise.

- The CEOs of these large corporations staked their personal reputations and corporate resources on the success of the Principles program. This ongoing and shared stake had the effect of minimizing the free-rider problem. The last thing these individual CEOs and their companies wanted was to be seen as exploiting the situation. Instead, they wanted to be seen as taking the "high road."

- The coalition of the original signatory companies came from diverse industries and were invariably the market leaders in their respective sectors. Thus, they had little incentive in forcing the standards to the "lowest common denominator." Instead, their market power, size, and reputation enabled them to "pull" many of the smaller, recalcitrant companies in their respective industries to a high level of compliance with the Sullivan Principles.

Unfortunately, though the Principles program derived considerable strength from the personal involvement of the CEOs and the resulting commitment of corporate resources, this same involvement also contributed to some of the program's weaknesses. Indeed, this confluence of strengths and weaknesses offers some important lessons for the creation and implementation of future "principles" or "codes" of good corporate practices, especially in the international arena.

1.1   Compromise or Consensus

The definition and scope of the Principles as initially formulated came about as a result of intensive discussions and negotiations between Leon Sullivan and the representatives of the companies. The final product was a result of mutual accommodation and reflected the interests—often complementary but just as often conflicting—of Sullivan and his constituencies, on the one hand, and of the corporate community, on the other.

The Principles were quite explicit in terms of their intended goals but equally vague in terms of the specifics of implementation. Taken together, these characteristics were highly desirable in that they provided the flexibility needed to adapt the Principles to actual field conditions, thereby maximizing their potential impact.

For the first time in the field of corporate social responsibility, the Principles program recognized the need for independent, outside monitoring and verification of corporate compliance efforts. These steps were both bold and unprecedented, forever changing the tenor of public debate and how corporations would respond to demands for greater corporate social responsibility. Even more importantly, the Principles program was successful in bringing the public's attention to bear on modes of corporate governance and on the need to develop more diversified and broadly defined notions of corporate accountability.

From the very outset of the initiative that led to the Principles program, there was a fundamental difference between Sullivan and corporate leaders—a difference rooted in the underlying "philosophy" or rationale that would justify the creation of that program. Sullivan advocated the Principles on moral grounds rooted in human rights. Thus, he wanted to justify the creation of the Principles program as transcending narrow economic grounds. That is, he felt that some injustices were so great (as in the case of apartheid) that they could not be tolerated and must be eliminated, no matter what the economic cost (or benefit). At the same time, he knew that economic concerns would inevitably play a significant role in corporate decisions. In the short term, he was therefore willing to accept the role of corporations in ameliorating the adverse consequences of apartheid for the disenfranchised Black majority of the people of South Africa. In the long term, however, he was unequivocal in wanting the corporations to become instruments of social change and important players in the abolition of apartheid. This agenda was one of which the corporations were fully aware, and his dedication to it was borne out by his decision to withdraw from the Principles program in 1987—even though United States corporations had by that time spent over $300 million in South Africa to comply with the Principles. Because his peaceful approach toward dismantling apartheid had not worked as well as he had hoped, he called for a total United States economic embargo against South Africa.

The signatory companies had a more conventional and limited agenda. They saw compliance with the Principles as a means of limiting external pressure on the companies to withdraw from South Africa. In addition, however, they saw the Principles program as providing them with a protective umbrella under which they could undertake some urgently needed reforms in South Africa—in particular, reforms concerning apartheid-related operational practices in their plants—without inviting retaliatory actions from the South African government. Finally, the corporations saw the Principles program as a means of undercutting the need for United States legislative intervention concerning the corporations' practices (or even presence) in South Africa.

Despite their participation in the Principles program, the signatory companies also shared the concerns of many other companies that, rejecting both the underlying premise and the scope of the Principles program, chose not to participate. These nonparticipating companies—and the business community, in general—were adamantly opposed to subjecting their actions to nonmarket forces and to nonmarket standards of assessing their activities and operations; such standards would both reduce the impact of market discipline on business conduct and impose nonmarket constraints on top management's freedom to run their enterprises. Indeed, extensive conversations with corporate executives, both in the United States and abroad, indicate that these concerns are broadly shared, to a greater or lesser degree, by senior executives of all ilks and persuasions.

The business community was also antagonistic to the notion that corporate decisions should somehow be judged in terms of specifically ethical norms. The arguments against applying ethical norms to business decisions are by now, of course, quite familiar. To wit, business decisions per se must

be value-free since market decisions already reflect ethical values as inter-
nalized by consumer choices. Shareholders do not hire managers to make
moral choices but to make economic decisions. It is beyond the scope of
managerial authority and even competence to make moral decisions on the
part of the owners of the corporation (that is, the shareholders).

Unfortunately, these arguments beg the question rather than answer it.
For the most part, the industrial sectors in which large corporations operate
are ones with highly imperfect markets. Corporations exercise considerable
bargaining power and thereby create extremely favorable operating conditions, neither of which would be possible under the scenario of the perfect—
that is, highly competitive—markets of neoclassical economics. Moreover,
the world of imperfect markets is not value-free. Large, publicly owned corporations have flourished mainly in democratic-capitalistic economic systems, where they are protected by democratic governments that create level
playing fields through a regulatory environment that assures private property
rights and freedom of commerce. And yet, these corporations seek out—and
support, either through benign neglect or indifference to local conditions—
antidemocratic and antimarket governments whose actions lead to economic
gains for the individual corporations. The corporations, that is, make every
effort to benefit from political and economic regimes that follow policies
adverse both to democratic political systems and market-based economic
systems.

1.2   Proponents of Two Ethical Theories Locking Horns

In 1977, when Sullivan announced the Principles, he was convinced that
business could use its power to advance the welfare of Blacks and ultimately
to help shape a society in which all South Africans would not only vote, but
also have jobs. This teleological ethic *(telos* meaning *goal* or *end)* was not
accepted by many of the religious groups represented in the ICCR coalition.
These groups often argued from an ethics of principle, declaring that it was
the duty of international investors to leave South Africa to avoid aiding and
abetting the evil apartheid regime (a position referred to as a *deontological*
ethic). In the late 1970s and early 1980s, however, numerous religious
groups may have been persuaded of the merits of Sullivan's teleological
position had business demonstrated a genuine moral concern rather than
merely an economic one. Unfortunately, business remained trapped in a
paradigm that precluded opposing the laws of a sovereign nation, even an
unjust one. As a consequence, religious and other anti-apartheid activist
groups remained convinced (in opposition to Sullivan) that total disinvestment in South Africa was required, and that attention to the economic plight

of Black South Africans must remain secondary as long as apartheid was still in place.

Most activists, although seldom engaged in the rigorous moral arguments that occupy scholars, were making an argument similar in form to that made by the philosopher Thomas Donaldson. Donaldson made a strong argument that full disinvestment was required since there was a systematic violation of the most basic human rights.[2] Citing Ronald Dworkin, he noted that consequentialist goals—for example, creating wealth and jobs—are ordinarily "trumped" by rights considerations unless "extraordinary moral horrors" could be expected to ensue from their exercise.[3] Developing a "condition of business principle," Donaldson also stated that "transactions are impermissible unless those transactions serve to discourage the violation of rights and either harm A or, at a minimum, fail to benefit A, in consequence of A's rights violating activity."[4] Since Donaldson found neither of these conditions present, he judged that doing business with an apartheid South Africa was wrong. Sullivan argued, however, that the moral course was for the companies to remain in South Africa, provided they took measures to assist the Blacks in their struggle for political and economic rights, and to prepare the way for job creation and investment in the new South Africa.[5] In this teleological view, which focuses on shaping a certain sort of community, Donaldson's "extraordinary moral horror" was, for Sullivan, that of a new Black government trying to lead a country with over 30 percent unemployment and little prospect for new investment because all foreign firms and capital had been forced out. Sullivan and others arguing this position, though not denying the great achievement of attaining political rights, continued to look forward during the struggle to the day when overcoming the economic legacy of apartheid would be the primary challenge.[6] That challenge, which is the current one, requires a well-developed infrastructure, a critical mass of multinational corporations to attract new investment and to create jobs, and a renewed emphasis on affirmative action. Sullivan argued that if the quest to attain economic rights failed in South Africa, there would be little hope for a democratic future and for a land of peace and justice.

Up until the mid-1980s, Sullivan saw sufficient movement in the dismantling of apartheid by the South African government to justify his remaining with the Principles program. P. W. Botha, in his initial years as state president, offered many signals that the end of apartheid was near. By 1985, however, Botha's resolve and strength of purpose were in doubt, and Sullivan began to have serious reservations that his gradualist program was on track. Two years later, of course, he announced his departure from the program.

To gather together the highlights presented in this volume, it may be helpful to adapt a model developed by the ethicist Ralph Potter.[7] Drawing on the work of the sociologist Talcott Parsons, Potter designed a model to understand how people come to disagree passionately over a matter of policy. That is, all of us have certain worldviews or assumptions about how the world works, as well as certain loyalties that influence our perceptions and decision making. Potter's model, as adapted in figure 9, provides a means of conceptualizing how this complex process influences our assessment of a policy proposal (using apartheid as a case in point). The model suggests that four elements shape our policy assessment: the definition of the situation (A); the loyalties of the decision maker (B); the values held, which reflect the type of ethical reasoning used (C); and the worldview or assumptions of the person or group involved (D).

Any policy proposal is based on certain facts or observations that are taken to be significant (figure 9: "Facts" highlighted). What one takes as a significant "fact" is influenced by one's values, which, in turn, reflect an implied, if not explicit, ethical theory. Our values provide the link between empirical observations and a normative policy prescription. Thus, if one's ethical theory focuses on helping to shape the sort of community where Blacks would have, in addition to the right to vote, both marketable skills and their share of the good jobs (figure 9, C2), and if one observes that international businesses can advance these ends (figure 9, A4), then one would argue that international businesses should remain in South Africa and advance these important values. (This teleological stance—one calculated to advance a just society—was Sullivan's position in 1976. As explained above, however, he was not able to persuade business leaders to accept that position and challenge the South African government until 1984.)

Alternatively, if one single-mindedly values the right to political participation as the essential right to achieve (figure 9, C1), and observes that business will do little to oppose a host government in that respect (figure 9, A2, A3)—especially a government that opposes the Soviet-Communist expansion in Africa—one would conclude that the only policy that makes sense is to pressure companies to leave. This position—a deontological stance, or ethics of principle—was that of the ICCR and others (figure 9, C1). The assumption here is that the departure of international businesses and the subsequent decline in the economy may serve as leverage to force the White South African government to the negotiating table. In any case, however, pressuring corporations to leave South Africa is the right thing to do, regardless of consequences.

For many church groups, a thirty-year struggle had convinced them that business leaders would do only what they were pressured to do on behalf of South African Blacks (figure 9, A5). And as we see, the factors that seemed to grip business leaders until the mid-1980s included: a business ideology that precluded political involvement in a host country; ideological and stra-

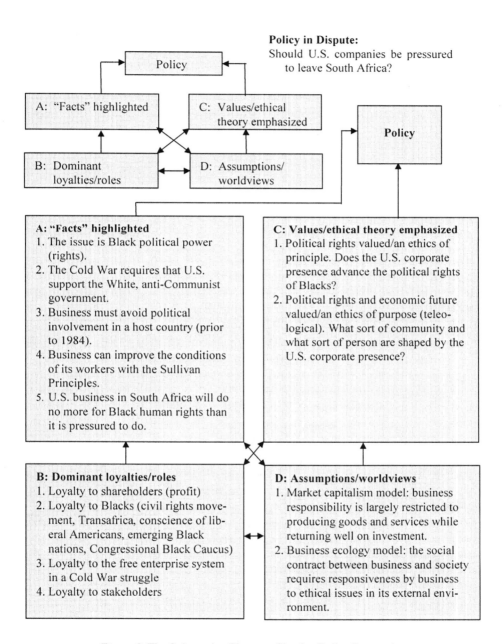

Figure 9. The Substantive Elements Shaping Policy Proposals

tegic considerations relating to the Cold War; and a notion of responsibility that was largely focused on creating shareholder wealth (figure 9, D1). Whereas business leaders seemed often to be very moral individuals and to be genuinely concerned about the plight of the Blacks, church groups found them to hold a worldview that precluded any significant, proactive involvement that would challenge or interfere with a government in a host country.

Beginning in the mid-1980s, in the wake of Sullivan's threat to leave the Principles program, business leaders finally did take an aggressive stand against the White South African government in support of Black economic and political liberation (the business ecology model; figure 9, D2). By that time, however, anti-apartheid church groups in the United States, with the blessing and encouragement of the South African Council of Churches, had already discounted business as a trusted ally in this struggle. Church groups consequently pressed all the more for complete disinvestment. This pressure was largely responsible for disinvestment by over 150 companies.

1.3   Some Lessons

We believe that because of their refusal to accept moral reasons as possible justifications for business decisions, corporate leaders missed an enviable opportunity to shape:

- The landscape of public opinion in ways that would have taken into account both the demands upon the corporations themselves to confront economic and market realities, and the ethical concerns of religious and public-interest groups

- Their corporations' internal decision-making processes, thus enabling the corporations to adept effectively to changing external environment

We also believe that in establishing a stance on matters of public policy, religious groups must not only consider the issue of political rights, but also the economic future of troubled nations. Keeping in mind the ultimate goal—the movement toward a just society—may inspire a less confrontational and more dialogic approach in dealing with business leaders.

It goes without saying that in the real world, a corporate action of any significance does not take place in a moral vacuum. And yet, instead of recognizing this unavoidable fact, many corporations assiduously avoid giving it any credence; they fear that doing so would lend further credibility to the claims of corporate critics. Consequently, corporations end up being perceived as ethically unresponsive, have actions and requirements imposed upon them from the outside, and have their choices narrowed within both the moral and economic arenas. They condemn themselves to repeating the same scenario again and again; witness, for example, the current public debate pertaining to the overseas operations of large multinational corporations in the developing countries and the attendant issues of sweatshop working conditions, abuse of child labor, and human right violations.

Unfortunately, Leon Sullivan did not fare any better. In his effort to create the broadest possible support level from the corporate community, he also downplayed the role of ethical values as the foundation for the Principles. Instead, he emphasized the economic power of the United States companies in terms of dismantling apartheid in the plant and in the communities where the majority of the Black people lived. Furthermore, he had hoped that the companies would use their economic influence with the South African government to hasten the process of political reform. He was sorely disillusioned on both counts, but he should not have been surprised. As we have noted elsewhere in the book, the United States companies had insisted from the very beginning that they would not directly challenge the South African government or become involved in the domestic politics of South Africa. Nor would they accept the suggestion that they there were under any sort of a moral obligation. By acceding to the corporations on the justification for going forward with the Principles program, Sullivan reduced the "moral" standing of the Principles to a largely economic calculus. This concession suited the corporations quite well. It also played into the hands of anti-apartheid activists—for the most part, religious groups—some of whom had derisively called the Principles "an exercise in triviality."[8]

It is ironic that, in the end, the parties that had the most to gain from the success of the Principles played such a critical role in undermining their viability and long-term sustainability. The corporations were unwilling to take the risk of going beyond the minimum that they felt they had to do to contain the problem. And Sullivan himself was willing to settle for what he he thought he could realistically achieve at the time when the Principles program was instituted. In the process, of course, he sacrificed the most fundamental—and ultimately, the most important—reason both for creating and for maintaining that program.

The above discussion holds four important lessons as we move into the future and consider creating new regimes—that is, modes of corporate governance and of external accountability—to address corporate activities that raise social issues of concern to the public. In order to be viable, any framework or set of principles intended to guide corporate conduct must

- have a cogent philosophy, or rationale, that transcends the immediate and direct interests of the current stakeholders. This philosophy should explicitly recognize and internalize the fundamental ethical norms and cultural attributes that underlie human societies.

- have a forceful individual sponsor whose integrity is unquestioned even by his or her critics. The sponsor must be seen as personifying—at least individually, if not as a representative of an institution—the moral values that are being advanced through the new framework.

- incorporate operational values and economic consequences that are sufficiently important to capture the attention of top management and become a matter of high priority on the corporation's strategic agenda.

- respect and address the sociopolitical and economic realities, as well as the diversity of goals and interests, that define the constraints within which solutions must be sought. By the same token, public-interest groups, nongovernmental organizations, and social activists will need to play a more constructive role in shaping public opinion and influencing corporate conduct. The landscape of public debate, including the controversies generated by crusades against the "big bad multinational corporations," is littered with the failed attempts of the well-meaning advocates of the poor—advocates who seek to impose codes of conduct that are more imbued with the intensity of their moral indignation and outrage than with a deeply moral understanding of, and response to, the complexities of the real world.

2.   IMPLEMENTATION PHASE

From its very inception of the Principles program, Sullivan was determined to ensure that the Principles were implemented in a manner to ensure there would be independent oversight, external monitoring and verification, transparency, and public reporting. He was concerned, and rightly so, that without these measures the Principles program would have no credibility with any of his constituencies, and would certainly be looked upon with disdain by anti-apartheid activists. The corporate community also shared Sullivan's concerns and was interested in creating systems to meet them.

A second aspect of the implementation phase involved the expansion of the scope of the Principles as all sides gained experience working with them. Sullivan viewed the initial formulation of the Principles as merely the starting point. He fully expected to incorporate new elements that would broaden the role of the signatory companies from the economic to the political arena. Thus, from his perspective, the primacy of the economic goals in the initial formulation of the Principles was a tactical device designed to get the corporations onboard at a level acceptable to them.

The implementation phase of the Principles program benefited from extensive involvement of midlevel corporate managers—both in the United States and in South Africa. With marching orders from top managers and with sufficient resources available, they brought their extensive operating experience and the knowledge of their respective corporate cultures to bear on the task of implementing the Principles. Implementation required the creation of new systems and operating procedures; there were no preexisting models. Thus starting with a clean slate, these executives developed systems that assured efficient use of resources, due diligence in the dispersal of funds, proper record keeping to minimize leakage of funds anywhere along the pipeline (which is the bane of many business-NGO partnerships), and accountability for performance. This approach also allowed for coordinated efforts by a group of companies to tackle large projects, and for the flexibility needed by individual companies to pursue specific projects that were best suited to their operations in South Africa. This effort was—in its own terms—remarkably successful. As we have noted earlier, United States companies spent more than $300 million on the Sullivan program over a seventeen-year period (1977–93), and the system was effectively free of any scandals involving the misuse of funds or other improprieties.

2.1   Independent Oversight Mechanism

Sullivan was well aware that the viability and credibility of the Principles program would depend on what the companies actually did and on the extent to which reports about corporate activities under the program were believed by the corporate critics and the public. Sullivan created a not-for-profit organizational entity called the International Council of Equal Opportunity Principles (ICEOP). It was composed of churchmen and educators who would oversee the overall functioning of the Principles program and assess the progress made by the signatory companies. The ICEOP structure was large and deliberately unwieldy. Sullivan wanted this group to be inclusive by bringing in leaders reflecting different constituencies and viewpoints. Such a large oversight structure, however, ran the risk of becoming splintered and unfocused, with different subgroups seeking to redirect the Principles' implementation to conform to their particular visions.

Sullivan was able to contain this risk through his strong personality and by maintaining centralized control. This centralization, however, compromised the deliberative process and undercut the input of diverse viewpoints, thus eroding the very reason for which the oversight function was created in the first place. As implementation gathered steam, the task of monitoring became more elaborate and time consuming; Reid Weedon of Arthur D. Little, Inc., the person responsible for creating and implementing the monitoring system, became the de facto policymaker. Moreover, as Weedon gained Sullivan's trust, he assumed ever greater responsibility for policy decisions. Eventually, Weedon would come to make virtually all the decisions—both major and minor—without prior approval from Sullivan.

The ICEOP was reduced to "window dressing" and played little, if any, role in the monitoring process, which robbed that process of its moral underpinnings. Since the ICEOP members did not, in fact, have the capacity to perform their oversight function, the implementation process came to be disconnected from the broader "moral" goals of the Principles program. Furthermore, the consequent failure of the independent oversight function had serious negative consequences not only as the Principles were interpreted and implemented by the companies, but also as their performance was evaluated and reported to the public.

There are three important lessons to be drawn from the above failure. An independent oversight monitoring function

- is an absolute necessity for ensuring that any new set of principles is effectively implemented and that public reporting of compliance with the principles has credibility.

- needs to be truly independent. It should not include advocacy-group representatives, who would be inclined to assess performance not in terms of what the principles demanded, but in terms of what the advocacy group believed that they should have demanded.

- must have people who are competent in evaluating activities that fall within the purview of monitoring, performance evaluation, and verification.

2.2   Objective Performance Measures

A second innovative measure in the Sullivan Principles was the recognition that standards must be created for objectively measuring the performance of individual companies in implementing the Principles. Objective standards would undercut the tendency of some companies to exaggerate their claims through rhetoric and hyperbole, and would also effectively prevent critics from throwing unsubstantiated charges at the companies for lack of performance.

The notion of performance measures was first introduced during the infant formula controversy and the Nestle boycott; the company had agreed to refrain from pursuing certain marketing activities in the promotion and sale of infant formula products.[9] The system, however, failed to deliver on its promise. The compliance standards were poorly articulated and insufficiently defined; there was a multiplicity of players—both Nestle's critics and its competitors—whose actions fell outside the monitoring domain of the Nestle Independent Formula Audit Commission (NIFAC); and the ponderous and unmanageable structure of NIFAC could not effectively perform its role of monitoring and auditing the activities of Nestle while also responding to the charges of the company's critics concerning Nestle's allegedly continuing violations.

The Sullivan Principles and the signatory companies, unlike Nestle and the infant formula controversy, had a highly favorable environment within which to create objective standards for performance measurement.

- The participating companies had a large cadre of experienced executives and knowledgeable professionals who could design standards that would meet the highest level of compliance with the Principles and yet remain within the acceptable limits of operational efficiency and financial feasibility.

- The signatory companies had the necessary incentive to comply with the Principles and have their performance evaluated in a manner that applied equally to all other companies and that would also pass muster with the external monitors. By thus minimizing the "free rider" problem, the companies would not have to worry about rogue competitors who would gain a competitive advantage at the expense of the companies who were diligently complying with the standards.

- Corporate critics were deterred from making unsubstantiated charges. The implementation standards were objective, and an independent monitoring system and oversight mechanism were in place.

In practice, the system fell short of its promise of imposing and utilizing objective performance standards. The companies preferred this flexibility in application, and Sullivan was either unwilling or unable to confront them over it. This lapse was, indeed, a pity because, like so many other aspects of the Principles program, the shortsighted and short-term orientation of the companies led them to fritter away a golden opportunity to increase both the public credibility and the effectiveness of the Principles program. Within a broader perspective, a more effectively implemented and enforced code could have lent strong credence to the viability of voluntary codes of conduct. It could also have immensely enhanced public trust not only in the signatory companies, in particular, but in the business community, in general.

In an effort to develop performance standards for compliance with the six Principles, the signatory companies did, of course, organize various task groups, but a system of measurement created by the very group whose performance it is designed to measure is likely to fall to the lowest possible level. This deterioration of standards is especially likely when, as here, the system has no independent, outside input. Such a system is prone to pressures from the recalcitrant members who would cite their "lack of resources" and plead for "gradualism in implementation," with the implied threat of "walking away" if the standards were held to be too onerous to implement.

Sullivan himself made mistakes. His strategic decision to downplay the "moral" rationale for the Principles and to view the Principles primarily in the economic context—as discussed earlier in this chapter—had an adverse impact on the development of performance standards. Although he had initially accepted the economic rationale as a necessary means to reach the ultimate goal of political reform, the result was that, in practice, the economic means became an end unto itself; the "moral" element of the Principles was barely invoked and was deemed more or less irrelevant by the companies. In addition, both Sullivan and Weedon constantly yielded to the companies' demands in terms of what was to be measured and how it should be measured; they were presumably overly anxious to see the Principles implemented and to thereby undercut potential criticism—for lack of progress—from anti-apartheid activists and even from Sullivan's own supporters. The situation was further compounded by Sullivan's own personality traits. He was a visionary and felt that he could move people and events by the sheer force of his personality and vision. He also lacked patience in dealing with nitty-gritty operational details and thus failed to see the implications of the so-called short-term accommodations that would eventually undermine the high moral values that were the heart of the Principles.

We believe that this situation might have been avoided had Sullivan utilized the very substantial resources of ICEOP and sought the advice and counsel of this eminent group. In the heat of the moment, however, Sullivan saw the ICEOP as more of an interventionist group whose impact should be minimized lest it slow down the process of implementation and bring unwarranted and unfavorable attention to the Principles program. This situation was further exacerbated by Sullivan's increasing reliance on Weedon, who saw his role in narrower terms: to make the Principles operational. This operational concern tended to overshadow—or even displace—the moral and value-laden concerns underlying the Principles.

The system devised by the signatory companies had all the appearance of objectivity and standardization, but in reality it fell short of its intended goals. The standards developed by the companies, and approved by Sullivan and Weedon, had the following characteristics:

- Among the most objective and verifiable standards were those pertaining to expenditure of funds.

- The companies would not be held to any objective measures of outcome, but would instead be judged by the standards of good-faith effort. The system was supposedly designed to give the member companies flexibility in the selection and implementation of projects, thus enabling the companies to pursue projects that most suited their particular strengths and were appropriate to their individual corporate cultures and circumstances.

- Companies were not required to adhere to any objective, outcome-based standards, even though the companies had substantial control over the outcomes and therefore should have been to demonstrate compliance. Of special note in this context were the goals pertaining to the training and promotion of Black employees to managerial ranks, and to the increased purchases—that is, corporate procurement—from Black-owned enterprises. Perhaps coincidentally, any progress in these areas would have necessitated making painful choices and a proactive deviation from "business as usual."

Under this system, the companies agreed to do what they felt they *had* to do in order to keep the Principles program alive and viable—and not what they *could* do in view of their resources and the moral standards implicit in the Principles. The low level of performance (at least if measured in terms of outcome, not just good faith or dollars) was sustained because Sullivan did not ask of the companies as much as he should have by way of moral commitment. Moreover, Weedon did not push for better performance even though he had every right and even obligation to do so.

The above discussion leads us to draw the following lessons in the area of establishing operational standards by which the implementation of any code should be measured. These lessons have to do with consistency, preciseness, objectivity, pertinence, and comparability.

- To the extent possible, standards must be outcome oriented; that is, they must measure the impact of an action rather than the good intentions of the parties involved. When and if process-oriented standards are used, they should be viewed only as interim measures to be replaced (in steps, if necessary) by a system of outcome-based standards.

- Every effort should be made to make the standards objective and quantifiable; different evaluators should be able to achieve consistently similar results when measuring the same activity.

- The standard-setting process must have expert input from sources independent of the companies that would be implementing the standards and that would be evaluated for their performance based on those standards.

2.3   Monitoring, Performance Evaluation, Verification, and Public Disclosure

From the outset, Sullivan wanted the task of monitoring, performance evaluation, and verification to be assigned to Arthur D. Little, Inc., a prominent consulting firm with considerable experience in field monitoring, especially in the area of environmental scanning. In particular, Sullivan wanted Reid Weedon of ADL to spearhead the Sullivan program's effort. The responsibility was a tremendous one and a heavy burden in terms of both time and resources.

As we have discussed elsewhere in the book, Weedon's system was essentially qualitative and group-oriented, although it had the appearance of objectivity and quantification. In our opinion, the system was designed with a view to meet certain criteria that were insisted upon by the companies and accepted by Sullivan. To wit, the companies refused to be evaluated in such a way that they would be perceived as competing against one another for performance ratings. The system that was adopted grouped the companies only in three broad categories—for example, making "outstanding" progress, making "considerable" progress, and "needs to become more active." The rating system was riddled, however, with subjectivity and qualitative judgments. By grouping more than 150 companies into three broad categories, the system appears to have been designed to protect individual companies from being accountable for their actions

The system failed to meet any of the criteria of objective measurement, independent verification, and transparency. The companies' financial contributions were not verified by independent outside monitors; the contributions were merely confirmed by the companies' own financial auditors, whose task was simply to confirm that the spending under the Principles met "generally accepted accounting principles." It takes no stretch of the imagination to believe that these financial auditors would have little incentive to go against the companies' interpretations of expenditures except in cases of gross violations. Morever, Weedon alone decided how many points a company should receive for undertaking certain activities. The criteria used by Weedon were never made public, and they were not open to external examination or validation. Finally, public disclosure did not identify individual companies or their relative performance.

Paradoxically, the so-called flexibility or qualitative evaluation created its own problem by negating any benefits it might have provided to the signatory companies, either individually or collectively. It introduced an element of arbitrariness into the evaluation process—no matter how benign or well intended—and made it difficult (or impossible) to make comparisons among companies. The monitoring system thus created a pernicious situation—and a fatal flaw: instead of evaluating performance as such, the monitoring system induced companies to orient their spending and project selection to whatever they considered to be the preferences and predilections of the system's monitor, Reid Weedon. Corporate executives, on their part, were unwilling to challenge Weedon in any significant manner for fear of angering Sullivan (and potentially receiving a poor rating from Weedon, as well). They were content to take the course of least resistance by doing Weedon's bidding and keeping out of trouble.

Admittedly, there were good reasons for this qualitative monitoring system. It created a spirit of cooperation among the companies by shifting their focus from individual performance to enhancing the validity and success of the Principles program. Nevertheless, the monitoring system was perceived by many outside observers—and also by executives of the signatory companies—as being entirely embedded in the person and preferences of Reid Weedon, whose work was not overseen by the ICEOP or by other external, nonindustry sources. This situation robbed the implementation process not only of the creative energy that would have come from constructive disagreements, but of the new initiatives that should have been generated by such an otherwise innovative venture as the Principles program. We believe that this gross discontinuity between governance and implementation prevented the Principles program from embarking on bold new initiatives. The insularity of the implementation process adversely affected the program's effectiveness. Furthermore, the aggregate and highly generalized nature of the publicly available reports effectively blocked any efforts to subject them to detailed analysis and evaluation.

There are important lessons that can be drawn from an understanding of the strengths and weaknesses of the system of monitoring, verification, and public disclosure used in implementing the Principles.

- The performance evaluation, or auditing, function needs to be handled separately from the assessment and verification function. The former is a technical function, whereas the latter involves both technical assessment and its relation to the achievement of a desired level of objectives.

- The assessment and verification function must have ascendance over the auditing function. The role and character of the auditing function must be based on the needs for verification and performance assessment.

- Public disclosure should be as comprehensive as possible and create maximum transparency except where it violates either trade secrets or standards of individual privacy. Moreover, both the manner and frequency of disclosure should be tailored to meet the needs of external constituencies and not the convenience of corporate members.

3.   ENHANCEMENT OF THE PRINCIPLES

From the very start, Sullivan believed that the Principles must be a dynamic, living document that would reflect a gradually expanding role for the corporations. He was also cognizant of the "art of the possible." Like many bold initiatives of Sullivan's vision, the enhancement or amplification of the Principles also fell short of its promise.

There was a fundamental confusion in relation to the amplification and enhancement of the Principles. Once the Principles were in place, was the further goal to *amplify* the principles and thus elaborate and clarify the existing Principles? Or was the further goal to *enhance* the principles and thus to expand the scope of the Principles program? As we have discussed elsewhere in the book, the enhancement (or amplification) process, in its actual operation, became highly unfocused and diffused.

- For the most part, the enhancements were aimed at making the implementation procedures and performance standards more precise, thus ensuring that all companies interpreted their performance expectations in a consistent manner. Thus, the so-called amplification process often degenerated into acrimonious debates between and among the companies, or between the companies and Reid Weedon.

- When the enhancements involved an expansion in the scope of the Principles, such enhancements invariably were reactive rather than proactive. Rather than leading and taking a forward-looking stance toward events in South Africa, the companies typically found themselves being dragged willy-nilly into accepting the new reality of changing political circumstances and expanded obligations.

Overall, the amplification program lacked a sense of direction, which was itself a product, at least in part, of the absence of strong moral leadership by the group of church leaders who were supposed to oversee the activities of the companies under the Principles program. In practice, the amplification program deteriorated into a series of discrete steps aimed at creating more specificity in the implementation process and in responding to short-term external pressures in South Africa. Of course, Leon Sullivan may have done the best he could—given the context in which he was working and the existing worldview of the business community at that time. Our interest here, however, is in drawing lessons for the future.

The above discussion, coupled with the evaluation of the amplification process as detailed in an earlier part of the book, would suggest the following lessons:

- Principles must have a firm vision of the future that their implementation would seek to accomplish. This vision must incorporate some lofty idea of human and cultural values that form the foundation of society.

- Principles or codes of conduct cannot be static. It is impossible to anticipate all the issues that might emerge during the implementation phase, and the changes in the external environment that might necessitate a reinterpretation of fundamental principles to make them more relevant to the evolving societal context.

- There should be a clear distinction between amplification and enhancement. The former pertains to making implementation more concrete and relevant, whereas the latter refers to transcending the prevailing understanding of the scope of the principles, and to raising them to a higher level of aspiration to meet changing societal expectations.

4.   SOME CONCLUDING REMARKS

We must now attempt to answer the final question. To wit, why is it that—despite the support of some of the largest corporations, enormous sums of money, the moral leadership of Leon Sullivan, considerable support of people and institutions in the United States and South Africa, and also the support of the United States government—the Principles program failed to deliver all of their stated promise or to mollify corporate critics in the United States and South Africa?

What, if anything, did the Principles program accomplish in terms of social good and public goodwill? In our opinion, the problem lay, first and foremost, with the thrust of the Sullivan Principles and, secondarily—but scarcely less significantly—with the United States companies.

The Principles program asked too much of the companies in areas in which "no level of activity," no matter how great, could possibly be sufficient. In developing the Principles program, we believe that Sullivan placed more emphasis in placating his critics, especially those in the United States, who advocated withdrawal of the United States companies from South Africa. In the process, he lost a major opportunity to mobilize the companies in areas where they could have played an important role as change agents.

Some of the critics in the United States could never have been appeased. Moreover, by delving into community-related activities, these companies became dependent on local groups whose activities and performance they could not control and whose ever increasing requests for funding and new project initiatives could never have been fully met. Based on our personal experience and close observation of a great many of these projects during our more than fifteen years of association with various NGOs in South Africa, it is clear that community-development projects—be they in housing, education, or health care—could never meet the entire community's needs. The projects, including those funded through the Principles program, insufficiently emphasized either "self-help" or communities' accountability for goal achievement. Thus, instead of treating such sponsored projects as sources for ideas or as seed money, communities came to depend on them as a continuing means of addressing their increasing needs in certain areas—a need so vast that it could only be satisfied through a massive influx of public funds. The funds required were, indeed, substantially beyond even the combined resources of all the United States corporations in South Africa.

The consequences of the above approach to the projects supported by the Sullivan program are all too clear. The dissolution of the program in 1994 left many NGOs and a vast majority of the program beneficiaries with fewer than ever resources to support continuing projects and to initiate new ones. In addition, many other sources of funding decided after 1994 to support South African government projects rather than NGO initiatives. The NGOs were suddenly left without much financial support and became, in effect, a depressed industry. The result has been a legacy of discontent with, and even anger at, the United States companies. This situation has persisted in the new democratic South Africa, and the NGO sector has continued to lose its position as a force for sociopolitical change in South Africa.

The Sullivan Principles did not ask enough of the companies in areas where they had the most capability to perform and produce tangible, long-lasting results; that is, in employment expansion, job training, upward mobility, and small-business development. By emphasizing accountability in dollars spent rather than goals accomplished, the Principles program offered the companies a simple measure of performance accountability. This approach lessened the need for the structural changes in the external and internal systems that would have been necessary to achieve most long-term, sustainable goals. The more than $350 million spent by the Sullivan signatory companies was a substantial sum both in absolute terms and when compared to the amount spent either by MNCs from other countries or by South Africa's own large corporations. From two other perspectives, however, the sum is small and ultimately unimpressive. Over a seventeen-year period, $350 million works out to an annual expenditure of less than $21 million. Assuming an average of one hundred signatories over the entire period, the amount spent by each company comes to approximately $210 thousand per year. Although that amount may appear to be a large sum for each of the companies to have spent, it is minuscule when considered in the context of "social needs." The money may have directly benefited a few, but in the larger scheme of things it is questionable whether the sponsored projects had any long-term, sustained impact on the Black communities.

Paradoxically, the two areas in which the signatories had the most control were also the areas of inadequate and indefensibly low progress by the United States companies. As noted earlier, Black representation in managerial and professional ranks remained extremely low. The situation in terms of Black entrepreneurship (supporting Black enterprises through directed purchasing programs) was similarly discouraging. A strong argument can be made that South African Blacks would have been better off if the signatory companies had been asked to focus their energies in these areas in which the companies had the greatest measure of direct control over the outcome—leaving other activities largely to the discretion and resources of other organizations. The issue, therefore, is not how, but where, the money was spent. In the future, we must look at alternative uses for such resources. The structure of the Sullivan program, its monitoring mechanisms, and the expectations of the activist constituencies in the United States caused the system to do poorly in those areas where it simply could not do well, and directed the companies away from the areas where they could have done better and should have been called upon to deliver more than they did.

ENDNOTES

1 This chapter draws from a number of ideas developed by the two authors and published previously as follows: S. Prakash Sethi, "Working with International Codes of Conduct: Experience of U.S. Companies Operating in South Africa under the Sullivan Principles,"

Business & the Contemporary World 8, 1 (1996): 129–50; S. Prakash Sethi, "American Corporations and the Economic Future of South Africa," *Business and Society Review*, Winter 1995: 10–18; S. Prakash Sethi, "Operational Modes for Multinational Corporations in Post-Apartheid South Africa—A Proposal for a Code of Affirmative Action in the Marketplace," *Journal of Business Ethics* 12, 1 (1993): 21–32; S. Prakash Sethi, "Black Economic Empowerment in South Africa," *Business & the Contemporary World*, 4. 4 (1992): 25–44; S. Prakash Sethi, "Economic Options for a Post-Apartheid Democratic South Africa: Learning from International Experience," *Development Southern Africa*, November 1990: 643–66; S. Prakash Sethi, "Economic Rights for the Disenfranchised Citizens of South Africa," *Development South Africa*, February 1990: 17–31; S. Prakash Sethi, "The Economics of Apartheid: Bringing Blacks into Business," *Business and Society Review*, Fall 1989: 27–31; S. Prakash Sethi, ed., *The South African Quagmire:* (Cambridge, MA: Ballinger, 1987). Also, Oliver F. Williams, *The Apartheid Crisis* (San Francisco: Harper & Row, 1986); Oliver F. Williams and Patrick E. Murphy, "The Ethics of Virtue: A Moral Theory for Business," in *A Virtuous Life in Business*, ed. by Oliver F. Williams and John W. Houck (Lanham, MD: Rowman & Littlefield, 1992); Oliver F. Williams, "The Apartheid Struggle: Learnings from the Interaction between Church Groups and Business," *Business and the Contemporary World* 8, 1 (1996): 151–57; Oliver F. Williams, "Business Ethics in South Africa," in *Encyclopedic Dictionary of Business Ethics*, ed. by Edward Freeman and Patricia H. Werhane (Cambridge, MA: Blackwell, 1997); Oliver F. Williams, "Capitalism," in *The New Dictionary of Catholic Social Thought*, edited by Judith A. Dwyer (Collegeville, MN: Liturgical Press, 1994); Oliver F. Williams, "Religion: The Spirit or the Enemy of Capitalism," *Business Horizons* 26. 6 (1983): 6–13.

2 See Thomas Donaldson, *The Ethics of International Business* (New York: Oxford University Press, 1989), 129.

3 Ibid., 134. See Ronald Dworkin, *Taking Rights Seriously* (Cambridge: Harvard University Press, 1978).

4 Donaldson, *The Ethics of International Business*, 133.

5 See, for example, Leon H. Sullivan, "Agents for Change: The Mobilization of Multinational Companies in South Africa," *Law and Policy in International Business* 15 (1983): 427–44.

6 An op-ed article succinctly stated the issue:

> The sanctions may well have hastened the denouement of 1994 when the ANC took power, but they also did serious damage to the South African economy. American multinationals closed down operations or sold them to South African interests. South Africa has had a rocky economic course in the 1990s. Mr. Mbeki ascended to the presidency of a country in which unemployment is 40% . . . and investors are diffident about putting money into new job-creating industries.

George Melloan, "In South Africa, A New Leader and New Hopes," *Wall Street Journal*, 28 September 1999.

7 Ralph B. Potter, *War and Moral Discourse* (Richmond, VA: John Knox Press, 1969). The use of this model was also informed by Marvin T. Brown, *The Ethical Process* (Berkeley, CA: Basic Resources, 1994).

8 The phrase is from George Houser. See chapter 1, p. 19.

9 S. Prakash Sethi, *Multinational Corporations and the Impact of Public Advocacy on Corporate Strategy: Nestle and the Infant Formula Controversy* (Boston: Kluwer Academic Publishers, 1994).

About the Authors

S. Prakash Sethi is University Distinguished Professor at Baruch College, the City University of New York, where he is also Professor of Management and Academic Director – Executive Programs, Zicklin School of Business. He holds a Ph.D. and M.B.A. from Columbia University, as well as a master's degree from Delhi School of Economics, Delhi University, India. He previously taught at the University of California, Berkeley and the University of Texas at Dallas, and held visiting appointments at Boston University and Rochester Institute of Technology. Professor Sethi has previously authored, co-authored, or edited twenty-three books and has published well over a hundred articles in scholarly and professional journals. His writings have also appeared in *Business Week*, the *Wall Street Journal*, and the *New York Times*. He is on the editorial boards of numerous scholarly journals, and is currently editor-in-chief of *Global Focus: An International Journal of Business, Economics, and Social Policy*. He is an internationally acknowledged expert in international business, economic development, corporate strategy, and business and social policy. He has had extensive experience in South Africa, sub-Saharan Africa, Asia, the Pacific region, Western Europe, and Russia.

He currently chairs an international monitoring commission responsible for conducting a social audit of the worldwide facilities of Mattel, Inc., the world's largest toy company. He presently serves as an advisor to the Executive Office of the Secretary-General of United Nations on international codes of conduct.

Oliver F. Williams, C.S.C., is associate professor of management in the College of Business Administration and academic director of the Notre Dame Center for Ethics and Religious Values in Business.

The author of *The Apartheid Crisis*, Father Williams also is an expert on economic and political issues in South Africa. From 1988 to 1994 he was a member of the National Advisory Council to the Sullivan Principles program. He served as a member of the U.N. Observation Mission in South Africa for the historic 1994 elections that brought an end to the country's 46-year policy of apartheid, and currently serves as chair of the U.S. board of the United States–South Africa Leadership Development Program (USSALEP). He facilitated a landmark 1991 meeting at Notre Dame between corporate and government officials from the United States and representatives of the African National Congress, the Inkatha Freedom Party, and the Pan-Africanist Congress. In recent years he has served each summer as a visiting professor at the University of Cape Town Graduate School of Business.

Father Williams is the editor or author of ten books, as well as numerous articles on business ethics in journals such as the *Harvard Business Review*, *California Management Review*, *Business Horizons*, and *Journal of the College Theology Society*. His most recent book is titled *Global Codes of Conduct: An Idea Whose Time Has Come.* He is a past chair of the Social Issues Division of the Academy of Management and a member of the editorial board of *Praxis: Journal for Christian Business Management* and *Global Focus: An International Journal of Business, Economics, and Social Policy.*

Bibliography

Africa News. "U.S. Firms Pledge Discrimination Ban in South Africa." *Africa News*, March 1977, 4–5.

Baker, Pauline. *The United States and South Africa: The Reagan Years*. New York: Ford Foundation, 1989.

Barber, Simon. "ANC in U.S. Row over Inkatha." *Business Day*, 17 September 1991.

———. "ANC's Two Faces Baffle Investors." *Sunday Times* (London), 13 October 1991.

Barrell, Howard. "The United Democratic Front and National Forum: Their Emergence, Composition and Trends." *South African Review* 2 (1984): 11–15.

Bellah, Robert N. *The Broken Covenant: American Civil Religion in Time of Trial*. New York: Seabury Press, 1975.

Booth, Helen E. "How Institutions Voted on Social Policy Shareholders Resolutions in the 1986 Proxy Season." Washington, DC: Investor Responsibility Research Center, 1986.

Borer, Tristan Anne, *Challenging the State: Churches As Political Actors in South Africa*. Notre Dame, IN: University of Notre Dame Press, 1998.

Bosch, David J. "Reconciliation: An Afrikaner Speaks." *Leadership* 4, 4 (1985): 64–65.

Botha, P. W. Abridged text of speech presented on 30 September 1985. Available from the South African Consulate General, New York, NY.

Branaman, Brenda M. *Sanctions against South Africa: Activities of the 99th Congress—Report no. 87–200 F.* Washington, DC: U.S. Government Printing Office, 1977.

Brown, Marvin T. *The Ethical Process.* Berkeley, CA: Basic Resources, 1994.

Bureau of National Affairs. *Daily Report for Executives,* 11 July 1991.

Business Week. "South Africa: Multinationals Are Caught in the Middle." *Business Week,* 24 October 1977.

―――. "South Africa—The Screws Are Tightening on U. S. Companies." *Business Week,* 11 February 1985.

Buthelezi, Mangosuthu G. "Black Demands." Paper presented at "Business International Conference on South Africa: The Evolving Challenge to International Companies," London, England, 5 June 1985.

Community Firms in South Africa. "Code of Conduct for Companies from the European Community with Subsidiaries, Branches or Representation in South Africa." *Bulletin EC* 11–1985.

Coons, Christopher A. "The Responses of Colleges and Universities to Calls for Divestment." Washington, DC: Investor Responsibility Research Center, 1986.

Cooper, Alison. "U.S. Business in South Africa." Washington, DC: Investor Responsibility Research Center, 1991.

Crocker, Chester A. *High Noon in Southern Africa.* New York: W. W. Norton, 1993.

―――. *State Department Bulletin* 85 (October 1985): 4–7.

―――. Testimony before the House Committee on Foreign Affairs, 17 April 1985.

de Gruchy, John W. *The Church Struggle in South Africa.* Grand Rapids, MI: Eerdmans, 1979.

de Villiers, Les. *In Sight of Surrender: The U.S. Sanctions Campaign against South Africa 1946–1993.* Westport, CT: Praeger, 1995.

Dole, Robert. Testimony. *Situation in South Africa: Hearing before the Senate Committee on Foreign Relations.* 99th Congress, 2nd sess., 22–24 and 29 July 1986.

Donaldson, Thomas. *The Ethics of International Business.* New York: Oxford University Press, 1989.

Dworkin, Ronald. *Taking Rights Seriously*. Cambridge: Harvard University Press, 1978.

Elbinger, Lee. "Are Sullivan's Principles Folly in South Africa?" *Business and Society Review*, Summer 1979: 35–40.

Eli Lilly S.A. (Proprietary) Ltd., South Africa. "Report on Health Care Involvement." August 1994.

"Eli Lilly & Company." In *The International Directory of Company Histories*. Vol. 1. Chicago: St. James Press, 1988–94.

Federal Republic of Germany. "Report on the Application of the European Code of Conduct for Companies with Subsidiaries, Branches or Representation in South Africa." Fall 1977.

Fenton, H. N., III, "State and Local Anti–Apartheid Laws: Misplaced Response to a Flawed National Policy on South Africa." *Journal of International Law and Policy* 19 (1987): 883–919.

Fernandez, Jose I. "Dismantling Apartheid: Counterproductive Effects of Continuing Economic Sanctions." *Law and Policy in International Business* 22, 3 (1991): 577–601.

Ford Motor Company. "Ford's Position on Sales to South African Police and Military." May 1980.

———. "Report of the International Labor Relations Staff." 30 November 1983.

———. "Report on Union Relationships." 1973.

Hauck, David, M. Voorhes, and G. Goldberg. "Two Decades of Debate: The Controversy over U.S. Companies in South Africa." Washington DC: Investor Responsibility Research Center, 1983.

Hengeveld, Richard and Jaap Rodenburg, eds. *Embargo: Apartheid's Secrets Revealed*. Amsterdam: Amsterdam University Press, 1995.

Hinchliff, Peter. *The Church in South Africa*. London: SPCK, 1968.

Hope, Marjorie and James Young. *The South African Churches in a Revolutionary Situation*. New York: Orbis Books, 1981.

Hufbauer, Gary Clyde, Jeffrey J. Schott, and Kimberly Ann Elliot. *Economic Sanctions Reconsidered*. 2nd ed. Washington, DC: Institute for International Economics, 1990.

———. *Economic Sanctions Reconsidered: Supplemental Case Histories*. 2nd ed. Washington, DC: Institute for International Economics, 1990.

Human Relations and the South African Scene in the Light of Scripture.
Cape Town: Dutch Reformed Church Publishers, 1975.

Huss, Donald C. Excerpt from "EEC Code of Conduct Regarding South Africa." 11 October 1977. Monograph.

Investor Responsibility Research Center. "How Institutions Voted on Social Policy Shareholders Resolutions in the 1992 Proxy Season." Washington, DC: Investor Responsibility Research Center, 1992.

————. "International Business in South Africa 1983." Washington, DC: Investor Responsibility Research Center, 1983.

————. "International Business in South Africa 1992." Washington, DC: Investor Responsibility Research Center, 1992.

————. "International Business in South Africa 1993." Washington, DC: Investor Responsibility Research Center, 1993.

————. "IRRC Finds Declining College Divestment Activity." *IRRC South Africa Reporter* 8, 4 (1989): 75–76.

————. "U.S. Business in South Africa 1991." Washington, DC: Investor Responsibility Research Center, 1991.

Jubinsky, Grace A. "State and Municipal Governments React against South African Apartheid: An Assessment of the Constitutionality of the Divestment Campaign." *University of Cincinnati Law Review* 54 (1985): 543–78.

Kahn, E. J. Jr., *All in a Century: The First 100 Years of Eli Lilly & Company.* Chicago: St. James Press, 1989.

Katayama, Frederick H. "Did Mobil Help or Hurt Apartheid? (Mobil Sells South African Operations to Gencor, Which Has a Reputation As a Harsh Employer)." *Fortune,* 5 June 1989.

Kibbe, Jennifer D. "Divestment on Campus: Issues and Implementation." Washington, DC: Investor Responsibility Research Center, 1989.

Kibbe, Jennifer and David Hauck. "Leaving South Africa: The Impact of U.S. Corporate Disinvestment." Washington, DC: Investor Responsibility Research Center, 1988.

Leadership. "Beyers Naude in Conversation with Alan Paton." *Leadership* 3, 4 (1984): 85–89.

Lewis, Kevin P. "Dealing with South Africa: The Constitutionality of State and Local Divestment Legislation." *Tulane Law Review* 67 (1987): 469–517.

Lipton, Merle. "Sanctions and South Africa: The Dynamics of Economic Isolation" (Special Report No. 1119, *The Economist* Intelligence Unit). London: *The Economist*, 1988.

Love, Janice. *The U.S. Anti–Apartheid Movement: Local Activism in Global Politics.* New York: Praeger Books, 1985.

Lugar, Richard. "Promoting True Democracy in South Africa." In *The South African Quagmire: In Search of a Peaceful Path to Democratic Pluralism*, edited by S. Prakash Sethi. Cambridge, MA: Ballinger, 1987.

———. Testimony. *Situation in South Africa: Hearing before the Senate Committee on Foreign Relations.* 99th Congress, 2d sess., 22–24 and 29 July 1986.

Massie, Robert Kinloch. *Loosing the Bonds: The United States and South Africa in the Apartheid Years.* New York, Doubleday, 1997.

McCardle, A. L. "In Defense of State and Local Government Anti–Apartheid Measures: Infusing Democratic Values into Foreign Policy Making." *Temple Law Review* 52 (1989): 813–47.

McClory, Robert J. "Notre Dame Divestment Divides School." *National Catholic Reporter*, 15 May 1986.

Moses, William F. "A Guide to American State and Local Laws on South Africa." Washington, DC: Investor Responsibility Research Center, 1993.

———. "S. Africans See Need for Corporate Code." *IRRC South Africa Reporter*, March 1992, 18–20.

Murray, Hugh. "A Moment in History." *Leadership* 4, 3 (1985): 30–35.

Mvubelo, Lucy. Foreword to *The Politics of Sentiment*, by Richard E. Sincere Jr. Washington, DC: Ethics and Public Policy Center, 1984.

Nel, D. J. Louis. Speech presented on 16 October 1985. Available from the South African Consulate General, New York, NY.

New African, Economic and Business. "Code Ignored." *New African, Economic and Business*, February 1979.

New Yorker. "Annals of International Trade: A Very Emotive Subject." *New Yorker*, 14 May 1979.

Paul, Karen. "U.S. Multinational Corporation in South Africa: Should There be a Conflict between Economic Interest and Political Imperatives." In *Up against the Corporate Wall: Corporations and Social Issues of the Nineties*, edited by S. Prakash Sethi and Paul Steidlmeier. Englewood Cliffs, NJ: Prentice-Hall, 1997.

Pifer, Alan. Summary of the Discussion on Labor Practices of American Corporations in South Africa, Carnegie Corporation of New York, 15 June 1979.

Potter, Ralph B. *War and Moral Discourse*. Richmond, VA: John Knox Press, 1969.

Roth, William V. Testimony. *Situation in South Africa: Hearing before the Senate Committee on Foreign Relations*. 99th Congress, 2d sess., 22–24 and 29 July 1986.

Schaufele, William E., Jr., "Steps by U.S. Business Community." *Department of State Bulletin*, 9 May 1977, 469–70.

Schlemmer, Lawrence and Charisse Levitz. *Unemployment in South Africa*. Johannesburg: South African Institute of Race Relations, 1998.

Schraeder, Peter J. *United States Foreign Policy toward Africa*. New York: Cambridge University Press, 1994.

Schultz, Geoge P. Testimony. *Situation in South Africa: Hearing before the Senate Committee on Foreign Relations*. 99th Congress, 2d sess., 22–24 and 29 July 1986.

Sethi, S. Prakash. *Advocacy Advertising and Large Corporations*. Lexington, MA: Lexington Books, 1976.

———. "American Corporations and the Economic Future of South Africa." *Business and Society Review*, Winter 1995: 10–18.

———. "Black Economic Empowerment in South Africa." *Business & the Contemporary World* 4, 4 (1992): 25–44.

———. "Economic Options for a Post–Apartheid Democratic South Africa: Learning from International Experience." *Development Southern Africa*, November 1990, 643–66.

———. "Economic Rights for the Disenfranchised Citizens of South Africa." *Development South Africa*, February 1990: 17–31.

———. "The Economics of Apartheid: Bringing Blacks into Business," *Business and Society Review*, Fall 1989: 27–31.

———. *Multinational Corporations and the Impact of Public Advocacy on Corporate Strategy: Nestle and the Infant Formula Controversy*. Boston: Kluwer Academic Publishers, 1994.

———. "A New Perspective on International Social Regulation of Business: An Evaluation of the Compliance Status of the International Code of

Marketing of Breast–Milk Substitutes." *Journal of Socio-Economics* 22, 2 (1993): 141–58.

———. "Operational Modes for Multinational Corporations in Post-Apartheid South Africa—A Proposal for a Code of Affirmative Action in the Marketplace." *Journal of Business Ethics* 12, 1 (1993): 21–32.

———. "Working with International Codes of Conduct: Experience of U.S. Companies Operating in South Africa under the Sullivan Principles." *Business & the Contemporary World* 8, 1 (1996): 129–150.

———, ed. *The South African Quagmire: In Search of a Peaceful Path to Democratic Pluralism.* Cambridge, MA: Ballinger, 1987.

Sethi, S. Prakash and Paul Steidlmeier, eds. *Up against the Corporate Wall: Corporations and Social Issues of the Nineties.* 6th ed. Englewood Cliffs, NJ: Prentice-Hall, 1997.

Siler, Julia Flynn. "The ANC To U.S. Investors: On Your Mark, Get Set . . . Not Yet." *Business Week*, 21 October 1991.

Smith, Timothy. "Whitewash for Apartheid from Twelve U.S. Firms." *Business and Society Review* 74 (1977): 59–60.

Spiro, Peter J. "State and Local Anti–South African Action As an Intrusion upon the Federal Power in Foreign Affairs." *Villanova Law Review* 72 (1986): 813–60;

Steiner, George A. and John F. Steiner. *Business, Government, and Society.* 5th ed. New York: Random House, 1988.

Sullivan, Leon H. "Agents for Change: The Mobilization of Multinational Companies in South Africa." *Law and Policy in International Business* 15: 427–44 (1983).

———. *Build Brother Build.* Philadelphia: Macrae Smith, 1969.

———. *Monitoring Report of the Statement of Principles.* August 1979. Unpublished monograph.

———. Statement. House Committee on International Relations. Joint hearing of Subcommittees on International Economic Policy and Trade, and on Africa. 95th Congress, 2d sess., 6 July 1978.

Sullivan Signatory Companies. *Annual Report,* 1977–93.

Tavis, Lee A. and Oliver F. Williams, eds. *The Pharmaceutical Corporate Presence in Developing Countries.* Notre Dame, IN: University of Notre Dame Press, 1993.

Temple University Archives. Acc. 654–6C. International Council for Equality of Opportunity Principles. Papers from 1974–1987.

Tutu, Desmond. "Sanctions vs. Apartheid." *New York Times*, 16 June 1986.

Unger, Sanford J. and Peter Vale. "South Africa: Why Constructive Engagement Failed." *Foreign Affairs* 64 (1985): 234–58.

United Kingdom. "Code of Conduct for Companies with Interests in South Africa, Government Guidance to British Companies on the Code of Conduct Adopted by the Governments of the Nine Member States of the European Community." London: Her Majesty's Stationary Office, 1978.

U.S. House of Representatives. Committee on Foreign Affairs. Joint hearing before the Subcommittees on International Economic Policy and Trade, and on Africa. 102d Congress, 1st sess., 30 April 1991.

————Committee on Foreign Affairs. *The Termination of Economic Sanctions against South Africa.* Joint hearing before the Subcommittees on International Economic Policy and Trade, and on Africa. 102d Congress, 1st sess., 31 July 1991.

U.S. Senate. Committee on Foreign Relations. *Situation in South Africa. Hearing before the Committee on Foreign Relations.* 99th Congress, 2nd sess., 22–24 and 29 July 1986.

————*U.N. Code of Conduct on Transnational Corporations: Hearing before the Subcommittee on International Economic Policy, Trade, Oceans, and the Environment.* 101st Congress, 2nd sess., 11 October 1990.

Walshe, Peter. *Church Versus State in South Africa.* New York: Orbis Books, 1983.

Ware, Gideon S. *A History of South Africa.* New York: Homes & Meier, 1974.

Weedon. Reid. "Report on the Signatory Companies to the Sullivan Principles," Nos. 1–17. Cambridge, MA: A. D. Little, 1978–93.

Weissman, Stephen R. *A Culture of Deference: Congress's Failure of Leadership in Foreign Policy.* New York: Basic Books, 1995.

Williams, Oliver F. *The Apartheid Crisis.* San Francisco: Harper & Row, 1986.

————. "The Apartheid Struggle: Learnings from the Interaction between Church Groups and Business." *Business and the Contemporary World* 8, 1 (1996): 151–57.

————. "Business Ethics in South Africa." In *Encyclopedic Dictionary of Business Ethics*, edited by Edward Freeman and Patricia H. Werhane. Cambridge, MA: Blackwell, 1997.

————. "Capitalism." In *The New Dictionary of Catholic Social Thought*, edited by Judith A. Dwyer. Collegeville, MN: Liturgical Press, 1994.

————. "Religion: The Spirit or the Enemy of Capitalism." *Business Horizons* 26, 6 (1983): 6–13.

————. "Who Cast the First Stone." *Harvard Business Review* 62, 5 (1984): 151–60.

————, ed. *Global Codes of Conduct: An Idea Whose Time Has Come.* Notre Dame, IN: University of Notre Dame Press, 2000.

Williams, Oliver F. and John W. Houck, eds. *Is the Good Corporation Dead: Social Responsibility in a Global Economy.* Lanham, MD: Rowman and Littlefield, 1996.

Williams, Oliver F. and Patrick E. Murphy. "The Ethics of Virtue: A Moral Theory for Business." In *A Virtuous Life in Business*, edited by Oliver F. Williams and John W. Houck. Lanham, MD: Rowman & Littlefield, 1992.

World Health Organization. *The International Code of Marketing of Breast–Milk Substitutes.* Geneva: World Health Organization, 1981.

Index